Gladstone and the Bulgarian Agitation 1876

Gladstone and the Bulgarian Agitation 1876

by

R. T. SHANNON

Lecturer in English History in the University of East Anglia

with an Introduction

by

G. S. R. KITSON CLARK

SECOND EDITION

THE HARVESTER PRESS
ARCHON BOOKS

This edition first published in 1975
by The Harvester Press Limited
Publisher: John Spiers
2 Stanford Terrace, Hassocks
Sussex, England
and in the United States of America
by The Shoe String Press, Inc.
Archon Books
Hamden, Connecticut 06514

Gladstone and the Bulgarian Agitation
first published in 1963 by Thomas Nelson

Copyright © R. T. Shannon 1963, 1975

The Harvester Press Limited
ISBN 0 901759 67 8

The Shoe String Press, Inc.
Library of Congress Catalog Card No: 74—22945
ISBN 0—208—01487—X

Printed in England by Redwood Press Limited
Trowbridge, Wiltshire
Bound by Cedric Chivers Limited, Portway, Bath

INTRODUCTION TO NEW EDITION

When this book was first published ten years ago, study in depth of Gladstone's post-1868 career was, in the words of Professor David Hamer (who has since himself contributed notably to the literature) 'astonishingly enough . . . conspicuous by its absence'. Apart from the present work Professor Hamer cited J. L. Hammond's monumental but emotionally over-Gladstonophile *Gladstone and the Irish Nation* (1938, reprinted 1964) as the outstanding exception to this rule. Perhaps he might also have allowed inclusion of Paul Knaplund's work on Gladstone's imperial (1927, reprinted 1966) and foreign (1935, reprinted 1970) policies. In the cases both of R. W. Seton-Watson's *Disraeli, Gladstone and the Eastern Question* (1935, reprinted 1962) and W. L. Medlicott's *Bismarck, Gladstone and the Concert of Europe* (1956) diplomacy swamps personality and politics. Even if the terms of reference are widened to embrace Liberalism generally, the list would not be greatly lengthened. Kenneth O. Morgan's *Wales in British Politics, 1868–1922* (1963) was by necessity a study in radicalism and Nonconformity. Likewise, Bernard Semmel's *Imperialism and Social Reform: English Social-imperialist thought, 1895–1914* (1960) investigated a theme inextricably bound up with Liberalism. Michael Hurst's extensive monograph, *Joseph Chamberlain and West Midland Politics, 1886–1895* (1962), helped to set new standards of detailed treatment. There was little enough intensive article-length scholarship in any case: C. H. D. Howard on Chamberlain and the 'Unauthorised Programme'; Michael Hurst, again, on Chamberlain and John Bright in Birmingham; J. F. Glaser on Liberalism and Nonconformity; John Roach on Liberalism and the Victorian intelligentsia; L. J. McCaffrey and W. H. Maehl on the 1874 election; Barry McGill and T. R. Tholfsen on Liberal organization; H. W. McCready on Home Rule. To these might be added Howard's edition of Chamberlain's *A Political Memoir, 1888–1892* (1953) and Agatha Ramm's edition of the Gladstone-Granville *Political Correspondence, 1868–1886* (1952 and 1962).

Still, by any reckoning, the literature was meagre; and *Gladstone and the Bulgarian Agitation, 1876* thus had the

v

fortune to enjoy a certain, modest, status as a pioneering work. That it was sponsored to the world by the doyen of research in nineteenth-century British history reinforced such academic or intellectual reputation as it could decently aspire to. It was achieved sympathetically, perhaps indulgently, by those who reviewed or noticed it. And certainly its author, ten years later, is better able than he was then to assess its merits (as well as its demerits) in presuming to offer, in its attempted integration of political and intellectual (including religious) history, a some- what original mode of comprehending the motives and personality of Gladstone and the dynamics of high Victorian Liberalism.

Since 1963 the state of Gladstone and Liberal scholarship has been entirely transformed. This transformation, of course, has depended to a great extent on work done outside or beyond the specific limits of post-1868 Gladstone and Liberalism. Much unexplored territory needed to be opened up, with contours surveyed and major bearings fixed. H. J. Hanham's *Elections and Party Management. Politics in the time of Disraeli and Gladstone* (1959) and Kitson Clark's classic *The Making of Victorian England* (1962) are outstanding examples of such surveying and fixing of bearings. The work of F. Barry Smith and Maurice Cowling on the Reform issue in 1866 and 1867 exhibits the findings of high intensity analysis. Indispensables understanding of pre-1868 politics came from D. C. Moore's work on community structures and political allegiance and John Vincent's studies of poll books. Nor could Gladstone and Liberal studies prosper without the clarifications of the Irish dimension of British politics provided by Cruise O'Brien's work on Parnell and F. S. L. Lyon's studies of the Irish parliamentary party and by L. P. Curtis, E. R. Norman, and D. A. Thornley. A completely new look at the implications of empire has been provided by Ronald Robinson, John Gallagher, and D. C. M. Platt. Equally indispensable are the insights offered into the working-class dimension of politics by Royden Harrison, Henry Pelling, Stedman Jones and Eric Hobsbawm. The significance of the relationship between the law and electoral practice has been brought out by W. B. Gwyn and Cornelius O'Leary; and the problems and possibilities of psephological techniques have been demonstrated by Henry Pelling, Trevor Lloyd, Neal Blewett, and J. P. D. Dunbabin. Sociological analysis of the nineteenth-century political elite has been offered by W. L. Guttsman. Nor are the contributions of the scholarship of nineteenth-century Conservatism to be overlooked: Robert Blake, James Cornford, E. J. Feuchtwanger, Paul Smith. The ramifications are indeed almost endless: The claims for a truly comprehensive social history urged by Harold Perkin; the growth of state intervention traced by David Roberts and Bentley Gilbert; the growth of cities illuminated by Asa Briggs, H. J. Dyos, M. Wolff, and Bruce Coleman, the government of cities by E. P. Hennock. And even then, one has not taken directly into account the dimensions of trade, industry, education, political ideas, or foreign policy.

For Gladstone and Liberal studies proper the post-1963 account opens with Peter Stansky's *Ambitions and Strategies. The Struggle for the leadership of the Liberal party in the 1890's* (1964), a close analysis of the manoeuvres of Rosebery, Harcourt, Morley and others to fill Gladstone's place. Although not strictly within the chronological limits here defined, John Vincent's *The Formation of the Liberal Party, 1857–1868* (1966) bears so directly on later nineteenth-century concerns as to command inclusion. Michael Hurst developed his studies of Chamberlain and Liberal Unionism into a form both large in scale and highly intensive in treatment: *Joseph Chamberlain and Liberal Reunion: the Round Table Conference of 1887* (1967). Paul Thompson's work on London as the crucial scene of Liberal-Labour relations matured in *Socialists, Liberals and Labour: the struggle for London, 1885–1914* (1967). David Hamer's *John Morley, Liberal Intellectual in Politics* (1968) established a reputation which was lived up to in *Liberal Politics in the Age of Gladstone and Rosebery* (1972), an exploration of the way Liberalism wavered between Gladstone's Low Church of Home Rule and Rosebery's High Church of Empire before settling for Harcourt's and Campbell-Bannerman's Broad Church of letting the Unionists decide. Jeffrey Butler in *The Liberal Party and the Jameson Raid* (1968), Bernard Porter in *Critics of Empire. British attitudes to colonization in Africa 1895–1914* (1968), Stephen E. Koss, *John Morley at the India Office, 1905–1910* (1969) Stanley A. Wolpert, *Morley and India, 1906–1910* (1967), R. J. Moore, *Liberalism and Indian Politics, 1872–1922* (1966), and H. C. G. Matthew, *The Liberal Imperialists, The Ideas and Politics of a Post-Gladstonian Elite* (1973), explored different aspects of Liberalism's problematical relationship with Empire. This theme was also the central focus of Geoffrey Searle's *The Quest for National Efficiency. A Study in British Politics and Political Thought, 1899–1914* (1971).

The theme of Liberalism, New Liberalism, social reform, the relationship with Labour, and indeed the whole question of how and why Liberalism later declined as a first-class political force, was opened up by Trevor Wilson's *The Downfall of the Liberal Party* (1966). Though Wilson commenced his story with the outbreak of war in 1914, this in itself spoke volumes for pre-1914 issues, since his argument was that Liberalism was killed by the war itself. He thus challenged the old-established if somewhat over-strained diagnosis of George Dangerfield's *The Strange Death of Liberal England, 1910–1914* (1935), which postulated a mortal disease whose symptoms were the rising tide of violence of Ulster, syndicalism, and feminism. Henry Pelling's interpretation of the rise of Labour challenged in turn both Dangerfield and Wilson: *Popular Politics and Society in Late Victorian Britain* (1968). Then appeared the powerful advocacy of P. F. Clarke in *Lancashire and the New Liberalism* (1971), which established on an entirely new footing of impressiveness the thesis that Liberalism's political health prior to 1914 was good and that its demise thereafter was explicable by misadventure rather than necessity. Peter Rowland's two volumes on *The Last Liberal Governments, The Promised Land 1905–1910* (1968) and *Unfinished Business, 1911–1914* (1971) argue that the Liberal leadership took up social reform reluctantly when they ought to have seen that it was their clear and bounden duty to do so enthusiastically. The theme of Liberalism, New Liberalism and state intervention is handled with rather more subtlety by H. V. Emy in *Liberals, Radicals and Social Politics, 1892–1914* (1973). The dynamics of post-Gladstonian Liberal revival are studied by Neal Blewett, *The Peers, the Parties and the People: the General Elections of 1910* (1972) and by A. K. Russell's analysis of the 1906 election, *Liberal Landslide* (1973).

Gladstonian politics have been recently scrutinized with a polemical insistence on the autonomy of 'high politics' by Andrew Jones in *The Politics of Reform, 1884* (1972). The edition of *Lord Carlingford's Journal. Reflections of a Cabinet Minister, 1885* by A. B. Cooke and J. R. Vincent (1971) has been expanded into *The Governing Passion. Cabinet Government and British Politics 1885–86* (1973).

The history of Liberal ideas in this period has been illuminated by a series of distinguished works. Maurice Cowling's examination of *Mill and Liberalism* (1962) exposed, with provocative acerbity, the underlying authoritarianism in a doctrine which presupposed an eventual rationalist consensus of opinion once reactionary social and political forces had been overcome. Melvin Richter's *The Politics of Conscience.*

T. H. Green and his Age (1964) handled one of Mill's successors with much more admiration and sympathy. Edward Alexander most pertinently raised the central problems of high Victorian Liberalism by confronting the two great allies and enemies, *Matthew Arnold and John Stuart Mill* (1965). John Burrow set up, in *Evolution and Society. A Study of Victorian Social Theory* (1966), a model of graceful scholarship. In *The Revolution of the Dons. Cambridge and Society in Victorian England* (1968) Sheldon Rothblatt discussed the influence of the prophets Mill and Arnold on efforts to adjust Cambridge to new Liberal purposes. *From Status to Contract. A biography of Sir Henry Maine, 1822–1888* (1969) by George Feaver enlivened the career of one of the Liberal intellectual grandees who grew increasingly disenchanted with Gladstonian Liberalism. It marches well with the edition by R. J. White (1967) of J. Fitzjames Stephen's assault on Mill, *Liberty, Equality, Fraternity* of 1873. J. D. Y. Peel's *Herbert Spencer, The Evolution of a Sociologist* (1971) is the best study of the greatest Victorian Liberal exponent of social science.

Liberalism and foreign affairs has, comparatively, been neglected. A. J. P. Taylor's *The Trouble Makers. Dissent over Foreign Policy, 1792–1939* (1957) set off many a hare which has yet to be run to ground. A. J. A. Morris's useful *Radicalism Against War, 1906–1914* (1972) (in collaboration with A. J. Dorey) is virtually the only recent thing in the field. For Gladstone one still has recourse to Paul Knaplund, *Gladstone's Foreign Policy* (1935, reprinted 1970). But there is, fortunately, the splendid study by D. M. Schreuder of the mixed world where empire and colonialism shade off into foreign relations: *Gladstone and Kruger. Liberal Government and Colonial 'Home Rule', 1880–85* (1969). Zara Steiner's *The Foreign Office and Foreign Policy, 1898–1914* (1969) and S. R. Williamson, *The Politics of Grand Strategy. Britain and France prepare for War, 1904–1914* (1969) cover the years of the last Liberal period of office, as to a lesser extent does George Monger, *The End of Isolation. British Foreign Policy, 1900–1907* (1963); and Keith Robbins's *Sir Edward Grey. A Biography of Lord Grey of Fallodon* (1971) adds depth and substance to a controversial issue.

Biography of major Liberal political figures is indeed another area where the gaps predominate. Gladstone himself remains a yawning chasm though one is grateful for the Royal Commission on Historical Manuscripts series of Prime Ministers' Papers, the *W. E. Gladstone, Autobiographica* volume of which has been edited by John Brooke and Mary Sorensen (1971). The great Oxford edition of the diaries, started off by M. R. D. Foot, will take a long time to get up to 1868. Meanwhile, *The Diary of Sir Edward Walter Hamilton, 1880–85*, edited in two volumes by Dudley W. R. Bahlman (1972), gives a vivid picture of Gladstone from the admiring point of view of his private secretary. Roy Jenkins, *Asquith* (1964), and John Wilson, *C.B. A Life of Sir Henry Campbell-Bannerman* (1973), provide competent studies. John Grigg's *The Young Lloyd George* (1973), is a more promising beginning of a long-needed extensive biography. *Rosebery* (1963) by R. R. James was a welcome re-assessment of that enigmatic Liberal. Peter Fraser's *Joseph Chamberlain. Radicalism and Empire, 1868–1914 (1966)*, though disjointed, as well as Julian Amery's completion of the massive Garvin biography (1951 and 1969), reminds one why the greatest Liberal Unionist was Lloyd George's major inspiration. The earlier chapters of *Lord Haldane, scapegoat for Liberalism* (1969) by Stephen H. Koss are useful for the pre-1914 period. *The Forerunner. The Dilemmas of Tom Ellis, 1859–1899* (1972) by Neville Masterman discusses the problems of the man who bore the twin burdens of being the 'Welsh Parnell' and Liberal Chief Whip. Alfred M. Gollin, *Proconsul in Politics: a study of Lord Milner in Opposition and in Power* (1964) is a weighty addition to the theme of Liberal Imperialism. Even weightier is the second volume of the grandiosely planned life of Winston Churchill, by Randolph S. Churchill, *Young Statesman, 1901–1914* (1967). The fecund S. F. Koss studies two different kinds of Liberal bigwig in *Sir John Brunner, Radical Plutocrat, 1842–1919* (1970), and *Fleet Street Radical. A. G. Gardiner and the 'Daily News'* (1973). T. J. Spinner, *George Joachim Goschen* (1973) is a useful addition to biographies of the older Liberal generation.

No survey of the recent literature of Liberalism should omit to notice and commend the welcome series of editions of classic texts being produced by various publishers. Gladstone's *Midlothian Speeches* of 1879 have been edited by M. R. D. Foot (1971); D. A. Hamer has edited *The Radical Programme* of 1885 (1971); and P. F. Clarke has edited L. T. Hobhouse's influential *Democracy and Reaction* of 1904 (1972). It is to be hoped that these are the forerunners of a copious library of such texts.

Within the context of what has thus become so extensive and complex a literature (at the level of articles in learned journals the volume of material would at least by doubled) on Gladstone and Liberalism, *Gladstone and the Bulgarian Agitation 1876* settles, on reprinting, into the category of an essay, possibly meritorious for its time but now a little dated, betraying expectable signs of a want of sophistication; but nonetheless still holding its place by virtue, perhaps, of the very unabashedness which characterizes enterprise by young scholars into very big and unexplored subjects.

Richard Shannon

Preface

IN MAY 1876 the Turks suppressed with atrocious severity an attempted insurrection of Bulgarian nationalists. Reports of these 'Bulgarian atrocities', as they soon came to be called, ambiguously but definitively, provoked a furious outburst of indignation in England against the Turks and, more to the point, against the pro-Turkish Eastern policy of Disraeli's government.

This 'Bulgarian atrocities agitation' deserves detailed study for two principal reasons. It was, in itself, by far the greatest and most illuminating revelation of the moral susceptibility of the High Victorian public conscience. And it was, in its effect on Gladstone, an event of profound political importance.

Yet these two aspects of the agitation have suffered undue neglect. Attention has been concentrated almost exclusively on observing the movement from outside, as a simple manifestation of 'public opinion'. For this purpose G. Carslake Thompson's *Public Opinion and Lord Beaconsfield, 1875–1880* (1886) and Professor David Harris's *Britain and the Bulgarian Horrors of 1876* (Chicago 1939) between them provide copious documentation of the metropolitan press, Blue Book, and *Hansard* sources. To these works, and of course to the late R. W. Seton-Watson's standard and authoritative study, *Disraeli, Gladstone and the Eastern Question* (1935), I refer those whose chief interest is in a chronological narrative of the Eastern question as it impinged upon the British public from 1875 to 1880. In the present study I have attempted to exploit the potentialities of a rather different kind of approach: I have tried, mainly through the reading of collections of private papers, to interpret the agitation from inside, as an entity with a life and character of its own.

The life of the agitation extended from July to December 1876, the period which defines the chronological scope of this book. With the collapse of the Conference of the powers at Constantinople in January 1877 collapsed also the prayerful aspirations of the public conscience which had sustained the atrocities agitation

to its last great effort in the National Conference on the Eastern
Question at St James's Hall in December 1876. Thereafter, the
student of the processes of opposition to the Eastern policy of Lord
Beaconsfield's government is concerned essentially with the more
restricted and, as I would argue, somewhat different phenomenon
of pressure groups. I have not attempted, therefore, to deal with
the career of the Eastern Question Association in 1877 and after.

I deliberately place the theme of the agitation as a phenomenon
in its own right before the theme of Gladstone in relation to it.
For the first conclusion of such a study as this, it seems to me, must
be the greatness of Gladstone's debt to the agitation and, conversely, the smallness of his contribution to it, despite the myth
to the contrary. Nowadays the agitation is remembered only by
virtue of Gladstone. The most instructive episode in later nineteenth-century English political history has been obscured by the
high drama of Gladstone's crusade on the Eastern question. An
interpretation which treats the agitation teleologically, merely as
the occasion of Gladstone's return to full political commitment,
ignores half the potential of the subject, and necessarily distorts
proportion and perspective. No doubt the fact that Gladstone
was called out of his retirement is, in retrospect, the point which
gives significance in a positive and pragmatic sense to the events
of 1876—for the agitation itself failed to attain its objectives. But
historians ought, if they wish to avoid presenting a distorted vision
of the past, to concern themselves as much with significant failures
as with significant successes. One purpose of this study is simply
to correct such a distortion. It attempts to restore the true colour
and shape of the events of 1876 by removing an incrustation of
misattributed cause and effect which has grown unavoidably in the
absence of close criticism. At the same time it tries to bring into
clearer perspective the wider political implications of Gladstone's
participation in the movement.

I am grateful to many people for their help. At Cambridge Dr
G. S. R. Kitson Clark first guided me into the field of nineteenth-
century studies, and has been ever since an unfailing source of encouragement. I owe much also to the generosity of Dr H. J.
Hanham of the University of Manchester, who helped to prepare
this work for the press. My manuscript benefited greatly from the
comments of three of my teachers, friends, and former colleagues

at Auckland, Professor Willis Airey, Professor Keith Sinclair, and Professor Robert Chapman. For the privilege of access to private collections of papers I have to thank the following: Mr W. K. Stead, of Little Beside House, St Day, Cornwall, for permission to read the papers in his possession of his grandfather, W. T. Stead; the Marquess of Salisbury, for permission to read and publish extracts from the Salisbury Papers housed at Christ Church, Oxford; the Very Rev. E. S. Abbott, formerly Warden of Keble College, Oxford, for making it possible for me to have access to the Liddon Papers stored in Keble Library; the Duke of Devonshire and the Trustees of the Chatsworth Settlement, for permission to read at Chatsworth the papers of the eighth Duke, and Mr W. S. Wragg, Keeper of the Devonshire Collections, for much assistance to that end.

Every effort has been made to get into touch with the owners of copyright material. In any case where this has failed, it is hoped that this general acknowledgment will be accepted as adequate.

May 1963   R. T. SHANNON

Contents

Introduction

What doest thou here, Elijah?

THE agitation in 1876 in condemnation of the atrocities inflicted by the Turks on their Bulgarian subjects has a double interest. It was one of the great semi-religious, semi-political agitations which aimed in nineteenth-century Britain at bringing the force of organised moral indignation to bear on the conduct of public affairs. These agitations are well worthy of study. Together with the purely religious revivals, which clearly tapped the same spiritual and emotional head springs, they reveal much about the nature of public opinion in a large section of society and about the stimuli to which it responded. Because they operated on parliament and public from outside the ordinary party system and did not need to employ the ordinary social influences which controlled the constituencies, they were an effective instrument for the self-expression of classes who had inherited little traditional political power. Moreover, this anti-Turk agitation has peculiar characteristics which give it a special interest. It developed suddenly and apparently spontaneously as the result of tragic events in a strange environment in countries remote from Britain; it was partly sponsored by men who did not normally take part in these agitations; it came remarkably quickly to boiling point; and it influenced an unusual cross-section of opinion.

However, the anti-Turk agitation has an additional interest of a different nature. Because it was what it was and came when it did, it probably affected the history of the Liberal party decisively, and it provided the prologue to the most interesting portion of the career of Gladstone, that ultimately tragic part which starts when he became Prime Minister for the second time and ends with the failure of the Second Home Rule Bill. It brought to him, in the retirement in which he had taken refuge after the failure of his first ministry, an inescapable challenge, and it committed him to the

xi

influence of heightened spiritual and emotional tensions which lasted till near the end of his life. It is indeed largely because of its influence on the career of Gladstone that it influenced the history of the Liberal party, for the fortunes of both are at this period inseparable; and it is because it affected both that the anti-Turk agitation may have a particular interest. For the course taken by the development of either of the great historic parties is of the greatest significance in British history in the nineteenth century. It was through the agency of these parties that powerful social and economic forces were able to influence politics. The condition of either of these parties, or of both of them, at any given moment, may explain the way things at that time worked, or failed to work. The development of the party system which they operated played a considerable part in determining the lines along which the constitution developed.

The problems which their development presented may however be easily missed owing to a rather common tendency to take too much for granted in these matters. The party system seems to most people so essential to the British polity, and the two parties which operated it before the intervention of the Labour party seem to have so continuous a past, going far back into English history, bound together in unceasing factious opposition to one another and forever presenting permanent factors in political discussion, that it is tempting to believe that here are phenomena whose development needs no explanation, or comment, because they are firmly grounded on the basic and permanent realities of English life. However, this sense of continuity is to a large extent a delusion. The issues of politics and the social and spiritual forces which activated politics changed drastically as history went forward, and as these changes took place so the parties which competed for power necessarily changed also, as did the terms and method of their competition and the prizes for which they competed. In fact the party system as we understand it is of comparatively recent growth. The conception of party, rather than of royal, governments in the form that we know them, does not go back before 1830. The first opposition party to be organised with the comprehensiveness of a modern party in opposition was probably the Conservative party that came into existence between 1833 and 1841. Even so, its leader, Sir Robert Peel, when he came into power did not understand what was expected of a party-created Prime Minister, and he tore his party into two by repealing the Corn Laws, which they thought they had placed him in power to preserve. Thereafter for about a dozen years the party system was at least partially in abeyance and neither controlled politics, nor provided lasting governments, nor gave adequate representation to the important interests of the country.

Politics began to straighten themselves out in 1859 when Gladstone finally joined the Liberal party, though the continued existence of Lord Palmerston slowed up their development till his death in 1865. In 1866, however, the crisis began which ended in the passing of the Second Reform Bill. This was followed by the general election of 1868 which gave the Liberals a majority and made Gladstone Prime Minister. Here then seems to be a turning point. Gladstone's first ministry has been called the first Liberal administration, and with reason. It was the first fruits of a reformed electorate, though the extent to which the Reform Act of 1867 had affected constituencies by 1868 has been exaggerated. Gladstone, not Palmerston, nor even Lord John Russell, was Prime Minister; Liberals had begun to take the place of Whigs in Cabinet and Parliament; and the government pursued what must be called a Liberal policy and passed a number of overdue reforms.

But the existence of a Liberal Prime Minister and the development of a Liberal policy did not mean that a Liberal party with sufficient organic unity to play a continuous rôle in British history had come into existence. Gladstone was supported in power by various groups. He was, as Prime Minister, leader of the old Whig Liberal party, and he was supported, at least at the beginning of his government, by the forces of organised Dissent. But the Dissenters had not learnt to accept the conditions which co-operation with a party, most of whom were not Dissenters, implied, and, on the other hand, it was not clear that the effective political future of the Whig Liberal elements would be long if they did not come to terms with the social and spiritual forces which the Dissenters represented. In fact it was not even clear that the political force behind Gladstone would long survive his defeat in 1874.

It is the part it played at that juncture which lends the anti-Turk agitation of 1876 much of its interest.

2

The problem of Liberal unity between 1870 and 1880, however, has a general relevance to a general problem which the development of the party system in the nineteenth century presents. Could a party system based on two historic parties, which had emerged from a very different past, adjust itself to the changing social structure of Britain? A two-party system such as exists in Britain depends on the existence of two parties with enough organic unity to enable them to play continuous rôles. If a party is going to maintain such a unity and to continue to play an effective part it must not only support causes which are likely to gain the assent of a majority of voters, it must not only develop an organisation to deploy its political resources to the best advantage, it must also be able to adjust itself to the social habits and relationships of a sufficiently large section of the nation to give it a stable nucleus of support. In aristocratic party politics this presents a comparatively simple problem. The party must possess enough influence through landowners and employers in a sufficiently large number of constituencies to give it a good start in the competition for power. But as wealth and political selfconsciousness increase among the voters the problem becomes more complicated. The methods of authority and patronage must be increasingly replaced by the more exacting techniques of persuasion, and the organisation which a party provides in the constituencies, the type of men which it puts forward as candidates, the language which its leaders use and the objects and principles they support, must be so adapted that they will remain congenial to the section of the country from which it hopes to gain its main support. If they do not do so the party will wither away, and another party will take its place.

Now, before 1830 politics had been a gentleman's game, a game played by noblemen and gentlemen for the advantage of noblemen and gentlemen. People from other classes had played their parts, but they played as auxiliaries and for minor rewards. The nobility and gentry took all the chief rôles and won all the best prizes. If someone from outside were successful he became by that action a gentleman, if he did not become a nobleman. This situation was traditional, but it also corresponded with the contemporary social structure of the country and with its political structure, since success in the constituencies largely depended on the kind of influence noblemen and gentlemen were most likely to possess. In these circumstances such political parties as there were were naturally tools in the hands of the upper classes.

In the nineteenth century with an ever greater diffusion of wealth and a continual increase in political selfconsciousness this situation was likely to become less secure. Indeed the Reform Bill of 1832 was, in part, a recognition of this fact; its object was to enfranchise a class, the 'middle class', which could no longer be excluded from all political power. It is important, however, not to exaggerate the change which the bill caused in the social structure of British politics. After the bill both the parties changed their names: 'Conservative' took the place of 'Tory' and 'Liberal' more slowly displaced 'Whig'; and it would be convenient to assume that the use of new names meant a shift in the social centre of gravity of politics. But this is not necessarily so. A 'Conservative' after the Reform Bill was likely to have the same social background as a 'Tory' had had before it. There was more sense of social contrast in the use of the words 'Whig' and 'Liberal'. But contemporary usage was not consistent. Both words are sometimes used on different occasions to describe the same statesman, and the implications of the words seem to have differed in different parts of the country. Meanwhile for another thirty years or so after the bill of 1832 the key to power in many constituencies still lay in the hands of members of the old aristocratic classes. As a result those classes continued to monopolise both the government of the country and the leadership of any party that had any chance to assume power.

The first effective attack on this monopoly after the Reform Bill was the attack on the Corn Laws between 1838 and 1846. Since the aristocracy were supposed to be responsible for these laws the attack on them was not only an attempt to get rid of them, it was also intended to be a general assault on the aristocracy. It was very ably conducted and sharply pressed home, and it had the significant characteristic that it was in its way a religious movement. From the very beginning Cobden saw that its best chance of success was that a 'moral and even a religious spirit' should be 'infused' into the subject, and he consciously modelled his campaign on the anti-slavery movement. It is indeed significant that so shrewd a judge as Cobden should believe that this was the note to which the classes to which he wished to appeal would most readily respond. The sequel showed that he was right. Nor as the century went forward did this phenomenon change at all quickly. For a long time in the nineteenth century the classes that were outside the aristocratic ring seem to have found it most easy to achieve effective unity of purpose in movements which invoked religious sanctions, which were directed towards objectives that seemed to be endorsed by Christianity, and which could draw upon the support of the Protestant nonconformist churches. It is quite true that some of these movements were attacks on grievances that seemed to be the direct result of the old aristocratic form of government, as were the privileges of the Church of England; but the arguments used were moral arguments, and the cause was always conceived as a religious one.

It is therefore significant that in the sixties there was a great deal of activity among the politically-minded Dissenters. The election of 1868 probably brought into the House of Commons more Dissenters and more men who were pledged to the disestablishment of the Church of England than ever before. Their appetite was immediately whetted by an act for the disestablishment and disendowment of the Church of Ireland promoted by Gladstone.

In the circumstances they naturally felt that the day of reckoning for the Church of England was at hand, that a breach in the curtain wall of privilege had been effected at last.

3

In 1868, however, the apparent strength of the politically-minded Dissenters was deceptive, for it depended on an alliance with a man whose objects and principles they were likely at that moment to misunderstand.

Indeed, it is relevant to suggest, at this point, how greatly the development of British parties and the British party system had been affected by the actions and idiosyncrasies of prominent individuals. At a critical moment Peel split the Conservative party into two. The continued existence of Lord Palmerston delayed the development of the Liberal party. By the same token after 1868 the nature of the party system, and the way it was to work, owed much to the character and behaviour of the two men who were to dominate the next chapter of political history—Disraeli and Gladstone.

They were very different men and the nature of their contributions was different. Disraeli's claim to have educated his party requires scrutiny and re-appraisal, but there is a strong case that it was due to him that there had survived a party to educate. In the slack period of the fifties Disraeli and Lord Derby by careful personal management had kept an effectively organised Conservative party in continuous existence. The feat was the more remarkable because not only was the party in a perpetual minority but there was no very obvious reason why it should exist at all. The political principles which it could afford to profess were hardly different from those of the Whigs who had supported Lord Palmerston, while the issues which it might have made its own were those on which any expression of its natural opinions would have meant political suicide. But by dexterous tactics Disraeli had led it round such pitfalls as an obstinate adherence to the policy of protection of agriculture by imposing taxes on food, or a conscientious refusal to take any part in the further reform of Parliament. As a result an organised Conservative party had survived to compete effectively for power after 1868, and, since organisation on one side in politics is likely to be answered by organisation on the other side, the existence of this party was probably one of the main reasons why by 1868 there also existed by that time something like an effectively organised Whig-Liberal party to compete for the control of government.

Disraeli's work had been that of a realist; indeed, his words and actions may seem at times to cross the shadowy boundary which separates realism from cynicism. It is difficult to see how it could have been otherwise. He had to be in close touch with those who were engaged in electoral management, which in the middle of the nineteenth century was not always a very savoury occupation. If he was to make something of the position of his party he needed a freedom of manoeuvre which might at times seem to require a flexibility of principle which was greater than the ordinary rules of political conduct might be held to permit. Moreover, the circumstances of his own spectacular ascent to power from the position of an adventurer of a despised race to the leadership of the Conservative party and his general insecurity at every moment of his climb must have left him with few illusions about some of

B

the harsher realities of the political game. Disraeli is a difficult man to understand and to judge, and he has at times been judged with great severity; but when judging any action of his, or trying to understand him, it is necessary to remember that at no time did the fates allow him much margin.

It was otherwise with Gladstone. He had not had to climb the steep and dangerous ladder which was Disraeli's only way up, and it may be doubted whether he would, or could, have done so. He was essentially the product of an aristocracy. Though he was of mercantile origin he was born into a position from which, if he received, as he did, the appropriate education, he could start his career with the privileges of an aristocrat. A seat in Parliament came to him early, without effort on his part. It was soon followed by office; indeed, not many years had passed before he was embarked on a career in which not even a sensitive, and at times unintelligible, conscience was likely to prevent him from reaching the high place in the councils of the state that his great abilities deserved. Moreover, even when he achieved power he seldom had had to do the work of political organisation or manipulation himself; that was normally done for him by others. Consequently he seems to have had surprisingly little traffic with the more sordid side of politics and at times to betray in such matters a surprising simplicity of outlook. This seems however to have been sometimes balanced by a strange intuitive knowledge, which he himself hardly recognised that he possessed, of what was likely to be politically effective.

Gladstone had also another characteristic which was to prove in its way a political asset. In an age when the political influence of religion was great, he was a profoundly religious man. He had been so since in early manhood he had deplored the kind of religion which he believed to be prevalent at Oxford and had written to his father at some length to suggest that he ought to take orders. His religion as a youth was evangelical and probably rather narrow and provincial; but foreign travel and an acquaintance with Catholic Europe enlarged his conceptions, and a study of his prayer book drastically modified his view of the tradition of the Church of England. Soon after this his friendships with Manning and J. R. Hope-Scott drew him into close touch with the Oxford Movement and its heart-troubling problems.

Probably religion provided him with the dominant interest of his life. But parliament and secular politics claimed him early. At first he tried to compromise with them by concentrating in politics on Church questions, and in 1838 he published a book called *The State in its Relations with the Church* which contained a reasoned justification for the existence of an established Church in England, and for that matter in Ireland. This is a much abler production than Macaulay's famous review of it would suggest; but it advanced principles which could no longer be sustained politically, as he himself was very soon to realise. Nor was he going to be permitted to remain eclectic in his approach to secular politics; they were to claim his whole life, not part of it. In 1841 Sir Robert Peel needed Gladstone at the Board of Trade, and he was immediately plunged into the problems of income taxes, import duties, and Corn Laws which were deeply interesting, but very different from the issues on which his mind had originally been set.

Thereafter Gladstone's mind can be divided into two. He was a working politician and financier, and much of his time was necessarily absorbed in a secular career of increasing importance. Yet his absorption in religion also never relaxed. He read about it extensively, as his library shows. He was punctual and devout in the performance of his religious duties. He engaged in Church controversies, and when moral or ecclesiastical questions intruded into secular politics the strength of his interventions showed what fires were banked underneath.

Religion and politics make uneasy bedfellows, and, as was to be expected, Gladstone was often accused of hypocrisy. In its simplest form this accusation is not worth consideration. Simple hypocrisy, the vice beloved of the old comic writers, the interested expression of sentiments which the speaker knows he does not entertain, must be one of the rarest vices as it must be one of the most difficult to practise. Without doubt Gladstone sincerely meant what he said, even if he sometimes said it with merciless particularity and elaboration, in such a way as to seem to bury his meaning in intricate verbiage. There is, however, one circumstance in Gladstone's life which may seem to require explanation; it is the variety, indeed the contrariety, of the opinions he had entertained. He was a High Churchman, his first book was in defence of the established Church of England and Ireland; but in later life he

disestablished and disendowed the Church of Ireland, he reduced
the privileges of the Church of England in the matter of Church
rates, and he supported a law which made it easier for atheists to
become members of the House of Commons. There was plenty of
material here for those who wished to quote Gladstone against
himself, with the pleasing addition that he changed his opinions to
suit the needs of his secular ambitions.

At the time of the Irish Church crisis, in 1868, he defended himself against such accusations in a pamphlet which he called *A
Chapter of Autobiography*, and his case is both interesting and convincing. But his fundamental consistency can be best realised by
reviewing not what he had been, but what he had not been. He
had been, he continued to be, a High Churchman; but he had never
been what was called a 'high and dry' Churchman, a Churchman
whose main interest was in the temporalities and privileges of the
Church rather than in its spiritual claims. He had defended
Established Churches, but he had not been an Erastian. That is,
he had believed that the state should maintain an established
Church because the Church represented that idea of truth which
the state as a moral entity existing for moral ends must possess;
but he had not defended religious establishments because they
might secure secular objects such as the promotion of social tran-
quillity, the endorsement of civil obedience, or the English connection with Ireland. He had abandoned his first position because
it was not politically practicable, and he had become increasingly
convinced of the impropriety of compulsion in religious matters;
but he had never adopted the facile nineteenth-century idea that
the state is a creation of mere secular convenience with little or no
spiritual significance.

In fact Gladstone's changing opinions were different views of
the same assumptions and of the same problem as presented to him
from different angles as he passed through life. The most important fact in life was for him, and in his view for everyone else, the
Christian religion. It announced truths which men could only ignore at their peril and a code of conduct which they must obey.
This mass of ineluctable truth and unquestionable command must
be related in some way to the institutions and needs and modes of
procedure of the secular society in which men live. How was this
to be done? He might as his experience lengthened give differing an-

swers to that question, but he never changed his mind about the nature of the challenge behind the question, nor yet about its urgency.

That challenge, the challenge of the relation of the eternal to the secular, must exist in any century for any Christian who takes his religion seriously; but there were two reasons why the problems it raised were likely to be peculiarly intrusive and difficult in the nineteenth century.

The old solution for this relationship was the conception of a Christian nation with institutions based on Christianity and a Christian Church established with acknowledged authority over the community. But it was not easy to maintain in the nineteenth century the conditions and institutions which this solution presupposed. Men were beginning to disagree too fundamentally. Moreover, established Churches, everywhere in the world, had become too closely identified with orders of society and systems of government against which men were in revolt. It was necessary therefore to make a slow and uncertain retreat from a state founded on a basic acceptance of one common form of Christianity, even when mitigated by toleration for those who could not accept it, apparently towards a state based on convenience with no common moral doctrine at all, if such a state were conceivable.

As a leading Churchman Gladstone had been from the beginning of his career closely involved in the problems of this retreat. But the circumstances of the period pressed the issue of the relationship of the eternal to the secular on contemporary politicians from an entirely different angle and in a different form. This was not only a time of increasing spiritual division, it was also a time of religious revival. In Britain many of the men who were to challenge the old aristocratic order had found through this revival their first self-consciousness, and had received through the movements which the revival inspired their first opportunities to organise and grasp at power. Indeed, since in the first half of the nineteenth century power in the constituencies was largely the monopoly of the aristocracy, such movements, the great semi-political, semi-religious agitations of the nineteenth century, provided some of the most effective means of action by men outside the aristocratic ring. But those agitations have a double aspect: they were not only attacks on aristocratic and ecclesiastical privilege; they also made claims on the policy of the country in the name of Christianity.

They were not only a bid for independence and power on the part of men who had been denied both by the old system; they were also an attempt to relate the secular to the eternal. Gladstone was unlikely to be drawn into these agitations. They were led by men to whom he was unlikely to listen, and directed towards ends he was unlikely to find attractive. But those who were involved in these agitations were often drawn to Gladstone. They recognised in the ring of his voice, in his choice of words, in the sanctions to which he appealed, the same spirit as that which possessed them. They seem often to have forgotten that his spiritual history was different from theirs.

His particular moral flavour was one reason, but not the only reason, why Gladstone's personality and position was of unique importance between 1860 and 1880. He had it in him, and possibly he alone had it in him, to provide continuity between the old party system, with all the parliamentary techniques it had developed and all the experience it had garnered, and the activities of the new classes who demanded a position of their own in politics. He was at the very centre of the old system. He moved with ease among the great nobility, he was related by marriage to some of the highest families in the land, his native ability had gained him some of the most important positions in the state, and after 1860 he was evidently in the succession to the position of Prime Minister under the old dispensation. Yet he was a reasonably advanced Liberal, as Liberals went in the middle of the century: he believed in the extension of the franchise, in free trade and economy, the abolition of jobbery in the civil service, the liberation of Italy and in due course of Ireland. Not only could he speak in a way that impressed Dissenters, he had discovered, probably at Newcastle in 1862, that he was a great popular orator. This in a strange way dovetailed in with his sense of the claims of the eternal in politics, for he detected in the crowds which listened to him so eagerly the influence of that moral force which did not seem to him to find its way so easily into aristocratic politics.

It might therefore be expected that when Gladstone became Prime Minister in 1868 the Dissenters would form a permanent alliance with the leader of the Liberal party. They had done unprecedentedly well in the elections; Gladstone was Prime Minister and had their confidence, and to show that his intentions were good he started proceedings by disestablishing the Irish Church and removing the sting of the grievance about Church rates. Yet the fusion did not take place; the old fissure did not close, it grew wider. In 1870 the government proposed a Bill to provide a system of public elementary education. An influential body of Dissenters had been agitating this subject and had demanded a system of public education which should be free, compulsory, and undenominational. The government's scheme fell short of the Dissenters' demands on each point; they found it impossible to make such compromises as might in some degree have conciliated the Dissenters; and the Dissenters were angry and attacked the government in the constituencies through the agency of a body called the Education League, which had been founded in imitation of the old model for this kind of warfare, the Anti-Corn Law League.

Thereafter things went wrong with the government in a good many matters. They proposed an Irish University Bill which was opposed by the Irish Roman Catholics and defeated. They tried to resign, but Disraeli would not take their place. They were involved by Gladstone in a series of curiously maladroit and avoidable difficulties, and ended their course by a reckless and ill-considered dissolution of parliament in 1874. At the general election the Liberals were generally beaten and the Conservatives came into power with Disraeli at their head.

It was a humiliating end to a hopeful beginning, and Gladstone personally was partly to blame. As he got older his tendency to be impetuous and masterful increased, and in the last years of this ministry he involved the ministry in several scrapes which were quite unnecessary and were made worse by his obstinacy. He also was responsible for the reckless haste with which they plunged into the dissolution. But there were causes for this failure which had a profounder and more general significance than Gladstone's follies. In fact the apparent promise of 1868 had been based upon misconceptions. It had seemed as if the Dissenters were coming into their own, it had seemed as if Gladstone would naturally provide an effective link between the social and spiritual forces which they embodied and the old Whig Liberal party. In fact the Dissenters had exaggerated the significance of their successes in the election of 1868. They believed that they could demand the acceptance of their principles in education, particularly the elimination of Church schools. They believed that they could press for the disestablishment of the Church of England and were affronted when Gladstone opposed it. But they were not nearly strong enough to carry either. They were probably not even in a position to give adequate support to the government to ensure success on either point supposing the government had been disposed to support their views.

But the government were not disposed to support their views. One of the most serious misconceptions about 1868 is to exaggerate the strength, at that moment, of the link which attached Gladstone to the Dissenters. He might attract Dissenters, but he was not a Dissenter. Nor in the past had he had much contact with Dissenters or known much about them. Such were the divisions of English society that, according to his own account, he had been 'astonished' to discover in 1851–2 how great was the multiplication of their chapels. Though he does not say so, he probably learnt this from the religious census of 1851; but not to have guessed what had been done shows a curious ignorance of a full half of England. In due course he had got to know John Bright, and apparently, in about 1864, Dr Newman Hall and through him R. W. Dale and other Nonconformist divines. But some of the proposals he supported while the Education Bill was before Parliament suggest that this contact had not given him very great insight into their minds.

However, it is probable that even if he could have fully understood them he would not have agreed with them. His differences with the Dissenters, certainly on the question of the disestablishment of the Church of England and probably on denominational education, were in effect on points of principle, and no amount of sympathy or mutual knowledge could have bridged them. In fact the moral of this ministry seems to be this. Whatever the personal qualities of Gladstone, the differences of old and new were so great that they could not be easily united under one leadership; so after the election the Dissenters prepared in anger to go their own way while Gladstone made up his mind to retire from his position at the head of his party. He led the opposition rather negligently for the rest of 1874. Then in January 1875 he retired from the leadership. A party meeting chose the Marquess of Hartington to lead them in the Commons. Earl Granville remained Leader in the Lords, with some sort of general responsibility for the whole.

4

It is significant that the two people who were closest to Gladstone, his wife and Earl Granville, seem to have deplored his resignation partly because they felt he might wish to come back and not find sufficient political resources to support him. He did not share this anxiety. The fact that he had not resigned his seat in parliament suggested that he had not closed his account with politics; but he had no intention of resuming his old position. For what remained of his life he would now turn to those religious problems which absorbed so much of his mind. It is, of course, fair argument that given Gladstone's temperament something would inevitably have drawn him back into the arena of secular politics before very long, and that once there, before he knew what he was doing, he would have found himself back again in the centre of things. What was clearly not in any way inevitable was that if he did so he would find an effective political instrument to his hand, or that he would be able to resume the old relationship with the Dissenters. The Liberal forces in parliament were in disarray. Before he accepted his position the Marquess of Hartington had calculated that there were no less than three parties among the Liberals, each of whom might properly have its separate leader: 'the Whigs or moderate Liberals', 'the Radicals', and 'the Irishmen'. About this time also Gladstone had listed nine subjects which excited keen interest. On none of them was there a real consensus of opinion and on one of them, education, his own opinion was not in unison with the rest of the party. But what was happening in the constituencies was even more significant.

The Education League had not been a great success. It had never secured sufficient support to make its impact really effective. Nevertheless it had important results. One of those who had been drawn into that agitation was a young Unitarian manufacturer from Birmingham named Joseph Chamberlain. Even before the general election of 1874 Chamberlain had recognised the weakness of the Education League and had seen that if anything effective was to be done it was necessary to turn to a more comprehensive political organisation with more general objects. As it happened, an effective instrument for his use to that end lay close to his hand. In the act of 1867 an attempt had been made to give the Conservative minority in Birmingham a chance to gain one of the three Parliamentary seats. In order to counter this it was necessary to distribute the Liberal vote with great particularity, and a very elaborate political organisation had come into existence which was largely the work of one William Harris, who must have been an organiser of genius. This organisation was, as far as membership was concerned, very democratic, though the control and direction remained in the hands of the wealthy and able men who were prepared to give time and trouble to the work, among whom Joseph Chamberlain rapidly became the leading figure.

From an electoral point of view the Birmingham organisation was very successful. In 1868 Birmingham returned three Liberals to Parliament, and when in 1874 the Liberal cause was failing everywhere else Birmingham again returned three Liberals. Meanwhile Chamberlain had captured the town council and was drastically replanning the town and developing an advanced policy of municipal reform. In 1876 he became one of the town's representatives in the House of Commons, but he had already lifted his eyes beyond Birmingham. He promoted the remodelling of other constituencies on the plan of the Birmingham caucus, and he gradually turned over the machinery of the Education League to the task of uniting all the newly furbished constituencies in one common organisation with Birmingham as its headquarters. In 1877 the Education League disappeared and the National Liberal Federation took its place.

It was a formidable movement, and the instrument of a formidable man. The electoral success of Birmingham in the year of defeat gave prestige to the organisation which had secured it. In a period when men were turning to the ideas of democracy the Birmingham model seemed to supply an essentially democratic way of organising politics. More important still, it provided a means by which men of wealth and ambition, whom earlier and more oligarchic forms of political organisation had excluded from influence, could gain control of a constituency. It could also respond to the old religious afflatus, as the force it derived from the anti-Turk agitation, when that developed, goes to show. But the ends it proposed to itself were by no means exclusively sectarian; for instance Chamberlain added to the attack on the Church of England and Church Education a violent assault on the great landowners of the country, Whig as well as Tory, and a demand for the emancipation of the agricultural labourer.

It is not easy to conceive this movement remaining for long a submissive component of a party led by the Marquess of Hartington, the son and heir of the Duke of Devonshire, one of the greatest landowners in the country. Nor in all probability was it in Chamberlain's mind that it should do so. 'I think', he wrote in 1877, while the National Liberal Federation was being formed, 'this may become a very powerful organisation, and proportionately detested by all Whigs and Whips.' Both prophecies were likely to come true, and it is interesting to speculate what in the ordinary course of events would have happened if they had done so. Conceivably the National Liberal Federation might simply have torn the Liberal party into two and so reduced it to prolonged impotence comparable to that of the Conservatives after 1846. And if that had happened what would have been the results for the development of the two-party system? Or it might have entirely replaced the existing Liberal party with another party much less inhibited in its attitude towards such relics of the past as the great landed aristocracy, or the established Church, or the monarchy. It would probably have developed a full programme of social reform and have been the exponent of a radicalism as dynamic, as hard, and as realistic as Chamberlain himself; for he would certainly have led it.

But these are idle speculations. Even before the National Liberal Federation had been fully formed the anti-Turk agitation had developed. It developed unexpectedly as the result of events in places far removed from the sphere of ordinary British domestic politics. It produced a cause that appealed to powerful religious emotions, but was not confused by the incidence of troublesome problems of principle connected with the position of the Established Church or the proper treatment of denominational schools. It excited the Dissenters, but from the first was sponsored by High Churchmen like Liddon, who were of all men closest to Gladstone. And it drew in Gladstone.

The case to be considered is whether there was not perhaps at this point a turn in the road both sharp and unpredictable. Certainly it would seem as if the future of several of the main figures was to be very different after 1876 from what it might have been expected to be in 1874.

In 1874 the Dissenters had repudiated the old Liberal party and were like to be led off into political independence by Chamberlain. In 1876 they had entered into a deeper communion with Gladstone than they had ever enjoyed before, which lasted till his death, and from which they gained something which they could not have gained from Chamberlain. They also probably received from the anti-Turk agitation, followed as it was by the Afghan and Zulu Wars, a clear picture of a common source of evil, to be named 'imperialism', of which the Conservative party and Lord Beaconsfield were alike agents.

In 1874 Chamberlain was already looking to what was likely to be an independent radical movement which would break the class control of the Liberal party. He did not share the indignations and enthusiasms of the anti-Turk agitation, but he welcomed them, for they greatly helped the extension of the National Liberal Federation, and he secured that Gladstone should be the chief speaker at the foundation meeting in Birmingham in 1877. He could not have foreseen that this rather old-fashioned Liberal statesman, who had already retired, would stay in politics long enough to stand in his way like a giant and in the end drive him out of both the Liberal party and the Federation which he had founded.

In 1874 Gladstone had left the centre of the stage of politics to turn his attention to religious problems which he reasonably felt were more important at that moment than any political ones. It was not revealed to him that after so short a respite the call of religion itself would drive him back into the thick of things to struggle against the forces of evil first in the actions of the Turks and then, so he conceived it, in the general policy of Lord Beaconsfield, and then, for long and in the end tragically, in the troubles of Ireland. Nor could he know that his final resignation would not be conceded to him for another twenty years.

It is not suggested that all these events inevitably derived from what happened in 1876. But it does seem probable that what happened played a considerable part in causing them. This is one reason why it may be very well worth while to give earnest consideration to what is the subject of this book.

G. KITSON CLARK

1

Foundations of the Atrocities Agitation

1 Prologue: Gladstone in Abdication, 1874–6

WHEN he formally resigned the leadership of the Liberal party in January 1875 Gladstone had recently celebrated his sixty-fifth birthday. For his age he enjoyed exceptionally good health. He still had more than twenty-three years of life before him unaffected almost to the end by disabling illness or infirmity. Yet it is unlikely that Gladstone's decision in 1875 would have been different even had he foreseen an unusually long and vigorous old age. He had no intention of retiring from serious political activity. He declined a peerage and kept his seat in the House of Commons. Stated baldly, Gladstone decided in 1874 to abdicate because he felt that the defeat of his party in the elections of that year had been in the nature of a betrayal of the trust which he had confided in the 'masses'. It was surely the most subjectively-inspired major act in the history of English politics. Gladstone was convinced that defeat meant the effective end of his career as the leader of a great party because the axis around which his politics had come to revolve—a sense of moral rapport with the 'masses'—was now broken. Like Antaeus, Gladstone felt strong only so long as he touched the earth. 1874 seemed to him to indicate that henceforth he could not draw on this source of strength. The abdication was thus an act conceived in bitterness and disillusion not at defeat itself, but at what defeat seemed to imply in terms of his great romance with the people of England.

Abdication was an act almost unknown to the conventions of English politics. The public not unnaturally tended to confuse it with normal retirement from active affairs, and so placed undue significance on Gladstone's occasional forays in 1874 and 1875. But such retirement Gladstone would have regarded as an irresponsible evasion of his natural obligations to parliament and the nation. He had argued this very point with Peel in 1846. Gladstone spoke often with envious admiration of a class of public men of long parliamentary experience and great influence who persistently refused office. This rôle he proposed to take henceforth.[1] He played it with great vigour in the sessions of 1874 and 1875. But these interventions were selective; this was the indulgence abdication allowed him. He would rise only to occasions which he deemed worthy of him.[2] Possibly there were elements both of selfishness and vanity in this; but his primary motive was simply economy of time. He was passionately anxious to devote the greater part of his remaining energies to the 'noblest, the most philanthropic, of all human enterprises', the defence of religious belief.[3]

Granville, upon whom Gladstone with doubtful propriety personally conferred the formal leadership of the party, had no faith in the permanence of Gladstone's abdication.[4] Effectively the party was managed by a collective leadership, Gladstone himself very often included. He still sat, indeed, on the front bench beside Hartington, the nominal Liberal leader in the Commons, and the rest of his former cabinet colleagues. The precise nature of his position—retired in principle from 'official' politics yet still intimate in the highest councils of the party and still reserving for himself the right to step in when he should feel an occasion worthy of him—was extremely dubious and embarrassing for everyone, even Gladstone in the end. The Radicals in particular could not be expected to remain content under the leadership of a duumvirate of Whigs; and every appearance of Gladstone in his old form aroused their wishful calculations.[5] Here again his highly subjective mode of thought made him self-centred and insensitive in matters of personal relationships. It was fortunate that his joint successors were men so equable and accommodating as Granville and phleg-

[1] Lord Kilbracken, *Reminiscences* (1931), p. 100.
[2] A. T. Bassett (ed.), *Gladstone to His Wife* (1936), pp. 209–10.
[3] E. S. Purcell (ed. E. de Lisle), *Life and Letters of Ambrose Phillipps de Lisle* (1900), vol. ii, p. 155.
[4] A. Ramm, *The Political Correspondence of Mr. Gladstone and Lord Granville, 1868–1876* (1952), vol. ii, p. 462; A. H. D. Acland (ed.), *Memoir and Letters of the Right Honourable Sir Thomas Dyke Acland* (1902), p. 319. For Gladstone's views on Granville as leader of the party, see F. E. Hamer (ed.), *The Personal Papers of Lord Rendel* (1931), p. 121.
[5] E.g. Mundella to R. Leader, 19 March and 24 April 1875, Mundella Papers, Sheffield University Library; L. Gordon Rylands, *Correspondence and Speeches of Mr. Peter Rylands, M.P.*, vol. i, *Life and Correspondence* (Manchester 1890), p. 241.

matic and unimpressionable as Hartington. The strain was eased for them by their complete lack of illusion as to their position. However impatient and annoyed they became with Gladstone in the following years, awe blunted their resentment.

Gladstone's abdication was an astonishing act by any but Gladstonian standards. There is no comparable instance of a great political leader insisting on laying down his leadership while yet in the fulness of his powers and against the pleadings of his chief lieutenants and the wish of the vast majority of his followers. Yet from Gladstone's point of view nothing could have been more logical. He was not a 'natural' politician like Disraeli. His first love had been the Church, and to the Church he remained ever faithful, in his fashion. His desire to consecrate his last years to its service expressed the striving for freedom and fulfilment which had hitherto been thwarted by the shackles of public conscience and public responsibility. Of the three Gladstone personae—the Peelite Gladstone, the demagogue Gladstone, and the Anglo-Catholic Gladstone—the first two were, as he hoped, laid to rest. For the third the struggle against Vaticanism, against Archbishop Tait, against the new infidelity, would provide more than enough scope.

Gladstone was always a politician in spite of himself. His strongest yearning was to achieve great expression in the spiritual sphere. But the sheer power of his public talents frustrated him. As a politician he achieved supreme greatness; his spirituality, by comparison, though intense, lacked subtlety and true profundity. The longing to be free to devote his life to religion places Gladstone's abdication in integral relationship with the deepest and most consistent undercurrent of his life. Yet its explanation remains political. Often during his career Gladstone had been faced with the choice either of continuing in a fully-engaged political life or of succumbing to a deeper personal desire for release. Hitherto the issue had never been really in doubt. The claims of politics were peremptory. 1874 posed another in this series of alternatives; but now the circumstances were such that Gladstone could with a relatively clear conscience convince himself that at last he had a right to choose the path of indulgence.

The great danger is that in the perspective of Gladstone's enormous career the abdication is apt to be dismissed without due consideration as a quirk, a miscalculation, a temporary aberration, the product merely of fatigue and pique at electoral defeat. So indeed it was regarded by Gladstone's contemporaries, few of whom accepted it as final—though equally few understood its true motivation. Historians, for their part, have tended to suffer from their occupational disease of hindsight. Morley is apologetic: the abdication was a false step. For Buckle it was something to be cynical about. This has been the pattern respectively for admirers and detractors of Gladstone.

Once a fallacious interpretation is accepted of the abdication as a simple impulsive mistake, an 'anticipation' by at least ten years of the 'natural course of events',[1] the 'Bulgarian atrocities' of 1876 becomes a wholly facile and misleading explanation of Gladstone's return to full political commitment. Gladstone in 1876 did not merely begin where he left off in 1874. The abdication signified a real interruption and a real change of course. Certainly the 'Bulgarian atrocities', in themselves, were not enough to induce Gladstone to go back on his decision. Something much more profound was required—no less indeed than an earthquake shaking the structure of English politics to its foundations; and to understand this it is necessary to understand the nature of Gladstone's evolution as a politician.

This evolution is characterised by two interlocking themes, derived ultimately from a single source. One is Gladstone the leader of the 'masses'; the other, Gladstone the European. The first was the dominant factor in determining the abdication; both were instrumental in his intervention in the Eastern question and the consequent cancellation of the abdication.

*

Gladstone's 'European sense' (to use the phrase of J. L. Hammond[2]), chronologically the senior and the more fundamentally creative of these themes, was a catholic largeness of vision and sympathy embracing Europe as a cultural and spiritual community. Gladstone conceived the European state system as a moral order, a family of nations, with a common public law. He conducted the policy of his own country in this spirit, and attempted

---

[1] H. W. Lucy, *A Diary of Two Parliaments, I, The Disraeli Parliament, 1874–1880* (1885), p. 115.
[2] *Gladstone and the Irish Nation* (1938), Chap. V.

to persuade or influence others, both inside and outside his own country, to do likewise.

This European sense Gladstone derived from moral and intellectual sources, principally the intense fervour of his Christianity, combined intimately with his devotion to Homer and Dante. In the fusion of Christianity and Hellenism Gladstone saw the soul and the mind of the European body. This body was to him a living reality, not merely a literary or political concept borrowed from past or current fashions of thought. It was the central feature of a coherent personal politico-religious vision. To Gladstone the European concert had to be the true expression of 'Europe' in the same way that Homer had to presage Christian revelation: to satisfy his personal moral system.

Gladstone reached the full development of his European sense by overcoming the limitations of his training in the strictest orthodox disciplines of Evangelicalism and Toryism. It was a painful process, for he was strong and tenacious of mind and deeply earnest and sincere in every opinion he held. Gladstone's religion was so much the dominating feature of his life that the first visions of broader horizons necessarily had to come through it. After a visit to Rome in 1832 he suddenly grasped the ideal of the unity of the Christian Church. This, and the influence of the Oxford Movement, began the disintegration of his Evangelicalism. But it also had repercussions outside the religious sphere. For Gladstone, the most valuable contribution of the Oxford Movement was that it did for England what Guizot, Villemain, Michelet, and Cousin had done earlier for France; it 'opened, broadened, deepened the issues and meanings of European history . . . reminded us that history is European; that it is quite unintelligible if treated as merely local'.[1] Gladstone's Anglo-Catholic Churchmanship was very much part and parcel of his catholic political outlook.

The High Toryism in which Gladstone had been educated began to disintegrate under the pressure of free trade. He abandoned protectionism and followed Peel. It is through Peelite Conservatism, and particularly through Aberdeen, that the pedigree of Gladstone's European sense is to be traced. It owed much more to Castlereagh than to Cobden. The doctrines of the Manchester School had little

---

[1] J. Morley, *The Life of William Ewart Gladstone* (2 vol. ed., 1905), vol, i, pp. 163–4.

C

appeal for Gladstone. He shared some of their assumptions, particularly a belief in free trade as a moral influence in international relations, a belief in the virtue of strict economy, and a disbelief in the economic advantages of empire. He shared with Cobden and Bright the credit for that 'great European operation', the Commercial Treaty with France in 1860. But fundamentally Gladstone and the Manchester School had little in common. The logic of Gladstone's European sense made him essentially interventionist, however much he might wobble on occasions; the Manchester Schoolmen tended to be simple isolationists. Free trade to Gladstone meant a true binding together of nations, a more intimate diplomatic concert; to the Manchester School it meant the end of the need to have a foreign policy at all. The Manchester School wanted to get rid of the colonies; Gladstone wanted to preserve the imperial connection in a system of free communities in free association, even if it involved some financial sacrifice. Gladstone and Bright fought together against the Crimean War and Disraeli's Eastern policy for quite different reasons and quite different objects.

In a very special and limited sense, however, Gladstone may perhaps be described as 'isolationist'; and this partial paradox has been the source of much misunderstanding. In 1876, under the stimulus of the Eastern question, Gladstone made a note on a text of Grattan on Ireland. Britain's special influence in Europe, Gladstone pointed out, derived from the husbanding of its 'moral strength' and by employing it in the interests of freedom, peace, and justice. This would not only maintain the dignity and fame of Britain but secure it also the unbought and spontaneous gratitude of the civilised world. Britain, insisted Gladstone, did not need to embark on a 'continental' policy of self-seeking, pride, prestige, and direct competition with other powers whose circumstances were quite different.[1] Britain thus had, in Gladstone's view, a peculiar capacity, and hence a peculiar obligation, to provide moral leadership for Europe. This deduction of 'selective interventionism' from a principle of a moral-husbanding quasi-isolationism raised many points of apparent contradiction; but in essence Gladstone's outlook remains intelligible and consistent.

Another intellectual revelation came to Gladstone when, in a

[1] Gladstone Papers, British Museum Add. MSS 44763, ff. 43–4.

conversation with Guizot, he realised how English treatment of Ireland appeared to intelligent foreigners. It is Hammond's opinion that had Gladstone then gone to Ireland instead of Italy there would have been results as important as those which followed his visit to Naples.[1] However, Gladstone went to Italy, and the squalid oppression he witnessed in Naples excited in him a reaction which in some ways foreshadowed his later outburst on the Bulgarian case. Gladstone was too distracted in the following years to give much time to the Irish question, but the impression made on him by Guizot remained. He wrote in 1872: 'It helped me on towards what has since been done.'[2]

Gladstone approved reluctantly but firmly the declaration of war against Russia in 1854 to vindicate, as he saw it, the public law of Europe. But later he opposed the continuance of the war, at the cost of intense unpopularity, when he became convinced that its original character had been lost in a scramble to assert national prestige. He advocated the restoration of the concert, and particularly a resumption of the so-called 'policy of Canning'—co-operation with Russia, or rather, intervention alongside Russia as a means of keeping Russia curbed—as the indispensable condition of a sane Eastern policy. This was to be the burden of his argument after 1875, when the Eastern question was re-opened once more.

On the Italian question Gladstone found himself in complete agreement with Russell and Palmerston. Much as he disliked and distrusted Palmerston, Gladstone disliked the Austrian and Papal sympathies of Derby and Disraeli even more. He joined Palmerston's Liberal cabinet in 1859 on European principles. His emerging Liberalism was not a necessary and integral part of his European sense—over Naples, as will be noted shortly, he appealed as a Conservative to the conscience of Conservative Europe—but it was certainly essential to its full and mature development. Paradoxically, Gladstone's distrust of Palmerston arose largely from the same reason that led him to join Palmerston's cabinet. Italy was almost their one common ground of agreement. This Gladstone chose to regard as decisive; but as he had become a Liberal on European principles, so he had to battle Palmerston continually in defence of those principles. Palmerston shared

[1] Hammond, *Gladstone and the Irish Nation*, p. 70.
[2] Morley, *Gladstone*, vol. i, p. 874.

nothing of Gladstone's sense of Britain's moral obligations as a great power. Gladstone clashed repeatedly with Palmerston: over the Chinese wars, the prosecution of the Crimean War, over the Suez Canal project (which Palmerston wanted to block as a threat to British imperial interests), over rearmament in the early eighteen-sixties; over everything, in short, represented in the doctrine *civis Romanus sum* of Palmerston's great speech in the Don Pacifico debate. Gladstone insisted that the object of British foreign policy should be 'to develop and mature the action of a common, or public, or European opinion . . . but should beware of seeming to lay down the law of that opinion by her own authority, and thus run the risk of setting against her, and against right and justice, the general sentiment which ought to be, and generally would be, arrayed in their favour'.[1]

Gladstone repudiated imperialism in every shape and form. The ideal of the beneficent sway of an imperial master race had no attraction for him. India seems hardly to have entered his thoughts. The grandeur of Imperial Rome left him cold. He was distinctly a Hellenist. It was the Greek idea as opposed to the Roman which appealed to him. His attitude to the colonies was Hellenic. The sort of thing that captured his imagination most readily was the spectacle of the Homeric Montenegrins fighting splendidly for their freedom against the Turkish hordes. Gladstone's concept of a beneficent pervasive power was that it should be moral and religious rather than civil: a moral order for the European concert and a union of the Christian churches. Hence his dismay at the tendencies represented by Bismarck on the one hand and Pius IX on the other.

Conversion to Irish disestablishment in 1865[2] may be said to mark the maturity of Gladstone's catholic politics. The rest of his career was essentially a working out, a deepening and widening, of this stream. He laboured assiduously and practically for his ideals. He insisted on Russia's seeking formal European confirmation of her abrogation of the Black Sea clauses of the Treaty of Paris—an unsatisfactory outcome, but at least an assertion of principle. Gladstone's persistent efforts to dissuade Bismarck from annexing Alsace-Lorraine expressed his desire to promote the principle of government by consent. His mind was beginning to

[1] *Ibid.*, p. 952.   [2] Hammond, *Gladstone and the Irish Nation*, pp. 78-9.

move towards the idea of Home Rule for Ireland as early as the eighteen-seventies.[1] His initiative in settling the *Alabama* claims expressed a highly practical wish to set a striking precedent for international arbitration. Constantly he urged his central political belief: 'the pursuit of objects which are European by means which are European, in concert with the mind of the rest of Europe and supported by its authority'.[2]

In the religious sphere Gladstone was active behind the scenes in attempting to moderate the ultramontane aggressiveness of the Vatican Council of 1870, though he had to wait until he had unburdened himself of office before making his attitude public. Of more immediate relevance to the Eastern question was the deep interest which Gladstone shared with the High Church party generally in the Reunion conferences between the Anglican, Old Catholic, and Eastern Orthodox Churches at Bonn in 1874 and 1875.

★

Meanwhile, Gladstone had become a leader of the masses. This, like his Liberalism, was not an integral part of his European sense; again like his Liberalism, it was more a result than a cause of his widening sympathies. Certainly in any case they were both very intimately related to his political catholicism. The difference made is best illustrated by comparing the Neapolitan and Bulgarian cases. In 1851 Gladstone, the disciple of the good Lord Aberdeen, appealed to the consciences of the 'established Governments of Europe as such', as 'a member of the Conservative party in one of the great families of European nations', who was 'compelled to remember that that party stands in virtual and real, though perhaps unconscious, alliance' with those established governments.[3] Gladstone made no appeal for the overthrow of the Bourbon régime. The gravamen of his charge was that the misgovernment of the Kingdom of the Two Sicilies was a standing encouragement to republicanism. He was shocked most profoundly at the barbarity of a judicial system by which cultured gentlemen were chained in double irons to ruffians of the ordinary criminal classes.

---

[1] *Ibid.*, p. ix; see also below, Chap. 8, §2.
[2] P. Magnus, *Gladstone* (1954), p. 175.
[3] *Two Letters to the Earl of Aberdeen on the State Prosecutions of the Neapolitan Government* (pamphlet, 1851), p. 6.

By 1876, however, Gladstone had outgrown his reverence for the principle that respect was due 'to Governments in general, whether they be absolute' or not[1]; he appealed to the conscience of the British democracy to vindicate the right of a people to revolt against oppression, advocating the sweeping away of the corrupt and vicious régime in Bulgaria.

Gladstone became a popular leader really against his will. It was the most conspicuous instance of his tendency to be carried to unwelcome conclusions, with great misgiving, by the logic of his mind. The deaths of his old Peelite friends Aberdeen, Newcastle, Graham, and Sidney Herbert, loosened the restraints which bound him to the old order. Of the others, Russell, eager for franchise reform, was hardly a restraining influence—quite the reverse, indeed, when the Eastern question arose. Granville, Gladstone's rising confidant, owed that position to his charm and complaisance rather than to strength of mind and willingness to be awkward. Soon only Palmerston himself was left; and he predicted trouble should Gladstone step into his shoes.

The masses themselves made a deep impression on Gladstone by their patient endurance of the cotton famine during the American Civil War and by their restraint during the great franchise agitation under Bright's leadership. In their turn, the masses came to recognise in Gladstone certain qualities they admired and respected. Palmerston had foreseen this: 'Enthusiasm, passion, sympathy, simplicity—these were the qualities which moved the masses; and Gladstone had them all.'[2] This was the meaning of the immense demonstration at Newcastle in 1862, when Gladstone received a popular ovation which affected him profoundly.[3] By 1864 Gladstone had come to accept in his own mind the principle of manhood suffrage. This, with his conversion to Irish disestablishment, naturally meant that he could not longer represent the University of Oxford. He was ejected, smarting, and found himself amid the popular constituencies, 'unmuzzled'.

The eighteen-sixties were the most important formative decade in Gladstone's career. The years 1864–5 were especially critical. His mature European sense was then fused with his new democratic sympathies. They formed a highly combustible compound. Palmer-

---

[1] *Ibid.*, p. 5.   [2] Hammond, *Gladstone and the Irish Nation*, p. 80.
[3] See G. J. Holyoake, *Bygones Worth Remembering* (1905), vol. i, pp. 289–90.

ston, commenting on the deplorable tendencies of Gladstone's development, predicted that he would 'always be more powerful out of office than in it'.[1] This judgment is prescient not only with regard to the period 1876–80. After 1865 the characteristic Gladstone is not the official Gladstone, the great reforming administrator and financier—though Gladstone certainly remained great in those spheres; the truly characteristic Gladstone is the leader of a popular crusade against what he conceived to be some fundamental moral evil: the Irish Establishment in 1868, 'Beaconsfieldism' from 1876 to 1880, the wrongs of the Union in 1885 and after.

This Gladstone was a true demagogue in the highest sense, but his demagogy had a strictly limited application. This, like his doctrine of selective interventionism, caused much misunderstanding. For Gladstone expected, once he had achieved the central object of a great political crusade, to be able to revert to his Peelite persona, finicking about with minor economies as if nothing had happened.

It is most misleading to describe Gladstone as a 'Radical' in any but a most carefully qualified sense. He never became a democrat, certainly never an egalitarian. His democratic sympathies had a moral origin. He came to believe, more and more, that the masses, once relieved of the burdens which debased them, had a simple capacity for unselfish righteous judgment on great controverted questions which the 'classes' evidently had not. But Gladstone emphatically did not enter, in any sense, into the great current of mass politics, the new phenomenon of the later nineteenth century. He had very little knowledge of the 'social problem' as a whole or in any aspect—much less than Disraeli, for instance. He had no real awareness of what the masses thought. He never modified his Peelite economic ideas. He had little understanding of and less sympathy with all the tendencies characteristic of the period after 1870. He was moving not from right to left in the conventional manner, but rather into a lofty station of his own, remote from the main political course. He did not attempt to base his power on mass support. He made no real effort to adapt himself to new political developments. He attended the inauguration of Chamberlain's National Liberal Federation in 1877, for instance; but his object was to capture it for his Eastern policy, not

[1] Hammond, op. cit., p. 80.

to endorse its programme, just as he swallowed the Radical programme in 1891 for the sake of Home Rule.

Gladstone's politics had become, in fact, sublimely self-centred.
He did not know the masses, or care very much what they wanted.
It was simply that on certain questions which Gladstone conceived
as turning on a moral issue, and which excited his imagination, he
found he could employ mass enthusiasm in a righteous cause. His
subjectivity, moreover, was complemented powerfully by the conviction that he was, in a direct and special way, however unworthy,
an instrument of God's will. His journals abound in expressions in
this sense. But Gladstone never became a simple fanatic. He never
ceased to be a politician, or assumed that the small necessary arts
of manoeuvre or minor opportunism could be dispensed with. His
politics, however, became essentially personal, almost idiosyncra-
tic, and in a strict sense irresponsible, to an extent incompatible
with the usages of English political life. As a rule, nothing is
more useless in studying Gladstone than the assumption that normal and conventional criteria of judgment will be adequate. Gladstone could never 'retire' from politics as any other statesman
could, in a manner conformable to the canons of recognised behaviour. For Gladstone politics was not a simple secular activity—
the vehicle of a great career, or even a means of effecting noble objects; it was an aspect of what, for convenience, has been called his
'European sense', which in turn was of the essence of his immensely
strong and pervasive Christian faith. Gladstone was an Early Father
of the Church embroiled in the questions of the nineteenth century.

Most people, not surprisingly, misconceived the drift of Gladstone's mind. Whig forebodings and Radical expectations were
equally irrelevant. How could Hartington and Chamberlain dream
that they would alike be driven into the cabinet of Lord Salisbury?
The event is so familiar that we are in danger of overlooking its
fantastic character and profound significance. Neither of them
could have been expected to read correctly the riddle of the ministry
of 1868–74, which follows the Gladstonian pattern with classic
precision. Gladstone is swept to power on a wave of popular enthusiasm, to all appearances the embodiment of the 'dangerous
character' of a democratic statesman. He employs that enthusiasm
for his own purposes, and lets it die away. He then goads the
Nonconformists, reduces the Radicals to incredulous despair, and

drives the trade union leaders to Disraeli's side. He is then re-
soundingly beaten in 1874 on a programme of extinguishing the
income tax and goes down with his Peelite colours flying. Abdication was a fitting sequel.

Blinkered by his subjectivity, Gladstone could not understand
how the bond of moral rapport which he conceived as existing
between himself and the masses, the inner mainspring of his political life, had come to be snapped. But he recognised that without it
there was no point in his continuing. Moreover, politics now
lacked the essential attribute which Gladstone's psychology had
come to demand of it: a great moral cause. He thought the Irish
question in both its religious and agrarian aspects was substantially settled, or at least, as far as it could be in his own time, which
he could not foresee would stretch on for more than twenty largely
vigorous years. He was aware, in a general way, that he was out
of touch with the spirit of the times. He could not easily imagine
any 'exceptional circumstances' worthy of calling him back,
though he was careful not to reject such a possibility entirely, for
he greatly distrusted Disraeli. He wrote to Granville on 25
November 1874: 'Nothing will rally the party but a cause: or
such portentous blundering as is almost beyond hope or fear.'[1]
But in any case, his reluctance to return wholly to political life
would be very great. The long process of his full engagement in
the Bulgarian question makes this clear.

2 The Spirit of British Eastern Policy

The Bulgarian atrocities agitation was an extraordinary manifestation of the tradition of popular moral protest which distinguished the public life of England in the nineteenth century. It
bore no formal resemblances to any of the agitations which had
gone before to emancipate slaves, achieve reform, or abolish corn
laws. It had—at least until the last phase of its existence—no
central organisation, no executive, no system of committees or
circuits. The proudest and most reiterated claim of its advocates
was that it was 'spontaneous'.[2] This claim, made with substantial

---

[1] Ramm, *Correspondence of Mr. Gladstone*, vol. ii, p. 461.
[2] See e.g. *Spectator*, 16 September 1876, p. 1150; E. A. Freeman, 'The English
People in Relation to the Eastern Question', *Contemporary Review*, February 1877,
p. 490; W. T. Stead, *The M.P. for Russia* (1909), vol. i, p. 247.

justice, became elevated into something more pretentious: a mystique, a confession of faith in the absolute purity of the agitation, a kind of dogma of immaculate conception and virgin birth. W. T. Stead, at this time editor of the halfpenny Darlington *Northern Echo*, in fact ascribed the agitation to the direct intervention of God.[1] Others less extreme were content to dwell on the 'mystery'[2] of the genesis of such a 'sublime national emotion',[3] or speculate on the problem of understanding the 'real secret' of the 'intensity of passionate excitement prevailing during the Bulgarian agitation'.[4] 'Men came together', wrote the historian Freeman, 'as if to deliver their own souls, as if their hearts could not rest within them till their tongues had spoken.' They came 'to wash their own hands clean from the deeds of which they had just heard the tale'. It seemed 'as if the common earth and the common human nature had received a defilement, which it needed some rite of lustration to wipe off from the consciences of all mankind'.[5]

Extravagant though Freeman's interpretation is, it expresses a fundamental truth about the agitation: the intensity which its moral indignation derived from a special sense of guilt and complicity created by the pro-Turkish policy of the British government. The atrocities presented a direct and unavoidable moral challenge as acts to which British policy made the British public, in a way, accessories. For practical purposes, the agitation was a movement of protest against the spirit and purpose of British Eastern policy; and an appreciation of the character of that policy and its implication in the events in Bulgaria is an essential prelude to a study of the atrocities agitation.

Equally essential is an appreciation of the moral sensibility of the society out of which the agitation came. The Bulgarian atrocities provoked the most convincing demonstration of the susceptibility of the High Victorian public conscience; and the agitation can be understood only in relation to the development and refinement of that public conscience. It was in the interaction between a special sense of complicity in the atrocities created by the circumstances of British policy and a peculiar refinement of public moral-

---

[1] J. W. Robertson Scott, *The Life and Death of a Newspaper* (1952), p. 104.
[2] *Nonconformist*, 13 September 1876, p. 905.
[3] Freeman, loc. cit.
[4] J. Guinness Rogers, *An Autobiography* (1903), p. 211.
[5] Freeman, loc. cit.

ity created by the circumstances of social development in nine-teenth-century England that the 'real secret' or 'mystery' of the genesis of the agitation lies.

*

Palmerston formulated in the eighteen-thirties a policy postulat-ing an independent, vigorous Ottoman Empire as a barrier against Russian and French ambitions in the Near East. The implications of this policy, especially after the diplomatic defeat and withdrawal of the French in 1840, were broadly Liberal. The Turks were to be bolstered to protect the liberties of Europe from Russia, and inci-dentally to secure the British position in India. Greek independ-ence, though far from complete, had largely removed the greatest source of irritation between English Liberal opinion and the Turks. Little was known of Serbs and less of Bulgarians. Indeed, the Turks themselves shared with the Poles, Italians, and Hungarians the benefits of the newly-developed English popular enthusiasm for oppressed peoples.

This enthusiasm was the greatest factor in making war between Britain and Russia in 1854. The Crimean policy, identified with Palmerston, of regarding Turkey as a link in the chain of European liberties, was imposed upon a reluctant cabinet by popular pressure. Palmerston's opponents—a 'miserable minority', as an eminent Liberal statesman recalled them in 1878 [1]—could make no effective resistance against the popular demand for war. Their leaders, Cobden (who knew Russia and the East well) and Bright, suffered political eclipse; Delane of *The Times*, strongly anti-Turkish, had to capitulate to the public mood.

The crisis of the eighteen-fifties, unlike the crises of the thirties and seventies, had its roots in Europe, not in the East; and both the Treaty of Paris of 1856 and the Tripartite Treaty between Austria, France, and Britain purporting to guarantee the Crimean settlement against Russian revisionism faithfully reflected this fact. The Ottoman Empire was treated much as if it had been Poland, liberated from Russian domination. Turkey, its independence and integrity guaranteed, was to be screened henceforth from Russian

---

[1] S. Childers, *The Life and Correspondence of the Right Hon. Hugh C. E. Childers* (1901), vol. i, p. 251.

pressure and penetration, a full member of the European system and a guardian of its civilised values, as symbolised by the Imperial Rescript (*Hatt-i Humayun*) of 1856, an imposing programme of enlightened reforms. As a contribution towards solving the real, underlying problems of the Eastern question, the Crimean settlement—certainly defensible and perhaps necessary in its own terms—was fundamentally irrelevant. Yet upon this irrelevance British post-Crimean policy was firmly founded; and for twenty years and more after 1856 the Foreign Office expended immense energy and ingenuity in ignoring obstinately the mounting evidences that its Eastern policy was getting increasingly out of phase with reality.

In spite of strenuous efforts by Stratford Canning (Lord Stratford de Redcliffe), architect of the British anti-Russian policy in Constantinople and chief begetter of the *Hatt-i Humayun*, Palmerston could not be persuaded to make the Turkish promises of reform an integral part of the Treaty of Paris, with machinery for enforcement and supervision given to the concert. Invincibly optimistic about Turkish capacity for self-reform, Palmerston wanted above all else to avoid giving the Russians any pretext whatever for further interference in Turkish affairs. Stratford then advocated that British policy be made a 'fulcrum' on which the Turks could be levered into reform; but he failed also in this. The logic of the Crimean policy was against him. That war was not fought to secure the good government of the Christian subject peoples of Turkey. The bulk of expert opinion, represented by Palmerston's particular protégé and later biographer, Lytton Bulwer, who intrigued against Stratford and ultimately succeeded him in Constantinople in 1857, held that reform must come in its own good time.

The Ottoman Empire, accordingly, continued to be misgoverned, despite the efforts of a few sincere reformers, in the most gross and fundamental manner. Muslim fanaticism nullified the promises of the *Hatt* to accord social equality to the Christians. A conspicuous feature of the misgovernment in the period after the Crimean War was extravagant borrowing in London and Paris, totalling nearly £200 millions by 1872, with investors often getting up to nine per cent. Most of this was hopelessly squandered; and by 1875 the Turkish government was bankrupt. Though the general economic condition of the Christians probably improved in this period, despite oppressive and corrupt tax-farming, this improvement in itself made the civil and religious disabilities imposed upon them correspondingly insupportable. Pan-Slav propaganda, mainly Russian in origin, encouraged the emerging national consciousness of the Serbs and Bulgarians. This added a further and powerful element to the increasing pressure for emancipation.

As the Ottoman régime declined steadily down the spiral of maladministration, corruption, oppression, and insurrection, British Eastern policy settled more and more rigidly into a Palmerstonian Turcophile orthodoxy. The name of Stratford de Redcliffe was used without justification as a symbol of this policy. While preserving Stratford's outward Russophobia it ignored his central thesis that Turkey must reform to survive. Stratford lived long enough to become, in 1876, a cordial supporter of the agitation against the policy ostensibly based on his tradition. He told Gladstone that he would 'rather have cut off his hand than subscribed the tripartite Treaty of Guarantee'[1]; and it was a stroke of ironic fitness on Gladstone's part to dedicate to Stratford his *Bulgarian Horrors*.

Increasingly also the Liberal implications of the Crimean policy faded away. Though given temporarily increased currency by the suppression of the Polish revolt in 1863, the myth of Russia as the gendarme of reaction wore very thin; and by the time of Disraeli's second ministry in 1874 the cause of Turkey had come to be identified predominantly with the maintenance of British imperial interests.

Despite occasional outbursts of impatience from Russell, British Eastern policy remained incapable of adjusting itself to meet changing circumstances. Those who, like Stratford, appreciated the hopelessness of unreformed Turkey, could put forward no feasible alternative policy of sufficient weight to overcome the inertia of the orthodox tradition. In the affair of the extensive massacres of the Maronite Christians by the Druses in the Lebanon and Damascus in 1860, British policy distinguished itself above all by a pathological suspicion of French motives in intervening on behalf of the Roman Catholic Maronites, protégés of France since the Crusades; and by consequent patronage of the Druses.

[1] Gladstone to Granville, 27 June 1876, Granville Papers, P.R.O., 30, 29/29.

In the Cretan insurrection and massacres of 1866–7 the Foreign Office maintained an undeviatingly pro-Turkish attitude. The protests of individuals like Argyll[1] and Freeman failed to arouse public indignation.[2] Balkan nationalism, when taken into account at all, continued to be deprecated as a subversive force fomented by Russian intrigue. Well expressive of the spirit of British Eastern policy was the notoriety enjoyed by Bulwer (Lord Dalling) as having recommended to the Turks the expediency of planting among the Bulgarians a horde of semi-barbaric, nomadic Circassians, fleeing from the restraints of Russian rule, to provide a permanent source of intimidation.[3]

Blue Books were carefully edited for public consumption to give as favourable as possible a picture of the Turks and a conversely unfavourable one of Christian insurgents.[4] So oppressive was the orthodox tradition that consuls tended to supply the ambassador with information agreeable rather than accurate. The case of Consul Skene at Aleppo provides an exceptionally revealing illustration of this tendency. In a circular with two enclosures Bulwer requested all consuls to supply answers to twenty-four questions for the implied purpose of providing evidence to rebut certain charges of misgovernment made by the Russians against the Turks. Unfortunately Skene did not get a copy of the first enclosure, which stressed the point that while H.M. Government wished for the well-being of Christians in Turkey, it wished also 'as you well know' to maintain the integrity of the Turkish Empire. Consuls were therefore urged to bear in mind when answering the questions in the second enclosure not to measure conditions by an 'impossible standard' and to take into consideration undoubted exaggerations in charges made against the Porte and undoubted

[1] Argyll republished in 1876 his speech of 1867: *Conduct of the Foreign Office During the Insurrection in Crete in 1867* (Glasgow).
[2] See the comment of the *Edinburgh Review*, October 1876, p. 550.
[3] See [H. Sandwith], 'The Servian War', *British Quarterly Review*, January 1877, p. 200. P. Brock, 'The Fall of Circassia: a Study in Private Diplomacy', *English Historical Review*, **71** (1956), pp. 401–27. deals with the background of the Circassian migration.
[4] For some insight into this see H. W. V. Temperley, 'The Bulgarian and Other Atrocities 1875–1878 in the Light of Historical Criticism', Appendix I, 'Excisions and Omissions in the Blue Books Dealing with 1875–6', *Proceedings of the British Academy*, **17** (1931); H. W. V. Temperley and L. M. Penson, *A Century of Diplomatic Blue Books, 1814–1914* (Cambridge 1938), 'The Eastern Question Papers of the Disraeli Administration, 1874–80'; W. N. Medlicott, 'Vice-Consul Dupuis' "Missing" Dispatch of June 23, 1876', *Journal of Modern History*, **4** (1932); and Duke of Argyll, *The Eastern Question* (1879), vol. i, pp. 38–9.

evidence of Slavonic intrigue.[1] Skene supplied Bulwer with the evidence ostensibly required, and then to his horror received the first enclosure by a later post. He hurriedly sent off a second series of answers better calculated to conform to prevailing official taste, with the apology: 'I thus furnished what information I could without being aware of the motives dictating the questions, and without being in possession of the valuable instructions conveyed by the other circular.' He hoped he would be forgiven for the 'crude notions' of his first and objective report.[2] This particular incident throws much light on consular and ambassadorial psychology at the time when British policy-makers needed above all to be informed fully and frankly of the nature of the Turkish operations in Bulgaria in May 1876.

Sir Henry Elliot, promoted from Florence to the embassy at Constantinople in 1867, continued the Turcophile tradition of Palmerston and Bulwer unchanged. Unlike the supple and adroit Bulwer, however, Elliot did not command much esteem. Salisbury, the Secretary for India, for one, thought him incompetent. After the Bulgarian scandal broke in 1876 Salisbury reminded his colleague Carnarvon that he had been 'preaching' for the past two years, privately and in cabinet, against Elliot's 'stupidity and caprices'.[3]

*

The long looked-for crisis came at last in 1875. Insurrections of Serbs, goaded by tax-farmers, broke out in July and August in the Herzegovina and Bosnia. Despite the agitated urgings of the British Foreign Office, the Turks could not stamp out the revolt. An investigation by a committee of the consuls of the powers, accepted with a very ill grace by Derby, the Foreign Secretary, reported that the insurgents' complaints were just and reasonable.[4] The affair dragged on, getting daily more dangerous as the Serbs in the autonomous principality and in Montenegro clamoured for intervention to liberate their oppressed brethren.

[1] *Accounts and Papers, State Papers*, LXVII (1861), *Reports Received from Her Majesty's Consuls Relating to the Condition of Christians in Turkey, 1860*, no. 1, Bulwer to Russell, 11 June 1860.
[2] *Ibid.*, no. 18, Skene to Bulwer, 20 August 1860. See also Sedley Taylor, *The Conduct of Her Majesty's Ministers on the Eastern Question* (pamphlet, 1877), pp. 8–9.
[3] Salisbury to Carnarvon, 13 September 1876, Salisbury Papers, Christ Church, Oxford.
[4] For criticisms of the bias of British policy at this time see the Duke of Argyll, *What the Turks Are, and How We Have Been Helping Them* (pamphlet, Glasgow 1876).

A new and genuine Eastern crisis was most unwelcome to all the powers. The Austro-Hungarian government feared that a general collapse of the Ottoman régime in Europe would result in a large South Slav state, with disastrous implications for the Habsburg monarchy; and therefore worked to get the Turks to come to terms quickly before further complications could arise. St Petersburg, careful above all else not to collide once more with a Crimean coalition and deprecating pan-Slav extremism, was quite prepared to be cautious and co-operative. Bismarck cared nothing for the Eastern question in itself but everything for continued good relations between Austria and Russia, and so worked with them for a quick solution. In December 1875 Andrassy, the Austro-Hungarian Foreign Minister, presented a Note to the Turks reminding them of their unfulfilled promises of reform and suggesting a series of practical concessions based on the consuls' recommendations. The French and Italian cabinets adhered cordially to the Note, but the British only with the greatest reluctance and distaste, and at the direct request of the Turks themselves, quite willing to have among their judges one who could be relied upon to sympathise with the Turkish point of view.[1]

Disraeli resented the initiative of the Imperial powers in presuming to take the matter into their own hands without prior consultation with the British government. He regarded the Andrassy Note as a dangerous breach in the spirit and letter of the clauses of the Treaty of Paris which disclaimed any collective right of interference in the internal affairs of Turkey. It was embarrassing also that certain agrarian reforms recommended in the Note bore unpalatable analogies to Irish demands.[2]

The Turks, strong in the knowledge of British sympathy, did nothing. When, in May 1876, the Imperial powers repeated their advice in stronger terms in the form of the Berlin Memorandum, Disraeli and Derby rejected it out of hand. As a riposte,[3] and probably in conscious imitation of previous British actions in 1849 and 1853, Disraeli ordered a squadron, shortly afterwards rein-

[1] For the general diplomatic background see David Harris, *A Diplomatic History of the Balkan Crisis of 1875–1878: The First Year* (Stanford 1936).
[2] R. W. Seton-Watson, 'Russo-British Relations During the Eastern Crisis', II, *Slavonic Review*, **3** (1924–5), pp. 657–8.
[3] Disraeli to the Queen, 29 May 1876, in G. E. Buckle (ed.), *The Letters of Queen Victoria*, 2nd Series, vol. ii, 1870–8 (1926), p. 455.

forced to a powerful fleet, to Besika Bay near the Dardanelles, where it was welcomed by the Turks as a symbol of British willingness to prosecute another Crimean War.[1] This, as later events indicated, Disraeli would have been quite willing to do had he thought it necessary; but his aim was to avoid a 'drift' to war in the alleged Crimean manner by an unmistakable show of firmness.[2] In June the Berlin Memorandum was withdrawn ignominiously.

Disraeli could claim a great successs in his new forward policy to restore British prestige after the Gladstonian period of concentration on domestic reform. He had already scored a coup by his purchase of the Khedive's Suez Canal shares. He now imposed on the surprised and discomfited Imperial powers the recognition that Britain would not henceforth accept the rôle of a mere subsidiary consenting party like France or Italy. Opinion in parliament and the country generally applauded Disraeli's action.[3] It came as a refreshing change to what was vaguely held to be a humiliating series of adverse international arbitration decisions during Gladstone's ministry. The strong misgivings of the Queen —always inclined to think Continentally—about rejecting the Memorandum[4] and sending the fleet[5] faded away in a glow of patriotic exultation.

It is difficult to assess what positive steps, if any, Disraeli would have taken at this point. He made sweeping and unconvincing claims later as to the policy he and Derby were preparing to put forward to settle the question, only to be forestalled by the Serbian and Montenegrin declarations of war on Turkey at the beginning of July,[6] declarations of war which they themselves in any case made almost certain by causing the withdrawal of the Berlin Memorandum. But, however this may have been, Disraeli's position was soon overwhelmingly compromised by news of events in Bulgaria.

★

---

[1] *Times*, 8 June 1876, p. 10.
[2] W. F. Monypenny and G. E. Buckle, *The Life of Benjamin Disraeli, Earl of Beaconsfield* (new ed. 1929), vol. ii, pp. 900–1.
[3] E.g. *Times*, 20 May 1876, p. 11; *Daily News*, 20 May 1876, p. 5; *Spectator*, 27 May 1876, p. 672.
[4] Queen to Disraeli, 25 May 1876, Disraeli Papers, Hughenden Manor.
[5] Ponsonby to Disraeli, 2 June 1876, *ibid*.
[6] *Times*, 21 September 1876, p. 9.

D

At the beginning of May Bulgarian nationalists, encouraged by the success of the Serb insurgents, attempted an insurrection in various parts of the *vilayet* of Eastern Rumelia.[1] It was a feeble effort, incompetently conducted. The Turks, however, harassed and exasperated, determined to crush it with exemplary ruthlessness. As many troops as could be spared in Constantinople were sent out; but the main part of the operation was conducted by a general levy of Muslim irregulars (*bashi-bazouks*), including many Circassians. These were let loose on an almost totally unarmed Christian population, of which only the smallest fraction was implicated in the attempted insurrection. Some fifteen thousand Bulgarian men, women, and children were massacred, with all attendant circumstances of atrocity. Over seventy villages, two hundred schools, and ten monasteries were destroyed.[2]

There was nothing new or unusual in the fact either of insurrection or massacre. Both were endemic features of Ottoman administration.[3] The massacres in Bulgaria were not unusually extensive, and there is no reason to assume that they were unusually atrocious. The one unusual and unexpected feature of the whole affair was that it provoked in England the movement of protest which very soon—deprecatingly at first—became known as the Bulgarian atrocities agitation.

To this movement of protest the practitioners of the orthodox policy returned an unyielding answer. The classic statement of their attitude is the dispatch of Sir Henry Elliot to Lord Derby of 4

[1] The most convenient survey of the insurrection is in David Harris, *Britain and the Bulgarian Horrors of 1876* (Chicago 1939).

[2] The principal sources are the official reports prepared in 1876 by Eugene Schuyler for the United States government and Walter Baring for the British government. See *Accounts and Papers, State Papers, Turkey*, XC (1877), *Correspondence Respecting the Affairs of Turkey, 1876*, no. 220, Elliot to Derby, 5 September 1876, enclosure 1 (Baring), enclosure 2 (Schuyler).

[3] K. Behesnilian, *Armenian Bondage and Carnage* (1903), Appendix, p. 16, gives estimates of Christians massacred in Turkey in the nineteenth century at the instigation or by the connivance of Turkish authorities.

1822	Greeks, especially in Chios	50,000
1850	Nestorians and Armenians, Kurdistan	10,000
1860	Maronites and Syrians, Lebanon and Damascus	12,000
1876	Bulgarians, Bulgaria	15,000
1894	Armenians, Armenia, Sassum	120,000
1896	Armenians, Constantinople	2,000

The figure for Constantinople in 1896 is certainly an understatement. The massacres in Crete in 1866–8 are omitted. After 1903 there were further massacres: 21,000 Armenians in Cilicia and Northern Syria in 1909; heavy massacres in Albania and Macedonia in 1910–12; nearly a million Armenians during the First World War.

September 1876. In this grave and indignant rebuke to those 'shallow politicians or persons who have allowed their feelings of revolted humanity to make them forget the capital interests involved in the question', Elliot conceded the justice of revulsion at the 'needless and monstrous severity' used by the Turks in suppressing the insurrection, but insisted that the 'necessity' which existed to 'prevent changes from occurring' in the Turkish Empire which 'could be most detrimental' to British interests was 'not affected by the question whether it was 10,000 or 20,000 persons who perished in the suppression'.[1]

3 The Moral Sensibility of the High Victorian Era

Elliot's dispatch of 4 September became a document of great notoriety, much quoted as the ultimate, flagrant revelation of the degradation of policy divorced from morality.[2] More than any other single statement, it made the debate on the Eastern question from 1876 to 1880 the most clearly-defined public conflict in English history on the fundamental problem of the moral nature of the state. The atrocities agitation protested against the attitude and assumptions represented by Elliot on two complementary principles: that states are bound by the same moral laws as individuals; and that it is not merely desirable but essential that decisions of policy should conform strictly and directly to absolute definitions of righteousness. There could be no more characteristic expression of the spirit behind the agitation than this comment by one leading agitator to another of another: 'Pusey says the exact truth. Our party is just the people, of whatever way of thinking about anything else, who believe in right and wrong.'[3]

The strongly anthropomorphic view of the state as a moral agent which distinguished this party can be illustrated aptly in two of its more prominent members, united perhaps in nothing

[1] *Turkey*, XC (1877), no. 221.
[2] E.g. E. A. Freeman, *The Ottoman Power in Europe* (1877), p. 251; Malcolm MacColl, *The Eastern Question* (1877), pp. 411–14; A. Boyle, *The Sympathy and Action of England in the Late Eastern Crisis and What Came of Them* (pamphlet, 1878), p. 7; Duke of Argyll, 'Morality in Politics', *Contemporary Review*, July 1877, pp. 325–6; Goldwin Smith, 'England's Abandonment of the Protectorate of Turkey', *Contemporary Review*, February 1878, pp. 603–4.
[3] Freeman to Liddon, 30 November 1877, Liddon Papers, Keble College Library, Oxford.

else. The formal doctrine of Henry Sidgwick on this point is expounded in his treatment of the 'Principles of External Policy' in
the *Elements of Politics*.[1] Sidgwick, the leader of the moderate
Liberal utilitarian tradition, defined the 'ultimate end and standard
of right conduct' for a state, as for an individual, as 'the happiness
of all who are affected by its actions'. All doctrines to the effect
that the state should not properly be subject to any restraint of duty
limiting the pursuit of its own interest, that its own interest was,
necessarily and properly, its paramount end, that conformity by the
state to rules of international duty can only be on the assumption
that such conformity will conduce to its national interests—all
such doctrines Sidgwick dismissed as 'essentially immoral'.

The Anglo-Catholic Canon Liddon deduced from a postulate of
religiously-derived 'virtuous action' the same conclusion arrived at
by Sidgwick from the greatest-happiness principle. Patriotism he
went so far as to define as 'the feeling which we have about our
relatives':

We wish our relatives to be good men in the first instance, and then
successful men, if success is compatible with goodness. I cannot understand how many excellent people fail to feel thus about their country too;
it would seem to me that exactly in the proportion in which we realise
the fact that a nation is only a very overgrown family . . . will be our
anxiety that this country should act as a good man would act; and that
patriotism consists in wishing this.[2]

Here the morality insisted on by the agitation is at its most
simplistic; but it is none the less cogent for that as the motive
force necessary to impel a massive popular intervention on a
question of foreign policy. Though the atrocities agitation became
unavoidably the vehicle of a good deal of politics, ecclesiastical as
well as secular, it remained in itself overwhelmingly an expression
of an intense moral sensibility in public life.

Certainly it is difficult to sustain the contention that the agitation derived significant strength from the resentment felt in in-
vesting circles at the partial repudiation by the Turks in October
1875 of the interest on their debt.[3] Investors were now to get only

---

[1] 2nd ed. (1897), pp. 297–8.
[2] J. O. Johnston, *Life and Letters of Henry Parry Liddon* (1904), p. 228.
[3] See e.g. W. L. Langer, *European Alliances and Alignments, 1871–1890* (New
York 1931), p. 94.

half the lucrative rate they had been getting[1]; but this did not make the integrity of the Ottoman Empire any less a desideratum. Disraeli, perhaps, could hardly have been expected to resist the temptation to assert, privately, that the agitation against his policy was 'partly produced by the Bulgarian outrages, and partly by the non-payment of Turkish dividends'.[2] And Carlyle, to be sure, had the dubious taste to denounce the Turks in 1876 for, among other things, swallowing up the tribute of the 'widows and orphans of England'.[3] It is possible also that certain of the people drumming up anti-Turkish feeling from the time of the Serb insurrections in 1875 may have been unfortunate in their investments.[4] Nor is it unlikely that the Turks, by their financial default, silenced voices that might otherwise have spoken up for them when the Bulgarian revelations broke on England.[5] But all this amounts to very little beside the indications that such positive influence as the repudiation did exert went predominantly against the agitation of 1876 and was more clearly evident in the jingo outbursts on behalf of the Turks in 1877 and 1878. Rehabilitation of Turkish credit remained the constant and natural aim of the bond-holding interest. The most prominent representatives of this interest, the Levy-Lawsons, proprietors of the Liberal *Daily Telegraph*, in fact slipped their political moorings on the Bulgarian question and became staunch defenders of Disraeli's Eastern policy and the Conservative party.[6] The Jewish community as a whole, traditionally prominent in Turkish investments, was an anti-agitation force.[7]

The very magnitude of the agitation as a popular movement proclaimed a phenomenon not easily to be accounted for on any conventional, or conventionally cynical, level of explanation. In less than six weeks nearly five hundred demonstrations throughout Great Britain, mainly city or town meetings, addressed to the Foreign Office expressions of abhorrence at the atrocities and re-

---

[1] Though even this undertaking was not honoured. See P. W. Clayden, *England Under Lord Beaconsfield* (1880), pp. 159–60; Spencer Walpole, *The History of Twenty-Five Years* (1908), vol. iv, pp. 6, 8–9, 73–4; and *Turkish Debt, a Report by Sir Philip Rose and Mr. John Staniforth* (pamphlet, 1876).

[2] Disraeli to Salisbury, 29 November 1876, Salisbury Papers.

[3] Eastern Question Association, *Report of Proceedings of the National Conference at St. James's Hall, London* (pamphlet, 1876), p. 122.

[4] See below, p. 37.

[5] See the comments of Clayden, *England under Lord Beaconsfield*, p. 160; A. Arnold, *Contemporary Review*, July 1876, p. 203; and G. Carslake Thompson, *Public Opinion and Lord Beaconsfield, 1875–1880* (1886), vol. i, pp. 88–9.

[6] See below, pp. 153–4.   [7] See below, pp. 198ff.

pudiation of the pro-Turkish policy of the government. The agitation culminated in the great National Conference on the Eastern Question in London, which assembled undoubtedly the most brilliant array of intellectual figures ever brought together to intervene in a question of politics in England. The *Spectator*, under Richard Holt Hutton, one of the more enthusiastic admirers of the agitation, saw in it incontrovertible evidence of an extraordinary 'moral healthiness'.[1] Even the *Saturday Review*, the most self-consciously 'anti-sentimental' of the intellectual organs, and hence with a special sense of obligation to resist the agitation, admitted that there was in it undeniable confirmation that 'in England' public opinion was 'greatly modified by moral feeling'.[2]

Agitation about the atrocities on a massive scale was (even allowing for the popular excitement in Slav, Orthodox Russia) indeed a peculiarity of England. There was of course one very obvious reason for this: the British government alone supported the Turks. Had Disraeli adhered to the Berlin Memorandum and sent the fleet to coerce instead of encourage the Turks, there would not have been a Bulgarian atrocities agitation on anything approaching the scale of the actual event. But there was never the slightest doubt about the direction British Eastern policy would take under Disraeli. The traditional policy was for him much more than a mere matter of Palmerstonian orthodoxy; it formed the basis of his personal vision of England as the centre of a great Oriental empire.

Quite apart, however, from the special feeling of complicity which British policy placed on a large section of the British public after the facts of the atrocities became known, the agitation derived its fundamental strength from qualities peculiar to nineteenth-century English civilisation. 'Foreigners', as Derby remarked to Disraeli, 'don't know what to make of the movement; and I am not surprised.'[3] The German theologian Döllinger, 'greatly struck' by the agitation, recognised that it would be almost inconceivable in any Continental country.[4] The German public remained unmoved by the revelations,[5] pointed to by English critics of the

---

[1] 16 September 1876, p. 1150.   [2] 12 August 1876, p. 185.
[3] Derby to Disraeli, 1 October 1876, Disraeli Papers.
[4] Johnston, *Liddon*, p. 208.
[5] See *Times*, 19 September 1876, p. 6; *Westminster Review*, January 1877, pp. 140, 150–1.

agitation like Alfred Austin as an example of admirable and enviable restraint.[1] In France Victor Hugo spoke out[2]; but there was, for all the outraged bond-holders, negligible response.[3] Strossmayer, the great Catholic Bishop of Diakovar and prophet of South Slav union, found himself compelled by the displeasure of the Hungarian government to tread warily in his work to assist the Serbs and Bulgarians.[4] The quietness of the United States was the subject of pleasantly surprised comment,[5] though certainly domestic issues, with the end of Reconstruction, were pressing. In Italy there was more of a stir. The Mazzinian tradition that Italy should be the special champion of national liberty was still strong. Garibaldi put himself at the head of a movement for the liberation of the 'Slavo-Hellenic peninsula', and denounced Disraeli as a 'man without a heart'.[6] And since Vatican policy was virulently anti-Russian and Orthodox Christian, and hence pro-Turkish, Italian anti-clericalism and freemasonry made a special point of taking up with ostentatious zeal the cause of the Serbs and Bulgarians.[7]

In Russia there was widespread religious excitement among the peasants,[8] egged on by the military in many cases, and a considerable amount of pan-Slav as well as religious fervour among the educated classes, patronised by members of the Imperial family. Officers volunteered with enthusiasm to serve in the Serb army against the Turks after the outbreak of the Turkish-Serbian war in July 1876. But popular agitation did not dominate the scene as it did in England. Though it was one of the more important considerations prompting the Czar Alexander and Gorchakov to adopt an interventionist policy in Turkey,[9] it by no means forced them against their better judgment.

*

[1] Alfred Austin, *Russia Before Europe* (pamphlet, 1876), pp. 70–1.
[2] *Bee-Hive*, 2 September 1876.
[3] *Spectator*, 14 October 1876, pp. 1272–3; *Times*, 20 September 1876, p. 9.
[4] See below, p. 192.
[5] G. J. Harney, *The Anti-Turkish Crusade: a Review of a Recent Agitation* (pamphlet, Boston 1876), pp. 4–5.
[6] *Northern Echo*, 28 August 1876, p. 5; 8 September 1876, p. 3; *Daily News*, 10 August 1876, pp. 5–6.
[7] *Catholic Times*, 15 September 1876, p. 5; *Daily News*, 4 September 1876, pp. 5–6.
[8] Most of whom, as Bryce pointed out, did not realise they were Slavs. E.Q.A., *Report*, p. 42.
[9] B. H. Sumner, *Russia and the Balkans, 1870–1880* (Oxford 1937), pp. 186–8, 196.

Without question religion formed the underlying basis of the singularity of English institutions reflected in the singularity of the English reaction to the atrocities. Two evangelical revivals and the Oxford Movement between them made mid-Victorian England a religious society in a deeper and completer sense than any western country since the Reformation.[1] Freeman's 'rite of lustration' is perhaps a little over-coloured, but certainly not hyperbolical.

The social and political consequences of this wide diffusion of religion in the national life are manifest in the great series of ameliorative movements beginning with anti-slavery. The first evangelical revival was the most important single influence in the development of what Jephson called the 'Platform', the tradition of public political controversy on a truly popular level.[2] It provided the moral energy directly of the anti-slavery agitation and indirectly of the anti-corn laws agitation. The Oxford Movement and the second evangelical revival from about 1859 (which tended to be predominantly a Nonconformist affair[3]) were two primary sources of inspiration for the Bulgarian atrocities agitation. The most striking impression given by the atrocities agitation was the prominence at every level of activity of Anglo-Catholic and Nonconformist divines. W. T. Stead, fugleman of 'atrocity-mongers', was himself a typical 'convert' of the second evangelical revival.[4] Later the campaigns of Moody and Sankey gave, in the words of the historian of the religion of the Victorian era, an undoubted 'general quickening' to English religious life in the eighteen-seventies.[5] An illustrative example: Samuel Smith, the Liverpool Presbyterian cotton merchant and one of the committee which invited Moody and Sankey to visit Liverpool in 1875, found himself forced to enter into political activity for the first time in his life to protest against the bolstering of Turkish misrule.[6]

When the *Spectator* asked for the cause of the 'moral healthiness' made so evident by the atrocities agitation, it answered its own question thus: 'the chief distinction of this generation has

---

[1] See the comment of the *Jewish Chronicle*, 1 September 1876, p. 344.
[2] H. Jephson, *The Platform, Its Rise and Progress* (1892), vol. i, p. 213.
[3] L. E. Elliot-Binns, *Religion in the Victorian Era* (1936), p. 213.
[4] F. Whyte, *The Life of W. T. Stead* (1925), vol. i, p. 15.
[5] Elliot-Binns, p. 212.
[6] S. Smith, M.P., *My Life-Work* (1902), p. 119.

been the revival of religious earnestness'.[1] As the *Spectator* went on to point out, this was a phenomenon observable in many countries, for instance in the rise of aggressive ultramontanism in the Catholic states; but in England it took a form of peculiar intensity and pervasiveness. Controversy over education and the Irish Church showed that religious commotion had sharpened the acuteness of political passion.

All the while the moral feelings of the country have been gathering purity and force from the growing interest in those religious strifes which take little account of political expediency, and make inconveniently sharp divisions between right and wrong. There is no better preparation for a period of heroic struggle or heroic folly. . . . Thus a large part of the nation has been silently, slowly, and unconsciously learning to apply more rigorous moral tests to political action. . . . Theological impulses are never unaccompanied by deep currents of morality. They are, indeed, only the dogmatic side of a growing wish to set up a higher standard of right and wrong.[2]

Acton, the most relentless of historians in his insistence on the necessity of pronouncing moral judgments, fittingly became a partisan of the atrocities agitation. Certainly he was very conscious of something like an ethical renaissance in the England of the 'Victorian era'.[3] Nor was the atheism or agnosticism of such friends of the agitation as Holyoake, Sidgwick, Bradlaugh, and John Morley less imbued than the religious denominations with the new moral rigorousness; and in Carlyle it had almost an official prophet.

The taut Victorian conscience found release in godly public activity. It was the golden age of the public meeting, and especially the philanthropic public meeting. Cobden based his techniques of agitation on precedents established by the Wesleyans on the assumption that the anti-slavery movement and the Reform Bill agitation had 'copied intentionally or unintentionally the Wesleyan model'.[4] The anti-corn laws agitation served as the school of political activity of the Nonconformist connections. With the anti-

[1] 16 September 1876, p. 1150.
[2] *Ibid.*
[3] See F. E. de Janösi, 'The Correspondence Between Lord Acton and Bishop Creighton', *Cambridge Historical Journal*, 6 (1940), p. 316.
[4] R. G. Cowherd, *The Politics of English Dissent. The Religious Aspects of Liberal and Humanitarian Reform from 1815 to 1848* (1959), p. 132.

slavery movement the atrocities agitation had many revealing links. The younger Sir Thomas Fowell Buxton was one of the speakers at the National Conference on the Eastern Question, his theme being the rather dubious 'fact' that the Turkish system of government was based on 'slavery and the slave trade'.[1] The analogy between Turks and slavery as two evils of the same order became very strong in Gladstone's mind.[2] The English sympathy for the Bulgarians, he told a deputation at Hawarden, was the same sympathy which ended in Negro emancipation.[3] F. W. Chesson, the journalist, prominent in many philanthropic organisations and especially important as an organiser of the later phase of the atrocities agitation, was in 1876 secretary of the Aborigines Protection Society; and Canada Building, King Street, Westminster, headquarters of the Society, became also the administrative centre of the Eastern Question Conference movement, and later of the Eastern Question Association.[4]

*

Two special aspects of the High Victorian moral sensibility contributed markedly to the atrocities agitation: the vision of progress and the veiling and exaltation of sexuality.

By the vision of progress in this context is meant the outlook represented by Liddon when he announced in a sermon at St Paul's that a hundred years after 1876 the massacres in Bulgaria would

---

[1] E.Q.A., *Report*, p. 21. See also the account of a meeting in September 1876 in Charrington's Great Tent at Mile End, where 2,000 people crowded to hear the Rev. Josiah Henson, the 'Uncle Tom' of Mrs Beecher Stowe's 'well known tale'. At the end a resolution condemning the Bulgarian atrocities was passed with enthusiasm. *Times*, 5 September 1876, p. 4.

[2] J. Bailey (ed.), *The Diary of Lady Frederick Cavendish* (1927), vol, ii, p. 199; Hartington to Duke of Devonshire, 28 January 1877, Devonshire Papers, Chatsworth 340/695. Disraeli's opinion on the anti-slavery movement gives a clue to much of his attitude to the atrocities agitation in 1876: 'The movement of the middle classes for the abolition of slavery was virtuous, but it was not wise. It was an ignorant movement. It showed a want of knowledge both of the laws of commerce and the stipulations of treaties; and it has alike ruined the colonies and aggravated the slave trade. But an enlightened aristocracy who placed themselves at the head of a movement which they did not originate, should have instructed, not sanctioned, the virtuous errors of a well-meaning but narrow-minded community. . . . The first duty of an aristocracy is to lead, to guide, and to enlighten; to soften vulgar prejudices and to dare to encounter popular passion' (*Lord George Bentinck, A Political Biography* (1851), p. 211 of ed. of 1905).

[3] *Times*, 21 August 1877, p. 4.

[4] See Chesson's pamphlet, *Turkey and the Slave Trade* (1877). The annual Report of the Aborigines Protection Society contains characteristic comments on the Eastern question (*Transactions of the Aborigines Protection Society, 1874–1878* [1878], p. 426).

'stand out in tragic relief'.[1] Englishmen of the middle nineteenth
century, aware of their industrial leadership, their freedom from
war and social revolution, the success of their liberal institutions,
took their progressiveness, like their moral earnestness, very self-
consciously. Frederic Harrison, the Positivist, in a typical phrase
attacked those who had 'a genuine contempt for the nineteenth
century'.[2] Dr Humphry Sandwith, famous as an associate of
Layard in the Nineveh excavations and an enthusiast for the
Crimean War, but now strongly anti-Turkish, asked himself on
hearing of the atrocities if he were 'really living in the nineteenth
century'.[3] The Duke of Argyll was shocked at the spectacle of the
horrors of African warfare in the heart of Christendom and the
horrid cruelties of Ghengis Khan 'in the days of Queen Victoria'.[4]

The attitude that the atrocities in Bulgaria constituted an
'anachronism'[5] would find particularly fit expression in Freeman
—at once a historian who conceived it his primary duty to defend
the concept of political liberty, a Liberal with Radical tendencies,
a Hellenophile, one who had made himself notorious as a self-
appointed censor of cruelty, whether in the form of field sports or
in Froude's intellectual defence of cruelty for reasons of state. In
an article on 'The Turks in Europe' in October 1876 Freeman
stressed the progress that had been achieved in the past twenty
years: slavery abolished in America, Italy united and free, France
rid of Bonapartist tyranny, Hungary no longer oppressed, Germany once more the Germany 'of Saxon and Frankish Caesars',
the Irish no longer bondsmen on their own soil.[6] Russia, Freeman
might have added, had emancipated her serfs; but the argument
needed no further pointing: Turkey remained the last great blot
on the face of Europe, a persistent and outrageous challenge to all
that nineteenth-century civilisation stood for.

In many ways the best, because the crudest, specimens of the
Victorian cult of progress are to be found, as R. G. Collingwood
pointed out, by 'slumming amongst the most unsavoury relics of
third-rate historical work'.[7] He selected *The 19th Century—A*

[1] *Nonconformist*, 16 August 1876, p. 817.
[2] *Autobiographic Memoirs* (1911), vol. ii, p. 6.
[3] *Daily News*, 13 September 1876, p. 3.
[4] *Hansard's Parliamentary Debates*, Third Series, vol. CCCXII (1877), c. 649.
[5] E.g. *Catholic Times*, 25 August 1876, p. 4; *Daily News*, 4 July 1876, p. 5.
[6] *British Quarterly Review*, October 1876, p. 29.
[7] *The Idea of History* (Oxford 1946), p. 145.

History, by one Robert Mackenzie, published in 1880, as his exhibit. This work, a panegyric interpretation of the nineteenth century as a tremendous surge of enlightenment and progressiveness after preceding millennia of darkness, ignorance, and error, is very apt for the purpose of illustrating the status of the Turks in the eyes of the self-consciously progressive Victorian. Starting from the basic assumption that 'the religion of the Turks forbids progress', Mackenzie launched into a violent condemnation of every aspect of the Turks and their life: their lack of education, of industry, of science, of constitutional advance, the degraded condition of their women. The atrocities in Bulgaria Mackenzie saw as a symptomatic climax of this barbarism. He criticised severely the British policy of supporting the Turks, and quoted from Sir Henry Elliot's notorious dispatch of 4 September 1876.[1]

More vividly indicative, however, of the deep currents of morality behind the Victorian consciousness of progress is the notice by Acton in the *English Historical Review* of the Rev. J. F. Bright's *A History of England, 1837–1880*, a popular text-book. Acton admired the work particularly because Bright found the keynote of the history of England in the nineteenth century in a sense of remorse, a desire for the settling of wrongs, a need to atone for misdeeds. 'He crowns the history of England with the age of conversion and compassion, of increased susceptibility in the national conscience, of a deepened sense of right and wrong, of much that, in the eye of rivalry, is sentiment, emotion, idealism, and imbecility.' There could not be a more precise and appropriate comment on the moral and historical context of the Bulgarian atrocities agitation. In support of his thesis, Acton offered the testimony of the liberal Roman Catholic theologian Gratry, who saw England in the nineteenth century as the admirable spectacle of a nation turning away from its sordid, carnal ways to make reparation for centuries of profitable wrong.[2] This kind of interpretation reveals more, perhaps, about Acton than about the atrocities agitation; yet it still reveals much about the agitation.

The Victorian vision of progress could not be divorced from Victorian preoccupation with religion in a situation where Christians were massacred by Muslims. As the Anglo-Catholic *Church Review* put it, the excesses of the Turks were an 'insult to European

[1] Pp. 398ff.   [2] *English Historical Review*, 3 (1888), p. 798.

Christendom'.[1] The agitation could not fail to draw on a good deal of simple bigotry against what one Anglican clergyman referred to in passing as that 'most nauseous of all abominations, Mohammedanism'.[2] Insistence that Christianity always carried with it the 'germs of progressive development' whereas Islam condemned the races which it 'cursed' to 'stagnate in evil',[3] was a dogma long established in the Christian West, but never more profoundly an article of faith than in the conventionally 'progressive' opinion of nineteenth-century England. Thus the Christian peoples of the Balkan peninsula were the 'predestined heirs of the future'.[4] The very progressiveness of 'this year of grace, of advanced civilisation, and of ennobling Christianity',[5] made Christian sentiment, as the Presbyterian *Weekly Review* pointed out, much more 'susceptible' and 'easily concentrated'[6] than it had been before, when distance, lack of communications, less enterprising journalistic techniques, would have left horrors such as the massacres in Bulgaria the subject at best of obscure and fragmentary rumours.

*

Perhaps there is no better commentary on the specifically Victorian attitude to sex in relation to the atrocities than the remark of an indignant correspondent to the *Spectator*, à propos of the news from Bulgaria, on that 'worst of all evils of war—outrages on women'.[7] The dishonouring of chastity, the debauching of the conjugal union, and prostitution, undoubtedly touched on the most sensitive of Victorian nerves. And the accounts of the atrocities provided by the newspapers placed before the Victorian public, in unprecedented fulness of detail, 'thrilling accounts'[8] of rapine on a vast scale.

Gladstone, who spent a good deal of time and money in personal work for the rescue and reform of prostitutes, is appropriately representative of the Victorian sensitivity to the sexual aspect of the atrocities question. In a speech condemning the Turks he asserted as one of the first duties of government the guardianship

---

[1] 15 July 1876, p. 357.
[2] Poole to Liddon, 4 February 1877, Liddon Papers.
[3] Johnston, *Liddon*, p. 222.   [4] *Ibid.*, p. 206.
[5] *Dame Europa's Remonstrance and Her Ultimatum* (pamphlet, 1877), p. iii.
[6] 16 September 1876, pp. 909–10.
[7] 21 October 1876, p. 1311.
[8] *Ross Gazette*, 13 July 1876, p. 4.

of the sanctity and honour of the family, 'and above all the sanctity and honour of women'.[1] Benjamin Waugh, founder of the Society for the Protection of Children, divulged that the thing about the Bulgarian atrocities that most affected W. T. Stead was the thought of outrages on women 'in the form of his own mother'.[2] In his *Northern Echo* at Darlington Stead had already entered enthusiastically into the agitation led by Josephine Butler and Stansfeld for the repeal of the Contagious Diseases Acts.[3] In 1877 he spoke of writing a novel about prostitution.[4] He was indeed well on the way that led to the 'Maiden Tribute of Modern Babylon' and the martyrdom of imprisonment.

Fitzjames Stephen, the most consistent and uncompromising of the *Saturday Review* school of writers,[5] accused the agitation of appealing to prurience as well as bigotry.[6] The atrocities certainly tapped an underlying current of rather morbid sensitivity, perhaps even sensuality—though it should be remembered that the most conspicuous example of prurient excitement in relation to the atrocities, Swinburne, opposed the agitation violently.[7] Some agitation leaders, Freeman and Sandwith notably, exploited in a crude though minor way the Turkish reputation for pederasty,[8] a reputation which gained widespread currency from the atrocities agitation. Even Gladstone thought it necessary to refer, in his speech at the Eastern Question Conference, to 'some gross and horrible vices' widespread among the Turks 'to a degree hardly to be exaggerated'.[9] But essentially the shock to Victorian sexual

---

[1] *Times*, 17 January 1877, p. 10. It was typical also of Gladstone that he should comment in a letter to Döllinger on the sad decline of the 'conjugal morals' of the highest class beside reflections on the 'unworthy part' played by Britain in the Eastern question. Gladstone to Döllinger, 11 August 1876, Gladstone Papers, Add. MSS 44140, ff. 421–3.

[2] *William T. Stead* [1885], p. 18. The book opens with an account of how Stead, at the age of twelve, knocked down another boy for watching a girl adjusting her garter (p. 7).

[3] *Ibid.*, p. 14. F. W. Chesson also: see his *Paper on How to Influence Members of the House of Commons . . . for promoting the Repeal of the Contagious Diseases Acts* (1870).

[4] *Stead*, pp. 15–16.

[5] Several *Saturday Reviewers* on the side of the agitation cut their connection with the paper. Freeman did so at a financial sacrifice of £400–500 p.a. See A. Peel, *Letters to a Victorian Editor, Henry Allon, Editor of the British Quarterly Review* (1929), pp. 131–2; and Freeman to Liddon, 22 June 1878, Liddon Papers.

[6] See below, p. 66.   [7] See below, p. 219.

[8] See e.g. Freeman at Cardiff (*South Wales Daily News*, 8 September 1876, p. 5). For Sandwith's proneness to this line of propaganda see Peel, *ibid.*, pp. 55, 57; and *British Quarterly Review*, January 1877, p. 196. Sir Charles Trevelyan also made a point of it in his letter to *The Times* of 11 August 1876, p. 10.

[9] E.Q.A., *Report*, p. 110.

sensitivity was quite contrary to any tendencies to prurience. It was the pudic reaction of an outraged puritanism overlaid with perhaps excessive sentimentality on the honour of women and enforced residence in what the Rev. Malcolm MacColl called 'those unspeakable hotbeds of vice—the harems of dissolute Turks'.[1]

*

There are good grounds for interpreting the eighteen-seventies as the period of highest refinement of Victorian moral sensibility. That decade on the whole provided far greater scope for the release of moral energy in a general political sense as opposed to specific political programmes than any other comparable period before or after. The second Reform Act marked the final end of the era in which fear of social revolution had been a political reality. By 1872 the great domestic and Irish programme of Liberalism had been substantially achieved. Of particular importance was the fact that, apart from irritation and dissatisfaction with the Education Act, the last major grievances of Nonconformity were now removed; so that the greatest single corporate embodiment of Victorian moral sensibility was free from the first time to direct its energies almost wholly in a moral cause outside its own restricted field of 'interests'. The campaign for disestablishment never provided such a moral cause: its aggressiveness contradicted the fundamental principles of Nonconformity. Even the education issue was not after 1874 a distraction, since the fall of the Liberal government had removed it from the range of practical politics. The tendency was rather for a reconciliation of Nonconformity with Liberalism.

The Liberal defeat seemed to imply in itself a sense of recognition of a moral exhaustion associated with the political exhaustion of the Liberal programme. Gladstone's resignation of the Liberal leadership in 1875 in turn recognised the validity of this sense of exhaustion. But the appearance was deceptive, as Gladstone belatedly came to realise in 1876. The moral energy hitherto consumed in political reform was now released to find its own cause. The great and absorbing political distraction of the Irish question in its new and fundamental phase had not yet arisen; the erosion of Liberal attitudes and assumptions involved in the rise of imperialism and socialism was not yet apparent. The Liberal victory of

[1] *The Sultan and the Powers* (1896), p. ix.

1880 seemed the crowning confirmation of Liberal moral vitality; and so in some ways it was. But as soon as energy had to be directed back into a political programme the old problems and the old malaise emerged once more.

The decline of the scope available to Liberal moral vitality after 1880 is best illustrated, with particular reference to the Bulgarian atrocities agitation, by the comparative insignificance of the movement of protest provoked by the far more extensive and heinous Armenian massacres of the eighteen-nineties. That movement, into which many veterans of 1876—Gladstone, Argyll, Westminster, Stead, MacColl, Clayden—entered with enthusiasm, left behind it, as one of them complained, 'only a sense of disappointment and humiliation'.[1] MacColl especially was confident that 1896 would be like 1876, 'so fresh in the memory of the public',[2] and that another Conservative government would face another spontaneous explosion of popular indignation against the Turks and alleged British patronage of them.[3] But MacColl found that 1896 was a world quite different from 1876. There was indeed a reversal of the pattern: the public generally remained apathetic in 1895–7, but Salisbury, though understandably reluctant to initiate unilateral British action against the Turks in the face of a hostile Continental 'concert', finally despaired of them; and the privilege and burden of patronage of the Ottoman Empire passed to the Germans.

4 Groundwork, May–July 1876

The Serb insurrections in the Herzegovina and Bosnia in 1875 aroused sympathetic interest in England in the general question of the position of Christians under Turkish rule. The curious situation in which the Turks rather than their Christian subject peoples had enjoyed the English sentimental solicitude for oppressed peoples was passing away; but the old tradition still had strength. There was little sense of incongruity, for instance, in the fact that the Duke of Sutherland, friend of Garibaldi and enthusiast for Italian liberty, should have led Turcophile society in 1876 and

---

[1] P. W. Clayden, *Armenia: The Case Against Lord Salisbury* (pamphlet, 1898), p. 1.
[2] M. MacColl, *England's Responsibility Towards Armenia* (pamphlet, 1895), p. 47.
[3] MacColl, *The Sultan and the Powers*, pp. 1, 7.

after. But Russell's call for subscriptions to aid the Serb insurgents symbolised the emerging maturity of a revised outlook in England on the Balkan nationalities. A public meeting of 'friends of the suffering Rayahs of Bosnia and Herzegovina' was held in September.[1] In December a League in Aid of the Christians of Turkey was founded, with Russell as patron and James Lewis Farley, Turkish consul in Bristol, as secretary.

Farley had been a senior officer of the Turkish State and Ottoman Banks and financial propagandist for Turkey.[2] A recent convert to the anti-Turkish cause, he defended his change of attitude by describing how he gradually became disillusioned with Turkish promises of reform.[3] It has been suggested that he may have lost money in Turkish investments.[4] In 1875 he published, at any rate, a pamphlet warning holders of Turkish bonds of their imminent fate.[5] Though there is no reason to doubt Farley's good faith in the cause of the Christians, his credentials as an agitator remained rather dubious,[6] and the finances of his League later became the subject of suspicion and criticism.[7] Farley failed to maintain a leading position when agitation against the Turks burgeoned into a mass movement under the stimulus of the revelations from Bulgaria.

Edward Augustus Freeman stands out as the most considerable figure in the proto-agitation on behalf of the Serbs. A scholar of comfortable private fortune, well-known as the historian of the Norman Conquest, Liberal politician *manqué*, relentless persecutor of Froude, Freeman had been a vociferous enemy of the Turks, from a Hellenist viewpoint, since the Crimean War.[8] He was converted to the Slav cause as well in 1875 while on a tour of Dalmatia. At Cattaro he met his future son-in-law, Arthur Evans, the archaeologist.[9] Evans, a veteran of Bosnia and an enthusiastic Slavo-

---

[1] *Times*, 10 September 1875, p. 8.
[2] There is a memoir of Farley in the *Dictionary of National Biography*. His last pro-Turkish propaganda work was *Modern Turkey* (1872).
[3] *Turks and Christians. A Solution of the Eastern Question* (1876), pp. vi–x.
[4] A. J. P. Taylor, *The Trouble Makers* (1957), p. 79.
[5] *The Decline of Turkey, Financially and Politically.*
[6] For Farley's unsuccessful attempts to get subsidies from the Russians see Seton-Watson, 'Russo-British Relations During the Eastern Crisis', I, *Slavonic Review*, **3**, pp. 430–1.
[7] See below, pp. 250–1.
[8] W. R. W. Stephens, *The Life and Letters of Edward A. Freeman* (1895), vol. i, pp. 150–1; and Freeman's preface to the new edition of his *History and Conquests of the Saracens* (2nd ed. 1876), pp. vii–viii.
[9] J. Evans, *Time and Chance, the Story of Arthur Evans and his Forebears* (1943), pp. 189–90.

E

phile, inspired Freeman to take up the Serb cause on his return to England. By October 1876 Freeman had collected, through individual appeals and letters to the press, nearly £5,000.[1]

The interesting feature about this Serbian proto-agitation is the way in which it drew together into a kind of preliminary association many of the principals of the later Bulgarian atrocities agitation. This was particularly the case with Freeman's campaign. In thanking Canon Liddon for a contribution Freeman remarked that it had come with one from P. A. Taylor, the Nonconformist Radical M.P.: 'glad you would pull together about anything'.[2] Freeman added a plea which may have influenced Liddon's later action on the Bulgarian atrocities: 'I wish you would preach about this.'[3] To his friend James Bryce, later also prominent in the atrocities agitation, Freeman commented on the 'oddness' of the juxtaposition in support of the Serbs of Taylor and Lord Glasgow, an Anglo-Catholic Conservative magnate, like Bryce and Taylor later a notable figure in the atrocities agitation.[4] So also were the Conservative philanthropist Lord Shaftesbury and James Fraser, Bishop of Manchester, both supporters of the Slav cause in its earlier phase.[5] The Rev. William Denton, an Anglo-Catholic clergyman with experience in the East, forms another notable link between the Serb and Bulgarian agitations.[6]

★

Rumours about the nature of the Turkish operations in Bulgaria began to filter through to England early in May. On 12 May Freeman remarked to Bryce, with rather misplaced jocularity, about a stray telegram in the papers referring to reports of Bulgarians being shot by *bashi-bazouks*.[7] On the same day Edwin Pears, correspondent in Constantinople of the *Daily News*, a Liberal London paper, sent off a dispatch relating that rumours current in Constantinople indicated that the Turkish forces putting down the insurrection in Bulgaria were 'acting with utter reckless-

---

[1] Freeman to Bryce, 22 October 1876, Bryce Papers, Bodleian Library, Oxford, E4.   [2] Freeman to Liddon, 10 May 1876, Liddon Papers.
[3] *Ibid.*   [4] Freeman to Bryce, 12 May 1876, Bryce Papers, E4.
[5] W. G. Wirthwein, *Britain and the Balkan Crisis, 1875–1878* (New York 1935), p. 41.
[6] *Times*, 10 September 1875, p. 8; and his book, *The Christians of Turkey, Their Condition Under Mussulman Rule* (1876).
[7] Freeman to Bryce, 12 May 1876, Bryce Papers, E4.

ness' and that 'horrible atrocities' had been committed.[1] Gallenga
of *The Times* later made similar reports.[2] The *Spectator* of 3 June
included an article which, while misconceiving the situation, did
have some claims to be the 'first alarm' of the Bulgarian atrocities.[3] It was probably this article which caused Carlyle, a day or
so later, 'quite well for Age', to be 'vehement against Darwin,
and the Turk'.[4]

Official Turkish sources announced that disturbances had indeed
broken out in the Philippopolis area, but they were hardly of the
order of an insurrection, and in any case the Imperial government
'hastened to take energetic and efficacious measures', which had
led to a 'favourable result'.[5] Thus Lord Derby was assured by
the ambassador of the Porte, the Greek Musurus Pasha.

Elliot, informed of the facts by teachers at Robert College, an
American missionary school in Constantinople with many Bulgarian connections, and furnished with confirmatory information
by his own consular agents,[6] yet preferred to take Turkish assurances at face value. Elliot's main preoccupation was rather to
urge upon the Turks his conviction that 'no exertion should be
spared' for assuring the 'immediate suppression' of the movement.[7] He told Derby nothing except that while the 'employment
of Circassians and Bashi-bazouks' had 'led to the atrocities which
were to be expected', reports of extensive massacres could be
safely discounted as Russian propaganda.[8]

By 16 June Pears could send off a reasonably full account of the
situation in Bulgaria. He reported that the more reliable estimates
of men, women, and children massacred ranged from eighteen to
thirty thousand, with upwards of a hundred villages wiped out.
This startling dispatch appeared in the *Daily News* of 23 June.[9]
The *Manchester Guardian* immediately took it up.[10] Gallenga's
version of the same reports appeared in *The Times* of 8 July.[11]

[1] 18 May 1876, p. 6.   [2] 26 May 1876, p. 8.
[3] '*The First Alarm*' *Respecting the Bulgarian Outrages*, reprinted from the *Spectator*
of 3 June 1876.
[4] W. A. Wright (ed.), *Letters of Edward Fitzgerald to Fanny Kemble, 1871–1883*
(1895), p. 111.   [5] *Times*, 16 May 1876, p. 5.
[6] See Medlicott, *Journal of Modern History*, 4 (1932).
[7] Elliot to Derby, 7 May 1876, *State Papers*, LXXXIV (1876), *Correspondence
Respecting the Affairs of Turkey, and the Insurrection in Bosnia and the Herzegovina*
(*Turkey*, No. 3), no. 254.   [8] Elliot to Derby, 8 June 1876, *ibid*., no. 443.
[9] Pp. 5–6.   [10] 24 June 1876, p. 7.
[11] P. 12. Gallenga's figures were: 25,000 massacred, 100 towns destroyed, 1,000
children sold as slaves, 10,000 imprisoned and undergoing tortures.

Elliot, the Foreign Office, and the government jointly became victims of their psychology of orthodoxy. Such rumours and reports as came out of Bulgaria from official sources were made to fit into a pattern of preconceived attitudes which deprived them of their significance and their warning value. Even when the fact that something extraordinary had indeed happened in Bulgaria could no longer be ignored or brushed aside, Elliot still neglected to send some one to investigate at first hand.[1] The initiative in sending an embassy official had to come from Derby, prodded by Carnarvon in the cabinet, and clearly under the pressure of rising public excitement.[2] Derby himself, monumentally phlegmatic, constitutionally prone to extreme scepticism in all things, failed to exert himself to keep Disraeli's tendencies towards extravagance within bounds.

Disraeli, for his part, was only too ready to improve on Elliot's rather excessive willingness to give the Turks the benefit of all doubts. He gave answers to questions in the Commons very much more positively contradictory of the *Daily News* exposé than even Elliot's reports, or lack of reports, entitled him to give. The fact that the first detailed accounts appeared in a leading opposition paper put him further off his guard[3]; and he was probably influenced by the memory that his sceptical attitude to somewhat similar atrocity reports at the time of the Indian mutiny had been justified.[4]

Forster raised the question of the *Daily News* accounts in the Commons on 26 June. Disraeli responded with a fantastic rigmarole based apparently on some consular dispatches inspired in the highest traditions of Sir Henry Bulwer. This grotesque version had it that mysterious 'strangers' had 'invaded' Bulgaria, burning villages indiscriminately, and that the Circassians, peaceful and indeed model settlers, with a 'stake' in the country, had been obliged to resort to self-defence. Disraeli had no doubt that the war between the 'invaders' and the 'settlers' had been carried out with great ferocity.[5]

---

[1] For a general critique of Elliot's attitude see Temperley, *Proceedings of the British Academy*, **17** (1931). See also S. Story (ed.) *The Memoirs of Ismail Kemal Bey* (1920), pp. 125, 130.

[2] A. Hardinge, *The Life of Henry Howard Molyneux Herbert, Fourth Earl of Carnarvon, 1831–90* (1925), vol. ii, pp. 340–1.

[3] Marquess of Zetland, *Letters of Disraeli to Lady Bradford and Lady Chesterfield* (1929), vol. ii, p. 58. Buckle, *Letters of Queen Victoria, 1862–1878*, vol. ii, pp. 471–2.

[4] Buckle, *Disraeli*, vol. i, pp. 1496–7.   [5] 3 *Hansard*, CCXXX, cc. 424–6.

In replying to a question from Argyll in the Lords put in the same terms as Forster's, Derby was much less fertile of explanations than Disraeli. He had no facts; but he thought one ought to be slow to believe such reports as appeared in the *Daily News*.[1] This was still his attitude on 7 July, in answer to Granville, though by this time he was aware that 'strong public feeling' had been excited, and he announced that he had telegraphed Elliot urgently for information.[2]

★

Such flat conflict of testimony between a reputable newspaper and the government on so important a matter of fact was bound to create public uneasiness. The government had committed Britain so unmistakably as the protector of Turkey from the attempted coercion of the European concert that even the possibility of the Turks having perpetrated massacres on a large scale, and implicating Britain in a sense as an accessory, would induce an immediate crisis of conscience. The great fleet riding at Besika Bay, dispatched at the very time when, if the reports were to be believed, the atrocities were taking place, became the special focus of this anxious feeling.[3] There was no doubt, despite the blustering disingenuousness of Disraeli[4] and the uncharacteristically flustered embarrassment of Derby,[5] as to how the Turks themselves interpreted its presence. This in itself was bad enough, quite apart from the honesty or otherwise of the official explanations that the fleet had been sent merely to protect British life and property in Constantinople and Salonika during the troubles attending the deposition and suicide of the Sultan Abdul Aziz and the deposition in turn of his incapable successor Murad V.

The responsibilities of their position certainly weighed heavily on the officers of the *Daily News*, both in London and Constantinople. At Pears' request it was decided to send out a special correspondent to make a full investigation.[6] Fortunately for the *Daily News*, the most brilliant correspondent of the time was available: Januarius Aloysius MacGahan, a young Irish-

[1] *Ibid.*, cc. 385–7.   [2] *Ibid.*, c. 1167.
[3] See e.g. Purcell, *Ambrose Phillipps de Lisle*, vol. ii, pp. 349–50.
[4] 3 *Hansard*, CCXXXI, c. 203.
[5] *Times*, 15 July 1876, p. 9.
[6] E. Pears, *Forty Years in Constantinople* (1916), p. 18.

American[1] whose offer of services had just been declined by *The Times* because of his reputation for 'sensational proclivities'.[2] As 'Special Commissioner' for the *Daily News* MacGahan made for the scene of the massacres, where he arrived on 25 July.

Evidences of a growing crisis of public conscience began to multiply early in July. Within the first week two meetings of Suffolk agricultural labourers, at Sudbury and Bury St Edmunds, passed resolutions protesting against British intervention on behalf of the Turks.[3] Joseph Arch himself spoke at Bury St Edmunds, thus beginning an association with the agitation which remained constant throughout.[4] Resolutions against the tendencies of the government's Eastern policy by the central committees of the Birmingham[5] and Manchester[6] Liberal Associations indicated a process of formulation of a specifically Liberal attitude in certain of the more aggressive sections of the party. Similar expressions in the *Methodist*[7] and Baptist *Freeman*[8] and the High Church *Guardian*[9] and *Church Review*[10] marked the beginnings of the special concern of Nonconformity and Anglo-Catholicism, which between them later gave the atrocities agitation so much of its shape, content, and character.

On 8 July the *Daily News* published a further dispatch from Pears confirming the substantial accuracy of the report published on 23 June, and amplifying details.[11] This, combined with Gallenga's dispatch in *The Times* of the same morning, caused a perceptible heightening of public anxiety. Symptomatic of this was the attempt of the Manhood Suffrage League to exploit the atrocities issue by calling a Trafalgar Square rally.[12] A. J. Mundella, the Radical M.P. for Sheffield, wrote on 12 July to Robert Leader, a proprietor

---

[1] There is a memoir of MacGahan (1844–78) in the *Dictionary of American Biography*. Noted as a 'vivid descriptive writer' with an 'eye for drama', he had reported, with conspicuous ability, the Franco-German War, the Commune, the *Alabama* Tribunal, and Sherman's Caucasus Expedition of 1872, which made him well-known in Russia; and in 1873 he distinguished himself especially in reporting the Russian campaign in Central Asia and became a warm friend of Skobolev. In 1874 he reported the Carlist war in Spain and in 1875 the Arctic expedition of the *Pandora*.

[2] *The History of the Times*, vol. ii, *The Tradition Established*, *1841–1884* (1939), p. 465.

[3] *Daily News*, 7 July 1876, p. 3.   [4] See below, pp. 166, 233.

[5] *Times*, 6 July 1876, p. 9.   [6] *Manchester Guardian*, 7 July 1876, p. 5.

[7] 30 June 1876, p. 3.   [8] 14 July 1876, p. 340.

[9] 5 July 1876, p. 887; 12 July, p. 904.   [10] 8 July 1876, p. 345.

[11] Pp. 5–6. Pears now put the lowest estimate of dead at 12,000. There were reports of a market in Bulgarian girls in Philippopolis at 3 or 4 liras each.

[12] *Times*, 10 July 1876, p. 10.

of the Sheffield *Independent* and president of the Sheffield Liberal Association, hoping that Leader had read the *Daily News* of the 8th with the details of 'the horrors in Bulgaria'. There had been, Mundella averred, 'no such bloody page in modern history'. He added that even old Lord Stratford de Redcliffe exclaimed on reading it: 'Good God! I would rather see Russia in Constantinople than the subjugation of the Principalities by such means.'[1] Mundella wrote also to Forster, urging him to follow up his original question to Disraeli, adding that if he did not, Mundella himself would.[2]

Mundella was prominent among a group of Liberals in the House of Commons, including Shaftesbury's son Evelyn Ashley, who were greatly dissatisfied with the answers given by the government. They signed a requisition to Gladstone, asking him to preside at a public meeting. Gladstone declined, wishing to reserve any pronouncement until the production of papers promised by the government and a clear statement from them of future Eastern policy.[3] This move was probably the result of efforts being made by Lewis Farley, of the League in Aid of the Christians of Turkey, to promote a public meeting[4] and also a deputation to Derby at the Foreign Office. Farley enlisted the aid of Auberon Herbert, former Radical M.P. for Nottingham, younger brother of the Colonial Secretary, the Earl of Carnarvon, and finest if somewhat eccentric flower of the Herbert tradition of brilliance, charm, and devotion to good causes. Herbert canvassed for support among his parliamentary friends.[5] The project for which Gladstone had been unsuccessfully requisitioned was retrieved and taken up under the auspices of Farley's League, with Shaftesbury as chairman. This 'preliminary meeting' to 'consider what steps should be taken to express indignation' was arranged for 20 July, but had to be postponed until the 27th.[6]

The *Daily News* gave a strong lead for action on 11 July, in a call to the country to make known its indignation against the attitude and policy of Disraeli and Derby 'through other channels' than parliamentary questions.[7] The call was taken up by the

---

[1] Mundella Papers. The principalities were Serbia and Montenegro.
[2] *Ibid.*   [3] *Daily News,* 11 July 1876, p. 5; 12 July, p. 5.
[4] Auberon Herbert to Dilke, 28 June [1876], Dilke Papers, British Museum Add. MSS 43898, f. 240.   [5] Auberon Herbert to Dilke, *ibid.*
[6] *Times,* 20 July 1876, p. 6.   [7] 11 July 1876, p. 4.

Liberal provincial press, notably Stead in the Darlington *Northern Echo*, already the ostentatious spokesman of the north country.[1] Freeman, still immersed until the beginning of July in his work for the Serb refugees,[2] now began to concentrate his attention on the Bulgarian aspect of the Slav cause. In a letter to the *Daily News* he pointed out that the tactic of the government was clearly to refuse information and evade questioning until the prorogation of the parliamentary session. Disraeli would then, Freeman was convinced, be rid of pressures and impediments and free to indulge in the wildest Turcophile adventures. Freeman urged the necessity of some demonstration outside parliament before the end of the session to impress upon the Commons and Disraeli the true state of public feeling.[3] The particular interest of this letter is that it reveals a complete absence of any conception of an agitation 'out of doors' replacing parliamentary pressure on the government.

But Disraeli had much more demanding personages to cope with than Freeman. The Queen telegraphed on the same day (13 July) praying that inquiries be made as to the 'Horrors described in the Foreign telegrams' in the *Daily News*. 'It is too awful', she added; it would turn everyone against Turkey. 'One ought to know what the other side have done.'[4] Derby, who had an audience that day, reported to Disraeli that the Queen was 'quite composed on the subject', and agreed readily to his suggestion that there was 'immense exaggeration in all the stories, and that they were put about for a purpose'. He concluded, rather less disarmingly: 'But I have not read my Daily News of today yet.'[5]

Disraeli sent for Tenterden, the Permanent Foreign Under-Secretary, and duly made inquiries. Tenterden asserted staunchly the orthodox Foreign Office viewpoint and succeeded in lulling any doubts that may have been forming in Disraeli's mind. Tenterden recounted, a little complacently, to Derby: 'I trust I explained clearly to him the real state of the case with regard to the Bulgarian atrocities', that is, that while atrocities no doubt had been committed, there was nothing to justify credence in the *Daily News*

[1] 13 July 1876, pp. 2–3. See also *South Wales Daily News*, 10 July 1876, pp. 4–5; 12 July 1876, p. 5; 18 July 1876, pp. 4–5; and Sheffield *Independent*, 18 July 1876, p. 2.
[2] *Daily News*, 1 July 1876, p. 2.
[3] 13 July 1876, p. 6.
[4] Queen to Disraeli, 13 July 1876, Disraeli Papers.
[5] Derby to Disraeli, 13 July 1876, *ibid*.

reports.[1] Derby reinforced Tenterden's soothing influence by assuring Disraeli that he had said nothing to retract or modify.[2]

Accordingly, emboldened by such expert testimony, Disraeli became even more reckless and dogmatic under increasing pressure from Liberal questioners in the Commons. He permitted himself a characteristically flippant turn of phrase (probably not meant to be flippant, but unluckily raising a laugh) on the question of certain alleged tortures; a phrase which he was never thereafter allowed to forget.[3] On 31 July he came out with his famous sneer at 'coffee-house babble'.[4]

★

The first major manifestation of the public uneasiness came on 14 July, in the form of two deputations to Derby at the Foreign Office. One, large and respectable, was led by John Bright, seconded by Henry Richard and several other prominent members of the Peace Society. It coincided with a series of public meetings throughout the country got up by local Peace Societies.[5] The deputation represented a strongly non-interventionist attitude—though several of its members attending as representatives of various Liberal Associations, as Henry Richard admitted to Derby, went far beyond the views it expressed.[6] Derby, extremely isolationist in outlook himself, found this deputation quite congenial. Bright, for his part, against the explicit advice of the *Daily News* that Derby was not to be trusted as a counterweighting influence in the cabinet against Disraeli,[7] declared full confidence in Derby's handling of affairs; and despite Derby's patently unconvincing explanations of the government's motives in dispatching the fleet,[8] the matter was not pressed.[9]

[1] Derby to Disraeli, 14 July 1876, inclosing memo by Tenterden of the same date, *ibid.* [2] *Ibid.*

[3] 3 *Hansard*, CCXXX, cc. 1181–2. Disraeli's words were: 'I doubt . . . that torture has been practised on a great scale among an oriental people who seldom, I believe, resort to torture, but generally terminate their connection with culprits in a more expeditious manner.'

[4] *Ibid.*, CCXXXI, c. 203. See on this point Spencer Walpole, *History of Twenty-Five Years*, vol. iv, p. 103, n. 4.

[5] Bridport (12 July), Stockton and Wrexham (13 July), Liverpool (14 July), Gloucester (17 July). Thompson, *Public Opinion and Lord Beaconsfield*, vol. i, p. 346. See *Daily News*, 13 July 1876, p. 6. (Liverpool), and *Northern Echo*, 14 July 1876, p. 3 (Stockton).

[6] See Mundella to R. Leader, 10 July 1876. Mundella Papers; Sheffield *Independent*, 14 July 1876, p. 3 [7] 12 July 1876, p. 4.

[8] See the comment of the *Saturday Review*, 22 July 1876, p. 91.

[9] *Times*, 15 July 1876, p. 9.

The second and smaller deputation, led by Farley in the name of the League in Aid of the Christians of Turkey, asked Derby to adopt a positive policy of patronising Christian autonomy in Turkey, and to give distinct assurances that he would withhold all support, moral and material, from the Turks. Derby dismissed these requests curtly with some remarks on the foolishness of impracticable ideas of autonomy in areas of mixed Christian and Muslim population and a reminder that reports about atrocities included 'a great deal of exaggeration and a great deal of pure invention'.[1]

The conflict made apparent by these deputations between the interventionist and non-interventionist attitudes on the Eastern question remained constant throughout the agitation. Though the non-interventionists led by Bright became decidedly the minority party, they were always prominent enough to give a 'perceptible flavour' to the whole movement, as the strongly interventionist Duke of Argyll regretfully remarked in criticising them for an inadequate sense of 'responsibilities'.[2]

A powerful expression of the interventionist spirit came from James Fraser, Bishop of Manchester, provoked by Derby's explanations, particularly on the question of the fleet, and Bright's eager readiness to accept them as satisfactory. In both the *Manchester Guardian* and *The Times* Fraser urged the public to speak out clearly against the Turks and the government's apparent willingness, as evidenced by the fleet at Besika Bay, to countenance them.[3] This caused an immediate stir in Anglican circles. One of Liddon's correspondents wrote to him full of enthusiasm for the bishop's 'delightful letter', very pleased that 'at last' people's sympathies were being worked up in the right direction.[4] Liddon himself and his lieutenant MacColl decided to travel to Serbia to see conditions at first hand and extend to the Eastern Christians the sympathy of the Anglican Church.[5] At the Assembly of the Convocation of Canterbury an unofficial petition signed by fifty-three members was presented, praying the Lower House to give expression to the Christian sympathy felt for the Bulgarians and to

---

[1] *Ibid.*   [2] Argyll, *The Eastern Question*, vol. i, p. xiii.
[3] *Times*, 18 July 1876, p. 5.
[4] Mirehouse to Liddon, 20 July [1876], Liddon Papers.
[5] MacColl to Gladstone, [20 July] 1876, Gladstone Papers, Add. MSS 44243, ff. 168-71.

address a resolution to the Eastern ecclesiastical leaders 'to free the Church of England from the scandal of appearing to look on unmoved at the atrocities'.[1] Another resolution, more directly political, asked the government to take steps to prevent any continuance or repetition of such massacres.[2] The resolutions were presented to the Upper House, but a prorogation intervened before they could be considered.[3]

★

By 20 July an acute, perceptive, and suspicious observer like Fitzjames Stephen could discern what seemed to him the deplorable phenomenon of an articulating popular excitement about the atrocities. He wrote to his friend Lord Lytton, the Viceroy of India, that though things seemed quiet enough,

I see, or think I see, the beginning of an outbreak of pseudo-Christian John Bullism about the Bulgarians and other people utterly unknown to us, who have been or are being, murdered and ravished by the Turks; not by any means without having murdered and ravished more or less on their own account.[4] I know of no more contemptible or disgusting spectacle in the world than excited Britons, headed by idiotic Bishops, roaring to belligerents 'Infamous barbarians fight with [?] holy water and patent Christian pastilles damn your heathen blood. We stand aghast at cutting throats, burning houses and outrages worse than death . . .[5] how can men with immortal souls dare to scandalise us.'

In one of Miss Edgeworth's novels, added Stephen, there was a heroine called Caroline 'distinguished from the rest of her sex by her capacity for feeling and expressing virtuous indignation'. She must, Stephen concluded, 'have become Miss Bull I think in later life'.[6] Stephen wrote less ironically, perhaps, than he intended.

The most significant expression of virtuous indignation to emerge at this time was the meeting on 27 July in Willis's Rooms, London, arranged by Farley and presided over by Shaftesbury, which had grown out of the original movement at the beginning

---

[1] See also Fraser's letter, in the name of the northern clergy, exhorting their southern brethren, in the *Guardian*, 26 July 1876, pp. 968–9.

[2] *Times*, 20 July 1876, p. 6.   [3] *Times*, 22 July 1876, p. 9.

[4] The number of Muslims killed in the insurrection, very few of them women or children, was well under 200. See Baring's Report, *Turkey*, XC (1877), no. 220, enclosure 1, p. 150.   [5] Words omitted in copy of text.

[6] Fitzjames Stephen to Lytton, 20 July 1876, Fitzjames Stephen Papers, Cambridge University Library Add. MSS 7349.

of the month to requisition Gladstone. Invitations were sent out in the names of forty-eight members of the House of Commons, led by Mundella, Ashley, and Fawcett, with twelve other gentlemen in association, including Auberon Herbert, George Dawson of Birmingham, John Morley of the *Fortnightly Review*, and the trade-union leaders George Howell and Henry Broadhurst.[1] Freeman made the decisive speech, and carried the meeting to endorse the principle of full autonomy for the Christians in Turkey.[2] The importance of this demonstration lay in its avowedly 'preliminary' character and the expectation that it would, as the *Spectator* hoped, be the first of a 'series'.[3]

Like its old contributor Fitzjames Stephen, the *Saturday Review* had an acute appreciation of the dangerous potentiality of the situation. The 'well-dressed mob' at Willis's Rooms, in a state of 'high Christian excitement', represented for the *Review* a popular feeling which very possibly and most unfortunately might 'determine the future policy of the country'.[4] Beginning on a theme which it maintained consistently throughout the agitation, the *Review* protested that such meetings were, by their nature, 'incapable of reasoning'.[5] Accepting the inevitability of an agitation, the *Review* yet demanded the impossible: that the agitation restrict itself to 'moral and sentimental considerations', and refrain from attempting to interfere in the direction of policy.[6] This was asking the agitation, in short, to renounce its very soul: the fusion of moral passion with the political issues; the recognition of, and protest against, the implication of British Eastern policy with the Turkish atrocities in Bulgaria.

[1] Howell Collection, Bishopsgate Institute, pamphlets, nos. 1–40.

[2] *Times*, 28 July 1876, p. 10. Freeman, who had recently written a long attack on Derby's answer to the deputations (*Daily News*, 20 July 1876, p. 5), and addressed a meeting at Bath (*Times*, 24 July 1876, p. 9), had pointedly not been invited to the Willis's Rooms meeting by Farley, with whom he seems to have been on far from friendly terms. Possibly Freeman distrusted Farley as a renegade; and a letter to the *Guardian* by 'M' (which might very reasonably be ascribed to Malcolm MacColl) suggesting that Freeman be put at the head of a 'Christian Defence League' to lead the agitation against the Turks, clearly represented a lack of confidence in Farley (5 July 1876, p. 887). Farley later accused Freeman of threatening at this time to wreck the League in Aid of the Christians of Turkey, out of jealousy for Farley's leading position (see below, p. 250). Freeman was invited to attend the Willis's Rooms meeting by Auberon Herbert, and decided to come only after 'much thought' (S. H. Harris, *Auberon Herbert: Crusader for Liberty* (1943), pp. 179–80).

[3] 29 July 1876, p. 937.

[4] 29 July 1876, pp. 123–4.

[5] *Ibid.*

[6] 5 August 1876, p. 152.

2

The Making of the Agitation, August 1876

DURING August public concern about the reports of Turkish atrocities in Bulgaria gathered momentum, at first slowly, then with almost dramatic swiftness. From the modest, easily overlooked affair represented by the Willis's Rooms meeting of 27 July, it burgeoned into a movement of national dimensions, compelling universal attention, extorting recognition and respect from the Foreign Office, even imposing upon Disraeli, for a time, considerations of a possible new point of departure in his Eastern policy. Above all, it captured Gladstone. This made it in one stroke securely an 'event of history'.

The process of Gladstone's involvement and commitment is, however, excepting for brief moments, parallel to, not part of, the central theme of the development of the agitation in August. As a prelude to an analysis of that development it is necessary to consider Gladstone's position at the end of July; but the pivotal theme of the agitation in August is neither Gladstone's presence nor his absence, but the means whereby rising public excitement was converted from struggling inarticulateness into a sustained campaign of 'atrocity meetings'. A considerable rôle in that conversion was played by what could for convenience be termed the 'Oxford group'—the three Oxford men, old friends, Bishop Fraser of Manchester, Liddon, and Freeman. But the principal agent of the conversion was the young editor of the Darlington *Northern Echo*, W. T. Stead. The inauguration of Stead's 'atrocity' campaign in the north on 23 August was the most important development in the actual process of agitation before the publication on 6 September of Gladstone's *Bulgarian Horrors*. Stead, of course, did not begin with nothing: he took at its flood a tide of public indignation which had been accumulating steadily since the early efforts of Freeman and Farley, and the momentum of which had been boosted notably earlier in August by Bishop Fraser and Canon Liddon. But it was Stead more than any other who supplied the great national movement emerging in the last days of August with a voice, a method, and a direction.

1 Gladstone's Speech of 31 July

The coming together of Gladstone and the atrocities agitation was a most natural conjunction; but it was slow to come about, and Gladstone's speech in the debate on the Eastern question on 31 July—his last major statement before he brought out his pamphlet —makes it quite clear that the movement which asserted itself so strongly in August owed nothing to him. Some of the agitation leaders, MacColl and Stead in particular, welcomed Gladstone's 'noble speech',[1] for indeed it condemned the character of the government's Eastern policy. But they welcomed it in default of anything better, for it was made without reference to the Bulgarian atrocities. Gladstone looked back, not forward. His speech of 31 July was the complement to the speech he had made at the beginning of the session, on 8 February, congratulating the government for its adherence to the Andrassy Note. It seemed to Gladstone then that Disraeli and Derby had at last recognised the reality of the 'European conscience' which in his view the Treaty of Paris substituted for Russian treaty rights on behalf of the Christians of Turkey. So solicitous was Gladstone to shelter and encourage what seemed to be a promising new departure in British policy that he cut across some criticisms made by Hartington in the ortho-dox Palmerstonian vein, and assured Disraeli that they were not to be construed in any way as representing an implied censure.[2]

Gladstone might well have saved himself trouble, Hartington annoyance, and Disraeli puzzlement; for the government's con-version to a 'European' policy was of course spurious, part of a Turkish manoeuvre to evade the execution of the Andrassy Note.

---

[1] *Northern Echo*, 3 August 1876, pp. 2–3.

[2] 3 *Hansard*, CCXXVII, cc. 102–4. Carslake Thompson, I think, tends to over-estimate the significance of this speech in relation to later events. He speaks of it as having cut the Liberal party 'adrift from the policy of supporting Turkey', and cutting also 'the official leaders of the Liberal party adrift from the old policy' (*Public Opinion and Lord Beaconsfield*, vol. i, pp. 265, 269). There is certainly not much evi-dence of this at the end of July. In any case, Hartington rarely took cues like this from Gladstone; and the Liberal party, as such, could hardly be credited with having a policy to be cut adrift from, either in February or July.

Gladstone expressed his disillusionment and disappointment on 31 July. He then condemned the policy of the government on exactly the same grounds as he had praised it in February. His consistent theme was the ideal of the concert. He regretted the policy of rejecting the Berlin Memorandum, of dispatching the fleet in a manner obviously open to misconstruction, of unworthy distrust of the good faith of Alexander II. He mentioned the Bulgarian atrocities in passing only to remark that it was a subject into which he would not enter.[1]

Why did Gladstone neglect to touch the specific Bulgarian issue? His refusal to preside at the meeting suggested after the debate of 10 July has already been noted.[2] He stated then that he would reserve an expression of his attitude for a parliamentary debate. But his attitude, as far as the agitation was concerned, proved to be negative. It was not that he was entirely unaware of the importance of the Bulgarian case; but it had not as yet, for him, moved out of the orbit of regular political issues. And it is clear that one reason for Gladstone's reluctance was his sense of the peculiar restraints of his personal responsibility—his 'historical' responsibility as a member of Lord Aberdeen's cabinet in 1854,[3] and, even more burdensome, the responsibility of his present public status as a composite retired elder statesman and active parliamentarian. Moreover, Gladstone's long-matured political instinct would be strongly against making any move before he was perfectly sure of his ground. He could not commit himself on the basis of newspaper reports, or of any informal evidence, however well authenticated or circumstantial.

Yet, allowing for all this, fundamentally Gladstone was disabled from taking the issue up by the simple fact that he had but little inkling of the potential of the question of Bulgaria in itself, and, more important, no inkling at all of its potential as a means of arousing a mass agitation. The most he hoped for was that the question might be revived in the next session, in February 1877.[4]

Gladstone's speech of 31 July was, consequently, wholly inadequate to the occasion. His attack on Disraeli's policy was unequivocal but irrelevant, in the sense that the Berlin Memorandum had

[1] 3 *Hansard*, CCXXXI, cc. 174–203.
[2] See above, p. 43.   [3] 3 *Hansard*, CCXXXI, c. 174.
[4] Gladstone to Granville, 7 August 1876, Granville Papers, 30, 29/29. For further discussion of this point, see below, pp. 96–7.

itself been made irrelevant by the events which occurred in
Bulgaria while the Imperial powers were formulating it in Berlin.
It was not merely that Gladstone was restrained, for instance, in
his studious politeness to Elliot, while expressing anxiety that an
investigation of the atrocities by one so closely associated with
Elliot's outlook as Walter Baring[1] might be unduly pro-Turkish
in bias; but his outline of the 'new measures' required by the circumstances can be described only as jejune in the extreme. Positive
that the Christians were the dynamic element in European Turkey
and that the Muslims were in decline, Gladstone yet did not go
beyond this further than a vague and rather perfunctory suggestion
that experience (not, apparently, principle) pointed to 'autonomy'
for the Christians as being the best solution. He was much more
definite, however, as to the desirability of maintaining Turkish
territorial integrity; and he went out of his way to emphasise that
he was 'not ashamed' to assert this. An independent Slav state,
Gladstone thought, would involve dangers too great to be contemplated. He concluded by expressing an earnest hope that the
government might yet discover a solution which would give 'consolatory assurance' that the efforts and sacrifices of the Crimean
War had not been in vain.[2]

This was emphatically not the speech of an 'atrocity-monger';
and Gladstone in fact was luckier than he deserved in having Disraeli deliver a rebuke which, in retrospect, became a cherished
compliment, something that Gladstone could present later as
evidence that he had not been completely without merit or insight
in his dealings with the Bulgarian question prior to the point
where awakening as to what was afoot was forced upon him.
Disraeli denounced Gladstone's speech as the 'only one that had
exhibited a real hostility to the policy of the Government'[3] merely,
of course, to emphasise the wide basis of support which his rejection of the Berlin Memorandum and dispatch of the fleet enjoyed
on both sides of the Commons. And Gladstone's speech was irrelevant to the developing situation in a deeper sense than its refer-

[1] A secretary of the Constantinople embassy appointed to report on the situation in
Bulgaria. See *State Papers*, LXXXIV (1876), *Turkey*, No. 5, no. 4, Derby to Elliot,
15 July 1876; and no. 8, Elliot to Derby, 19 July 1876.
[2] 3 *Hansard*, CCXXXI, c. 201.
[3] See Gladstone's autobiographical fragment of 1896: Gladstone Papers, Add.
MSS 44790, ff. 112–14.

ence to the Berlin Memorandum. To the atrocity agitation leaders the Treaty of Paris was the 'wicked Treaty'.[1] And 'consolatory assurance' that the Crimean War had not been fought in vain was at bottom, after all, the very mainspring of British Eastern policy; the ultimate source of all the conscious and unconscious dishonesties and evasions of its ambassadorial prognostications, its consular misrepresentations, its Whitehall complacencies and unrealities.

Bishop Fraser of Manchester, disdaining the wishfulness of MacColl and Stead, made public his exceeding irritation at what he regarded as Gladstone's quite gratuitous obsession with the need to maintain Turkish territorial integrity: to him this seemed to strike at the very heart of what the agitation stood for.[2] Freeman, an even stronger advocate of Slav independence, 'trembled for a moment' when he read the speech. Nothing, in Freeman's view, but the 'freedom of all lands north of Haemus' would ensure even temporary peace in the Balkan peninsula.[3] The only real consolation which those agitation leaders more disposed to make the best of a poor bargain could salvage from the speech was that, in attacking Disraeli's policy in general terms, Gladstone had made possibly a first public step in their direction. But it soon became depressingly clear that Gladstone did not contemplate a second step.

2 The End of the Session

The debate of 31 July gave very little positive encouragement to the agitation. Shuvalov, the Russian ambassador, reported to St Petersburg that the long-awaited 'parliamentary tourney' indicated a general indifference in the House to the Bulgarian issue and a general support for the policy of aloofness from the Berlin Memorandum.[4] Hartington, far from being 'cut adrift' from the orthodox policy, declared his agreement with the broad lines of the course of action taken by the government.[5] Granville, in the Lords, made but the faintest echo of Gladstone's critique.[6] Dis-

---

[1] Liddon to Freeman, 31 August 1876, Liddon Papers.
[2] See below, pp. 56, 61.
[3] *South Wales Daily News*, 9 September 1876, pp. 4–5; Freeman to Bryce, 27 August 1876, Bryce Papers, E4.
[4] Shuvalov to Gorchakov, 20 July/1 August 1876, *Slavonic Review*, **4**, p. 178.
[5] 3 *Hansard*, CCXXXI, cc. 216–25.
[6] *Ibid.*, cc. 83–94.

raeli himself was perfectly confident that the situation was well in hand, and continued to indulge in a strain of sarcasm about his alleged 'want of sympathy with the sufferers by imaginary atrocities'.[1]

Even as Disraeli congratulated himself that the affair had almost blown over, MacGahan, the Special Commissioner of the *Daily News*, had arrived at Batak, a town thirty-five miles south-west of Philippopolis. The place was a ghastly shambles. Six of the eight thousand inhabitants had been massacred after submitting peacefully to the Turkish commander, Achmet Aga. MacGahan's first dispatch, a telegraphic but sufficiently horrifying account of the scene at Batak, appeared in the *Daily News* of 7 August. On the same day, while this distasteful bolus was being digested, Bourke, the Parliamentary Foreign Under-Secretary, read to the House a letter from Walter Baring describing his initial impressions of the Bulgarian scene. This letter, though dwelling on journalistic exaggerations, confirmed the general accuracy of the earlier reports in the *Daily News*: about twelve thousand Bulgarians had perished and sixty villages were wholly or partly destroyed; the province was utterly ruined.[2]

The combination of MacGahan and Baring gave the British parliament and public the most profound stir it had experienced since the opening of the Bulgarian question. Even Hartington was roused to demand more papers promptly, before prorogation.[3] The Queen, restless again, telegraphed to Disraeli that she was 'shocked at the details of the Bulgarian massacres'. Mr Baring, she added, with a touch of revealing naiveté, 'admits 12,000'. 'I cannot rest quiet without urging the prevention of further atrocities which Sir Henry Elliot apprehends possible henceforth.'[4] Disraeli evidently still imagined that he had said his last word on 31 July, for on 7 August he left Bourke to bear the brunt of the attack by the Radicals Mundella (primed with first-hand information from Sandwith),[5] Anderson of Glasgow, P. A. Taylor, and Jacob Bright. But the tone of this debate made Disraeli aware that his confidence had been altogether misplaced. He could now

[1] Buckle, *Disraeli*, vol. ii, pp. 909–10; 3 *Hansard*, CCXXXI, c. 215.
[2] Enclosure, Elliot to Derby, 25 July 1876 (received 4 August), *Turkey*, no. 5, no. 27.   [3] 3 *Hansard*, CCXXXI, cc. 721–46.
[4] Queen to Disraeli, 11 August 1876, Disraeli Papers.
[5] W. H. G. Armytage, *A. J. Mundella, 1825–1897* (1951), p. 169.

plainly see all his sarcasms rebounding against him; and he reflected thankfully to Derby after the 'very damaging debate' that the session was luckily near its end. 'It is a very awkward business', he added wryly, 'and, I fear, a great exposure of our diplomatic system abroad and at home.'[1]

The unfortunate effect was heightened by the appearance soon after of the official Turkish report on the alleged atrocities, with its unintelligently sweeping denials and its derisory figures of Bulgarian victims.[2] Nor were matters mended by the new Blue Book got out hurriedly by the Foreign Office on 10 August. This selection again was edited on the accepted principle of shielding the Turks and discrediting Christian insurgents; but the time had gone by when this kind of deception, or self-deception, could pass without protest. Together with the Turkish report Tenterden included an extract from the *Levant Herald*, notoriously in the pay of the Porte, and an accompanying comment by Elliot that it supplied 'interesting details' 'to some extent justifying the severe measures'.[3] Elliot, as late as 25 July, was still trying to discredit Pears's original sources of information, and spoke of the correspondent's 'credulity' being imposed upon.[4] All this read very oddly beside Baring's letter, forwarded on the same day (25 July) and the dispatch of Vice-Consul Dupuis of Adrianople to Derby on 21 July, supplying information which Derby had urgently requested on 14 July, prior to his interview with the deputation led by Bright and Richard. Dupuis reported that although great atrocities undoubtedly had been committed, newspaper estimates were exaggerated. As regards the Philippopolis area, Dupuis added with unconscious irony, the lives 'sacrificed' were 'below 15,000'; in a greater stroke of unconscious irony, he added a '(*sic*)'.[5]

★

The shocks of 7 August provoked three immediate and significant reactions. The first was from *The Times*, hitherto vacillating and trimming. Delane had been disgusted by the effrontery of the

[1] Buckle, *Disraeli*, vol. ii, p. 918.
[2] Musurus Pasha to Derby, 4 August 1876, *Turkey*, no. 5, no. 29, enclosing Report to Sublime Porte by Edib Effendi.
[3] Elliot to Derby, 25 July 1876 (received 1 August), *Turkey*, No. 5, no. 24.
[4] *Ibid.*   [5] Dupuis to Derby, 21 July 1876, *ibid.*, no. 11.

Turkish report.[1] MacGahan's dispatch and Baring's letter proved to be the last jolts necessary to push him clearly into a position of countenancing outspoken condemnation by his writers of Disraeli's flippancy and Elliot's incompetence, and thus effectively of patronage of the agitation. The rather clumsily pro-Turkish Blue Book of 10 August confirmed Delane in this new editorial policy.[2] He was never an active advocate of the agitation in the same sense as Stead of the *Northern Echo* or Frank Hill of the *Daily News* or even C.P. Scott of the *Manchester Guardian*. He abandoned the agitation, moreover, just as soon as it really needed support in the face of declining enthusiasm and something of a Russophobe counter-agitation. But, for the critical weeks to come, the sympathetic commitment of the most powerful daily paper was an asset of immense utility for the agitation.

Then came a public meeting at Manchester on 9 August, convened by the mayor to 'make known the opinion of the people of Manchester as to the duty of England with regard to these barbarities'. The *Manchester Guardian* gave it enthusiastic backing.[3] The Dean of Manchester delivered the main address, calling for nation-wide expression of the demand for an end to the old Eastern policy; and the Anglo-Catholic Churchman Knox-Little got in a hit at the apathy of the bishops in the House of Lords. The most important feature of the occasion, however, was a letter from Bishop Fraser referring to the horrors of MacGahan's dispatch and denouncing the government's policy of non-interference as 'interference on the wrong side'. Fraser also took the opportunity to attack sharply Gladstone's doctrine on the territorial integrity of Turkey. He concluded by repeating his earlier appeal for the English people 'to speak their minds loud and clear' if they 'would stand before the bar of European opinion acquitted of complicity in some of the most dreadful crimes which history records'.[4]

The third reaction to the events of 7 August was the last spasm of the dying parliamentary session. Evelyn Ashley—all the more sensitive, perhaps, to the issue in that he had just completed his *Life of Palmerston*, based on the early volumes of Lytton Bulwer —watched Disraeli's 'studied silence' on 7 August with mounting

[1] *Times*, 7 August 1876, pp. 8, 9.   [2] *Ibid.*, 11 August 1876, p. 9.
[3] 8 August 1876, p. 4; 10 August 1876, p. 5.   [4] *Times*, 10 August 1876, p. 6.

exasperation.[1] He determined to force a debate for the 11th. This presented Disraeli with a serious challenge for the first time. Gladstone was quite out of the running, and Hartington still declined to attack; but Ashley received strong support from Forster and Harcourt on the Opposition front bench.

Disraeli, who in January, after due hesitation, had laid it down deliberately that 'We can't be more Turkish than the Sultan—*plus Arabe que l'Arabie*',[2] now denied with solemn indignation that Britain had given the Turks any moral support. He dismissed as erroneous and baseless the thesis that Britain had a 'peculiar alliance' with Turkey, or that the British government deserved to be regarded as the Turks' 'peculiar friends' any more than the other European allies of the Sultan. From this premise Disraeli rejected Harcourt's charge that the British government was morally implicated in the atrocious massacre of twelve thousand Bulgarians. Disraeli could no longer deny the fact of extensive massacres, but he justified his earlier scepticism on the ground that Baring's letter clearly established that some newspaper estimates were exaggerated. That twelve thousand had indeed perished was, he agreed, a deplorable event; but it could not justify a change in the fundamental policy of the British Empire, enshrined in the Treaty of Paris and the Tripartite Treaty of Guarantee. On this note of legality and imperial interests Disraeli closed, as he thought, the question of the East, as far as parliament and the public were concerned.[3]

Most people would certainly have agreed with Disraeli on this point—Gladstone for one. As late as 23 August Freeman lamented that in the recession of parliament Disraeli and Derby would 'practically have it their own way'.[4] The post-sessional atmosphere was naturally one of political relaxation. Although MacGahan's dispatch had helped to provoke a debate in the Commons, it did not provoke the politicians to continue the debate outside. Dilke, one of the few who did so, revealed himself so stolidly unimpressed[5]

---

[1] Ashley to Gladstone, 12 September 1876, Gladstone Papers, Add. MSS 44451, ff. 174–5.   [2] Buckle, *Disraeli*, vol. ii, p. 891.

[3] 3 *Hansard*, CCXXXI, c. 1146. He said after the debate to Lord George Hamilton: 'I think Burke's [*sic*] answer and mine covered the ground, and we shall not have much further trouble on the subject.' Lord G. Hamilton, *Parliamentary Reminiscences and Reflections, 1868 to 1885* (1917), p. 118. Disraeli also closed his career in the Commons on 11 August. It was announced on the following morning that he was to become Earl of Beaconsfield.

[4] *Daily News*, 23 August 1876, p. 6.   [5] *Times*, 16 August 1876, p. 6.

as to earn the reputation of an 'unexpected ally' of Disraeli and an indignant rebuke from the *Methodist*.[1] On the other hand, the small group of Liberals who had pressed the atrocities issue in the Commons were determined that it should not be allowed to pass completely out of sight during the recess. At the end of the session they formed themselves into a committee to 'watch the position of the Eastern Question'.[2] Those most prominent in this committee appear to have been Mundella, J. Holms, Evelyn Ashley, Wilfrid Lawson, Henry Richard, and Jacob Bright. Henry Fawcett was also associated closely with the group.[3] Auberon Herbert and F. W. Chesson acted as secretaries.

This committee is interesting and important as evidence of a consistent and continuing parliamentary concern with the atrocities issue, linking the earlier proposals for a demonstration after the debate of 10 July which led eventually to the Willis's Rooms meeting to the later development of the St James's Hall Conference committee under Mundella and the Eastern Question Association. For both of these the committee formed at the end of the 1876 session was the germ. But it is clear that the committee had, at the beginning of the recess, no more conception than Gladstone of the immediate possibilities of keeping the question alive which the state of public opinion, as represented by the Manchester meeting, offered them. On the contrary, they assumed that the issue would fade away during the recess unless special efforts were made to keep it in being, ready to be raised again in the next session. They were a corps purely of observation, not of pursuit.

The cases of Mundella and Herbert, the two members of this group who later became most prominent in the agitation, best illustrate the paralysing effect of the prorogation on the activity of the politicians generally. Both had shown an exceptional depth of interest in atrocities question.[4] Mundella in particular prided himself on his part in bringing the atrocities before the notice of the Commons.[5] Immediately after the debate of 11 August Mundella went off to stay at Herbert's place, Ashley Arnewood, in

---

[1] 25 August 1876, p. 3.
[2] Gladstone Papers, Add. MSS 44452, ff. 47–8.
[3] See Mundella to R. Leader, 1 November 1876, Mundella Papers; *Northern Echo*, 28 August 1876, p. 4.
[4] On their correspondence with Humphry Sandwith see Harris, *Auberon Herbert*, p. 179.
[5] Mundella to R. Leader, 26 August 1876, Mundella Papers.

Hampshire.[1] Also at Ashley Arnewood that season[2] were Frank Hill, the editor of the *Daily News*, and Sir George Campbell, a Liberal M.P., former Indian administrator, and strong opponent of Disraeli's Eastern policy.[3] On the face of it, four more likely conspirators of agitation against the government's attitude and policy could hardly have been assembled. Yet nothing came directly from any discussions at Ashley Arnewood. Hill shortly afterwards left for a lengthy vacation in Italy, not foreseeing, as he later explained to the equally unforeseeing Gladstone, 'the clearing storm which was about to break'.[4] All eyes were on the next session. But in little more than a week Mundella and Herbert were deeply involved in the process of agitation. This was the result of the initiative of others who did appreciate the potentialities of the public mood.

3 The Oxford Group: First Phase

The curious fact about the public response to MacGahan's dispatch and Baring's corroboration of the reality of an extensive massacre was the slowness of its development. Between the Willis's Rooms meeting of 27 July and the first of Stead's northern atrocity meetings on 25 August, there was but one notable public demonstration, at Manchester on 9 August. No 'series' of demonstrations was set in motion at Willis's Rooms, as the *Spectator* had hoped. It is clear, on the evidence of the Manchester meeting, that MacGahan's report did have a direct impact on public opinion. But the absence of similar meetings for a period of two weeks suggests also that atrocity reports were not enough, even when supported by strong exhortation in general terms, to provoke in themselves a consistent campaign of public manifestations against the government's policy. Stead greeted the Manchester meeting with enthusiasm: 'England is being roused at last.'[5] The Anglo-Catholic

---

[1] Mundella to R. Leader, 12 August 1876, *ibid.*
[2] Harris, *Auberon Herbert*, p. 178.
[3] See his *Handy Book on the Eastern Question, being a Very Recent View of Turkey* 1876). Campbell was especially valuable to the agitation as an expert who could answer with authority the argument that the British position in India depended on bolstering the Sultan's political and religious prestige.
[4] Hill to Gladstone, 19 September 1876, Gladstone Papers, Add. MSS 44451, f. 220–1.
[5] *Northern Echo*, 11 August 1876, pp. 2–3.

Church Review was equally hopeful that such meetings would be 'multiplied throughout England'.[1]

But their optimism, like the *Spectator*'s optimism about Willis's Rooms, was premature. The Manchester demonstration remained rather awkwardly isolated. It was the result clearly of special local conditions: principally, no doubt, the known views of a bishop exceptionally active in local affairs, the incitement of the *Manchester Guardian*, and, on the primary level of activation, it would appear, an energetic committee of ladies.[2] These factors, between them, provided a catalyst which resolved the particular elements of latent indignation and public expression of it in Manchester. The problem was to find a catalyst of some kind in every locality. The politicians were obsessed by their assumption that the end of the session meant the end of serious political activity; and in any case most of them were away on vacation.[3] The function of local agitation-making was eventually taken up, in the overwhelming majority of cases, by Nonconformist ministers and Anglican clergy.[4] The testimony of the Rev. J. Guinness Rogers, a leading Congregationalist divine, is typical:

> Personally, I never had any hesitation as to the course which, as a Christian man, I ought to take in relation to the Bulgarian atrocities. When the first report of them reached this country, I happened to be spending a quiet vacation time at Whitby. The story at once touched the imagination and the hearts of the townspeople, as well as of a great many visitors. . . . A meeting was held—the forerunner of many—and the enthusiasm in opposition to the Turk was intense.[5]

Rogers, in association with local ministers and clergy, took a leading part in the demonstration. This kind of clerical presence

---

[1] 12 August 1876, p. 405.

[2] *Manchester Guardian*, 15 July 1876, p. 9.

[3] See Gladstone's comments on this point, *Times*, 11 September 1876, p. 10: and Joseph Cowen, M.P. for Newcastle, who was recalled by his constituents from a holiday in France, *Newcastle Daily Chronicle*, 7 October 1876. One of the very few cases where the local M.P. played a decisive part in getting up a demonstration was in Ross (Herefordshire), where Thomas Blake, the Liberal member, took the lead (*Ross Gazette*, 28 September 1876, pp. 3–4).

[4] Bedford is a typical example of this pattern. The *Bedfordshire Times and Independent* (9 September 1876, p. 6), in reporting the meeting at Bedford on 4 September remarked on the great regret expressed that the shortness of notice made it impossible to get the county and borough members back from their vacation in time for the meeting. The dynamic force behind the Bedford demonstration was obviously clerical there were no less than eight clergymen or ministers on the platform.

[5] *Autobiography*, p. 210. See also *Whitby Times*, 1 and 8 September 1876.

was not, however, merely *faute de mieux*; it was a very natural consequence, as the demonstration at Manchester indicated, of the essentially moral character of the issue raised by the atrocities.

Liddon, Canon of St Paul's as well as professor at Oxford, did his best to give a lead in the metropolis such as Bishop Fraser had given in Manchester. He congratulated Fraser warmly on his letter to the Manchester meeting, though echoing Knox-Little's strictures on the supineness of the other bishops. Fraser responded by emphasising his feeling that he had been under a moral obligation to do what he had done. He felt also an obligation to defend his fellow prelates. He begged Liddon not to be 'too hard on the poor Archbishop, or on the rest of the bench in this matter'. Fraser's situation in a centre such as Manchester gave him, he claimed, a 'greater opportunity in a matter of this kind than most of them enjoy. I should be false to my convictions if I did not use the opportunity when Providence put it in my way'.[1] Liddon remained unconvinced. It seems also that he rather deprecated Fraser's attack on Gladstone. Fraser regretted this, but insisted that the question of Turkish territorial integrity concerned him 'very much'; and he could 'not help noticing it'.[2]

These differences were greatly outweighed by general agreement in principle, as Liddon's sensational sermon at St Paul's on 13 August on the theme of a 'moral, Christian, humane' Eastern policy made clear.[3] The sermons of Liddon, the most celebrated Anglican preacher of his day, were something of a national institution, almost on the same level as C. H. Spurgeon's in the Baptist Metropolitan Tabernacle. Liddon's violent denunciation, from the first pulpit of the Establishment, of Disraeli's immoral policy, his 'light-hearted incredulity', his 'heartless epigrams', achieved a most gratifying scandal. More important was Liddon's powerful warning and appeal to each individual conscience that avoidance of responsibility before God for a share in the evil of the atrocities could be attained only by public action against the government's pro-Turkish policy.

This 'inflammatory harangue'[4] caused many repercussions. In the congregation at St Paul's was a young inspector of schools,

---

[1] Fraser to Liddon, 11 August 1876, Liddon Papers.
[2] Fraser to Liddon, 16 August 1876, *ibid.*
[3] *Guardian*, 16 August 1876, pp. 1086-7.
[4] *Rock*, 18 August 1876, p. 643.

Ellis Ashmead Barlett, whose case is exceptionally revealing and valuable. Bartlett had recently distinguished himself at Oxford as a leader of the Conservative party in the Union, and especially as a strong champion of Disraeli.[1] Yet such was the impression made on him by Liddon's sermon that the broad blue stripe of his Tory consistency was briefly but decisively interrupted. The sermon was not the only factor involved: it appears that Bartlett was emotionally unstable and excitable, and this temperamental weakness later barred him from a serious political career. The atrocities question had also been on his mind for some time. Liddon's sermon came as the final emotional shock needed to push Bartlett into activity.

Bartlett wrote to Liddon that day, 'impelled' by feelings 'excited' by the sermon. For 'weeks past', he related, his 'indignant sympathies' had been aroused 'on behalf of fellow Christians in Bulgaria now experiencing such horrible and unprovoked oppression'. Liddon's 'great appeal' to all of his hearers to 'do something to protest against the barbarity of the Turk' made Bartlett wish more than ever to do what he could to 'contribute towards the overthrow' of the Turks in Europe.

It has occurred to me that I might be able to speak or lecture in some of the principal Towns on the evils of the Ottoman rule and on behalf of these wretched victims.

Of course however such a scheme would require influential introduction and interest to secure success.

I doubt my power to do very much, but I might do something, having read some history and having had some practice in speaking at the Oxford Union.

I am sure that in this cause, if any, I might speak with effect, for on no other have my feelings been more deeply aroused. If you think my plan in any way feasible, and can do anything to advance it I shall be most

---

[1] He defeated H. H. Asquith handsomely for the presidency in 1873. Bartlett's later political career was vehemently Conservative. After a visit to the East in 1877–8 he returned violently Russophobe and took up propaganda work for Disraeli, who rewarded him in 1880 with the patronage seat of Eye. He held minor office under Salisbury, and was knighted in 1892. He became noted as an imperialist of the fullest-blooded variety. He served with the Turkish army against the Greeks in 1897 and rounded off his career by fighting in South Africa. (There is a memoir in the *Dictionary of National Biography*.) Undoubtedly one cause of his later reversal of attitude on the Eastern question was the influence of his brother William, secretary and later husband of the philanthropist Baroness Burdett-Coutts, who promoted a 'Turkish Compassionate Fund' in 1877. See C. B. Patterson, *Angela Burdett-Coutts and the Victorians* (1953).

rejoiced to give my best services freely during the leisure time I am about
to have in my vacation.[1]

Bartlett explained that he was a Conservative in politics, and could
not understand how so many Conservatives remained unsympathetic to the Eastern Christians. He certainly had a strong
crusading urge. 'Would that but for two months I could have the
name of Gladstone or the unleashing enthusiasm of Peter the
Hermit.'[2] In default of both these qualifications Bartlett was yet
prepared to sacrifice his vacation in Switzerland. Liddon responded
with an offer of an introduction to the Bishop of Manchester; but
the bishop was not optimistic enough about prospects to attract
Bartlett, so the newly-launched agitator decided to divert his attention elsewhere.[3] He reported to Liddon on 4 September the success
of his first meeting.

The more typical and conventional response to Liddon's sermon
is illustrated by the Rev. Henry Tozer, a former Fellow of Exeter
College, Oxford. As one who had personal experience of conditions
in the East, Tozer felt 'humiliated' as an Englishman by the
actions of his government. In thanking Liddon for his advocacy of
the cause of the Eastern Christians, Tozer remarked that the
English people were beginning to awake to the iniquity of Turkish
rule; 'but it will require that every possible means of influence
should be brought to bear' to counteract the 'traditional philo-
Turkism' of British policy. Tozer was very anxious to do what he
could to help Liddon. 'In particular', he added, 'I am anxious that
the clergy should make such a cause their own.'[4] This was indeed
very much to Liddon's heart.

It soon became apparent, however, that the clergy would present
a far from united front in this cause. The *Rock*, the aggressive
organ of the Low Church, had hitherto been fairly orthodox in its
anti-Turkish expressions, though by no means particularly cordial
to the atrocities agitation itself. Criticism of Disraeli, that pillar
of Protestantism, remained muted; and the sympathy of the Anglo-
Catholic party with the apostate Orthodox Church caused concern.
t was comforting, on the other hand, that the Romans and

[1] Bartlett to Liddon, 13 August 1876, Liddon Papers.
[2] Bartlett to Liddon, 18 August 1876, *ibid.*
[3] Fraser to Liddon, 16 August 1876, *ibid.*, and Bartlett to Liddon, 18 August 1876,
ibid.   [4] Tozer to Liddon, 15 August 1876, *ibid.*

Ritualists could not agree on this point; and Shaftesbury's presence at the Willis's Rooms meeting was reassuring. The *Rock* contented itself by announcing that it had no other policy on the Eastern question than of waiting until events should have provided the answer to it.[1]

Faced suddenly with Liddon's sermon at St Paul's, however, the *Rock* instinctively smelt a Ritualist plot. Matters immediately took on a very different and decided aspect. If, as could not be doubted, 'the Moslem power was commissioned by God to chastise the apostate idolatrous Christians of the East and West', the English people must be very careful what they did. 'Besides, we have some difficulty', added the *Rock*, 'in satisfying ourselves that Dr. Liddon's impassioned appeal is an outburst of *genuine* humanity. Is he quite sure that his yearning for reunion with the Greek Church may not have something to do with it?'[2] It was a sign of the times that the Baptist paper, the *Freeman*, should have leaped passionately to Liddon's defence, despite the 'momentous' nature of its own struggle against Ritualism.[3]

The shrill and hostile outburst of the *Rock* was in some ways the most significant consequence of Liddon's sermon. The *Rock* represented, in its extremist, most bigoted form, the basically evangelical tone of the Church of England in the mid-Victorian era. The attitude of the *Rock* was certainly symptomatic of an outlook widely held among clergymen who, if not entirely prepared to accept the Turks as a providential dispensation to chastise idolatry, were quite prepared to accept them as providential to the fundamental interests of the British Empire. The *Rock's* outcry proclaimed not only that Fraser's and Liddon's hopes of a united Anglican approach to the atrocities question were definitely to be disappointed; it indicated also that the divergence over this issue would tend to follow the pattern of the discords about the nature of the Church which had agitated it since the emergence of the Tractarian movement—at a time, moreover, when the wounds of the latest struggle over Ritualism were still fresh and sore.

That Liddon's own wounds were very fresh and very sore is evident in a letter to Freeman at the end of August.

[1] 4 August 1876, p. 605.
[2] 18 August 1876, p. 643.
[3] 25 August 1876, p. 412.

It is good, no doubt, to stir up us parsons. But why not the Bishops? Why are they in the House of Lords, except to represent the cause of humanity and justice, when 'statesmanship' and red-tapism are silent or hostile? But alas! the Public Worship Regulation Act represents the highest efforts of modern Archiepiscopal genius; and it has completely succeeded in deepening all our divisions, and in threatening little less than disruption in the years before us. I may do him an injustice; but I have a shrewd suspicion that Archbishop Tait sees in the Ottoman Porte the Judicial Committee—in the Bulgarians and Servians, the refractory Ritualists—and in the Circassians and Bashi-Bazouks the wholesome and regenerative influences of Lord Penzance.[1]

The occasion of this rather unconsciously amusing outburst was the publication in the *Guardian* on 30 August of the correspondence between Tait and the Archbishop of Belgrade. The Serbian archbishop had written to Tait in July enclosing a letter from the leading inhabitants of Bosnia-Herzegovina to the people of England, supplicating their Christian sympathy and active charity, and begging them not to be deterred by unwarranted distrust of Russia. Tait replied on 3 August, cool and 'statesmanlike' to the point of being positively chilling. He assured the Serbian archbishop of the sympathy of the English people; he also assured him that the government of Mr Disraeli would do its best to diminish the sufferings of the Christian peoples; and he took the opportunity to emphasise his own faith in the assurances of the government that the dispatch of the fleet to Besika Bay had behind it absolutely no motive but the protection of British life and property in Constantinople.[2]

This somewhat dampening exchange was published just at the time when Liddon was preparing to leave, with MacColl, for his journey to Serbia and other disturbed areas of the East to give to what the *Rock* invariably called the 'wafer-worshipping' so-called Eastern Christians personal and direct assurance of the warm and active sympathy of the English Church. There was, perhaps, a certain dramatic aptness, if little justice, in Liddon's identification of the cruelly-oppressed Ritualists with the down-trodden Christians of the East.[3]

★

[1] Liddon to Freeman, 30 August 1876, Liddon Papers. Lord Penzance was the judge appointed under the Public Worship Regulation Act.

[2] *Guardian*, 30 August 1876, pp. 1147–8.

[3] Liddon, describing later to Lady Salisbury his journey to the East, remarked a trifle sardonically on the tactlessness of the Archbishop of Belgrade in proposing the

On the same day that Liddon delivered his sermon at St Paul's Fitzjames Stephen reported once more to Lytton the curious spectacle of English feeling veering around to the 'sentimental point of view'. His diagnosis of the situation, though heavily biassed, is not entirely without point or usefulness:

If you want to drive John Bull mad the plan is to tickle (rather delicately—yet not too delicately) his prurience with good circumstantial accounts of 'insults worse than death' inflicted on women, then throw in a good dose of Cross and Crescent, *plus* Civilization v Barbarism, plus a little 'Civil & Religious liberty all over the world', & there you have him, as the Yankees say, 'raging around like a bob-tailed bull in fly-time'. I am much mistaken if during the long vacation he does not yet get worked up into that noble condition, poor old beast.[1]

With his usual acuteness, Stephen saw much more clearly, if more narrowly, than most. It was not until 24 August that the 'veer' became sufficiently pronounced to encourage Liddon to thoughts of careful optimism. He wrote to Freeman that there appeared to be, as he hoped, 'a turn in the tide of English opinion about the Turks', though the said Turks were 'very strong in the Clubs, and in military circles'. It was, indeed, very likely in a club that Liddon got into 'hot (or anyhow warm)' water with Russell Gurney, the Recorder of London, who, Liddon recounted, 'talked about "exaggerations", defended Disraeli through thick and thin, and would not allow that we were indirectly answerable for the horrors in Bulgaria'. Gurney was a type, Liddon concluded regretfully, of a large class: 'men who don't mean to be inhuman or anti-Christian, but they give their support, nevertheless, to a race which is both one and the other'.[2]

Though there had been as yet no signal demonstration on the scale of the Manchester meeting, there were increasing evidences of stirrings and preparations. A 'Christian Minister' called in a letter to the *Daily News* for a meeting in Exeter Hall to keep the metropolis level with the preparations in the provinces, declaring that 'myriads' were straining for an opportunity to give 'vent to

health of the Archbishop of Canterbury, at a dinner in Liddon's and MacColl's honour in a 'fervid speech'. Liddon to Lady Salisbury, 30 September 1876, Salisbury Papers

[1] Fitzjames Stephen to Lytton, 13 August 1876, Fitzjames Stephen Papers, Cambridge Add. MSS 7349.

[2] Liddon to Freeman, 24 August 1876, Liddon Papers. Doubtless, also, Liddon' feelings on this particular incident were all the more acute in that Gurney was a prominent advocate of the Public Worship Regulation policy.

their anger and abhorrence'.[1] The first move towards activity in the metropolis came in fact from a committee of working men, guided by Auberon Herbert, who planned a demonstration in Hyde Park to denounce the Turks and demand Elliot's recall.[2] Freeman, invited to take part, rather deprecated the idea of Hyde Park, discredited in his eyes by the activities of the supporters of the Tichborne Claimant[3]; and the demonstration took place ultimately in the Hackney Working Men's Institute on the 29th. There were reports that some leading citizens of Greenwich were trying to get Gladstone to address his constituents.[4]

The *Daily News*, meanwhile, had begun to publish letters from MacGahan much more elaborate and detailed than his earlier telegrams. The first, a general survey of events, came out on 16 August; the second, a fuller version of the telegram of 7 August decribing the harrowing scene at Batak, appeared on 22 August, and caused an immense stir.[5] The details, commented the *Manchester Guardian*, were 'horrible and repulsive', but it was 'incumbent upon Englishmen to read them in order that they may rightly understand what their duty is in the matter'.[6] Auberon Herbert had the letter reprinted and distributed as a pamphlet at his own expense about his part of Hampshire.[7] The Queen noted in her diary on 23 August that the recent news was causing 'dreadful excitement and indignation'.[8] The *Daily News* announced on 24 August that it was overwhelmed with letters from all parts of the country and all classes of persons of all shades of politics.[9]

Derby referred later, with perhaps pardonable bitterness, to the

[1] 19 August 1876, p. 3.
[2] Harris, *Auberon Herbert*, p. 180, and *Daily News*, 18 August 1876, p. 3.
[3] Freeman to Bryce, 27 August 1876, Bryce Papers, E4.
[4] *Times*, 22 August 1876, p. 9.
[5] MacGahan's dispatches are gathered together conveniently in pamphlet form: *Turkish Atrocities in Bulgaria.* [6] 23 August 1876, p. 5.
[7] *Outrages in Bulgaria: the Latest Authentic Details* (26 August 1876). Harris, *Auberon Herbert*, p. 179.
[8] Buckle, *Letters of Queen Victoria, 1862–78*, vol. ii, p. 475.
[9] P. 4. An interesting point which might be noticed in this connection is the surprising paucity of illustrations of the aftermath of the atrocities. The *Illustrated London News* had a picture in its issue of 12 August (p. 149), and some rather bigger and better pictures on 19 August; but the whole is rather less than one would expect. The *Graphic* does not appear to have anything on the Bulgarian atrocities, though it had artists in Serbia who sent sketches of similar atrocities in that quarter. The *Irish Times*, indeed, commented on the remarkable fact of the absence of depictions of the scene at Batak which had been so minutely described, 'and yet these would have commanded an enormous sale'. The *Irish Times* inclined to deduce from this that the narratives supplied by MacGahan were exaggerated and unreliable (7 September 1876, p. 4).

'skilful and artistic narratives' of MacGahan.[1] The skill and artistry of these narratives certainly helped greatly to bring the crisis of public conscience to a head. MacGahan set out deliberately to project his own sense of passionate indignation. The protest of the *Saturday Review* that this infringed the conventions of the higher English journalism[2] was rather beside the point. MacGahan had found at last a subject for which his talent for sensationalism could do full justice, but yet not more than justice.

The perceptible heightening of tension produced by Mac-Gahan's dispatch of 22 August enabled Liddon to write on the 24th with fair confidence that the blood of the murdered Bulgarians had made it impossible for Britain to go to war with Russia, if Russia, as Liddon trusted she would, declared war on Turkey 'in the name of Christ and humanity'.[3] This was reading events with remarkable accuracy; for only two days previously Derby had succumbed to the combined pressure of a further letter from Baring, describing the scene at Batak,[4] and a letter received on the 22nd from Dupuis confirming and amplifying his earlier telegram.[5] Derby immediately telegraphed to Elliot that the 'universal feeling of indignation' in England against the Turks had reached such a pitch that in the extreme case of Russia declaring war against Turkey the British government would find it 'practically impossible to interfere'. The danger of such an extreme case grew greater with every successive Serbian defeat at the hands of the Turks. He instructed Elliot therefore to put such pressure on the Turks as to secure a speedy conclusion of hostilities as 'a matter of urgent necessity'.[6]

Bourke announced publicly the sense of this somewhat revised attitude at the end of the month.[7] He carefully avoided any implication that the revision had been imposed upon the government by the pressure of public opinion; but the terms of Derby's dispatch to Elliot make it clear enough that, as Liddon claimed to know from 'trustworthy quarters', the government had become con-

---

[1] *Times*, 12 September 1876, p. 8.
[2] 16 September 1876, pp. 353–4.
[3] Liddon to Freeman, 24 August 1876, Liddon Papers.
[4] Encls. 1, 2, Elliot to Derby, 9 August 1876, *Turkey*, XC (1877), no. 39.
[5] Dupuis to Derby, 7 August 1876, *ibid.*, no. 57.
[6] Derby to Elliot, 22 August 1876, *ibid.*, no. 159 (in dispatch form of 5 September). Temperley, I think, attributes rather too much significance to this when he describes it as a 'tremendous change in British policy' (*Proceedings of the British Academy*, **17** (1931), p. 118).
[7] *Times*, 2 September 1876, p. 8.

cerned at the growing strength and persistence of the criticism of its policy.[1]

The interesting point about Derby's despatch of 22 August is that the public indignation of which he seemed to be so impressed had hardly begun to assume a menacing air. Derby appears to have taken fright before being seriously threatened. This may be accounted for partly as a tactic to coerce the Turks by an appeal to domestic exigencies. Doubtless also Derby had read MacGahan's Batak letter in that morning's *Daily News*, and appreciated that it would hardly act as oil on the troubled public waters. But the tone of his dispatch, and the tone of Disraeli's letters a little later,[2] indicate clearly that they had no conception of the dimensions of the storm that was about to break over their heads.

Indeed, had he known what was coming, Disraeli very probably would not have countenanced even the modest effort of 22 August to outflank public criticism. Disraeli was capable of almost infinite elasticity so long as he was not openly under duress. Once threatened, however, he immediately stiffened. The tragedy of the situation at this moment was that a popular agitation which would unavoidably exacerbate relations between Disraeli and public opinion was irrevocably in the process of eruption. For in the week following 22 August the character of the movement critical of the government's Eastern policy was altered decisively from an affair of the newspapers—editorial articles, dispatches, and letters to editors—the pulpit, and occasional demonstrations, into a sustained campaign of 'atrocity meetings' originating in the north and quickly sweeping the whole country.

4 Stead and the Northern Atrocities Campaign

It is one of the very minor ironies of history that the part played in the atrocities agitation by W. T. Stead, who alone of the leading agitators wrote extensively of his activities, and actually contemplated writing a study of the agitation itself,[3] should have been

[1] Johnston, *Liddon*, p. 207.
[2] Buckle, *Disraeli*, vol. ii, pp. 923–4.
[3] Stead began collecting materials for this at least as early as November 1876. See Liddon to Stead, 15 November 1876, Stead Papers, Little Beside House, St Day. See also Stead to Gladstone, 1 July 1878, Gladstone Papers, Add. MSS 44303, ff. 298–9; Gladstone to Stead, 19 August 1878, Stead Papers; Freeman to Stead, 25 December 1879, *ibid.*: 'You once spoke to me of a little sketch of the movement since 1876.' It

so little and so grudgingly recognised by later historians.[1] Stead was to some extent a victim of circumstances. An obscure provincial figure in 1876, he worked anonymously through the medium of the *Northern Echo*. But he was a greater victim of his own manner. He was psychologically incapable of balance and restraint, and almost everything he wrote is infected to some degree with hysteria. In many ways he was a pro-Russian counterpart of the Turcomaniac David Urquhart. R. W. Seton-Watson dismissed Stead's book *The M.P. for Russia* as an 'interesting literary extravaganza'.[2] This dismissal is undoubtedly warranted on the larger issue of Stead's extravagant interpretation of the political importance of Madame Novikov; but it tends to involve in the same discredit the claims which Stead made incidentally for the importance of his rôle in the agitation. These claims also were inflated,[3] but not absurdly. The first Bulgarian National Assembly convened after the foundation of the new state knew what it was about when it selected Stead as one of the three Englishmen who deserved the thanks of the Bulgarian nation for extraordinary services in the cause of its independence. The other two were the editor of the *Daily News* and Gladstone.[4]

Stead had been consistently and enthusiastically Slavophile since the beginning of the Serb insurrections in 1875. His zeal for this cause made the *Northern Echo* at Darlington something quite outside the run of ordinary provincial journalism. Stead had learned his Russophilism in the office of a Newcastle merchant who was

---

was to have been entitled *The History of the Nation in Revolt against [the] Turkish Alliance* (Robertson Scott, *Life and Death of a Newspaper*, p. 107). Despite Carlyle's encouragement Stead never managed to put it together. His researches were eventually employed in the biography of his friend Madame Olga Novikov, pan-Slav and Orthodox propagandist in England. *The M.P. for Russia*, written to celebrate the Anglo-Russian entente of 1907, contains much of the material originally loaned by Gladstone to Stead for the agitation study.

[1] Stead figures in neither G. Carslake Thompson's *Public Opinion and Lord Beaconsfield, 1875–1880* nor Professor David Harris's *Britain and the Bulgarian Horrors of 1876*. (Professor Harris alludes to Stead once, indirectly, in his text, and to *The M.P. for Russia* in a footnote.) He is mentioned only once, incidentally, by Wirthwein, *Britain and the Balkan Crisis, 1875–1878*. R. W. Seton-Watson, *Disraeli, Gladstone and the Eastern Question* (1935), does him rather more justice on the whole, but leaves his real achievement substantially unrecognised. Mr A. J. P. Taylor in *The Trouble Makers* is rather more willing, indeed somewhat uncritically, to take Stead at his own valuation.

[2] *Disraeli, Gladstone and the Eastern Question*, p. 116.

[3] E.g. 'The Bulgarian atrocity agitation was in a great measure my work.' Robertson Scott, *The Life and Death of a Newspaper*, p. 104.

[4] Estelle Stead, *My Father* (1913), p. 57.

also Russian vice-consul, and from the writings of Cobden.[1] Not yet thirty, bursting with rather frantic energy, ambitious, able, a proud and intensely pious Nonconformist, a strong Radical, a natural crusader, Stead in 1876 was ripe for just such a cause as the atrocities offered. Everything combined irresistibly in an impulse wholly genuine and wholly advantageous. Stead's religious fervour was particularly important. He launched himself into the atrocities agitation as the recipient of a 'clear call of God's voice'.[2]

From the first Stead made the *Northern Echo* a champion of the agitation, a disseminator of the *Daily News* reports, of anti-Turkish and anti-government propaganda of every kind. Stead's was not the only lesser provincial paper to do this kind of thing during the early agitation period: the *South Wales Daily News* at Cardiff is a notable instance of much the same attitude and activity. But only the *Northern Echo* became eventually a power far beyond its normal provincial circulation. Stead made it the favourite reading of Gladstone,[3] Madame Novikov ('Who is this man who writes just like a Russian?'),[4] and Freeman, who extolled it widely as the 'best paper in Europe', and posted it to Russia and Montenegro.[5] It gave him the entrée to the circles about Novikov, Gladstone, and Carlyle. In the atrocities agitation Stead founded the reputation that led him directly to the reformed *Pall Mall Gazette* under Morley and the *Review of Reviews*.

Stead's coming to the front meant a significant alteration in the general character of the agitation leadership. Freeman, Fraser, and Liddon—even Farley—were all products of the Anglican, literary culture of the universities, the Church, the upper class, the metropolis. The strategic weakness of their position was that these were not the spheres in which agitation could most effectively be mobilised. Stead represented and asserted the part of democracy,

---

[1] A. Watson, *A Newspaper Man's Memories* (n.d.), p. 63, and Stead, *The M.P. for Russia*, vol. i, pp. 380–1.

[2] 'I felt the clear call of God's voice, "Arouse the nation or be damned". If I did not do *all* I could, I would deserve damnation.

I had a terrible afternoon [date unspecified: probably after the Batak dispatch of 22 August]. It was like a Divine possession that shook me almost to pieces, wrung me and left me shuddering and weak in an agony of tears. I went out determined to do this and nothing else until such time as my mission was revoked.'

Stead added that the absence of the proprietor of the *Echo* in Switzerland at the time was an initial advantage. Robertson Scott, *The Life and Death of a Newspaper*, p. 104.

[3] Gladstone to Hill, 6 April 1877, Gladstone Papers, Add. MSS 44454, ff. 24–5.

[4] Stead to Dowager Empress of Russia, 17 March 1908, Stead Papers.

[5] Freeman to Liddon, 31 March 1877, Liddon Papers.

Nonconformity, the provinces. By profession, by temperament, above all by environment, Stead was in a far more favourable position to inspire and direct a popular movement on something approaching a massive scale. When Liddon wrote to Freeman on 30 August: 'You are certainly to be congratulated on the present condition of public opinion',[1] he was doing Freeman no more honour than he deserved for his tireless work since 1875; yet, in strict justice, Liddon ought to have been congratulating Stead, of whom neither he nor Freeman had as yet heard.

For it was Stead's decision to seize the opportunity provided by MacGahan's Batak letter in the *Daily News* of 22 August which gave by far the strongest lead to the country before Gladstone committed himself to the agitation. Just as Stead represented a new kind of agitation leader, so he contributed to the agitation a new method and spirit. Though he had applauded the activities of Freeman, Fraser, Liddon, and Farley, Stead was quite remote from the agitation as it had hitherto developed. Freeman, Fraser, and Liddon exhorted in high moral terms. They appealed to people in an almost abstract way to demonstrate. They did not organise meetings. They did not know how.[2] To Bishop Fraser the Manchester meeting of 9 August was an opportunity put in his way by Providence, not the result of his own efforts. Simple moral exhortation produced only sporadic results. In Stead's phrase, it had no 'immediate effects'.[3] Stead's achievement was that in a situation of mounting excitement but very little defined and practical sense of purpose on a large scale, he took the initiative and set in motion a series of 'atrocity meetings' over as wide an area as he could direct and inspire by his personal and political influence, and by means of a pushing provincial newspaper. His expectation was that the ball, once set rolling, would gather pace and size under its own momentum.

Stead's watchword was 'There must be no waiting for notables to lead the way.'[4] For an effective agitation on a large scale it was necessary to rouse into activity the primary level of petty local

---

[1] Liddon to Freeman, 30 August 1876, *ibid.*

[2] Thus, in the following year, Freeman wrote to Liddon that, to save the country from a war with Russia on behalf of Turkey, another agitation must be got up like the one in the autumn of 1876. 'But how do you go about it? You know better than I' (Freeman to Liddon 12 March 1877, Liddon Papers). There is nothing to suggest, however, that Liddon in fact knew any better than Freeman.

[3] *Northern Echo*, 27 September 1876, p. 3.   [4] *Ibid.*, 28 August 1876, p. 3.

leadership, political and religious, a class to whom notables of the standing of the Bishop of Manchester, Canon Liddon, and Dr Freeman were remote and, to Nonconformists, alien. Stead emphasised again and again the necessity of the small local meeting. He urged especially that the initiative of one organiser in each town and village was the sole pre-requisite for a demonstration. The essential thing was to go ahead without worrying about the chances of success; support would assuredly come, Stead insisted, once a strong lead was given.[1] This was excellent advice. Of the forty-seven protest meetings counted by Stead in the northeastern region up to 22 September, including Carlisle, Ripon, Durham, Whitby, Sunderland, Morpeth, and Newcastle, two were summoned by ratepayers' associations, the rest got together by handbills issued by a few individuals.[2]

One of Stead's first steps was to provide a brief programme for the agitation—'a clear and definite duty to perform'—in a series of useful heads of resolutions for the guidance of organisers of meetings.[3] Stead did not by any means neglect moral exhortation, but the most valuable and serviceable features of his propaganda were appeals to Nonconformist sentiment and tradition, to north-country patriotism, and to Liberal partisanship. Cromwell (for whom Stead had something of a cult), Milton, and the Vaudois formed the central theme of the first appeal, the north's not entirely mythical millennium as the 'vanguard of English liberties' in the second, and in the last the alleged Tory instinct to uphold indefensible tyrannies.

Stead of course always claimed that his agitation had no political bias. 'We have laboured', he announced piously on 16 September, 'to divest this great outburst of national indignation of a party character.'[4] He certainly made a point of noticing and commending any of the comparatively rare manifestations of sympathy with it from Conservative sources; but partisanship in some form or other was unavoidable if sufficient petty local leadership was to be

---

[1] 'One organiser in each town and village throughout the length and breadth of Durham, Northumberland, and Yorkshire is all that is needed to elicit an unprecedented outburst of sympathy and indignation.' *Ibid.*

[2] *Ibid.*, 27 September 1876, p. 3; 29 September, p. 3.

[3] These comprised expressions of horror at the atrocities; denunciation of the Turks, and the whole system which made such atrocities possible; condemnation of the policy of the government; the recall of Sir Henry Elliot; and renunciation of the Turkish alliance once and for all. In form, if not in spirit, neutralist feeling was thus catered for.   [4] *Northern Echo*, 16 September 1876, p. 2.

mobilised to sustain such a popular effort as he had in mind.[1] He indeed had golden visions of the widest political implications arising from the agitation. 'The nation', he declared on 28 August, 'is waking up'; the 'soulless inertia' that enabled Disraeli to insinuate himself into office had 'disappeared'.[2]

The notables were not neglected. Stead canvassed them indefatigably. Especially, he did not hesitate to canvass the greatest notable of all—Gladstone. He wrote to a great many peers, prelates, and members of parliament in the north.[3] There were some encouraging replies. The Duke of Cleveland and the Earl of Durham sympathised; Earl Grey regrettably did not. The Archbishop of York responded well, and Stead's prodding may have had something to do with his attendance at an atrocity meeting at York early in September.[4] The Archbishop's good will, however, faded early. Baring, Bishop of Durham, a great stamper-out of Ritualism, did not unbend to the agitation; and it was perhaps tactless of Stead, in attempting to prod him, to announce that much hope would be excited by the Bishop's coming visit to Darlington, 'for as yet no prominent Evangelical has spoken out', beneath a report warmly commending the pro-agitation activities of the High Church clergy of Exeter.[5] Stead had to console himself with the thought that at least some of Baring's clergy spoke out.[6] On the whole, Stead was greatly disappointed by the response of the notables.[7] The Bishop of Manchester was, of course, sound; and so also were some members of parliament like Backhouse, Samuel Morley, C. M. Palmer, and Stansfeld. But Stead clearly indicated that most of the politicians, and most of the peers and clergy, were neglecting their duty.

Stead's decisive contribution to the agitation was the example of his own demonstration at Darlington on 25 August inaugurating, as far as he was concerned, the Bulgarian atrocities agitation

---

[1] An interesting confirmation of this point, as well as an indication of the radically different circumstances in which the Armenian atrocities agitation in 1896 attempted to operate, is the resolution passed by the conference on 11 November 1896: 'This Meeting is of opinion that the policy of non-party agitation in relation to the Armenian Question has been a failure, and that the Question should be taken up by the Liberal Party, on Party Lines.' Clayden, *Armenia: The Case Against Lord Salisbury*, p. [25].

[2] *Northern Echo*, 28 August 1876, p. 2.

[3] *Ibid.*, 6 September 1876, p. 3.

[4] E. H. Thomson, *The Life and Letters of William Thomson, Archbishop of York* (1919), p. 255.   [5] *Northern Echo*, 30 August 1876, p. 3.

[6] *Ibid.*, 6 September, 1876, p. 3.   [7] *Ibid.*, 28 August 1876, p. 3.

'proper'.[1] In the *Northern Echo* of 23 August, beside a reprint of MacGahan's Batak letter of the previous day's *Daily News*, Stead had the 'satisfaction' to announce that a demonstration would be held at Darlington, the first, it was hoped, 'of a series of town's meetings which will be held in the North', not only in the immediate vicinity—Middlesbrough, Stockton, Durham, and the Hartlepools—but 'wherever North Countrymen, in church or chapel, public hall, or village green, can be assembled'. The north country, Stead insisted, would betray all humanity if it shirked its hereditary duty to lead the way.[2] On the following day Stead was able to report a definite response. Meetings were spoken of from every quarter, 'even quiet Richmond', though as yet only Darlington had formally announced.[3]

The Darlington meeting, Stead promised, would be the first blast of the trumpet of the north country, sounding again the heroic note of Milton's sonnet to the Piedmontese.[4] The demonstration was in fact a great success. The most notable feature of the occasion was a strong call for Gladstone to intervene.[5] Stead almost certainly inspired this himself, for immediately after the meeting he forwarded a copy of the *Northern Echo* report of it together with an excited letter to Gladstone telling him that a series of such atrocity meetings in the north had begun, and begging Gladstone to lend the sanction of his 'mighty name' to the movement.[6] Gladstone replied less promptly and more briefly and guardedly than might have been expected, for Stead was enthusiastically tactless enough to express the hope that recent events would bring Gladstone back to the leadership of the party.[7]

Looking back from the heights of September, Stead reviewed the course of his campaign. He designated the Darlington meeting of 25 August as the commencement of the atrocity agitation which became the 'characteristic feature of the recess'. Stead justified his claim on the grounds that his meeting was the first held after the rising of parliament (15 August), and was announced 'simultaneously' with the publication of the first really detailed report of the atrocities. Stead conceded that it was 'only fair to admit' that there

---

[1] *Ibid.*, 16 November 1876, p. 3.   [2] *Ibid.*, 23 August 1876, pp. 2–3.
[3] *Ibid.*, 24 August 1876, p. 3.
[4] *Ibid.*, 25 August 1876, pp. 2–3.   [5] *Ibid.*, 26 August 1876, pp. 3–4.
[6] Stead to Gladstone, 26 August 1876, Gladstone Papers, Add. MSS 44303, ff. 230–1.   [7] Gladstone to Stead, 2 September 1876, *ibid.*, f. 232.

had been a notable atrocity meeting held before the Darlington meeting, at Manchester on 9 August. But this, he argued, was not really significant, since it took place before the prorogation and before the publication on 22 August of MacGahan's second Batak dispatch, 'from which the outburst of national indignation may be said to date'; it stood alone and did not produce 'immediate effects'. To clinch the matter Stead pointed out that Manchester recognised the unsatisfactory nature of the first demonstration by holding another later in September.[1]

In his eagerness to corner as much credit as possible Stead does less than justice to the agitation before 25 August. Nevertheless his claim remains substantially justified. Only where Stead was in the centre of things was there an impressive series of atrocity meetings before the beginning of September. Stead's activity provided the essential complement to MacGahan's revelations in bringing the agitation to the point of full and sustained articulateness.

By 28 August Stead could proclaim that a 'great change' was passing over the nation. The 'keynote sounded so clearly at Darlington' seemed 'destined to reverberate all over England'. There had been demonstrations at Saltburn and Liverpool.[2] By 1 September Stead could cite fourteen atrocity meetings, ten held north of the Humber, in most of which he could claim a direct or indirect part.[3] The success of the movement in fact surprised Stead himself, who had not anticipated quite such a rapid succession of demonstrations. His next step was to announce that it had been thought desirable, 'in order to give greater effect to the expression of public opinion which is now going on spontaneously in the North', to form a 'central organisation' at Darlington, 'the headquarters of this movement', or at any other central position thought more convenient, to direct the efforts being made 'with every prospect of success' to array the north of England. This central body, he suggested, could be affiliated to the League in Aid of the Christians of Turkey. It would be the duty of the north to lead the way in forming branches.[4] It is quite likely that Stead had approached

---

[1] *Northern Echo*, 27 September 1876, p. 3. In fact, atrocity agitators in Manchester boasted of four meetings: two city meetings, and two demonstrations in the Free Trade Hall. See E.Q.A., *Report*, p. 51.

[2] *Northern Echo*, 28 August 1876, pp. 3–4.

[3] *Ibid.*, 4 August 1876, p. 3.   [4] *Ibid.*, 28 August 1876, p. 3.

Farley with such a suggestion. Nothing, however, appears to have come of it, though Stead never let the idea drop completely.

Success was assured by 31 August. The south was coming up strongly, though the north remained 'nobly to the front'.[1] On 6 September the movement was still gaining intensity. Two-thirds, if not three-quarters, of the meetings, Stead proudly claimed, had been held north of the Humber. Newcastle, a little tardy compared to South Durham and Cleveland, at last prepared to join in. Demonstrations continued to be held about Darlington itself where, as Stead never tired of harping, 'this great national movement was cradled'. Stead noted sternly that Durham still remained 'dumb'. It was pleasing, however, to observe the spread of the movement from the larger towns to the country towns and villages: Stokesley and the Shildons, Marske and Crooke, South Bank and West Auckland.[2] Next to catch fire were the country towns of the North Riding: Ripon, Richmond, 'even Malton'. Thirsk alone remained silent, but the Cleveland region continued to be a 'hotbed of agitation'; and Bishop Auckland was at length beginning to move.[3] Of the great industrial cities of Yorkshire Stead was pleased to see Leeds shaking off the 'deadening influence of an apathetic press'—a hit at Wemyss Reid of the *Leeds Mercury*, a Liberal but a great admirer of Derby.[4] In Sheffield Mundella was also active by this time, together with Robert Leader of the Sheffield *Independent* and H. J. Wilson, secretary of the Sheffield Liberal Association.[5]

The seal was set on this new state of affairs by the publication in the *Daily News* of 29 August of the United States Consul-General Schuyler's Preliminary Report. This, an impeccably official counterpart to MacGahan (another of whose dispatches, describing the devastated town of Panagurishte, had appeared on the 26th), established formally the facts of the atrocities. Baring's official report was strangely delayed—a mystery puzzling even to Bourke and members of the cabinet[6] as well as *The Times*.[7] Carnarvon especially was impatient for its appearance; and the embarrassed

---

[1] *Ibid.*, 30 August 1876, pp. 2–3.   [2] *Ibid.*, 6 September 1876, pp. 2–3.
[3] *Ibid.*, 8 September 1876, p. 3.
[4] *Ibid.*, 6 September 1876, pp. 2–3. See T. Wemyss Reid, 'Lord Derby at the Foreign Office, 1876–1878', *Macmillan's Magazine*, May–October 1879.
[5] Sheffield *Independent*, 6 September 1876, p. 3.
[6] A. E. Gathorne Hardy, *Gathorne Hardy, First Earl of Cranbrook* (1910), vol. i, pp. 369–70.   [7] 30 August 1876, p. 7.

Derby had to explain on 8 September that it had not yet reached the Foreign Office, though he believed it was on its way; and he assured Carnarvon that it would be published immediately on receipt.[1] Though Elliot belatedly enclosed it with a dispatch dated 5 September, Baring's report was not in fact officially received until the 14th and not published until the 19th. This additional delay was important, for it gave Schuyler's report an extended official monopoly; and Schuyler was markedly more sympathetic to the Bulgarian point of view than Baring proved to be. Though not polemical in form, Schuyler's report had a distinctly polemical effect in the context of the agitation in England. Gladstone later inclined to attribute to it more importance than MacGahan's dispatches in arousing English sentiment[2]; but this is undoubtedly a reflection of the bias of his own as opposed to the popular mind.

*

By the beginning of September the strength of the northern atrocities agitation had become a phenomenon noteworthy to observers outside the north. Freeman wrote from his Somerset home to Mundella: 'You in the North are, I am sorry to say, always ahead of us in these parts of England; but I trust the example of Sheffield, Liverpool, and Darlington may not be lost upon us.'[3] It was not. The working men's meeting at Hackney on the 29th opened the campaign in London, and soon midland, western, and southern towns began to move: Nottingham (where Auberon Herbert was prominent),[4] Stoke, Birmingham, Wolverhampton, Bristol, Exeter, Norwich, Brighton. By the end of the first week of September the movement was snowballing at an extraordinary pace.[5]

[1] Derby to Disraeli, 8 September 1876, Disraeli Papers.
[2] Gladstone to Elliot, 3 September 1876, Gladstone Papers, Add. MSS 44451, ff. 116–7.   [3] Sheffield *Independent*, 4 September 1876, p. 3.
[4] Harris, *Auberon Herbert*, p. 179.
[5] For example see *South Wales Daily News*, 29 August 1876, pp. 4–5: 'Although we have received several letters earnestly requesting that steps should be taken in the principal towns of South Wales . . . so far as we know nothing has yet been done towards the accomplishment of that object . . . it is difficult to believe that the inhabitants of the important commercial centres of South Wales can be less sensitive to horrors of such a description than is the population of other parts of the Kingdom. Nevertheless, whilst a general movement is spreading throughout England, Wales, from one end to the other is silent. . . . Should Cardiff move with alacrity in the matter . . . other towns . . . will doubtless soon follow. . . .'
Similarly in a long letter to the Sheffield *Independent* (1 September 1876, p. 3) the Rev. Greville J. Chester wrote as one who, though no longer a resident, took a 'lively

The meeting at Hackney on 29 August demands particular notice as the occasion of the first public indication by Gladstone of his attitude to the agitation. He had been asked to advise some supposedly perplexed working men whether or not they ought to join in the agitation. Gladstone, on 23 August, duly conferred the desired benediction in a letter criticising the way in which Disraeli had treated the question as being so 'inadequate and unsatisfactory' that he could not but think it 'well' that the people should 'seek opportunities to speak for themselves' in order to 'assist' the government to judge the best course for future policy.[1]

This was at least markedly more encouraging than the hapless speech of 31 July; and it certainly made a significant contrast to the grudging benediction given to the agitation by John Bright, roused out of his vacation in Scotland. Bright clearly revealed an apprehensive sense of the interventionist spirit and tendencies of the movement. The question, he wrote to the citizens of Rochdale, was not one to be 'treated hastily', and he confessed that he almost feared to 'say anything about it'. Bright in fact said very little about it, and reverted to his favourite theme of the wicked folly of the Crimean War.[2] A. V. Dicey, discussing this point later with Bryce, remarked that since 1854 there seemed to have been a growing desire on the part of the nation as a whole to take a more active interest in foreign affairs. 'Even the catching at the Bulgarian massacres seems to me', Dicey wrote, 'a proof of this and Bright instinctively felt this and discouraged the agitation.'[3]

Agitation began to spread outside England. The *South Wales Daily News*, after a good deal of pushing and prodding, at last succeeded in getting up a meeting in Cardiff on 7 September, with Freeman giving the main address.[4] The rest of Wales followed on

interest in the credit of Sheffield', and who was disturbed during a recent visit to learn that no atrocity meeting was being organised, as in other towns, to protest against the Turks and the policy of the 'Jew Earl'. A meeting was in fact shortly afterwards arranged for 5 September (*ibid.*, 2 September, p. 2).

And, again, the *Bedfordshire Times and Independent* (9 September 1876, p. 5) congratulated Bedford on having 'at last honoured itself' by joining in the agitation. At Ross (Herefordshire) T. Blake M.P. pointed to the shame which would come to Ross if it remained silent while the north of England was on fire (*Ross Gazette*, 28 September 1876, p. 3).

[1] *Times*, 30 August 1876, p. 7.   [2] *Ibid.*, 5 September 1876, p. 4.
[3] Dicey to Bryce, August [? 1877], Bryce Papers, E2. A notable instance of Bright's dampening influence is to be observed in his brother Jacob's fading enthusiasm for the agitation; see below, p. 232.
[4] *South Wales Daily News*, 8 September 1876, p. 5.

strongly from this lead. There had already been a demonstration in Edinburgh on 29 August, but Scotland was noticeably more sluggish to follow up than Wales. Ireland, despite a meeting at Belfast on 5 September, never really started to agitate. Liddon's sermon had awakened a faint echo in a Dublin canonry earlier in August, but this evoked an even fainter response.[1] To none of the dynamic forces in Irish life was the atrocities issue congenial. To nationalism it was English and hypocritical. To Orange Toryism it was of course factious and unpatriotic. Above all, to Roman Catholicism it conflicted with the most emphatically expressed canons of Vatican policy, bitterly hostile to Greek Orthodox pretensions.[2]

Fitzjames Stephen noted that the 'Pope's newspapers' had 'begun to remark that the Bulgarians and Servians represent "the Revolution"'.[3] Indeed the *Catholic Times* had pronounced as early as July that Roman Catholics must brace themselves to be reproached for subordinating everything to the law of God and the welfare of their Church.[4] Cardinal Manning, if he represented anything, represented the voice and spirit of the Roman Curia; and he was the voice, if not entirely the spirit, of Irish as well as English Catholicism. To Manning the Orthodox Church was merely 'the basest delusion of 1000 years'; and he feared above all to see it restored at Constantinople with Russian power at its back.[5] Manning set the official Roman Catholic attitude towards the agitation with sufficient clearness at the end of August when he refused to attend a demonstration on the grounds that it represented no settled and definite policy.[6]

But Ireland and Roman Catholicism were remote from Stead's calculations. 'We begin', he wrote on 4 September, as news of meeting after meeting poured in, 'to appreciate the naturalness of what has hitherto appeared most unnatural': an 'extraordinary manifestation of national righteousness' in the apparently materialist nineteenth century. The Crusades, Stead declared, were no longer an enigma.[7] Certainly, if Freeman was the Bernard of

---

[1] Dublin *Daily Express*, 25 August 1876, p. 3; 28 August, p. 2.
[2] *Voce Della Verita* quoted in *Catholic Times*, 21 July 1876, p. 4.
[3] Stephen to Lytton, 13 August 1876, Fitzjames Stephen Papers, Cambridge Add MSS 7349.   [4] 21 July 1876, p. 4.
[5] Manning to Ripon, 4 October 1876, Ripon Papers, British Museum Add. MSS 43545, ff. 22-3.   [6] *Times*, 1 September 1876, p. 8
[7] *Northern Echo*, 4 September 1876, pp. 2-3.

Clairvaux of the atrocities agitation, Stead was its Peter the
Hermit.[1]

5 The Oxford Group: Second Phase

Freeman was aware that a considerable impulse had been given to
the agitation from the north, but he was not clear how or where
this impulse originated. A 'grand meeting at Darlington'[2] caught
his attention, but when he wrote commending the spirit of the
north it was to Mundella, not Stead. The Darlington meeting,
together with preparations for a Hyde Park demonstration and a
meeting at Liverpool under the auspices of the Working Men's
Reform Association to which Freeman had been invited, first gave
him hope of a decisive turn of events. He wrote on 27 August to
Bryce, then touring in the Caucasus, on a note of slightly incredu-
ous triumph, as if a dream of hope long deferred were about to
come true. 'I really believe that the nation is at least stirring.
Meetings to denounce the Turk and the Jew are getting common.'
He added: 'I had a very good letter from your Pollock [Sir W. F.
Pollock] today about Turks. You may suppose I have an endless
lot from all kinds of people, wise and foolish, mostly admiring,
some abusive.'[3]

Freeman was by far the most widely known figure among the
agitation leaders.[4] His range of operations grew steadily more extensive. His trenchant letters had become a familiar feature of the
metropolitan journalism of the time. Freeman was in many ways
a very effective agitator. A master of variant repetitiveness, he
possessed also a certain talent for scurrility. He salted his propaganda heavily with bitter abuse of Disraeli and Derby. Their

---

[1] Stead himself was very conscious of this rôle: 'I realised the feelings of Peter the
Hermit. God was with me.' Robertson Scott, *The Life and Death of a Newspaper*,
p. 104.
[2] Freeman to Bryce, 27 August 1876, Bryce Papers, E4.   [3] *Ibid.*
[4] See Bartlett to Liddon, 4 September [1876], Liddon Papers. Some indication of
Freeman's prestige is given in the order of precedence in the ironic dedication of an
anonymous pamphlet, *Revelations from the Seat of War. Russians, Turks, Bulgarians
and Mr Gladstone* (1877), dedicated to
    'The Right Hon. W. E. Gladstone
    Mr E. A. Freeman
    "The Times" and "Daily News"
    The Ritualists
    And Political Dissenters
    And all Crusading Philanthropists, English and Russian'.

existence Freeman could not account for, he once wrote in all
seriousness to Bryce, 'but by supposing the existence of an Ahri-
man of very considerable power. The Turk I can understand; he is
simply a bad man; but these wretches are pure fiends.'[1]

This rather unbalanced violence put strict limits on Freeman's
sense of the profitable in propaganda. An example of this is his
'Appeal to the English Clergy' published in the *Guardian* of 30
August. The inadequacy of the response of the clergy to the atrocities agitation was a theme to which Freeman continually reverted
in later months. 'Here is the plain fact', he once expostulated to
Liddon. 'Through all this matter, the Nonconformists, as a body,
have been prophets of righteousness. So have doubtless A, B, C, D,
a great many of them one by one, of the Established clergy, but
not as a body.' The two convocations, added Freeman, ought to
have protested 'in the name of Christian morality'.[2] Freeman
found himself led reluctantly but firmly to the conclusion, of which
he had informed Allon, editor of the Nonconformist *British
Quarterly Review*, that, though he could not undertake to support
disestablishment, he would no longer oppose it. He would gladly
'purchase Christian St. Sophia at the price of disendowed Canterbury'.[3]

The contrast which Freeman found so painful between the
divided Anglican clergy and the outspoken solidarity of the Nonconformist connections had already become plain before the end
of August. Freeman was not a narrow Churchman, though his
general sympathies lay with the High party, by virtue of history
rather than theology. Freeman loved the Church whose Saxon
beginnings he knew so well. That this Church should not, as a
Church, share his fervour on behalf of the Eastern Christians—
again a historical rather than a theological sentiment—was to
Freeman doubly deplorable.

The passion and sincerity of Freeman's 'Appeal to the Clergy'
are unmistakable; but so also is his addiction to the damaging habit
of injecting into his propaganda a partisanship much more violent
and open than that necessary even for the consumption of Liberals,
and quite out of place in an appeal for the support of Tory parsons.

[1] Freeman to Bryce, 27 August 1876, Bryce Papers, E4.
[2] Freeman to Liddon, 7 April 1878, Liddon Papers.
[3] Freeman to Bryce, 21 December 1877, Bryce Papers, E4.

Were the clergy satisfied, Freeman demanded, to uphold the Tory government now that its leaders appeared plainly as the 'sworn allies of Antichrist'? For good measure, Freeman dragged in the fate worse than death to which the maidens of Bulgaria were doomed by the 'clients of Lord Beaconsfield'. 'Western delicacy', he added with characteristic indelicacy, 'the inborn feelings of lands who are unaccustomed to the doings of the Turk, will not allow me to point out in plain terms what becomes of the brothers of those maidens.' Were not the Liberals, though despoilers of the Irish Church, yet preferable to men who maintained such 'clients'? Would not the clergy arise and follow the Bishop of Manchester and Canon Liddon?[1]

Freeman undoubtedly mishandled the affair. He quite point-lessly converted an appeal on behalf of the agitation into an appeal on behalf of the Liberal party. Liddon indeed assured Freeman that he was 'deeply moved' by the Appeal.[2] But the publication of Tait's correspondence with the Archbishop of Belgrade in the same issue of the *Guardian* was an unmistakable sign that no positive lead was to be hoped for from the primate.[3]

It had by this time also become clear that the atrocities agitation made a comparatively slight impression outside the High Church party. Without a strong lead from the bench the bulk of the Church —the Establishment within the Establishment—would not move.[4] Dean Stanley of Westminister quite early damned the agitation with faint praise by insisting that virtuous indignation against the atrocities was not the monopoly of one party in either Church or state.[5] It was not merely theological sympathy with the Eastern Churches which moved the Anglo-Catholics and the High Church in general to endorse the agitation. Their party formed the natural 'opposition' in the Church, the unpopular, distrusted, rebellious element, fruit of the deplorable Tractarian movement,

---

[1] *Guardian*, 30 August 1876, p. 1136. For clerical criticism of Freeman's article see *Guardian*, 6 September 1876, p. 1167; 20 September, p. 1232; and Freeman's reply, 13 September 1876, p. 1199.

[2] Liddon to Freeman, 31 August 1876, Liddon Papers.

[3] E.g. one of Freeman's critics in the *Guardian* (6 September 1876, p. 1167) com-mended Archbishop Tait's letter on the question of the fleet and its recognition of the wider problems of international law and political considerations involved, in contrast to the dangerously 'hysterical' Freeman-*Guardian* approach.

[4] See e.g. the attitude of the Rector of Ross (Herefordshire) in answer to a call for action by the M.P., Blake (*Ross Gazette*, 28 September 1876, pp. 3–4). Blake was strongly supported by the Wesleyan and Baptist ministers.

[5] *Primitive Methodist*, 7 September 1876, p. 603.

villains of the Public Worship Regulation policy—the very last party, in short, to need a lead from the upper and respectable levels of the hierarchy.

The Church managed, none the less, to make a creditable contribution to the function of providing leadership on a primary level beneath the secondary level of the *Daily News*, Freeman, Liddon, Farley, and Stead. If only three English bishops other than Fraser of Manchester (Mackarness of Oxford, Woodford of Ely, and Temple of Exeter) came out in full support of the agitation, on the other hand the clergy who took in the *Guardian*, the *Church Review*, or the *Church Times*,[1] with the Nonconformist ministers who took in the *Nonconformist*, the *Methodist*, or the *Freeman*, formed between them by far the greatest body of initiative in agitation. Sometimes clergy and ministers dominated meetings entirely; such was the case, for instance, at Southwark.[2] A more typical instance would be Chesterfield. Apart from Admiral Egerton, Liberal M.P. for East Derbyshire, the speakers were the Vicar of Newbold, and the Unitarian, Free Church, and Primitive Methodist ministers.[3] The conveners of the Folkestone meeting of 5 September were the Vicar of Folkestone, the Vicar of Christ Church, the Vicar of Holy Trinity, the Congregational, Baptist, and Primitive Methodist ministers, at the head of an assortment of laymen.[4] The Folkestone meeting brought out also the difficulties that could sometimes arise from the unwonted proximity of Anglo-Catholic clergymen and Nonconformists. The *Church Review* commented sourly on the Folkestone meeting that the local Baptists were in strong force, 'owing to their presiding genius, Mr. Sampson, having been instrumental in getting up the demonstration, a fact which he made the most of' with speeches of 'self-laudation', abuse of the *Folkestone Chronicle* and eulogy of the *Daily News*. He was seconded by the vicar in an 'earnest speech' which 'contrasted well'.[5]

★

---

[1] Strongly pro-agitation after the publication of MacGahan's second Batak dispatch; see 25 August 1876, pp. 426–7.

[2] *Times*, 6 September 1876, p. 8. See also the case of Burnley, *ibid.*

[3] Sheffield *Independent*, 14 September 1876, p. 3.

[4] Public Record Office, F. O., 78, *Turkey, General Correspondence Respecting Atrocities in Bulgaria*, 2551.   [5] 16 September 1876, p. 469.

Freeman's 'Appeal to the Clergy' did have one practical result: it inspired the idea of getting up an address to be presented to the Queen on behalf of the clergy. A request for support was circularised under the names of Liddon, Canon George Williams, C. F. Lowder, and W. Denton, all prominent on the Catholic wing of the High Church and all members of the Eastern Church Association.[1] Denton, writing later on the response to the circular, apologised that the four sponsors were, it was true, members of one theological school; and he could only express regret if this 'mere' fact kept back those of differing schools. These others no doubt felt their suspicions confirmed when Denton revealed that among the names of clergy supporting the circular was that of the Rev. Dr Pusey.[2]

Liddon busied himself also in recommending Freeman's fund-raising campaign on behalf of the oppressed Slavs, at the same time warning his fellow-clergy off funds being raised by people like Lady Strangford, widow of the diplomatist and Oriental scholar, whose philanthropy extended to wounded Turks as well as Christians. Their first duty, Liddon pointed out, was to the 'household of faith'.[3] This was less an expression of bigotry than an appreciation of the underlying pro-Turkish sympathies of the relief funds which made a virtue of their neutrality and conformity to the rules of the Geneva Convention.[4]

On 31 August, the date by which Stead was fully assured of the success of his campaign in the north, Liddon arrived rather tardily at the realisation that the agitation would have to be equipped with something like a common or standard programme. The difference in outlook between Stead and Liddon is clear and instructive: for Stead a practical programme was the starting point, almost a condition, of his campaign; for Liddon it was a refinement to be added once the movement had really got under way. 'The danger now is', Liddon wrote to Freeman, 'lest all this agitation should end in nothing for want of a definite object.' The 'need of

[1] *Guardian*, 6 September 1876, pp. 1169–70.
[2] *Ibid.*, 13 September 1876, p. 1199.
[3] *Ibid.*, 30 August 1876, p. 1136.
[4] E.g. *Times*, 16 August 1876, p. 6. See in this connection Sir E. Lechmere to Liddon, 14 August 1876, Liddon Papers; Lady Strangford in *The Times*, 25 September 1876, p. 10; Freeman to Liddon, 15 October 1876, Liddon Papers, on Lady Strangford's complaints that her fund was being adversely affected. For Lady Strangford's pro-Turkish attitude see Pears, *Forty Years in Constantinople*, p. 23.

H

the moment' was that 'somebody' should formulate a 'humane and Christian policy to be *enforced* on the Government'. Liddon suggested a programme including the immediate recall of Elliot, the autonomy of all the European provinces of Turkey, and a conference of the powers 'with a view to the essential modification' of the 'wicked Treaty' of 1856. 'A great deal might be done', Liddon added, 'if these or some substantially similar demands could be repeated, again and again, in great public meetings all over the country.'[1]

Liddon followed up this suggestion with a letter in the *Daily News* of 2 September, 'What to Insist On', where he repeated for the guidance of meetings his programme of 31 August, with the addition of a resolution demanding compensation for sufferers and punishment for culprits.[2] Freeman, independently, did substantially the same in a letter to the *Daily News* of 5 September, 'Points for Public Meetings', with a special warning for the benefit of the followers of John Bright against any meeting committing itself to the 'phantom of neutrality'.[3]

Did Liddon have Gladstone in mind as the 'somebody' to meet the 'need of the moment' and formulate a national policy for the agitation? He was certainly careful in his *Daily News* letter to allow for correction of his suggested programme 'from those who know better'.[4] Liddon's letter to Fraser after the Manchester meeting of 9 August indicates that he felt more optimistic about Gladstone's outlook than either Fraser or Freeman. And the circle closest to Liddon personally, especially MacColl and Denton, were strong for urging Gladstone to put himself at the head of the agitation. This was an attitude shared by Stead, the *Spectator*, the *Freeman*, the *Methodist*, and many others, more particularly after the publication of Gladstone's letter to the Hackney meeting of 29 August. Undoubtedly Liddon had Gladstone at least partly in mind. The fact that Manning could, with some show of reason, dismiss the agitation as being without a clearly formulated policy pointed to the need of a source of definition much more nationally commanding than the Oxford group and Stead combined.

[1] Liddon to Freeman, 31 August 1876, Liddon Papers.
[2] Thompson, *Public Opinion and Lord Beaconsfield*, vol. i, p. 400.
[3] *Ibid.*, pp. 401–2.
[4] *Ibid.*, p. 400.

6 The 6th of September

In the first week of September Fitzjames Stephen, with a kind of melancholy satisfaction, saw his worst predictions only too completely realised. That 'poor old beast' John Bull was indeed working himself into a truly noble condition. By 6 September nearly all the considerable towns in the north and more than half in the whole of England had held protest meetings. Shaftesbury wrote in his diary for the 6th: 'The anger—I rejoice in it—against the Turks is an universal fever at blood-heat!'[1] On the same day Fitzjames Stephen wrote more sourly than ever to Lytton: 'My prophecy as to John Bull and the Bulgarians is coming true. Bishops, Lords, Professors, all sorts and conditions of men are swarming about the country as to the atrocities.'[2] John Morley had written to Dilke from Brighton on the previous day: 'If there were an election in this noble borough this week, the two Tories would be expelled with a fork.'[3] Members of the government could not, in private, conceal their apprehension. Derby consoled himself by writing to Disraeli on 7 September: 'I am not more discouraged than you by the Bulgarian agitation: which as far as it is sincere, is directed against the Turks rather than against the Cabinet: though naturally it is utilised by the enemy.'[4] Bryce, in the Caucasus, rejoiced at the tale of Freeman's glad tidings. 'Curious people, the English: they smouldered all those months & now have got into a blaze at last. It is verily well; and must affect the behaviour of those cold-hearted shortsighted fellows who unfortunately represent us.'[5]

Stephen concluded his jeremiad on the triumph of mass irrationality by announcing that since fools in his age and country controlled public opinion, which must run its course, he would simply hold his tongue and congratulate himself on having 'no call to express any opinion journalistically or otherwise on the subject'.[6] Others would find in such circumstances an irresistible call. Of these the greatest, and the last to commit himself, was Gladstone.

---

[1] E. Hodder, *The Life and Work of the Seventh Earl of Shaftesbury, K. G.* (1886), vol. iii, p. 375.

[2] Stephen to Lytton, 6 September 1876, Fitzjames Stephen Papers, Cambridge Add. MSS 7349.

[3] Morley to Dilke, 5 September 1876, Dilke Papers, Add. MSS 43895, f. 137.

[4] Derby to Disraeli, 7 September 1876, Disraeli Papers.

[5] Bryce to Freeman, 10 and 22 September 1876, Bryce Papers, E5.

[6] Stephen to Lytton, 6 September 1876, Fitzjames Stephen Papers, Cambridge Add. MSS 7349.

After a long period of apathy, then of mental conflict, he had at length, on 5 September, completed a pamphlet, and seen the first printed and finished copies. On the 6th, *Bulgarian Horrors and the Question of the East* was selling as no other pamphlet had ever sold.

Gladstone and the Agitation, to 6 September

1 The Process of Involvement

GLADSTONE's involvement in the atrocities agitation, sooner or later, can be taken, for all practical purposes, as an inevitable outcome of the situation as it developed in August. It is difficult indeed to conceive that he could have held himself aloof when the Bulgarian affair flared out and ignited the moral passion of a great section of the British public on an issue which engaged every major element of his politico-religious existence—his Catholic Christianity, his European sense, his Liberalism, his democratic sympathies. Persistent aloofness would have been little short of a fundamental contradiction of Gladstone's life and career.

The cumulative inducements to intervention, in fact, seem so overwhelming that a mere recital of them has hitherto been regarded as sufficient to explain Gladstone's alleged coup of 'right timing' of 6 September 1876. A Christian, subject people were being cruelly oppressed by an anti-Christian, alien, despotic régime. The solemn promises given by that régime to the concert of Europe to accord its Christian subjects social and religious equality had been treated as waste paper. The concert, the central feature of Gladstone's international outlook, was being flouted brazenly; and Gladstone had been a member of the Cabinet which had entered the war of 1854 to deprive Russia of its claims to interfere on behalf of the subject Christians of Turkey. Worse, the Turks were being emboldened to defy the concert by the government of the very power which, in Gladstone's view, had a special moral obligation to do precisely the contrary. Gladstone also shared the High Church party's solicitude for the fortunes of the Eastern Churches—a relatively minor consideration, but by no means insignificant.

Nevertheless, even such a catalogue is quite inadequate as a means of understanding Gladstone's mind and motives in August and September 1876. For, far from being a decisive agent, Gladstone was practically carried into the agitation by others. Far from being the conscious meditator of a diabolically cunning coup of right timing against Disraeli, Gladstone was, at most, absent-mindedly waiting for something to turn up; and then remained for long unconscious of the fact that something had turned up. Far from being excited into activity by the atrocities in Bulgaria, Gladstone's excitement was related almost exclusively to the popular movement in England. Far from being an impatient crusader against Disraeli, Gladstone, even after committing himself on 6 September, wasted a vital and precious month in delays and vacillations. Far from deliberately boosting forward the agitation in September, in effect Gladstone did more than anyone else to put a drag on its impetus. And Gladstone was a latecomer: 'late it is true', as Ellis Ashmead Bartlett remarked to Liddon, 'but still in time to do immense good'.[1] It is only the grandeur of unforeseeable events to come which gives this statement its grotesque and comically patronising air. It was perfectly natural and legitimate in its time.

It is this lateness above all which sums up these qualifying considerations about the nature of Gladstone's involvement in the agitation. It poses a problem not adequately solved by such suppositions as that Gladstone must have 'waited for nearly two months in a mood of very dangerous calm'.[2] Gladstone did not 'wait' in any sense conformable with such a supposition. His mood of calm was, in fact, simple nonchalance; and it was embarrassingly innocent. Freeman, always jealous of his precedence as an 'atrocity-monger', was later at some pains to impress upon Stead, à propos of the 'little sketch of the movement' projected by the latter, that if there were to be 'any mention' of Freeman in it, he would like Stead to 'bring out' the point that, contrary to the blurred view of events publicly received by 1879, Gladstone had joined the movement long after it had got under way, and far behind Freeman.[3]

---

[1] Bartlett to Liddon, 17 September [1876], Liddon Papers.
[2] Magnus, *Gladstone*, p. 239.
[3] Freeman to Stead, 25 December 1879, Stead Papers.

It is not difficult to ascribe reasons for this backwardness. Gladtone himself was afterwards profuse with excuses. He pleaded hat his slowness to observe the 'real leanings' of Disraeli, and)israeli's dominance over the Cabinet, derived from clinging long ɔ the meritorious hope that the government would recognise ɪeir moral obligations to the Eastern Christians under the Treaty f Paris. For himself: 'I shrank naturally but perhaps unduly from ecognising the claims they made on me, on me individually', as a ɪember of Aberdeen's cabinet.[1] Then there was the problem of is relationship to Granville and Hartington as official leaders of ɪe party. And there was the absence of formal confirmation of the trocity reports.

These were all good and genuine inhibiting considerations; yet nderlying them were two far more fundamental and important ircumstances. The first was that Gladstone's mind was not irectly attuned to the Eastern question. He had no serviceable ʳamework of intellectual or political attitudes into which he could ɛadily fit the Bulgarian case. He had not really faced the Eastern uestion squarely since giving up the Crimean War as a lost cause. ˉhere had been enough, and more than enough, to occupy his ttention in the eighteen-sixties and early seventies. Gladstone ɛrtainly never was, as his critics who opposed the atrocities agitaon very correctly pointed out, the leader of a movement to revise ɪe orthodox Eastern policy. In the later eighteen-fifties he had isplayed capacity, in the cases of Romania and the Ionian Islands, ɔr criticism of the Turks and appreciation of the potential of ˙hristian progress and nationalism; but this criticism and appreciaon soon became noticeably cursory. Though always ready enough ɔ challenge Palmerston, Gladstone raised no recorded protest ɡainst the bizarre extravagances of the policy which in 1860–1 ⱡcrificed the interests of the Lebanese and Syrian Christians to ritish fears of French aggression. Freeman, engaged in 1877 in ɔme characteristic dispute, applied to Gladstone for an assurance ⱡat Gladstone had not approved Stanley's (the Lord Derby of ʒ76) conduct during the Cretan insurrection of 1866–7 in refusing ylum on British ships to Cretan refugees.[2] Freeman thanked

---

[1] Gladstone Papers, Add. MSS 44790, ff. 112–14.
[2] Freeman to Gladstone, 12 August 1877, Gladstone Papers, Add. MSS 44454, 326–7.

Gladstone for his 'full' answer, but regretted that he would not be able to make a very strong point of it, and thought perhaps it would be better to let the matter drop.[1]

Gladstone sympathised readily enough, if somewhat perfunctorily, in 1875 and 1876 with Christian insurgents against Turkish rule.[2] The Turkish financial default loomed 'very large' in his view as 'one of the greatest political events'. But it did not excite him to activity. On the contrary, he reassured himself that Disraeli would handle it 'rationally'.[3] He noted in April 1876 that 'great events' seemed to be 'drawing near in the East'[4]; but he remained curiously remote and detached, absorbed in Homer and theology. Before his mind became excited to a pitch where he could commit himself to engage wholeheartedly in the Eastern question, he had to be convinced that the question promised, for him, the element of a moral crusade; and the basic element of a moral crusade was a significant manifestation of moral sentiment on a popular level and scale. Essentially, the aspect of the Bulgarian affair that excited Gladstone most profoundly was not the horror of the atrocities themselves but the realisation that they had provoked a great mass movement of popular moral passion. The central function of the atrocities agitation, for Gladstone, was that it restored the moral rapport between himself and the masses which the defeat of 1874 had snapped.

This was the second fundamental circumstance which inhibited action. Until the realisation came to Gladstone that such a moral passion was in being, his attitude to the question raised by the atrocities was distinguished by no very extraordinary quality except perhaps for a persistent tendency to think of it as the possible occasion of the 'portentous blundering' on the part of the government for which he hardly knew whether to hope or fear; the possible 'cause' of a political 'reaction' in favour of the Liberal party.[5]

★

[1] Freeman to Gladstone, 15 August 1877, *ibid.*, ff. 332–3.
[2] Purcell, *Ambrose Phillipps de Lisle*, vol. ii, pp. 151–2.
[3] Gladstone to Granville, 3 November 1875, Granville Papers, 30, 29/29.
[4] Purcell, *op. cit.*, vol. ii, p. 151.
[5] See e.g. his remarks to Granville, B. Holland, *The Life of Spencer Compton Eighth Duke of Devonshire* (1911), vol. i, p. 176.

The atrocities issue seems to have been first presented to Gladstone in a direct way by Stratford de Redcliffe. Stratford wrote a
very agitated note to Gladstone on 26 May, wanting to see him
very much and asking him to call.[1] From what can be seen of their
counsels later, there seems little doubt that news of the situation
in Bulgaria had reached Stratford. And in fact reports of rumours
of extensive massacres were shortly afterwards filtering into the
newspapers. It seems likely that Stratford impressed upon Gladstone his general sense of anxiety.

It was Forster, not Gladstone, however, on the strength apparently of the *Spectator* article of 3 June, who prodded the sluggish
Hartington into movement.[2] Disraeli easily eluded Hartington's
very half-hearted effort to extract information.[3] Gladstone was
indignant at Disraeli's evasion,[4] but Granville was not encouraging,[5] and the government's triumph on the withdrawal of the
Berlin Memorandum sent Gladstone back to his Homer and
theology. It was not until 20 June that Granville, faced with the
prospect of a debate on the Eastern question, proposed a meeting
of party leaders, including Gladstone. Possibly he was a little nervous about tendencies in Gladstone's mind, for he was very careful
to insist on the acceptability of the official government explanation
that the action in sending the fleet to Besika Bay, 'which is popular
now as a proof of vigour against Russia', was only decided upon
after urgent appeals from Elliot 'for protection for the Greeks
against the Turks'.[6]

Pears' first detailed dispatch in the *Daily News* of 23 June and the
questions and answers it provoked in parliament on the 26th
brought Gladstone and Stratford de Redcliffe once more into consultation. They discussed Derby's latest speech, and agreed on a
'critique' along the lines that the government were 'quite wrong'
to allow themselves to be excluded from the initiative on the plea
of non-interference in Turkey's domestic affairs, that to treat the
insurrections as a 'civil war' begged the whole question, and that

---

[1] Gladstone Papers, Add. MSS 44450, f. 117.
[2] Hartington to Granville, 8 June 1876, Granville Papers, 30, 29/26.
[3] Hartington to Disraeli, 8 June 1876, Devonshire Papers, Chatsworth, 340/670;
Disraeli to Hartington, 9 June 1876, *ibid.*, 671.
[4] Gladstone to Granville, 9 June 1876, Granville Papers, 30, 29/29.
[5] Granville to Gladstone, 10 June 1876, Gladstone Papers, Add. MSS 44170, ff.
216–17.
[6] *Ibid.*, ff. 220–1.

the dispatch of the fleet to Besika Bay had a 'distinct tendency to encourage' the Turks in their wrong-doing.[1]

There is nothing as yet to suggest that Gladstone's outlook was coloured to any marked extent by the revelations of the events in Bulgaria. The larger question of the treaties of 1856, and the obligations of Britain in relation to them, still remained uppermost in his mind.[2] Possibly, however, he was jolted into a rather more receptive frame of mind by Stratford's remark on 29 June that he had received 'sad accounts of the Turkish atrocities in Bulgaria'.[3] But whatever the influence on Gladstone of this endorsement, in effect, of the newspaper reports by the English name most revered in connection with the Eastern question, he still remained withdrawn. He declined, as has been noted, an invitation pressed on him by a group of members of the House of Commons to preside at a public meeting. He did not join the deputation to Derby on 14 July led by Bright, principally because, as he later explained, he disagreed with its non-interventionist viewpoint.[4] This is not a particularly convincing explanation. Had he felt strongly on the question he could either have registered dissent from Bright on the score of non-intervention, or joined Farley's deputation to Derby which immediately followed Bright's.

Gladstone began to come under pressures more urgent and insistent, however, than those either of the *Daily News* or Stratford de Redcliffe. Of the original 'atrocity-mongers' the Rev. Malcolm MacColl, Liddon's lieutenant and a long-standing acquaintance of Gladstone, was the first to appeal directly to Gladstone, and he remained the most persistent. MacColl informed Gladstone that he and Liddon were shortly to go to the East to sift the evidence of the atrocities. 'I believe', he told Gladstone, 'that they are substantially accurate, and the shameful efforts of Dizzy and Lord Derby to palliate them are intolerable.' Unlike Bright and Granville, MacColl was not at all prepared to accept the government's explanation of the sending of the fleet to Besika Bay; this was just another example of their 'indifference to truth'. Disraeli, it hardly needed saying, was one of the 'most inveterate liars in Christen-

---

[1] Gladstone to Granville, 27 June 1876, Granville Papers, 30, 29/29.
[2] See Stratford de Redcliffe to Gladstone, 29 June 1876, Gladstone Papers, Add. MSS 44450, f. 219.
[3] *Ibid.*
[4] *Bulgarian Horrors and The Question of the East* (pamphlet, 1876), p. 22.

lom'. MacColl concluded: 'I sincerely trust you may find it convenient to speak on the Eastern question, and tear away the mask
rom the fanciful pictures of Turkey wh. the Government & a
ortion of the press have presented to the public.'[1]

Perhaps this, together with the production of a new Blue Book
on 22 July which covered the operations of the Foreign Office from
January to 17 July, contributed to the somewhat more alert and
impatient attitude displayed by Gladstone in the last days of July.
He was very indignant on the 27th that a debate on the Eastern
question was to be postponed, a debate which, in his view, would
assume 'distinctly and unequivocally the character of a Vote of
Confidence'.[2] On the previous day he had protested strongly to
Granville against letting the Liberal party be seduced into support
of a motion by the Hon. T. C. Bruce, a Conservative and chairman
of the Imperial Ottoman Bank, which involved approval of the
government's proceedings. 'This', Gladstone added, 'I for one
cannot do. I can hardly suppose you or H. will do it.' Gladstone
forwarded a copy of the motion to make sure that Granville could
see the 'tuck' the Liberals were invited to join in. 'My digestive
organs are not strong enough.' Gladstone instead wanted an
amendment lamenting the refusal of the government to adopt the
principle of the concert.[3]

This outburst was the first of many jolts which Granville was
to receive from Gladstone in the following months. Gladstone's
new, rather aggressively independent tone, though not yet related
specifically to the atrocities themselves, clearly perturbed the
Liberal leaders. Granville hurriedly telegraphed back that he and
Hartington thought it better to 'avoid praise or blame' by resort-
ing to a technical evasion.[4] But Gladstone had already passed beyond the point where technical evasions were acceptable.

Yet Gladstone's attack on Disraeli's policy in his speech in the
debate of 31 July was not at all the speech for which MacColl had
pleaded. Old Lord Russell, indeed, dismissed it almost with con-
empt for timidity and 'want of earnest purpose'. He demanded
hat the fleet be sent to Constantinople and made a knife at the

---

[1] MacColl to Gladstone, [20 July 1876], Gladstone Papers, Add. MSS 44243,
f. 168–71.
[2] 3 Hansard, CCXXX, cc. 1975–6.
[3] Gladstone to Granville, 26 July 1876, Granville Papers, 30, 29/29.
[4] Granville to Gladstone, 27 July 1876, Gladstone Papers, Add. MSS 44170, f. 224.

throat of the Sultan as the first move towards a restoration o
Canning's policy of co-operation with Russia.[1]

Pears' dispatch in the *Daily News* of 7 August and Baring's
preliminary letter read in the Commons on the same day, however
brought Gladstone somewhat nearer to the realisation that per
haps he had been missing the point. 'There were two subjects or
which I should have *dwelt*', he now wrote to Granville on '
August, 'but for the belief that the debate must last and that other.
would handle them: the Bulgarian atrocities, and the pretende
colonisation of European provinces with Circassians, one of the
worst things the Turks have done.'[2] The note of *esprit d'escalier*
and exculpation continues as Gladstone answers Russell's com
plaints: he thought Russell made too light of the 'difficulty' tha
the charges against the Turks were not yet 'formally proven'; bu
he stressed to Granville his hope that it was clearly recognised
among the party leaders that if, and when, the charges were show
to be valid, 'we shall all come down upon Turkey pretty freely in
respect of them'. Gladstone added, with a rising if somewhat be
lated note of feeling: 'There is something horrid in reflecting that
while horrors were going on, our fleet was at Besika Bay within a
few hours sail & not only was not there to arrest them but was
believed by the perpetrators to be there for the purpose of securing
their impunity.'

The Bulgarian question was indeed just beginning, for Glad
stone, to move beyond the plane of politics in which, for the las
two years, his major concern had been the search for issues likely
to restore the fortunes of the party. 'As a party question', he tol
Granville, 'this affords no despicable material, but there are mucl
higher interests involved.' The shift to a new plane was as yet im
perceptible. At this juncture the 'higher interests' were high to
the point of remoteness. The question was 'party', but not even o
immediate importance from that point of view. Though Gladston
trusted that Granville would make sure before the impending
prorogation that the results of Baring's inquiry would be publishe
at once, and not 'bottled up' until the next session, his genera
assumption remained undisturbed that the atrocities would, witl
luck, be an affair of that session. 'The subject *might* even come up'

---

[1] *Times*, 4 August 1876, p. 5; Russell to Gladstone, 2 August 1876, Gladston
Papers, Add. MSS 44294, ff. 270–1.   [2] Granville Papers, 30, 29/29

he went so far as to prompt Granville, 'in an amendment to the Address next February.'[1]

*

Gladstone later excused the feebleness of his opposition to the government's Eastern policy in July and August on the grounds that it was an opposition 'without hope'.[2] Certainly, on no occasion was the feebleness and hopelessness of his opposition more nakedly displayed than in his refusal to join Evelyn Ashley's 'gallant effort' of 11 August. Gladstone afterwards explained that his motive in not doing so was the want of 'clear and responsible evidence' of the atrocity charges[3]; but this, like the explanation of his not joining Bright's deputation, has a distinct *ex post facto* ring about it. If Forster and Harcourt could both support Ashley, there was nothing to prevent Gladstone from so doing except a simple lack of will. In fact, there is little doubt that uppermost in Gladstone's mind as the session faded out was the thought of getting back to Hawarden as soon as possible and sinking himself in much more congenial literary occupations. On leaving for Harwarden, he 'mentally postponed all further action to the opening of the next Session'. It never occurred to Gladstone, any more than to his parliamentary colleagues, that a popular agitation would or could replace parliament as the arena of the Eastern question—that it would, in fact, eventually set up an alternative 'parliament' of its own.

With Gladstone in this rather hopeless frame of mind, it needed a very considerable accumulation of pressures to make him start revising his attitude. Such mild applause as his speech of 31 July drew[4] would hardly begin to make any permanent impression on him. MacColl did his best to see in it a response to his plea of 20 July that Gladstone should 'tear away the mask' with which British policy had covered Turkey. But in fact MacColl's major concern was to smooth down the Bishop of Manchester's irritation at Gladstone's stress on the necessity of maintaining formal Turkish integrity.[5]

---

[1] *Ibid.* [2] Gladstone Papers, Add. MSS 44790, ff. 112–14.
[3] *Bulgarian Horrors*, p. 18.
[4] E.g. H. Skinner to Gladstone, 2 August 1876, Gladstone Papers, Add. MSS 44451, ff. 9–10; J. L. Hanly, editor of the *Journal Stamboul*, to Gladstone, 10 August 1876, *ibid.*, ff. 38–9. [5] MacColl to Gladstone, 23 August [1876], *ibid.*, ff. 177–8.

Perhaps the most important immediate influence on Gladstone at this point was Russell's call for a return to the tradition of Canning. Granville dismissed this as mere senile raving.[1] Very probably he was worried at the seductive influence Russell in his present mood might exert on Gladstone. He had good cause to be To Gladstone, Russell stood above all for the sacred cause of Italy And, apart from anything else, an evocation of Canning was sure to attract Gladstone. The best indication of Russell's general in fluence on Gladstone at this time is Gladstone's later proposal to dedicate the *Bulgarian Horrors* to him, until dissuaded by Gran ville.[2] Granville had a good case for this. Russell was too dodder ing to be reliable; and it was embarrassing that Elliot, whose head the agitation demanded with increasing vociferousness, was Lady Russell's brother. Gladstone's politeness to Elliot in his speech brought forth warm thanks from Lady Russell[3]; and Elliot himself thought he might insert a note of caution for Gladstone's benefit He added to a letter relating to Schliemann's recent excavations a Mycenae his regret at noting that Gladstone was 'rather an advo cate for autonomy in the Insurgent Turkish Provinces'. For Elliot did not think that 'those who brought forward that view' had 'properly weighed the practical difficulties in the way of it in Province where the populations are divided into several hostile sects, likely to lead to a perfect state of anarchy'. He concluded 'It will not be easy to devise any tolerable solution.'[4]

Such slight influence as this may have had on Gladstone would have been more than counterbalanced by the information sent to him by Hanly, the editor of the *Journal Stamboul*. This consisted mainly of copies of his paper, which was threatened with sup pression by the Turkish authorities if it continued to expose Turkish conduct or criticise Elliot.[5] And the Turkish official report on the alleged atrocities, issued early in August, shocked Glad stone in its cynical effrontery: 'a sheer & gross mockery', he told Granville.[6] Then Argyll, Gladstone's colleague of 1854, wrote 'in

---

[1] See Granville to Gladstone, 2 July 1876, *ibid.*, Add. MSS 44170, ff. 222–3. Also Granville to Gladstone, 1 September 1876, *ibid.*, ff. 236–7.
[2] Granville to Gladstone, 1 September 1876, *ibid.*
[3] Lady Russell to Gladstone, 2 August 1876, *ibid.*, Add. MSS 44451, ff. 7–8.
[4] Elliot to Gladstone, 5 August 1876, *ibid.*, ff. 22–3.
[5] Hanby to Gladstone, *ibid.* The *Courrier d'Orient* had already been suppressed for protesting against Disraeli's contradiction of one of its reports.
[6] Gladstone to Granville, 20 August 1876, Granville Papers, 30, 29/29.

ıry' after reading the Blue Book put out on 10 August.[1] This
oused from Gladstone on 14 August a faint hope that the subject
f the massacres in Bulgaria might not 'slumber through the re-
ess'[2]; but it was a hope without faith.

★

The crucial turning-point in Gladstone's outlook on the Bul-
arian question was now, however, almost at hand. Indications
multiplied that he was coming under pressures too intense to let
is attitude of 31 July, even as modified, remain intact. An impor-
ant contribution to the mounting pressure on Gladstone came
rom Madame Novikov, who had cultivated him since 1873 on the
asis of common religious interests, and now counted him as a
member of her London salon. Madame Novikov's brother,
Nicholas Kireev, an officer in the Russian army, was the first
volunteer to die fighting the Turks in the Serbian campaign of
1876, in circumstances of conspicuous heroism. His death at once
became a popular legend in Russia. Madame Novikov, afflicted by
her loss and at the same time moved with deep indignation at what
he conceived to be the utterly immoral character of British policy,
simply lost her head', in her own phrase,[3] and wrote bitterly to
her many English friends—Napier, Froude, Kinglake, Freeman,
Villiers, Harcourt, and of course Gladstone.[4] Of all her friends
Gladstone alone sent no reply.[5] This surprised and grieved her.
But Gladstone had come to the conclusion that he might prepare a
worthier testament of his regard for the memory of Nicholas
Kireev, as well as a statement of his own convictions as to the moral
character of British policy, than a mere letter of condolence. When
Madame Novikov did receive acknowledgment, it was in the form
of a copy of his pamphlet on the *Bulgarian Horrors*.

It is not quite clear when Gladstone first began to think of
writing a pamphlet as a means of meeting the case. It was a per-

[1] Argyll to Granville, 25 October 1876, *ibid.*
[2] Morley, *Gladstone*, vol. ii, p. 159.
[3] Madame Olga Novikov, *Russian Memories* [1916], p. 39.
[4] Novikov to Gladstone, 10 August 1876, Gladstone Papers, Add. MSS 44268, ff.
29–30 (from Milan): 'You always sympathised with what is noble & heroic! Allow
me therefore to give you a little description of my brother's death in Serbia. . . . But
tell me, how is it, that Europe, who professes to be Xian, how can she not only remain
perfectly indifferent to the atrocities committed against other Xians, but even support
& sympathise with Mahometans. It is a dreadful riddle! and all out professions of
faith seem to be an impious humbug!'   [5] Novikov, *Russian Memories*, p. 39.

fectly predictable reaction on his part, but it is unlikely tha
Madame Novikov's letter was the decisive stimulus, much as he
appeal to his Christian, European sense would have touched Glad
stone's susceptibilities. Liddon's powerful and sensational sermon
in St Paul's, it will be remembered, was delivered on 13 August
just about the time when Gladstone would have been pondering
Madame Novikov's letter. Its trumpet-call to Christian action
must have sounded loudly in the ears of one who shared so much
of the religious outlook of Liddon.

But above all, there was Gladstone's discovery, with a shock of
surprise, that despite the prorogation, the Bulgarian question
persisted among the people themselves, that it had a life indepen
dent of parliament and politicians. At Hawarden, on 18 August
reading that day's *Daily News*, Gladstone's eye fell upon an article
headed 'Working Men and the War in the East', which announced that a rally in Hyde Park was being organised to con-
demn the government's policy and demand Elliot's recall. Glad
stone suddenly realised that, as he put it in terms which Morley
thought best to expurgate, 'the game was afoot and the question
yet alive'.[1] Many years later Gladstone wrote to Henry Broadhurst, the trade-union leader, that he had 'never hesitated to aver
that in 1876, at a time when he thought the Bulgarian question 'for
the moment dead, and had (mentally) postponed action upon it'
it was the 'tidings of an intended working men's meeting in Hyde
Park' that altered his 'plan' and made him 'at once perceive that
the iron was hot and that the time to strike had arrived'.[2]

The important point is Gladstone's surprise and sense of sudden
enlightenment. He said later of the agitation as a whole: 'I admit
to me it has been an unexpected movement. I have been astonished
at its commencement and its progress.' It came, as Gladstone saw
it, 'suddenly', and at a time when the 'natural leaders of local
parties' were dispersed. It commenced, survived, and expanded
essentially as an affair of the masses, unaffected and uninfluenced
by sophisticated calculations of policy and party prospects.[3] This
was to Gladstone its supreme virtue and attraction. His whole

[1] Gladstone Papers, Add. MSS 44790, ff. 112–14. Morley's version is in *Gladstone*
vol. ii, p. 158.
[2] Gladstone to Broadhurst, 20 September 1896, Broadhurst Papers, L.S.E., vol. v
no. 1. See also T. Wemyss Reid (ed.), *The Life of William Ewart Gladstone* (1899)
p. 619.   [3] See his comments, *Times*, 11 September 1876, p. 10

approach to the Eastern question began a process of revolution. In inception it was almost nakedly opportunist—'the game was afoot' and 'the time to strike had arrived'; but Gladstone's opportunism now transcended the purely political plane. The critical and decisive moment in the process of his commitment to the agitation came when he realised that a stirring of truly popular moral passion was in being. This process of commitment was not a continuous one; there was a definite break, a distinct shift to a new level, though the old level of 'party question' still continued, and, indeed, in some respects gained vigour.

The idea of a speech rather than a pamphlet seems to have occurred to Gladstone first. His Greenwich constituents had asked him to address them, and he replied on 18 August, probably after reading the *Daily News* article, that if there were a widespread demand he would not fail to consult those without whose 'concurrence' he could not take any steps, 'as the matter is far from being a purely local one'.[1] He then informed Granville that there was to be 'a meeting for the Bulgarians in Hyde Park'. The letter which notified it asked for 'subscriptions for the expences'. Gladstone had 'half a mind to send them a trifle'. Did Granville object? And altogether Gladstone felt 'more inclined to say something, during the recess, on the Turkish policy', than he had been 'for any such escapade during the last four years'.[2]

Granville, busy superintending the campaign in the Bucks. by-election following Disraeli's recent translation to the Lords, delayed replying until the 25th. He preferred a speech, 'which may be very useful', to a subscription.[3] Possibly Granville calculated that Gladstone would be obliged to be more circumspect in a speech than a subscription might encourage the public to think him. But he was too late: Gladstone had already sent a subscription of £5—which Granville had no doubt, as he remarked to Hartington not without a touch of waspishness, would be of 'great assistance to the cause'.[4]

★

MacColl was soon joined by other leading figures in the agita-

[1] *Ibid.*, 22 August 1876, p. 9.
[2] Gladstone to Granville, 20 August 1876, Granville Papers, 30, 29/29.
[3] Gladstone Papers, Add. MSS 44170, ff. 228–31.
[4] Granville to Hartington, 1 September 1876, Devonshire Papers, 340/672.

I

tion in keeping pressure on Gladstone. He still needed to be worked on. The delights of theology held him in a powerful attraction. He was working on the problem of future punishment, 'a chief and favourite point of attack', inadequately met, in his view, by the Early Fathers up to St Athanasius. Possibly his letter of 23 August to the working men made public at the Hackney meeting of the 29th was stimulated by MacGahan's second Batak dispatch in the previous day's *Daily News*; yet as late as 26 August Gladstone could answer Ambrose Phillipps de Lisle, who had written full of zeal for the continuance of atrocity meetings, with details of his theological preoccupations and add almost as a foot-note: 'But I have room in me to feel about the Bulgarian horrors.'[1]

Prominent among MacColl's fellows was the Rev. William Denton, who wrote to Gladstone on 24 August, two days after MacGahan's famous dispatch on Batak appeared in the *Daily News*: 'I don't know what part you may take in guiding the burning in-dignation—surely the righteous indignation—of Englishmen about the Bulgarian atrocities. That you will be called upon and will feel it right to speak out I don't doubt.' Denton concluded powerfully that he was sure Gladstone would 'see as a large matter of policy [what] ought to be done'. And there was 'a third con-sideration, that of duty'. It was to the ministry to which Gladstone belonged that 'a promise was made by the Vali of equal rights to the Christians'.[2] This appeal was no less powerful for the fact that the last statement was not quite accurate.

Hutton, of the *Spectator*, played very skilfully on Gladstone's susceptibilities in the same manner as Denton. He referred to the request of the electors of Greenwich for Gladstone to address them. He trusted that Mr Gladstone would yet, and speedily, see his way to accept this invitation. 'It is for him and his colleagues to judge whether a speech from him would advance the interests of the Opposition, but it is hardly for them to decide whether in remain-ing silent on Turkish affairs, he does not become in some degree *particeps criminis* with the Cabinet.' That, Hutton concluded, was 'a matter of individual conscience'.[3] Nothing more precisely cal-culated to jolt Gladstone could have been conceived.

---

[1] Purcell, *Ambrose Phillipps de Lisle*, vol. ii, p. 155.
[2] Gladstone Papers, Add. MSS 44451, f. 77.
[3] *Spectator*, 26 August 1876, p. 1084.

MacColl wrote again on 26 August, pleading with Gladstone to 'find or make' an occasion of delivering a speech. MacColl found it impossible to get the scenes described in the *Daily News* out of his mind. He concluded: 'Do please, raise your powerful voice against the bestial government of Turkey & the degrading policy of our own Government.'[1] And MacColl was in very close liaison with Hutton. He wrote to Gladstone on 30 August, having just come from the editor of the *Spectator*, who had received 'direct information from the Russian embassy' that the Russians intended, in the event of a conference of powers, to propose the autonomy of Bosnia, the Herzegovina, and Bulgaria. Clearly, MacColl insisted, England had been deeply moved by the atrocities, 'and will be satisfied with nothing less than Russia's proposal, if it can only be made to understand the question'. All the more important, then, that Gladstone should deliver a 'great speech' at this moment.

MacColl carefully forwarded papers to Hawarden, including, on 30 August, the *Daily News* of the previous day, containing Schuyler's preliminary report. Gladstone would see that it not only confirmed the accounts supplied by the *Daily News* but that it added 'frightful details wh. did not come out before, such as the violation of an old man upon an altar. In Turkey we really seem to be face to face with a modern Sodom & Gomorrah.'[2] Yet again, relentlessly, on 1 September: 'I do hope you will make a speech on the Eastern question.' The nation's aroused feelings desperately needed guidance. 'Its aspirations are all in the right direction, & all it requires is to have its ideas & wishes put into shape & order.' As an additional incentive MacColl pointed to the 'immense capital' to be made at Disraeli's expense, not only on account of the atrocities, but also because he was playing Russia's game—'assuming that she is engaged in a bad game'.[3]

Stead also of course had written on the 26th from Darlington, with an account of the atrocity campaign which had been inaugurated there, asking for some word of endorsement. 'It is still', Stead added, 'the cherished hope of the North Country that you may once more lead us to victory, & that hope has certainly not been weakened by recent occurrences abroad.'[4] Distasteful

---

[1] Gladstone Papers, Add. MSS 44243, ff. 179–82.
[2] *Ibid.*, ff. 183–6. [3] *Ibid.*, ff. 187–90.
[4] *Ibid.*, Add. MSS 44303, ff. 230–1.

as Gladstone must have found this approach, he could not have remained unimpressed by the news of such a demonstration in the north, with promise of more to come. It was exactly the kind·of confirmation that he needed to stimulate his developing conception of the post-sessional popular movement heralded by the Hyde Park announcement.

An impassioned appeal came from Ellis Ashmead Bartlett, Liddon's earlier and eager disciple, 'imploring' Gladstone to put his 'great name & influence' at the head of the 'almost unanimous demand of the nation' that the 'maddening' spectacle of unredressed oppression by the Turks must be ended. 'We owe a great and conspicuous expiation to the oppressed Christians of the East.' Bartlett stressed especially that this was 'not a question for party'; he was a strong Conservative, 'but if our Government will not do what mere humanity demands', he would only pray that they 'may be compelled by any means available to act as the nation is now resolving they shall'. Above all: 'Our old bad policy must be reversed.'

> I do not exaggerate the feelings of the country, but write from personal knowledge of what I have seen at many great meetings in the North & West, where I have made it my privilege to attempt to advance if possible this great & righteous cause.
>
> The enthusiasm & unanimity among all ranks and classes is most unparalleled. *Half* measures will not satisfy the people now. . . .
>
> No wonder that the enthusiasm and indignation of the English nation is unbounded & unparalleled. It is for you Sir to formulate, to direct to lead this great wave of righteous indignation, to save a suffering & outraged people, & render an inestimable service to religion & humanity.[1]

2 'There is now . . . a virtuous passion'

All this was preaching to one already more than half-converted; but it was none the less necessary, not merely to clinch for Gladstone the solid existence of the popular movement itself, but to give him final assurance that he alone could provide the agitation with the guidance it needed if it were not to falter and die in futility.

---

[1] Bartlett to Gladstone, 6 September 1876, Gladstone Papers, Add. MSS 44461, ff. 128–31.

Gladstone's need for assurance was all the greater in that he had yet to overcome the difficulty of his relationship to Granville, Hartington, and the party as a whole. This problem was becoming increasingly embarrassing. Gladstone could no longer disguise from himself the fact that a considerable section of the party 'out of doors', led by such as Stead, eagerly hoped to take advantage, among other things, of 'occurrences abroad' to have him return to the leadership. This was a much more formidable power than the manoeuvres of parliamentary Radicals like T. B. Potter or Peter Rylands had been able to exert on him. It was easy for Gladstone to ignore the matter in his reply to Stead; it was not so easy to evade when excursionists to Hawarden raised it with tactless persistence. Gladstone objected that he was 'too old'.[1] Rather later, Gladstone privately rejected the importunities of another Radical, the historian Goldwin Smith, in the terms that 'no circumstances would justify my taking any sort of step to replace myself in the leadership out of which I forced myself in a manner which gives the existing leaders the strongest claims on me'. Gladstone added a catalogue of lesser objections.[2]

This was written in November 1877. There is no doubt that Gladstone finally committed himself to the agitation in 1876 without the slightest premonition of the consummation of 1880. Yet for all his catalogue of objections, there is no compelling reason to assume that he would have acted differently had he been able to foresee the result. He was certainly very conscious in 1876 of the grave risks which the Eastern question involved for the integrity of his unofficial status. He told Granville that he had declined a request from Lord Carington, the brother of the Liberal candidate for Bucks., for him to speak there, mainly because he did not want speculation 'on my position in the party, and thus possibly to produce mistrust & division'. Gladstone added deprecatingly that he had supplied some suggestions on the Eastern question: 'he asked for them'. He concluded: 'I really hope that on this Eastern matter the pot will be kept boiling.'[3]

It need not be assumed that Granville was at all loth to see the pot kept boiling. He did not need Gladstone to point out to him

---

[1] *Times*, 22 August 1876, p. 9.
[2] A. Haultain, *A Selection from Goldwin Smith's Correspondence* (n.d.), p. 62.
[3] Gladstone to Granville, 27 August 1876, Granville Papers, 30, 29/29.

the party advantages involved. Thus he reported gleefully to
Gladstone that in the Bucks. campaign he had recommended to
Rupert Carington 'a very clever little lawyer' who would 'get
up the Bulgarian atrocities well'.[1] But Granville seems to have had
no adequate appreciation of Gladstone's growing state of excitement under the stimulus of the sudden burgeoning of the popular
movement of moral protest and the incessant pressure of appeals
for him to take action. Charles Wordsworth, Bishop of St Andrews,
noted on 29 August after a visit to Hawarden the striking impression Gladstone made of being a 'busy, restless-minded man,
if ever there was one'.[2] It was indeed on the 28th that Gladstone
had started work on 'a beginning for a possible pamphlet on the
Turkish question'.[3] In 1879, sorting his papers, he marked in
pencil on a pile of notes headed 'Future Retribution': 'From this
I was called away to write on Bulgaria.'[4]

★

Gladstone was apparently pleased with the beginning of the
pamphlet; but there were two immediate impediments in the way
of bringing it to a conclusion. He was still without the 'clear and
responsible evidence' for which he had earlier stipulated. This was
provided on the 29th by the publication of Schuyler's preliminary
report in the *Daily News*.[5] More difficult was the problem of
squaring Granville and Hartington. Gladstone began to prepare
the ground in a letter to Granville on the 29th. He started by indicating his pleasure at the assiduous way in which Granville continued to 'nurse' the Bucks. election, now assuming for the first
time a special significance in Gladstone's mind. He agreed with
the *Spectator* that 'the existence of the Government should be
challenged in this Election on the ground of the Bulgarian massacres
—and of their conduct about them & what hangs on to them'.
And he went on to observe, in a moment of inspired reflection:
'Good ends can rarely be attained in politics without passion: and

[1] Granville to Gladstone, 25 August 1876, Gladstone Papers, Add. MSS 44170,
ff. 228–31.
[2] J. Wordsworth, *The Episcopate of Charles Wordsworth* (1899), p. 210.
[3] Morley, *Gladstone*, vol. ii, p. 159.
[4] Gladstone Papers, Add. MSS 44698, f. 367.
[5] Buckle's complaint (*Disraeli*, vol. ii, pp. 931–2) that Gladstone 'would not wait
for Baring's detailed report' and that he based his pamphlet entirely on 'the most
horrifying stories of the unverified newspaper reports', is quite unfounded. The delay
in the publication of Baring's report had in any case already become a scandal.

there is now, the first time for a good many years, a virtuous passion.'[1]

Gladstone was 'much struck' with the indications of feeling brought to him daily by the post as well as the newspapers. So far as he was concerned, he told Granville, the question of speech or subscription had 'gone by'. But he was in 'half, perhaps a little more than half, a mind to write a pamphlet'—mainly, Gladstone explained lamely, on the ground that 'Parliamentary action was all but ousted'. Gladstone concluded by inquiring whether Granville was 'shocked' at his proposal and requesting information as to how a copy of Schuyler's report could be got.[2]

Certainly Granville was 'a little startled'. He replied briefly that he had already primed Carington to 'open up the Bulgarian case' in Bucks.—indeed, he ranked it as an electoral asset with the 'dash, wealth & popularity of the Caringtons'[3] and with the triumph in getting the reluctant Rothschilds to support by threatening them with reprisals in the next general election.[4] While, however, Granville felt that he must veto a speech, he could not object to a pamphlet.[5] Granville's assent leaves a distinct impression of reluctance and a calculation that a pamphlet, as opposed to a speech, would have the advantage of seeming less official and compromising to the party. His only specific plea at this stage was: 'Pray be merciful to Elliot'; and he advised against dedicating it to Russell: 'It is too late.'[6]

Granville relayed the disturbing news to Hartington, with his own opinion that Gladstone and his friends were 'rather exaggerating' the government's share of responsibility for the atrocities. Granville was, however, prepared to concede that 'it was not our business to countenance their conduct, & that it was obvious the feeling of the country was getting much excited on the subject'.[7] Hartington was 'sorry' that Gladstone thought it necessary to write a pamphlet, and could not imagine (with good reason, considering Gladstone's conspicuous neglect to take advantage of the opportunity offered him by Evelyn Ashley on 11 August) what

---

[1] Granville Papers, 30, 29/29.   [2] *Ibid.*
[3] Granville to Gladstone, 2 September 1876, Gladstone Papers, Add. MSS 44170, ff. 239–40.
[4] Carington to Gladstone, 6 September 1876, *ibid.*, Add. MSS 44451, ff. 132–7.
[5] Granville to Gladstone, 31 August 1876, *ibid.*, Add. MSS 44170, ff. 234–5.
[6] Granville to Gladstone, 1 September 1876, *ibid.*, ff. 236–7.
[7] Granville to Hartington, 1 September 1876, Devonshire Papers, 340/672.

Gladstone meant by parliament being 'ousted' from discussion of the subject, 'as we had two debates on the "atrocities" besides the general one'.[1]

By 1 September the pamphlet was more than half finished. Gladstone wrote to P. W. Clayden, acting editor of the *Daily News* in Frank Hill's absence: 'In the matter of the Bulgarian outrages, you have led the people of England: and I am about to walk as best I can in your steps, by an immediate publication, in which I shall hope to pay the Daily News a just acknowledgement.'[2] He asked for facilities among the paper's files; the British Museum, alerted, also prepared itself to receive Gladstone with everything laid to hand.[3] Gladstone set off for London on Sunday the 3rd, in a state of high excitement, exclaiming to his wife: 'This is the most extraordinary moment of my recollection.'[4] In London he completed his draft, resisting some objections from Granville against the principle of complete autonomy for the Christians with only titular Turkish suzerainty.[5] 'Between ourselves,' as he later wrote to Bright, 'I may mention that G. who received my pamphlet in proof wished me to generalize the concluding part but I thought that with the purpose I had in view it was absolutely necessary to propose something that the country would understand.'[6]

On the 5th Gladstone held a final consultation with Granville and Hartington, who seems to have accepted the distasteful business in a spirit of stolid resignation. Finished copies of the pamphlet were ready that evening. The trio, Gladstone in a high

[1] Hartington to Granville, 3 September 1876, Granville Papers, 30, 29/26.

[2] Gladstone to Clayden, 1 September 1876, Gladstone Papers, Add. MSS 44451, f. 102.

[3] Bullen to Gladstone, 2 September 1876, *ibid.*, f. 112.

[4] G. Battiscombe, *Mrs. Gladstone* (1956), p. 169.

[5] Basset, *Gladstone to his Wife*, p. 218. Gladstone also took the occasion to answer Elliot's warning of 5 August:

'When I wrote to you, I was under the impression that by the beginning of next year the public feeling would exhibit a new movement.

Since that time, I think principally owing to the American Report on Bulgaria, such a change or growth has been witnessed as I have not known in all my life, & the only question now is how far it will go.

You justly observe on the difficulties of provincial autonomy. I hope they may be overcome. For if they cannot, *more* and not less will be demanded by the people of this country, & it is far from unlikely, that they may have ability to obtain their demands' (Gladstone to Elliot, 3 September 1876, Gladstone Papers, Add. MSS 44451, ff. 116–17).

[6] Gladstone to Bright, 27 September 1876, Bright Papers, British Museum Add. MSS 43385, ff. 257–9.

good humour of intellectual and emotional release, went off to the Haymarket Theatre to see a farce. A friend of Disraeli witnessed the curious spectacle of three empty stalls in front of him being occupied successively by Granville, Gladstone, and then, trailing somewhat disconsolately, Hartington. Gladstone 'laughed very much' at the performance; Harty-Tarty 'never even smiled'.[1]

★

So was born what a Darlington committee, with pardonable infelicity, hailed as the 'well-timed pamphlet'.[2] MacColl, on the eve of his departure for the East with Liddon, was enchanted at the prospect of the 'no less glorious fruit' it would bear than the pamphlet on the 'far less heinous' atrocities of the Neapolitan régime.[3] Clayden also rejoiced to be able to announce its publication, 'as I see day by day', he told Gladstone, 'from the vast number of letters wh. come by every post how people are everywhere wishing for some statement from you'.[4] George Anderson, a Radical member of parliament for Glasgow, expressed perhaps the general judgment of the supporters of the agitation: 'It was the one thing wanted to guide rightly the grand spontaneous outburst of national indignation.'[5] Granville remained cheerful, despite his qualms: 'I wish you joy of the receipt of *the* pamphlet.'[6] Its 'receipt' became of course a legend. After the first day of public sales Gladstone could report proudly to Granville that it was 'alive & kicking: four & twenty thousand copies now printed, & they think it is not at an end'.[7] Within four days forty thousand copies were sold, within a month two hundred thousand.

Bulgarian Horrors and the Question of the East was a rehash of Schuyler, MacGahan, the Blue Books, and Gladstone's speech of 31 July, mingled with virulent abuse of the Turks. It contained no revelations. On Granville's advice there was no attack on Disraeli 'individually'.[8] It had no particular literary merit except perhaps for the 'bag and baggage' phrase in the famous rhetorical perora-

---

[1] Buckle, *Disraeli*, vol. ii, p. 933.
[2] Gladstone Papers, Add. MSS 44451, f. 165.
[3] MacColl to Gladstone, 2 September 1876, *ibid.*, Add. MSS 44243, ff. 191–2.
[4] Clayden to Gladstone, 3 September 1876, *ibid.*, Add. MSS 44451, ff. 114–15.
[5] Anderson to Gladstone, 8 September 1876, *ibid.*, ff. 146–7.
[6] Granville to Gladstone, 8 September 1876, *ibid.*, Add. MSS 44170, ff. 243–4.
[7] Gladstone to Granville, 7 September 1876, Granville Papers, 30, 29/29.
[8] Gladstone to Granville, 6 December 1876, *ibid.*

tion derived, fittingly enough, from Stratford de Redcliffe,[1] but which, in any case, obscured rather than illuminated the issue. Gladstone demanded merely the extinction of Turkish 'administrative action' in Bosnia, the Herzegovina, and Bulgaria; the fame of the bag and baggage phrase led to the widespread misapprehension that he had called for the expulsion of the Turks from Europe. This misapprehension, fostered deliberately or mistakenly, undoubtedly did the agitation more good than harm. It helped to conceal the fact that beneath the rhetoric the substance of Gladstone's programme remained moderate. Turkish territorial integrity was still the foundation, though Gladstone did not, as on 31 July, go out of his way to assert that he was not ashamed to stipulate this. His main practical point was the necessity of reaching an understanding with Russia. Well might Derby sneer in a note to Disraeli: 'a small result for so large a document'.[2]

But Derby's sneer was beside the point. The significance of the *Horrors* lies in its character as a unique response to a particular series of stimuli which coloured its form and content and made it the supremely representative expression of a passionate moment of history. Had it been more original and informative—as, say, in the Neapolitan case—it would have been correspondingly less effective. The *Bulgarian Horrors* succeeded so completely because it concentrated into a single utterance a profoundly excited public mood struggling for articulation. The essential point is that it was far less a case of Gladstone exciting popular passion than of popular passion exciting Gladstone. The realisation that he and a great mass movement were in a state, or potential state, of moral rapport must have been rather intoxicating for him—'the first time', in his own words, 'in a good many years'.

*

The widely-held assumption that the *Bulgarian Horrors* constitutes Gladstone's classic exercise in the art of 'right timing'[3] needs fundamental revision. That there was a strong element of

---

[1] See R. W. Seton-Watson, *Britain in Europe, 1789–1914* (Cambridge 1937), pp. 102, 520. Gladstone would probably not have read the original reference; and Stratford undoubtedly quoted it to Gladstone in their conversations of May and June 1876. See also S. Lane-Poole, *The Life of . . . Viscount Stratford de Redcliffe* (1888), vol. i, p. 307.
[2] Derby to Disraeli, 7 September 1876, Disraeli Papers.
[3] E.g. by his latest biographer, Sir Philip Magnus, *Gladstone*, p. 242.

opportunism involved is obvious. It was not the opportunism, however, of one who watches events and waits for the moment to intervene. It was the opportunism of very belated enlightenment, of one standing absent-mindedly at a bus stop, and then having to scramble hurriedly to catch the bus which has almost passed by. Gladstone told the acting editor of the *Daily News* nothing less than the simple truth: that he was following in the footsteps of that paper, catching up.

That Gladstone himself continued to recognise fully this character of his 'opportunism' in 1876 is indicated in the fragment which he entitled 'General Retrospect', written as late as 1896.

I am by no means sure, upon a calm review, that Providence has endowed me with anything which can be called a striking gift. But if there be such a thing entrusted to me, it has been shown, at certain political junctures, in what may be termed appreciation of the general situation and its result. To make good the idea, this must not be considered as the simple acceptance of public opinion, founded upon the discernment that it has risen to a certain height needful for a given work, like a tide. It is an insight into the facts of particular eras, and their relations one to another, which generates in the mind a conviction that the materials exist for forming a public opinion, and for directing it to a particular end.

Gladstone then expounded the four occasions of his life with respect to which he thought these considerations 'applicable': the renewal of the income tax in 1853; the proposal of 'religious equality for Ireland' in 1868; the proposal of Home Rule for Ireland in 1886; and his attempt to secure a dissolution in 1894 and 'the determination of the idea of the issue then raised between the two Houses of Parliament'.[1]

The omission of the intervention of 1876 is certainly striking and equally certainly not accidental. In fact 1876 has nothing in common with the four stated occasions—when the question of 'right timing' might well be raised. Gladstone was always precise in his definitions. In the first place, Gladstone in 1876 clearly had no appreciation of the 'result', and, indeed, almost until the last moment, hardly any true appreciation of the 'general situation'. Secondly, the formation of public opinion owed nothing to him. He was merely a part of it. Thirdly, all the examples given by Gladstone are acts of volition, a conscious taking of the initiative

[1] Gladstone Papers, Add. MSS 44791, f. 51; Morley, *Gladstone*, vol. i, pp. 874-5.

by a parliamentary leader. In 1876 the initiative was not in Gladstone's hands—probably never before or after was he so much in
the grip of circumstances, so little in control of events; and he was
not a parliamentary leader, both officially and in the sense that the
conditions for his eventual leadership *de facto* necessarily did not
emerge until after the prorogation. Buckle's dramatically Glad-
stonophobe picture of the 'old hunter, once more sniffing the scent',
stalking his noble quarry with cunning patience, waiting for the
moment to strike and pull down his too 'successful rival', is a
legend wholly without foundation; it does Gladstone far too much
credit for perspicacity. Equally legendary are the Gladstonophile
versions: Gladstone's breast, according to Morley, agitated by a
'mighty storm', lit by the 'lurid glare' of the atrocities, determining, according to Sir Philip Magnus, to 'direct public opinion
towards the end which he desired'. The *Horrors* was indeed, in the
phrase of the Darlington committee, 'well-timed'; but only in the
sense that the timing was imposed upon Gladstone by external
pressure, not determined by him as a free agent, a stalking hunter,
an independent exploiter of opportunities. It is in this sense that
his 'call' away from Future Retribution has full and undeniable
validity.

★

The state of Gladstone's mind at this moment is illuminated indirectly but with great clarity in an exchange with his old friend
Sir James Hudson, former ambassador at Turin. A propos of a
recent conversation, Hudson wrote to Gladstone on the day after
the appearance of the *Bulgarian Horrors*: 'Yesterday evening at
Panizzi's I put Fagan on the scent of "Vox Populi" and here is his
answer'—and forwarded to Gladstone Fagan's report on his researches about the 'quotation or proverb "Vox populi vox Dei"'
in *Notes and Queries*, from which he extracted a list of nine references for Gladstone's solemn consideration.[1]

---

[1] Hudson to Gladstone, 7 September 1876, Gladstone Papers, Add. MSS 44451,
f. 142; and Fagan to Hudson, 7 September 1876, *ibid.*, f. 143. Panizzi was a former
Principal Librarian of the British Museum.

4

Gladstone as Reluctant Leader of the Agitation, to 7 October

1 Gladstone at Blackheath

IN 1896 Gladstone wrote in a biographical fragment of his decision to publish the *Bulgarian Horrors*: 'From that time forward until the final consummation in 1879–80 I made the Eastern question the main business of my life. I acted under a strong sense of individual duty without a thought of leadership: nevertheless it made me leader again whether I would or no.'[1] Gladstone's excitement was sufficient to carry him to the point of bringing out the pamphlet, but it did not carry him, for the moment, beyond that point to a full acceptance of the logic of the situation created by his own action. For a month after 6 September Gladstone attempted to evade the fact that he was leader of the atrocities agitation and, in a sense, of the Liberal party. Most of the forward and pushing elements of the party had got the Bulgarian issue as a bit between their teeth; and with Gladstone's tractive weight now added, the party wagon would be dragged along with the agitation no matter how hard the Whigs and 'moderate men' pulled on the brakes. Gladstone, 'deeply sensible', as he wrote on 15 September, that his 'personal position in politics' was 'inconvenient in many ways to the public',[2] attempted to manoeuvre Granville and Hartington into taking up the Eastern question in a manner more or less agreeable to the agitation. He tried to give the government an opportunity to revert, genuinely, to the policy represented by its earlier adhesion to the Andrassy Note. Only when finally convinced that both these aims were hopeless did Gladstone accept the necessity of going forward independently.

[1] Gladstone Papers, Add. MSS 44790, ff. 112–14.
[2] Gladstone to Alfred Austin, 15 September 1876, *ibid.*, Add. MSS 44451, ff. 196–7.

It was this hesitation that made the speech delivered by Gladstone on 9 September[1] to a great demonstration on Blackheath in
his Greenwich constituency so curiously indecisive an event. In
essence, it was a declaration by Gladstone that he still hoped for
satisfaction from the government. His immediate object was to
coax Granville into some kind of open endorsement of his attitude
and action. He completed arrangements for the Blackheath meeting
in Granville's dining-room in Carlton House Terrace, which place
he found more convenient to use as his field headquarters than his
own house in Harley Street. He reported transactions to Granville
with a subtly baited hook: 'The [Greenwich] people asked if you
would go. I said I thought if you did you would like to have the
option of going quietly.'[2] Gladstone confided to his wife: 'Will
Granville go I wonder.' If he did it would be 'a proof that his mind
is working on and that he sees more ripeness in the time'.[3] But
Granville refused to be drawn. Not less than ten thousand people
gathered under dripping umbrellas on Blackheath, but Granville
was not among them, even 'quietly'.[4]

Granville saw little 'ripeness' in the time. He had written to
Hartington at the beginning of the month about the letters he received, as Hartington probably did also, 'reproaching the leaders
of the party for remaining mute'. Granville had not answered
them, and thought it 'very unlikely' that he would 'avail' himself
of 'any opportunity to speak on the matter'. It was a question as
to whether Hartington had 'better do so, or not'.[5] It happened that
Hartington was engaged to speak at the Sheffield Cutlers' dinner,
and supposed he could not avoid saying something about the
'atrocities'. He consulted Granville on the best 'line' to take[6];
and the outcome was that he treated the agitation and Gladstone
very respectfully but yet made no outright condemnation of the
government's Eastern policy. Hartington's own contribution to-

[1] See *Times*, 11 September 1876, p. 10.
[2] Gladstone to Granville, 7 September 1876, Granville Papers, 30, 29/29.
[3] Bassett, *Gladstone to his Wife*, pp. 219–20.
[4] MacColl, perhaps over-anxious in his insistence in 1878 that Gladstone acted
after 'consultation with the leaders of his party', states that Granville was present on
Blackheath (*Three Years of the Eastern Question* (1878), p. 133). Spencer Walpole
seems to have followed MacColl (*The History of Twenty-Five Years*, vol. iv, p. 107).
But no contemporary report mentions Granville's presence; and the *Standard* remarked that Granville and Rupert Carington were expected to have been present,
'but neither was visible' (11 September 1876, p. 3).
[5] Granville to Hartington, 1 September 1876, Devonshire Papers, 340/672.
[6] Hartington to Granville, 3 September 1876, Granville Papers, 30, 29/26.

wards a settlement was a call for a special autumn session of parliament.[1] This, though viewed with distaste by both Gladstone and Granville as an 'intolerable nuisance',[2] did coincide with the desires of agitation leaders like Freeman, MacColl,[3] and Stead. In the *Northern Echo* Stead welcomed Hartington's statement as 'reserved' but on the whole aligning him behind Gladstone.[4] Gladstone himself also interpreted the speech with an eye of faith[5]; but in fact it represented no real advance on Hartington's orthodox Palmerstonian position of 8 February or 31 July.

The scepticism of the Liberal leaders was powerfully reinforced by their Whig associates. Lord Halifax wrote to Granville in a state of disquiet. 'Of course you will see Gladstone before he appears on Blackheath & I hope that you will impress on him the wisdom of looking before he leaps.' The populace, it seemed to Halifax, were 'running a little wild on the Bulgarian atrocities'.[6] Henry Reeve, editor of the *Edinburgh Review*, also wrote indignantly in the same vein.[7] Harcourt, willing enough to attack the government but full of distaste for the possible return of Gladstone to a leading rôle,[8] formed a link between the Whigs and those Radicals such as Dilke who also disliked the idea of Gladstone's return. Dilke wrote to Harcourt after the Sheffield Cutlers' dinner speech: 'Isn't Hartington doing his work splendidly.'[9] However, Lord and Lady Sydney were pleased and proud to put their house at Frognal, Foots Cray, at Gladstone's disposal for the Blackheath meeting, and even tried to persuade Granville to attend.[10] In the event, Sydney was able to report to Granville that the demonstration was a 'great success'; the 'Assemblage was large & respectable. Not Rags but people in Cloth Coats & Top Hats . . .'.[11]

Despite the respectability of the assemblage, the Blackheath demonstration had about it much of the character of a great re-

---

[1] See *Times*, 8 September 1876, p. 8.
[2] Granville to Gladstone, [4] October 1876, Gladstone Papers, Add. MSS 44170, ff. 257–61; and Gladstone to Granville, 7 October 1876, Granville Papers, 30, 29/29.
[3] MacColl to Gladstone, 26 September 1876, Gladstone Papers, Add. MSS 44243, ff. 199–202.   [4] 9 September 1876, p. 2.
[5] Gladstone to Granville, 7 October 1876, Granville Papers, 30, 29/29.
[6] Halifax to Granville, 7 September 1876, *ibid.*, 29/26.
[7] Reeve to Granville, 9 September 1876, *ibid.*
[8] Dilke to Harcourt, 9 September 1876, Dilke Papers, Add. MSS 43890, f. 80.
[9] *Ibid.*
[10] Lady Sydney to Gladstone, 7 September 1876, Gladstone Papers, Add. MSS 44451, f. 144.
[11] Sydney to Granville, 10 September 1876, Granville Papers, 30, 29/26.

vivalist rally.[1] In this respect it exhibited much of the inner nature
of the atrocities agitation. W. T. Stead was an easily impression-
able young man, but it still counts for something that to the end
of his days he placed Blackheath among the most memorable
scenes of his life.[2] Stead travelled down from Darlington in a fever
of anticipation on his 'first political pilgrimage', sustained as he
sped through the dark fen country with visions of Hereward the
Wake and Oliver Cromwell and by thoughts of Gladstone's un-
impeachably clear line of political succession from them.[3] George
Holyoake, who had witnessed Gladstone's first great reception at
the hands of the masses at Newcastle in 1862, came down from
Bedford to hear the 'mighty protest'.[4] Under the spell of enlightenment cast upon him by the *Daily News* report on 'Working Men
and the War in the East', Gladstone made of the Blackheath
demonstration a solemn affirmation of his conviction that the agitation sprang, pure and undefiled by party and political motives,
from the very bedrock of morality and righteousness in public
affairs, the simple, undesigning conscience of the masses.

But the almost religious intensity of the occasion tended, as in
the case of the *Bulgarian Horrors*, to obscure the moderation of its
content. The real significance of the Blackheath speech, as far as
Gladstone's personal relation to the agitation is concerned, lies in
what he did not say, or refused to say. The cry 'We want a leader!'
burst spontaneously from the crowd, ringing out again and again,
according to Stead's report.[5] Gladstone evaded the demand by re-
joining that when a nation had a good purpose in view a leader
would always be found. These words, wrote Stead, were caught
up eagerly by the crowd to mean that Gladstone was willing to

[1] An interesting example of this spirit is a long poem in Wordsworthian blank
verse, presented to Gladstone: *Lines Written by a Young Man*, (*a London Clerk*),
*One of the Multitude which, on Saturday Last, Assembled on Blackheath, to see and to
Hear Mr. Gladstone*. Gladstone Papers, Add. MSS 44451, ff. 172–3.
[2] Estelle Stead, *My Father*, p. 70.
[3] *Ibid.*, pp. 62–3.
[4] Holyoake to Gladstone, 9 September 1876, Gladstone Papers, Add. MSS 44451,
ff. 157–8: 'It was a great & generous thing to come & speak to us in the rain, & mist,
& wind. Voices in the streets speak only of gratitude and gladness. Horror-stricken,
indignant, articulate, but aimless, the nation craved direction it could trust. It seems
now as though the Humanity of the world had spoken in your voice.' See also *The Life
of Hugh Price Hughes* by his daughter (1905), p. 113; G. Lansbury, *My Life* (1928),
p. 40; *A Memoir of the Right Hon. William Edward Hartpole Lecky* by his wife (1909),
p. 112.
[5] *Northern Echo*, 11 September 1876, p. 2. The *Daily Telegraph* report refers to the
'perfectly logical cry' of 'We will have you for our leader' (11 September 1876, p. 2).

take his place at their head,[1] whether or not he actually meant this.[2] Gladstone remained silent in the face of continued importunities. Stead, to whom Gladstone's resignation from the leadership had been a 'personal sorrow, a grief akin to that of bereavement',[3] consoled himself by reflecting that Gladstone at least did not directly repudiate the crowd's salute. He also realised that any decision by Gladstone ultimately to declare himself would depend mainly on the course taken by the government.[4] Perhaps the clearest expression of the paradoxical nature of Gladstone's position in the speech is to be found in the mixture of surprise, relief, and bewilderment evident in the comments of the leading pro-government organs.[5]

Gladstone continued to be importuned privately as well as in public. A workman of Hertford wrote to him on the theme that it was 'time we had a Leader': 'You told us we Must Be up and Doing and we must have our old Statesman for our Leader.'[6] 'O Sir,' cried the Warden of Cavendish College, Cambridge (in his 'private capacity'), 'will you not hear in this great crisis the voice of God in the voice of the people?'[7] There was indeed little likelihood of Gladstone's failing to do this sooner or later, if the interest he had evidently displayed in the *Notes and Queries* references to *Vox populi vox Dei* was any indication.

2 Gladstone and the Liberal Party

Gladstone wrote to Adam, the Liberal Chief Whip, on 4 October 1876:

I am a follower & not a leader in the Liberal party and nothing will induce me to do an act indicative of a desire to change my position. Any such act would be a positive breach of faith on my part towards those whom I importuned as I may say to allow me to retire, and whom I left to undertake a difficult and invidious office.[8]

---

[1] *Daily Telegraph, ibid.*: 'We will go back to you, Mr. Gladstone.'
[2] *Northern Echo*, 11 September 1876, p. 2.
[3] Stead to Gladstone, 23 September 1876, Gladstone Papers, Add. MSS 44303, f. 238.   [4] *Northern Echo*, 11 September 1876, p. 2.
[5] E.g. *Standard*, 11 September 1876, p. 3; *Daily Telegraph*, 11 September 1876, p. 4.
[6] Taylor to Gladstone, 13 September 1876, Gladstone Papers, Add. MSS 44451, ff. 180–1.
[7] T. J. Lawrence to Gladstone, 21 September 1876, *ibid.*, ff. 226–31.
[8] *Ibid.*, Add. MSS 44095, ff. 23–4.

K

Gladstone's problem was, in short, that while the voice of the people was the voice of God, the official voice of the Liberal party remained the voice of the duumvirate, Lords Granville and Harting-ton. The embarrassment which Gladstone felt in his position in relation to the party leaders and to the party as a whole was now matched by a determination to see that the Bulgarian question should have full political justice done to it. This uneasy equilibrium of conflicting feelings, characteristic scruple and reluctance against equally characteristic tenacity and persistence, sets the theme of Gladstone's conduct as a 'follower & not a leader in the Liberal party' not merely for the period immediately after the *Horrors* and Blackheath, but for the years up to 1879–80 also. Nevertheless, though a long drawn out process to its final conclusion, the central issue of the problem was for all practical purposes worked out in the few weeks following 6 September.

Gladstone's difficulty in persuading Granville and Hartington into a more 'advanced' view of the Bulgarian question was much increased by the absence of a strong atrocity-conscious group in the upper levels of the party. The Duke of Argyll alone approached Gladstone in the warmth of his feelings. Lowe was also warm, but his personal hatred of Disraeli was so notorious and the decline of his reputation so complete as to make him a dubious asset at best.[1] Bright's sympathies were, at best, strictly limited. Stafford North-cote, the Chancellor of the Exchequer, fell in with Bright on a railway journey in mid-September and reported to Disraeli: 'He was far from satisfied with Gladstone, though he did not like directly to abuse him; but he tried to impress on me that the true thing for England to do was to withdraw altogether . . . and let "natural forces" have full play.'[2] Harcourt remained essentially Hartingtonian.[3] Neither Childers[4] nor Goschen[5] looked with favour upon the agitation. The peers generally were apathetic.[6]

[1] See Granville to Gladstone, 15 September 1876, *ibid.*, Add. MSS 44170, ff. 247–8; Gladstone to Granville, 16 September 1876, Granville Papers, 30, 29/29; and Ailesbury to Granville, 12 October 1876, *ibid.*, 29/26.

[2] Northcote to Disraeli, 19 September 1876, Disraeli Papers.

[3] See Harcourt to Granville, 10 October 1876, Granville Papers 30, 29/29.

[4] Childers, *Childers*, vol. i, pp. 242–3; though it appears that Childers did preside at a protest meeting at Knottingley (*Times*, 27 September 1876, p. 6).

[5] A. D. Elliot, *The Life of George Joachim Goschen, First Viscount Goschen* (1911), vol. i, p. 183.

[6] There were twenty Whig or Liberal peers among the conveners of the Eastern Question Conference of December 1876, who could thus be regarded as sympathetic to the atrocities agitation: Acton, Ailesbury, Airlie, Blachford, Camoys, Cowper, De

As Argyll expostulated to Granville, his firm belief was that had he been in London when the Blue Book of 10 August appeared, and attacked the government's Eastern policy on the basis of it, he would have met with no support on his own side of the Lords, 'and wld. probably have been replied to by Kimberley!'[1] Kimberley's view, in truth, was that while the Palmerstonian policy seemed clearly 'played out', and while the government had mismanaged the affair badly, transition to a new policy of patronising the Eastern Christians must be 'cautiously managed'; and meanwhile the 'violent & unreasoning agitation' rendered the question 'immensely more difficult'.[2]

Forster, who made the only really weighty Liberal front-bench speech attacking the government other than Gladstone's speech of 31 July, is a special case. There seems little doubt that he thrust himself forward in the Bulgarian question at least partly, and possibly primarily, for the purpose of asserting his political status against Hartington. He still smarted from the rejection of his claims to the party leadership in 1875. He went to great lengths to assert himself in the Eastern question; as far, in fact, as Constantinople itself.[3] This ostentation caused comment, though Forster insisted that his conscience did not rebuke him.[4] Joseph Chamberlain, the political spokesman of the irreconcilable Nonconformists who could never forgive Forster for his 'treachery' over the Education Act, needed no convincing that Forster's tactic in the Bulgarian question was to 'dish the radicals' by bidding for 'the whigs & moderates'.[5] Whatever Forster's motives may have been in the actions he subsequently took, their effect certainly gave colour to Chamberlain's suspicions.

Lacking support from the front benches, Gladstone was yet unable, with parliament prorogued, to mobilise a back-bench pressure group. In any case, the session of 1877 revealed that Tabley, De Vesci, Ducie, Durham, Fitzhardinge, Lyttelton, Kinnaird, Lanerton, Monck, Portsmouth, Robartes, Russell, Waveney, and Westminster. Argyll, though not technically a convener, could also be included. A few others, like Spencer, were Gladstonian in sympathy, but remained reserved.

[1] Argyll to Granville, 25 October 1876, Granville Papers, 30, 29/29.
[2] Kimberley to Ripon, 23 September 1876, Ripon Papers, Add. MSS 43522, ff. 253–6.
[3] He was in Budapest, on a vacation tour, when he heard news of the agitation, and decided to go on rather than back (*Times*, 9 October 1876, p. 9).
[4] T. Wemyss Reid, *Life of the Right Honourable William Edward Forster* (1888), vol. ii, p. 126.
[5] Chamberlain to Dilke, 10 October 1876, Dilke Papers, Add. MSS 43885, f. 49.

Gladstone over-estimated greatly the amount of thoroughgoing support he could call on from the rank and file. And the situation was complicated further by the fact that those at the head of the section of the party more or less aligned with Gladstone on the Eastern question were Radicals like Mundella, Fawcett, and Chamberlain, men eager for Gladstone to supplant Granville and Hartington. Eventually, in 1877, Gladstone found himself obliged, for the sake of the Eastern question, to strike a bargain with the most important of them, Chamberlain[1]; and this was certainly not the least significant of the consequences implicit in the situation of September 1876.

Chamberlain himself had only very recently joined the Liberal party in the House of Commons, but he entered it with nothing to learn. With Birmingham solidly behind him and through his control of the Education League, which he was preparing to use as the nucleus of a national Liberal organisation, Chamberlain was a major political force in his own right. In conjunction with John Morley of the *Fortnightly Review*, he was planning the coming Radical campaign on the basis of disestablishment and the county franchise.[2] But the Bulgarian atrocities provided even better grist to Chamberlain's mill. He does not appear to have paid any attention to the Eastern question or the special Bulgarian aspect of it for its own sake. All his comments were related strictly and pragmatically to the domestic implications involved in the question. 'What a hole Dizzy has put his Party into!' he wrote to Dilke on 26 September. 'At this rate the Liberals will be in again before many years are over.'[3] This attitude was reflected in Morley, whose cool approach in the *Fortnightly* contrasts strikingly with the moral excitement of Hutton in the *Spectator*.

Chamberlain calculated that Gladstone, if not exactly usable, could not fail to be useful. He wrote to Dilke: 'If he were to come back for a few years (he can't continue in public life for very much longer) he would probably do much for us, & pave the way for more.'[4] Chamberlain's confidences in this matter to Dilke were indiscreet, for Dilke took the Eastern question seriously for its own sake. Though willing to work with Chamberlain for the success

[1] See below, pp. 268 ff.
[2] F. W. Hirst, *Early Life & Letters of John Morley* (1927), vol. ii, pp. 3–6.
[3] Dilke Papers, Add. MSS 43885, f. 46.
[4] Chamberlain to Dilke, 10 October 1876, *ibid.*, f. 49.

of the Radical programme, he also took his Radicalism too seriously to imagine that Gladstone would be its unwitting agent.[1] Dilke reported to Harcourt that Chamberlain wished Gladstone ' "formally to resume the reins"—and shows profound dislike of Hartington, founded on no reasons at all'.[2] This confirmed Harcourt's suspicions that the 'extreme crew' were using the opportunity provided by the atrocities agitation to demand the deposition of Granville and Hartington and the recall of Gladstone; which consideration he passed on to Granville.[3] Harcourt remained confident, however, that Gladstone was a spent force, and that there would be no 'return from Elba'.[4]

Harcourt's and Dilke's hopes of keeping Gladstone out were ruined by the intransigence of both the Whigs and the government, who thus cancelled each other out and let Chamberlain's thesis emerge victorious by default. As Gladstone tried to entice Granville into patronage of the Blackheath affair, so Carnarvon attempted to draw Disraeli back to a more conciliatory attitude. Carnarvon had close connections with the agitation, both as brother of Auberon Herbert and through him well known to Mundella, and as fellow High Churchman and intimate friend of Liddon. Carnarvon also had a long record of opposition to Disraeli, notably over the franchise reform of 1867 and the Public Worship Regulation Act of 1874—opposition which Disraeli repaid with steady contempt.[5] On 5 September, 'so impressed' with what he heard 'on all sides' as to the 'general feeling with regard to the Turkish excesses', Carnarvon felt 'bound' to write to Disraeli:

I have been for a long time past, as you are aware anxious on the subject. . . . But after every deduction has been made, I feel satisfied that the public feeling on the subject is very strong, that it exists in classes which we cannot afford to overlook, and that it will grow, unless some early means of checking it are found. If indeed it runs its course much further, it will, I fear, become ungovernable and will either drive us into some precipitate and undignified course or will end in a serious catastrophe.

Some 'decided action' to reassure the public mind was, Carnarvon

[1] Dilke to Chamberlain, 5 October 1876, *ibid.*, f. 48.
[2] Dilke to Harcourt, 16 October 1876, *ibid.*, Add. MSS 43890, f. 90.
[3] Harcourt to Granville, 10 October 1876, Granville Papers, 30, 29/29.
[4] Harcourt to Dilke, 10 October 1876, Dilke Papers, *ibid.*, f. 82.
[5] E.g. Buckle, *Disraeli*, vol. ii, p. 815.

insisted, essential. The government must take the initiative; it would not do to be dragged at the tail of a European combination. Supposed 'connivance' in the horrors—'which admit of no doubt' —must be scotched immediately. Surely Baring's report had arrived by now? But it has not been communicated to Carnarvon. Could not a cabinet be called?[1]

Stafford Northcote had also written on 30 August from Balmoral, where he reported the Queen 'excited'; and advocated 'some demonstration' to convince the public that the government 'seemed' to be working for better things; otherwise their hand might be forced.[2] Thus he argued again, at greater length, on 2 September, and once more on the 7th. And Salisbury had earlier led off with a scathing indictment of Elliot's 'stupidity'[3] as a prelude to putting forward a comprehensive scheme for a completely new Eastern policy.[4]

But Disraeli would not be budged. He had accepted the advisability of Derby's warning to the Turks of 22 August; but he would concede nothing substantial under overt coercion of a popular agitation. His comments on 'little Carnarvon' were sardonic; and he found in the inert Derby, who was shown all the correspondence, a willing collaborator in a negative policy of doing as little as possible. The Turks, as Derby pointed out, had already been most sternly reprimanded; the Foreign Office was actually preparing certain proposals towards a possible measure of local autonomy for the Christians; and there could be no official statement on the 'atrocities' until Baring's report arrived. So what more was there to be done?[5] Derby added an echo of Disraeli's steady opinion: 'We have nothing to unsay or undo, and we must not make things look as if we had.'[6]

*

The government's answer to the invitation made by Gladstone at Blackheath took the form of a reception by Derby of some workmen's deputations at the Foreign Office. Derby defended the policy and good faith of the government elaborately, with further disingenuous arguments about the fleet at Besika Bay and the matter of

[1] Disraeli Papers.
[2] *Ibid.*
[3] Salisbury to Disraeli, 29 August 1876, *ibid.*
[4] See below, p. 131.
[5] Derby to Disraeli, 5 September 1876, Disraeli Papers.
[6] Derby to Disraeli, 8 September 1876, *ibid.*

noral support. He declined to be a party to what he called 'quack' chemes for Christian autonomy which overlooked the ethno-ogical complexities and international difficulties of the problem. Ie put out a vague hint that constructive proposals would shortly be put forward for the consideration of the Porte.[1]

Derby was acclaimed in government circles as having 'thrown lust in their eyes successfully'.[2] Derby himself was well pleased with his effort, contemptuous of 'cranks and pacifists', irritated only by the one man who made himself 'objectionable': 'a parson, one Denton, who had got in without belonging to the deputation, and insisted on being heard'.[3] Disraeli was convinced that Derby's explanations would 'quench' the agitation[4]; but neither Salisbury nor his friend Carnarvon were reassured, though conceding that Derby's statement, for the moment, was 'as much as can be said'.[5]

Gladstone, however, was unwilling to make even this concession. He declined to be blinded by dust, and agreed with Panizzi's judgment of Derby's statements as 'mystifications'. Under cover of them', he told Granville, 'they may contrive to act in the old spirit. There is nothing for it but "the polls".'[6] Gladstone was clearly moving towards disillusionment with aspirations of satisfaction from the government. 'Polls' meant, for immediate purposes, the Bucks. by-election to be held on 21 September. Gladstone's watchword was now 'Bucks Bucks Bucks'.[7] He appreciated fully that the prospect of winning was remote[8]; but a notable reduction of Disraeli's former majority would be worth working for. Gladstone gave careful and fussy instructions to Granville as to how the campaign should be conducted. 'Pray', he concluded, on a curiously imperious note, as if once more issuing directives in cabinet as Prime Minister, 'continue to give your mind to this.'[9]

Gladstone was looking also, however, beyond Bucks. to 'polls' in a wider sense. He kept pressing and coaxing Granville with what must have been the rather irritating technique of assuming that Granville was really in substantial agreement with him:

---

[1] *Times*, 12 September 1876, p. 8.
[2] Hardinge, *Carnarvon*, vol. ii, p. 338.
[3] Derby to Disraeli, 12 September 1876, Disraeli Papers.
[4] Zetland, *Letters of Disraeli to Lady Bradford and Lady Chesterfield*, vol. ii, p. 74.
[5] Salisbury to Carnarvon, 13 September 1876, Salisbury Papers.
[6] Gladstone to Granville, 14 September 1876, Granville Papers, 30, 29/29.
[7] *Ibid.*   [8] *Ibid.*   [9] *Ibid.*

'Ought you not however to think of County meetings now
Yorkshire should begin. Middlesex would I should think be safe
Lancashire ought to be well considered but I am not so sure
whether it is safe to lead off with.'[1] As it happened, the county
meeting idea would have been fruitless in any case. Lords
Lieutenant, gentry, squires, and rural parsons remained, predict
ably perhaps, unaffected by emotional zeal for the Bulgarians. The
significant point is Gladstone's deliberate assumption of Gran
ville's good will towards the agitation. He pressed Granville
again: 'I suppose the Pope has kept Ireland quiet. But a line to
Law[2] would cause them I think to move in the North.'[3]

This assumption on Gladstone's part was unwarranted. It is
extremely unlikely that Granville ever thought about county
meetings or took the cue to write to Hugh Law. As he told the
Duke of Argyll, in the course of rebuking him gently for his 'rather
ostentatious repudiation of party ties', he could not agree with
Gladstone's wish to turn the Turks out of Bulgaria; and even if it
were possible, he could conceive nothing less desirable at the
moment. Nor could Granville agree with Gladstone's tendency to
make 'too light' of giving the Russians a 'material standpoint' in
European Turkey and inviting them to advance. Nor was Granville
at all convinced that the anti-Turkish feeling in the country had
superseded entirely the traditional anti-Russian sentiment; and he
feared a reaction which the government could exploit.[4]

Gladstone also made a determined effort to carry Bright with
him.

It may seem inconsistent in me to have been very active up to a certain
point and then to speak of stopping short. This however is as I think my
unavoidable position. My old Crimean responsibilities forced me forward
my position in the party as a leader who has abdicated holds me back.
In my original pamphlet . . . I did all in my power to keep off the ground
of party, for if the matter is decided on that ground I have some fear of
being dragged out of a retirement which though partial I had made real

Gladstone desired therefore 'to leave the further prosecution of
this great business', if he could, in the hands of 'others'. Bright

---

[1] Ibid.
[2] Hugh Law, Liberal M.P. for Londonderry, former Attorney-General for Ireland
[3] Gladstone to Granville, 14 September 1876, Granville Papers, 30, 29/29.
[4] Lord E. Fitzmaurice, The Life of Lord Granville (1905), vol. ii, pp. 165–6.

position, Gladstone pointed out, was 'far more free'. Bright had neither the 'old responsibility' to drive him forward, 'nor exactly the same limiting considerations' to hold him back.[1] Bright, however, felt himself no less bowed down under a sense of limiting considerations; and clearly, as indeed he had already indicated to Gladstone,[2] he was not to be lured into this 'great business'.

Gladstone remained very unwilling to come forward again personally. He was being pressed strongly by a group in London, including Denton, to attend a City meeting being arranged at the Guildhall.[3] Gladstone declined this and all other applications which, as he related virtuously to Granville, he had not 'a proper capacity to appear in'.[4] The Guildhall meeting committee persisted to the point of flushing Gladstone out at Hawarden itself. Trapped, Gladstone was forced to hear their plea. Unsatisfied with his apology, they contended that he had a duty in this question as the 'leader of the whole of England', and no mere party. Gladstone had to confess that he could plead no prior engagements, no reasons of health. But he protested that after his efforts so far, he did not want to be accused of 'over-activity', which the public would soon get suspicious of 'on his part'. His decision, he insisted, was irrevocable.[5]

For all his vehement firmness, Gladstone remained extremely restless, warm for action, yet apologetic. If he spoke again, Gladstone told Granville on 14 September, he would finally be obliged to deal with the question of the attitude of the government, 'which throws upon us if we acquiesce [in it] all the responsibility of what may happen'.[6] Gladstone was resigned to the fact that sooner or later he would have to 'acquit' himself by getting this out. He noted, as an additional hint for Granville's benefit, that Argyll was soon to speak at Glasgow. 'He is full, and warm.'[7] Argyll, in fact, was, as he told Granville, 'boiling', and not at all inclined to listen to Granville's 'word in season'. He had a 'rattling good' speech in his head, and though he had never before tried to 'act

[1] Gladstone to Bright, 27 September 1876, Bright Papers, Add. MSS 43385, ff. 257–9.
[2] See below, pp. 139–40.
[3] Denton to Gladstone, 14 September 1876, Gladstone Papers, Add. MSS 44451, f. 187.
[4] Gladstone to Granville, 14 September 1876, Granville Papers, 30, 29/29.
[5] Times, 16 September 1876, p. 10.
[6] Gladstone to Granville, 14 September 1876, Granville Papers, 30, 29/29.
[7] Ibid.

agitator', he was going to try now. 'Speaking for myself,' he added, 'I mean to speak freely. In substance I agree with Gladstone.'[1]

Argyll's brushing aside of Granville's attempt to restrain him undoubtedly encouraged Gladstone to keep steady pressure on Granville. He concluded his letter of 14 September to Granville on a note of apology which became increasingly present as the days went by: 'At Wycombe Abbey I had an Address from the Liberal Association and could not refuse to write them an answer to be used as they may find it discreet.'[2] But behind the reserve and apology there was always present a sense of impending action. Gladstone could not refrain from writing to *The Times* and *Daily News* of 16 September assaulting Derby's 'mystifications' of the 11th on eight counts,[3] and adding support for Hartington's call for an autumn session 'as a lever', as he explained to Granville.[4] The pro-government press greeted this letter as a most ominous sign that Gladstone was preparing to jettison the moderation he had displayed at Blackheath.[5] Certainly it meant that Gladstone would not henceforth be much restrained by considerations of the need to give the government an adequate opportunity to reformulate a more acceptable Eastern policy. It was encouraging also that Granville could find no fault with it.[6]

Gladstone's next move was to embark on a series of private country-house visits in the north. He still adhered to his doctrine against 'over-activity'; and his motives in undertaking such a tour were undoubtedly more innocent than otherwise. But it did not require much perspicacity to predict—and Hartington so predicted[7]—that a 'private' tour by Gladstone in the north in such circumstances had no chance of remaining private. Possibly Gladstone had half-consciously at the back of his mind a vague idea of testing the state of public feeling and perhaps helping to jog Granville a little into a less negative approach.

The situation was getting too tense for Hartington's comfort. Delaying only to attend the Doncaster races, he departed for Con-

---

[1] Argyll to Granville, 15 September 1876, *ibid.*
[2] Gladstone to Granville, *ibid.*   [3] *Times*, 16 September 1876, p. 5.
[4] Gladstone to Granville, 16 September 1876, Granville Papers, 30, 29/29.
[5] E.g. *Pall Mall Gazette*, 18 September 1876, pp. 1–2.
[6] Granville to Gladstone, 16 September 1876, Gladstone Papers, Add. MSS 44170, ff. 249–50.
[7] Granville to Gladstone, 15 September 1876, *ibid.*, ff. 247–8.

tantinople via Vienna on the night of 14 September, 'with the Duchess of Manchester, accompanied by the Duke', as *The Times* chose to put it, to Chamberlain's rather malicious amusement.[1] Gladstone apparently had no inkling of this escapade; he asked Granville whether by a slip of the pen he had written 'Constantinople' instead of 'Kimbolton'.[2] Harcourt commented to Granville: 'H. did (as he always does) the wisest thing he could in going away. But the situation is very uncomfortable.'[3] Apart from the question of comfort, Hartington was also undoubtedly influenced by the example of Forster; and very probably was being egged on in this respect by his ambitious mistress. Forster obviously would return, and perhaps consciously intended to return, as the great Eastern expert. By following him Hartington could trump Forster's trick. Also, of course, there could just be a little practical value in such a tour; Delane himself at one time seriously considered going, but decided finally that he was really more at the centre of things in London.[4]

Hartington saw Granville briefly before departing and expressed anxiety that Gladstone's going north would cause demonstrations that would 'put the rest of the country the wrong way'. Granville immediately passed this consideration on to Gladstone, though probably with little hope that it would deter him.[5] Other Whigs were nervous about Gladstone's attitude and intentions. Lord Bessborough told Granville that Gladstone seemed to have 'gone wild'. No doubt the Turks were 'naughty'; but Lord Bessborough understood that the Christians were just as bad, so he could not 'quite go' with his party in the 'present crisis'.[6] It must have been galling for Granville to see the 'party' thus naively identified with Gladstone's viewpoint rather than his own. Bessborough was pleased to see that Granville had declined to attend the Guildhall demonstration on the grounds that the non-partisan and spontaneous character of the agitation must not be compromised[7]; but many Whigs failed to be reassured. The Roths-

---

[1] Chamberlain to Dilke, 10 October 1876, Dilke Papers, Add. MSS 43885, f. 49.
[2] Gladstone to Granville, 16 September 1876, Granville Papers, 30, 29/29.
[3] Harcourt to Granville, 10 October 1876, *ibid.*
[4] Delane to Granville, 12 September 1876, *ibid.*, 29/26.
[5] Granville to Gladstone, 15 September 1876, Gladstone Papers, Add. MSS 44170, 247–8.
[6] Bessborough to Granville, 15 September [1876], Granville Papers, 30, 29/26.
[7] *Ibid.*

childs, resentful at the pressure put on them in Bucks., were prac
tically in open revolt, and by the beginning of October had 'gon
Tory altogether'.[1]

The Liberal figures in the Bucks. election were creditable, bu
the Conservatives held the seat, much to the Queen's relief.
Granville pointed the moral to Gladstone that anti-Russian feeling
was still strong and that, according to reports he had received
many Liberal votes had been given to the Conservative candidate.
He pointed out that the Liberal party would probably face simila
defections in a vote of censure in a special autumn session, cer
tainly more than from the Conservative side.[4] Such Conservativ
participation in the agitation as there had been was now dwindlin
rapidly. Sydney wrote to Granville on 2 October that a propose
non-partisan meeting at Bromley would have to become a part
meeting 'as the Tories have backed out of their Philanthropi
views'. He added that the Liberals themselves were far from united
Some did not like to 'force the Executive in Foreign Policy'
others thought that the time had gone by for sensational meetings
Sydney himself agreed with the latter, and also objected to
'Slavonic Empire'. 'I confess I do not see', he concluded, 'that w
should do much good by an Autumn Session. . . . I think we ar
playing the Russian game too much & do not care for mor
meetings.'[5] Harcourt was full of accounts of the restlessness of th
'Brooksites' and the 'Commercial men like Norwood Samuels &
C. who find their pecuniary interests greatly damaged by th
present state of things taking very adversely to the agitation'.
And Hartington reported from Constantinople to his father th
Duke that Christian autonomy was out of the question. He unde
stood (or so the British consul in Rustchuk assured him, for h
never himself actually visited any Christian areas) that th
Christians were 'utterly unfit for public duties of any kind'.[7]

[1] Harcourt to Granville, 12 October 1876, ibid., 29/29.
[2] Queen to Disraeli, 22 September 1876, Disraeli Papers.
[3] See Grenfell to Granville, 23 September 1876, Granville Papers, 30, 29/26. C
six Whig or Liberal voters in one parish, two Whigs and two Liberals voted for th
Conservative; and one Catholic Liberal did not vote.
[4] Granville to Gladstone, [5] October 1876, Gladstone Papers, Add. MSS 4417
ff. 257–61.
[5] Sydney to Granville, 2 October 1876, Granville Papers, 30, 29/26.
[6] Harcourt to Granville, 10 October 1876, ibid., 29/29. Norwood was an 'extensiv
shipowner' trading with Russia, in which trade the freight rates had apparently 'rise
enormously'.
[7] Hartington to Devonshire, 25 September 1876, Devonshire Papers, 340/674.

It was an unusual High Whig indeed, like the old Marquess of
Ailesbury, who sympathised outspokenly with the agitation and
with Gladstone's efforts to influence the party in the direction of
policy of emancipation. Contriving to button-hole Hartington
in the Doncaster race-stand as the latter was donning his overcoat
to start for Constantinople, Ailesbury took the opportunity to
assert bluntly that it was to be 'regretted very much' that Hartington and Granville had both remained cold to the agitation.[1]
Ailesbury later told Granville that his rôle should have been to
encourage Derby into right paths; and Granville's silence seemed
to 'discountenance' the agitation which alone could exert sufficient
pressure to make such encouragement effective.[2]

★

With Hartington prudently retired with his 'Harem'[3] in the
East, Argyll 'full and warm' in Glasgow, and Gladstone becoming
the centre of a furious movement in the north, Disraeli made his
first move. His immediate object was to make sure of the Bucks.
election. To assist in this cause Baring's report was at last published.[4]

The *Report by Mr. Baring on the Bulgarian Insurrection of 1876*[5]
made a generally bad impression. Those who hoped to find in it
substantial contradiction of Schuyler's report and the *Daily News*
dispatches were disappointed. It corroborated the facts alleged
against the Turks; but in so querulous and graceless a manner as
to disgust even the *Saturday Review*.[6] There can be no doubt, however, that the explanation of what the *Review* called the 'puzzling
delay'[7] in its publication was Disraeli's calculation that it would
be useful in Bucks. Its superficial aspect as the unmasking of a
Pan-Slav plot could be exploited before the less obvious fact that it
confirmed the details of the atrocities had time to make a deep
impression. Some Liberals for a brief moment thought that in
publishing it on the eve of the election Disraeli had played into
their hands[8]; but Disraeli did not make mistakes like that.

[1] Ailesbury to Granville, 12 October 1876, Granville Papers, 30, 29/26.
[2] *Ibid.*
[3] Harcourt to Dilke, 10 October 1876, Dilke Papers, Add. MSS 43890, f. 82.
[4] It came out as a supplement to the *London Gazette*, 19 September 1876.
[5] Schuyler's report, to indicate the contrast in approach, is entitled *Report by Mr.
Schuyler on the Bulgarian Atrocities.*   [6] 23 September 1876, p. 369.   [7] *Ibid.*
[8] Carington to Gladstone, 20 September 1876, Gladstone Papers, Add. MSS
44451, ff. 224–5.

At Aylesbury on 20 September, in a speech of deliberate vio
lence 'much admired' by the Queen,[1] Disraeli used Baring's repor
as the basis of an assertion to the effect that the atrocities in Bul
garia were the work of the 'Secret Societies of Europe'.[2] Dis
daining to pretend that the Eastern policy of the government ha
the support of the nation, Disraeli defied the agitation and de
nounced Gladstone's activities as 'worse than any of those Bul
garian atrocities which now occupy attention'.[3]

This 'outrage'[4] put into extreme peril any chance of concilia
tion between the government and the agitation on the basis of th
instructions by Derby to Elliot, made public on 21 September
outlining a scheme for a very modest degree of local administra
tive autonomy for the Christians.[5] This, though very far from th
substantial political autonomy or tributary status demanded b
the agitation, was at least susceptible to the interpretation tha
the government had begun to follow the path marked out for
by Gladstone.[6] Even Disraeli came near to allowing somethin
like this when he wrote to Salisbury: 'Our great object, wh. Derb
& myself have had during what Ld Overstone calls "a franti
ebullition of public excitement", has never been to admit that w
have changed our policy, & that we have adopted the views of th
Opposition. This greatly irritates them. . . .'[7] Disraeli had, in fac
simply covered a minor tactical withdrawal by the smokescreen o
his Aylesbury outburst.

[1] Queen to Disraeli, 22 September 1876, Disraeli Papers.
[2] Seton-Watson, *Disraeli, Gladstone and the Eastern Question*, p. 89, observ
severely and justly on Buckle's omission of this phrase in his version of the spee
(*Disraeli*, vol. ii, pp. 936–9). That Disraeli was perfectly serious in this interpretatio
is indicated by the letter of 29 September to Lady Bradford (Zetland, *Letters of Di
raeli to Lady Bradford and Lady Chesterfield*, vol. ii, p. 78). Professor Harris's doub
on this point (*Britain and the Bulgarian Horrors*, pp. 317–18) are hardly warrante
especially as he seems to think that in addressing the Royal and Central Buck
Agricultural Association Disraeli was talking down to 'yokels'.
[3] *Times*, 21 September 1876, p. 9.
[4] See Lawrence to Gladstone, 21 September 1876, Gladstone Papers, Add. MS
44451, ff. 226–3, and Baring-Gould to Gladstone, 23 September 1876, *ibid.*, f. 238.
[5] Derby to Elliot, 21 September 1876, *Turkey*, XC (1877), no. 316.
[6] See e.g. H. E. Carlisle, *A Selection from the Correspondence of Abraham Haywar
Q.C.* (1886), pp. 265–6. Stratford de Redcliffe, who remained throughout in gener
agreement with Gladstone (see his letter in *Times* of 9 September 1876, p. 8, and
Gladstone, 10 September 1876, Gladstone Papers, Add. MSS 44451, ff. 161–2, a
14 September, *ibid.*, ff. 190–3), wrote to Gladstone on 29 October 1876 (*ibid.*, Ad
MSS 44452, ff. 88–9): 'Many mouths to my regret have been opened against yo
pamphlet & speeches, but no one, I think, can deny you the merit of having draw
from our Foreign Secretary his instructions of September 21 to Sir H. Elliot.'
[7] Disraeli to Salisbury, 26 September 1876, Salisbury Papers.

In any case, Derby's offer was too little and too late, despite Gladstone's eagerness to grasp at any straw promising a fresh departure which '*may* give a wholly new turn to the affair'.[1] As Freeman pointed out, it would have been creditable a year earlier, but by September 1876 was quite inadequate to satisfy either the Eastern Christians or the agitation in England.[2] And Salisbury pressed for more: 'The Bucks election shows that the agitation has not been without effect on our party', he wrote to Disraeli. 'It is clear enough that the traditional Palmerstonian policy is at an end.' Derby's proposals of the 21st were good enough for an 'emergency', but much more would be required for a permanent arrangement. Salisbury went on to outline a comprehensive project for a 'Protector of Christians' to be nominated by the concert and appointed by the Porte, with adequate powers, who would in turn nominate Christian governors for provinces and make subsidiary arrangements for autonomous provincial councils.[3] Derby blenched at this 'large and new' scheme: 'It amounts to a new constitution for the Turkish empire.'[4] Disraeli would not hear of going beyond the almost derisory proposals of the 21st; anything more would make the government look 'contemptible'. A 'great reaction', he assured Salisbury, would soon set in.[5]

★

Aylesbury certainly diminished greatly Gladstone's lingering hopes for a change of heart on the part of the government. Despite Derby's statement, as Gladstone remarked to Bright, it was 'not possible to assume as yet that the Government has come up to the mark'. Gladstone was now convinced that a special autumn session would be necessary; only 'within the walls of Parliament by hook or by crook we can force them forward'. Gladstone insisted that he would 'very much rather they should come forward without it', for he was 'selfishly anxious' to avoid a 'ministerial crisis', though he could not say that it would in his judgment be a 'public

[1] Gladstone to Bright, 27 September 1876, Bright Papers. Add. MSS 43385, f. 257–9.
[2] *Daily News*, 17 October 1876, p. 6.
[3] Salisbury to Disraeli, 23 September 1876, Disraeli Papers.
[4] Derby to Disraeli, 26 September 1876, *ibid.*
[5] Disraeli to Salisbury, 26 September 1876, Salisbury Papers.

evil'. He coaxed Bright in the same manner as he coaxed Granville: 'It may be a question whether a county meeting or two, say
in York & Middlesex, would now be advisable.'[1]

Meanwhile, Gladstone's round of northern visits threatened to
become a triumphal progress. He described to Frank Hill of the
Daily News his impressions of the immensely strong popular
feeling in the north and how he was having the 'utmost difficulty'
in preventing his visits from changing into a 'tour of propagan-
dism: which under the circumstances would be extremely objectionable'.[2] He refused numerous invitations to appear or speak on
the grounds of avoiding political 'notoriety', a consideration, he
insisted, which applied 'in a peculiar manner' to himself.[3] In particular, he declared that he would not let himself be provoked into
public altercation by Disraeli's Aylesbury speech. In reply to a
committee organising a workmen's meeting in St James's Hall,
he announced that, now that he had laid his views before his constituents and the public, the question ought to be left to the 'calm
but resolute' consideration of the country.[4]

In fact Gladstone found it impossible to let Disraeli's provoca-
tion pass wholly without protest.[5] At Staindrop station in South
Durham, on the 23rd, he allowed himself to be 'carried away'
into self-vindication[6] by the frantic importunity of the crowd. His
main theme clearly pointed a moral for Granville. He protested
against Disraeli's demand, in effect, that the Liberals should efface
themselves as a party on the Bulgarian question. If the Liberal
party had been at fault, Gladstone asserted—and here he spoke
with an only too full consciousness of his own fault—it had been
in the direction of 'too great reluctance, too great reserve, too
great tardiness'.[7]

[1] Gladstone to Bright, 27 September 1876, Bright Papers. Add. MSS 43385,
ff. 257–9.
[2] Gladstone to Hill, 28 September 1876, Gladstone Papers, Add. MSS 44451, f. 258.
[3] Gladstone to Melrose, 27 September 1876, *ibid.*, ff. 256–7.
[4] *Times*, 27 September 1876, p. 6.
[5] Stead was convinced that Disraeli must have been under the influence of strong
drink. 'It would be charitable to think so', he suggested to Gladstone (21 September
1876, Gladstone Papers, Add. MSS 44303, f. 237). Gladstone declined to comment
on the suggestion, having been 'too much in personal conflict on political matters with
Lord B. to be altogether a fair judge of incidents connected with his utterances' (to
Stead, 21 September 1876, *ibid.*, ff. 235–6).
[6] *Times*, 26 September 1876, p. 7.
[7] *Ibid.*, 25 September 1876, p. 6. See also Ramsay, secretary of the Blaydon Open
Air Demonstration, to Gladstone, 23 September 1876, Gladstone Papers, Add. MSS
44451, ff. 246–7.

Staindrop was a premonitory indication that Gladstone's restraint was wearing thin. He wrote to Granville of his many refusals to address public meetings, but was careful to make allowance for prospective contingencies: at any time 'a local case might arise'; and 'a new question has come up, raised by Dizzy's declaration that he is not backed by the country conjoined with the fact that they are persevering in a disapproved policy without dissolving or consulting Parliament'. And Gladstone's particular desire was to hear what Granville was now thinking on the Bulgarian question and whether he had 'advanced' any further in considering the matter, 'that I may have regard to it even in charging my pocket pistols in the shape of short letters which I cannot altogether avoid writing & which sometimes struggle into notice'.[1] It was clear that Gladstone's demand for 'decisive measures' would eventually force a more or less definite breach with Granville.

The Times was quick—ominously quick—to see the implications of Staindrop, and press them heavily upon Gladstone. 'To rouse the country against the Ministry without being prepared, if necessary, to accept the place and task of the Ministry would be unworthy of a serious politician.'[2] Delane was beginning to trim again. He emphasised now the need to give the government time and freedom to implement its policy. He had already congratulated Granville for the 'safe-footed caution' which had kept Granville out of 'the pools into which others have stepped'.[3] Staindrop was a small, but a very deep and splashy pool indeed. One of those spattered with mud was Lord Halifax. Alarmed, he wrote off to Granville full of misgiving that Gladstone would not 'do himself much good' by what he said. 'One outbreak of his feeling might have passed—but it has come now, to what quiet people even on our side may not unjustly characterise as an agitation.'[4]

Granville's attitude matched Delane's. He declined to accept Ailesbury's thesis that though Gladstone's idea of a direct parliamentary challenge to the government was unwise, 'Pressure but above all *unanimous* pressure from our side . . . is what we want'. He refused also Ailesbury's advice to express publicly some kind

[1] Gladstone to Granville, 3 October 1876, Granville Papers, 30, 29/29.
[2] *Times*, 26 September 1876, p. 7. See also *Saturday Review*, 30 September 1876, pp. 408–9.
[3] Delane to Granville, 12 September 1876, Granville Papers, 30, 29/26.
[4] Halifax to Granville, 25 September 1876, *ibid.*

of approval of Gladstone's efforts.[1] Forster returned from Constantinople early in October as a further buttress to Granville's
negative attitude. He impressed Granville with his conclusion that
autonomy for the Christians would be impossible to establish
without a military occupation by the powers.[2] In general he was
pessimistic; and this coincided conclusively with the judgment
agreed on by both Granville and Ailesbury that Gladstone was
'*much too sanguine*'[3] as to the readiness of the party as a whole to
go ahead in a policy of emancipation in co-operation with Russia.
In reply to Gladstone's request for a statement of the 'advance'
of his outlook, Granville rejected the idea of pressing the government with a demand for a special session and suggested that Gladstone keep himself quiet: 'Your progress in the North has been
an immense triumph, & the greater for the privacy which you have
endeavoured to maintain. But if I were you, I should continue to
avoid further utterances for the present moment, which appears
critical.'[4]

This uncompromising negative forced Gladstone to declare
himself. He remained extremely sensitive on the personal level:
His 'repeated assurances', Ailesbury reported to Granville, 'that
he looked upon you as the Leader of the Liberal party were quite
touching to listen to'.[5] But he realised that the logic of his opinions
and his conscience made it essential for him to assert full freedom
of action. He was not impressed by Forster's doubts. 'Reflection',
he told Granville, had already brought him to the conclusion that
'in all likelihood, after the practical emancipation of the three
Turkish Provinces, a temporary military occupation on a small
scale might be necessary, for purposes of police'. He had already
been 'driven', he added, to the conclusion that he must make a
further 'utterance' following the course of transactions. He decided to adhere to this conclusion notwithstanding Granville's
opinion, to which he attached 'great weight'. He felt himself
compelled to advise 'upon the career of that national movement'
which he had 'tried hard to evoke and assisted in evoking'.

[1] Ailesbury to Granville, 12 October 1876, *ibid.*
[2] Granville to Gladstone, 3 October 1876, Gladstone Papers, Add. MSS 44170,
ff. 254–6.
[3] Ailesbury to Granville, 12 October 1876, Granville Papers, 30, 29/26.
[4] Granville to Gladstone, [5] October 1876, Gladstone Papers, Add. MSS 44170,
ff. 257–61.
[5] Ailesbury to Granville, 12 October 1876, Granville Papers, 30, 29/26.

Gladstone recognised Granville's special responsibility for the party, but asserted his own special responsibility as a maker of the Crimean War. He shared Ailesbury's regret that Granville had not been able to see his way to a 'more advanced and definite policy', but he was not at all inclined to recriminate. He abandoned all immediate hope that Granville would see a 'ripeness' in the time, though he could not help interpreting wishfully that Granville thus held himself in hand only for the purpose of holding his party in hand.

Nevertheless, whether willing or not to accept finally the painful fact that Granville really was in fundamental disagreement with him, Gladstone was quite ready to accept the consequences of it. He told Granville that he no longer felt under an obligation to attempt to keep in step with the party. He would be henceforth an 'outside workman', preparing 'materials' for Granville and the party to 'manipulate' and then to 'build into a structure'. For though he did not wish to 'shut the door' upon the government, he despaired of them, 'after so many invitations and so many refusals'. He was 'convinced that a virtual emancipation ought to take place'. and he rather believed it would; and at any rate he felt himself 'bound to promote it as one of the public'. 'The distinction involved in these words may be fine,' he concluded, 'but I think I have only to observe it as well as I can.'[1]

All was infinite gentleness. Few clashes of opinion on an important political issue have been so muted. It was none the less a real clash, and it involved a real break. Gladstone entered into what promised to be a distinctly new phase in his part in the atrocities agitation and the Eastern question.

3 Gladstone and the Agitators

To the original fomentors and prophets of agitation the tremendous explosion of public indignation from the end of August was far too prodigious and dazzling a reality to allow them to concern themselves greatly with the precise state of Gladstone's mind. Undoubtedly the Blackheath speech was much less forthright than many had hoped; but it was enough for the moment that he had written the *Horrors* and addressed a great throng. He was, in Free-

[1] Gladstone to Granville, 7 October 1876, Granville Papers, 30, 29/29.

man's words, the voice of truth and righteousness, worthy of Isaiah castigating the corrupt ministers of Hezekiah, or Demosthenes denouncing the hirelings of Philip.[1] To Newman Hall, one of the leading metropolitan Nonconformist divines, he was 'our great Leader of Progress, Freedom & Humanity'.[2] Stead gushed gratitude.[3] With characteristic presumption he chose to regard Gladstone's pamphlet as an answer to his letter of 26 August.[4]

With Liddon and MacColl abroad, and Fraser retired into more proper episcopal reserve, Freeman remained the only active agitator among the Oxford group. To him especially, as one old in the anti-Turkish cause long before it had become popular, the atrocities agitation was a wonderful windfall. Unable, as he boasted to Bryce, to go to a tenth of the places to which he was asked, Freeman entered with naive gusto into his inheritance. He was received at Cardiff triumphantly—an epoch-making event, in the opinion of the *South Wales Daily News*, in the social history of the city.[5] Freeman was indeed acclaimed there, as he told Bryce, as an 'angel of light', and later at Frome and in a workmen's meeting in St James's Hall, London also. At Oxford, however, he had to fight 'after the manner of men' with 'beasts'—the undergraduates in particular were not respectful.[6] 'Beer and Koran', he wrote to Gladstone, thanking him for a copy of the *Horrors*, were too strong among the Oxonians; 'they should go to learn manners at Cardiff.'[7]

But it was still Stead in Darlington who made the running, who provided ideas. His next was a project for a 'Bulgarian Sunday', a day of national mourning and humiliation. The inspiration came from Cromwell's example. He proposed his idea eagerly to Gladstone immediately after reading the *Bulgarian Horrors*. 'I have a practical suggestion to make which I hope you will deem to be

[1] *Guardian*, 13 September 1876, p. 1199.

[2] Newman Hall to Gladstone, [13] September [1876], Gladstone Papers, Add. MSS 44188, ff. 150–3.

[3] Stead to Gladstone, 6 September 1876, *ibid.*, Add. MSS 44303, ff. 233–4: 'In words of entreaty I now write to you to thank you with an earnestness which words cannot express for your noble pamphlets [sic]. You have fulfilled & more than fulfilled our utmost expectations. You have justified & more than justified the unshaken devotion which the North has ever placed in your leadership. You have once more taken your proper place as the spokesman of the national conscience as the exponent of the sentiments which animate every man worthy of the name.'

[4] Robertson Scott, *Life and Death of a Newspaper*, p. 104.

[5] 9 September 1876, pp. 4–5.

[6] Freeman to Bryce, 22 October 1876, Bryce Papers, E 4.

[7] Freeman to Gladstone, 14 September 1876, Gladstone Papers, Add. MSS 44451, ff. 188–9.

not unworthy of your attention.' In indicating the possible sources of subscriptions in aid of the Bulgarians Gladstone had omitted, Stead pointed out, 'the most important of all, the Churches & chapels which cover the land'.

When the Piedmontese were slaughtered a day of intercession & of humiliation was ordained throughout the land & in every church sermons were preached & collections made. . . . Is the occasion less urgent now? Is it not still more pressing? I am a Nonconformist, a Radical, an advocate of the Anti-State Church doctrines & a steady supporter of the Birmingham League, but in spite of these things, I would hail—in common with all Englishmen irrespective of creed or party—the appointment by the Crown of a solemn day of humiliation—'a Bulgarian Sunday'—in which collections should be taken alike in crowded city & in rural village for the sufferers whom we have been the unwitting means of destroying. Nonconformists would vie with Churchmen in making such a Sunday a national memorial of our sorrow and sympathy.

All that was needed to make the Bulgarian relief fund truly such a memorial of 'our national repentance', Stead concluded, was the proper utilisation of the 'elaborate machinery of the Churches & Chapels'.[1]

It is most unlikely that Gladstone shared either Stead's zeal or optimism in this project. In any case, it was not until 14 September that Stead publicly disclosed the elements of his new campaign. He pointed out that all the churches of the Commonwealth testified on behalf of the Piedmontese, while only a fraction of the churches in Britain in 1876 had testified on behalf of the Bulgarians. But there was still time, he urged, for the present feeble and intermittent protests of Establishment and Nonconformity alike to be converted into a universal testimony. For this purpose a special Sunday should be set apart. There was no need, Stead insisted, for politics to become involved.[2]

He pressed ahead, organising the north. Within a few days he announced that the Bishops of Durham, Ripon, and Carlisle were 'considering' his idea. One can assume at least that they had received letters from Stead advocating it. Manchester was working on the idea through the local relief fund committee. A recent letter from the Archbishop of Canterbury calling for collections in

[1] Stead to Gladstone, 6 September 1876, *ibid.*, Add. MSS 44303, ff. 233–4.
[2] *Northern Echo*, 14 September 1876, pp. 2–3.

churches to relieve suffering in the East gave Stead hopes of better, more dramatic things. He was particularly pleased to report an enthusiastic response to the idea from the Rev. R. W. Dale, the most important figure in Birmingham Nonconformity. C. H. Spurgeon, the great Baptist notability, did not, however, as Stead had to admit, 'appear' to appreciate the necessity for such a national demonstration.[1] But in the north, at any rate, 'practical steps' would be taken to secure concerted action on the part of the several denominations. The question had for some time been under the consideration of a Darlington committee, which issued a circular to all ministers of religion. The propriety of the idea was being studied also, for instance, in South Shields.[2]

It soon became clear to Stead that there was little chance that any particular Sunday could be set aside as a national, or even a regional, day of atonement. The best that could be hoped for was collections in most places.[3] No doubt Stead's idea provided a useful stimulus in this direction; but nothing more appears to have come of it. Only a lead from the highest circles—the court, the established hierarchy—could have ensured success; and R. W. Dale's not too tactful hints that the Queen would do well to follow Cromwell's example would have been little inducement.[4]

In any case, Stead's attention was diverted by the defiant insolence of Disraeli's Aylesbury speech of 20 September. He had just rebuked the government, as represented by Stafford Northcote at Edinburgh,[5] for failing to see the futility of further resistance to the popular will.[6] His natural reaction to Aylesbury was to conclude that Disraeli had 'pronounced the doom of his Ministry' by challenging the nation directly.[7] It was encouraging to find Gladstone in full agreement with his strictures[8]; even more encouraging that the Staindrop episode should soon follow.

Northcote's speech roused in Stead the suspicion, confirmed fully by Aylesbury, that the government was losing its awe of the popular wrath, and apparently sitting tight to watch the series of atrocity meetings out. More than a hint of incipient frustration

[1] *Ibid.*, 18 September 1876, pp. 3–4.
[2] *Ibid.*, p. 3.   [3] *Ibid.*, pp. 3–4.   [4] *Ibid.*
[5] See *Times*, 18 September 1876, p. 11.
[6] *Northern Echo*, 20 September 1876, p. 2.
[7] *Ibid.*, 21 September 1876, p. 2.
[8] Gladstone to Stead, 21 September 1876, Gladstone Papers, Add. MSS 44303, ff. 235–6.

becomes evident in Stead's indignant declaration that such meetings could not be continued indefinitely 'merely for the sake of impressing simpletons'.[1] If, as it would seem, the atrocity meetings had not yet quite succeeded in their immediate purpose, to Stead the remedy was clear. A 'fresh series of indignation meetings' would have to be held. If it was to come to a direct struggle between the government and the nation it would be more necessary than ever to secure an earlier session of parliament. He looked with confidence to the north to 'speak out first'.[2] In a letter to the *Northern Echo*, 'Darlingtonian'—more than likely Stead himself— argued ingeniously that the Conservatives ought to support the call for an early session, for it was the 'utterly disorganised and hopelessly outnumbered' Liberals who had least to hope from it.[3] Such arguments were too innocent for their own good, and while they proved no inducement to Conservatives they frightened not a few Liberals. John Bright wrote to Gladstone that his friends in Birmingham proposed to call a great meeting to petition the Queen to call an early session, and were speaking also of a possible national petition. The latter idea seemed to Bright a 'cumbersome method', which he judged unlikely to succeed. Instead he made the same proposal as Stead, that if anything were to be attempted, it should be a fresh series of meetings to pass resolutions and agree to memorials to the Queen.[4]

But in fact Bright had little faith in this or any other project. He had no moral zest for the work. He recognised that the Aylesbury outrage 'ought' to make some movement possible, but he had 'not much confidence in popular fervour in a matter of this kind'. He was convinced that the Tories and the clergy would withdraw from any movement likely to endanger the government. Failure, moreover, would strengthen the government in their present views and policy. And if parliament met, 'what then?' What could the Liberals as a united party propose? Even a programme of co-operation with Russia, Bright thought, would be unlikely to have much success, for he thought an immediate settlement involving 'small changes' would be more convenient for the powers than 'anything great' such as Gladstone had suggested. Bright concluded on a

[1] *Northern Echo*, 20 September 1876, p. 2.
[2] *Ibid.*   [3] *Ibid.*, 25 September 1876, pp. 2–3.
[4] Bright to Gladstone, 23 September 1876, Gladstone Papers, Add. MSS 44113, ff. 105–6.

note which expressed well his outlook of mingled pessimism and smugness: 'I have not spoken yet, for reasons that will occur to you. I advised the Cabinet 22 years ago not to get into a hole, & how to keep out of it, but it is difficult, when once in, to show them how to get out.'[1]

It was difficult to deny Bright a right to be smug, still more difficult to prove his pessimism unjustified. Stead informed Gladstone confidently on 30 September that a second series of indignation meetings was being organised in the north, with the special purposes of encouraging the Serbs in their struggle for the liberation of the Slav peoples and of demanding an autumn session.[2] Gladstone was encouraging but reserved. He was not surprised that the moral energy of the north should cause it to take the lead in a 'supplemental movement' as it did 'to a great extent' in the former one. But though he approved of more meetings, Gladstone was reluctant to commit himself publicly on specific issues, especially at a time when Derby was trying to arrange an armistice between the Turks and the Serbs,[3] and when he was attempting also to manoeuvre Granville into a more positive attitude. Stead inaugurated the new movement in the *Northern Echo* of 29 September. His 'Important Announcement' included details of arrangements made with Lewis Farley's League in Aid of the Christians of Turkey to assist in the movement. Darlington would lead off with a meeting on 2 October, 'when, we need hardly say, we expect the capital of South Durham will once more justify her claim to the initiative of the North'.[4]

But despite the optimism unfailingly displayed by Stead in the succeeding days this second series of meetings does not appear to have been anything like as impressive as the series which commenced on 25 August. Partly, no doubt, this was an inevitable consequence of the inherent weakness of doing everything over again. As Stead himself remarked later, it was not consistent with dignity and self-respect to go on repeating the same resolutions.[5] But the vital missing element which most debilitated the agitation in this phase was the absence of active leadership by Gladstone.

[1] *Ibid.*
[2] Stead to Gladstone, 30 September 1876, *ibid.*, Add. MSS 44303, f. 239.
[3] Gladstone to Stead, 30 September 1876, *ibid.*, ff. 240–1.
[4] *Northern Echo*, 29 September 1876, p. 3.
[5] *Ibid.*, 16 November 1876, p. 3.

The simple fact was that Gladstone had failed to fulfil the implicit promise given to the agitation in his pamphlet. The energy and impetus which in the nature of the case it was Gladstone's special function to contribute faded away in the weeks of futile effort to persuade Granville to accept the rôle of leadership which Gladstone at Blackheath had deliberately left vacant. Leaving the question to the 'calm but resolute' consideration of the country was not enough to sustain the agitation past the first week or so of October. Thus, at the very point where Gladstone came at last to the conclusion that he would have to go ahead without the active assistance of the leaders of the party, the atrocities agitation, the instrument he was to use, had exhausted its natural momentum.

Consequently the paradox emerged that Gladstone, the great leader of Progress, Freedom, and Humanity, remained for almost the whole of the remaining three months of the agitation period essentially a figure in the background. The saving element of the agitation was found in the idea of a national convention or conference, based on the precedents of the anti-slavery and anti-corn law agitations. This idea provided a far better alternative to the abortive scheme of a second full-scale series of protest meetings. It was much more practicable than either the project for a 'Bulgarian Sunday' or the proposal for a national petition. This latter was, as Bright objected, 'cumbersome', and moreover the very principle had been discredited by the Chartist fiasco. Anti-slavery and anti-corn laws, on the contrary, presented precedents of success to be in every way emulated. There were many natural connections, moral and personal, between the Bulgarian agitation and the anti-slavery and corn law movements; and nothing could be a more logical climax and culmination of a nation-wide series of local meetings than a great central national demonstration. This concept had a further advantage: it would to a very great extent, if successful, compensate for the absence of parliament, for the prospect of forcing the government's hand in this respect became increasingly recognised as doubtful. A national demonstration would, in effect, be a kind of substitute parliament, all the better for not containing a majority hostile to the agitation and its programme, and a minority including many whose attitude was at best lukewarm.

★

The impulse in this new direction originated towards the end of September in Sheffield, in the person of Henry Joseph Wilson, the secretary of the Sheffield Liberal Association. Wilson deserves special attention not so much for what he did in and for the agitation—which was very considerable—but in himself as a representative, in its highest and purest form, of the tradition of high-principled public activity which was one of the noblest legacies of the evangelical revival. The son of a wealthy Congregationalist cotton-spinner of Nottingham, educated in an intense atmosphere of Nonconformist piety, fervent Liberalism, and devotion to the causes against slavery and for temperance, Wilson's participation in the Bulgarian atrocities agitation was very much in the natural course of things.

Natural also was his reference to the great precedents of the anti-slavery movement for guidance in the present case. He discussed the idea of a national meeting with Robert Leader, the president of the Sheffield Liberal Association and co-proprietor of the Sheffield *Independent*. Leader endorsed the idea enthusiastically, and together they embarked upon preliminary moves. Wilson wrote on 25 September to the Liberal Associations of Manchester, Liverpool, Darlington, Birmingham, Bradford, and Leeds:

> The first outburst of feeling in all parts of the country in reference to the Turkish atrocities, & the foreign policy of this country, has been thoroughly spontaneous & unorganised, but it seems to Mr. Leader . . . & to myself, very important that it should be followed up by concerted action, so as to secure the utmost unity of aim and purpose.

With this in view, Wilson and Leader thought it would be desirable to have some interchange of opinion among a few of the Liberal Associations, and they invited two or three delegates from each Association to meet at the Victoria Station Hotel in Sheffield on 30 September.

> Our own present opinion is that the best course to pursue is to arrange for a Representative Conference, Congress, or Assembly somewhat like those which did such good service in Anti-Slavery, & Anti-Corn Law days; but if this should not commend itself to others, we shall be equally anxious to concur in some better plan which may be propounded.[1]

[1] Wilson to president and secretary of Manchester Liberal Association, 25 September 1876, H. J. Wilson Papers, Sheffield Central Library, M.D., 2588/1.

The meeting took place as arranged, with delegates present from Manchester, Leeds, and Darlington.[1] The significant gap, as it later turned out, was Birmingham. Leader took the chair, and after a long discussion the idea sketched by Wilson was adopted. Sparks of Leeds proposed and Blacklock of Darlington seconded a motion that it was 'necessary to enforce upon the Government the duty of yielding to the wishes of the people'; and Blumer of Darlington and Balcer of Leeds proposed that Leader and Wilson of Sheffield and Green of Manchester be a sub-committee to make necessary arrangements. Consultation was to be opened immediately with the Congregational Union, the Baptist Union, the Wesleyans and the Methodists, the New Methodist Free Church (whose stronghold was in Sheffield), and a wide range of Nonconformist and Liberal local associations.[2] The advice and aid of Samuel Morley, the Nonconformist philanthropist and politician, would also be sought.[3]

The formal public announcement of the general lines of the new project was made in the *Daily News* of 6 October[4] and more fully in a supplement to the Sheffield *Independent* of 7 October.[5] The full approval of the Manchester Liberal Association had been communicated by Green on 2 October; and on the 3rd the Sheffield resolutions were commended (and disclosed prematurely) by the London committee which had arranged the Guildhall demonstration. The *Independent* announcement stressed particularly the idea of falling back on the precedents of the anti-Slavery and anti-Corn Law agitations' for the holding of a 'national Convention (or Conference)' in London. Leader and Wilson proceeded to sound Liberals by circular as to a date and a place.[6]

Stead, meanwhile, pending further developments in this new direction, pressed on with his scheme for a fresh series of meetings, primarily as a counter to rising anti-Russian sentiment.[7] As for the proposed 'National Convention', Stead was inclined to regret that such a demonstration could not be organised without recourse to party machinery, though he appreciated fully Gladstone's

---

[1] There were three delegates from Darlington, three from Leeds, and one from Manchester. Six Sheffield delegates attended.
[2] H. J. Wilson Papers, Sheffield Central Library, M.D., 2588/3.
[3] *Daily News*, 6 October 1876, p. 2.   [4] *Ibid.*
[5] P. 11.   [6] *Ibid.*
[7] *Northern Echo*, 9 December 1876, p. 1.

declaration at Staindrop that the continued intransigence of the government would force the question more and more into party lines.[1] He seems also to have regretted that London should have been regarded as the inevitable venue. Perhaps he dreamt of Darlington as the capital of England for a day. Stead's mind ran more in the direction of a self-consciously substitute parliament, or National Convention, than of a party demonstration. He sent Gladstone a copy of the *Northern Echo* containing a sketch of a 'somewhat daring scheme' which differed in 'essential points' from the Sheffield project. 'I want', he told Gladstone, 'to see an informal Parliament.'[2] Stead's outline plan to achieve this end was that the present constituencies of the country would assemble in public meeting under some responsible chairman to elect delegates to the 'Convention' in the same numbers as they had members of parliament. Thus a 'thoroughly representative Assembly' might be elected, which would be able to address ministers with authority as undoubted representatives of the national will.[3] It went without saying, of course, that this will coincided with the programme of the agitation.

It was indeed a 'somewhat daring' scheme. Stead was extremely optimistic, even for Stead, if he expected Conservatives to join in the spirit of the thing and take the mock 'elections' seriously. In reality the local Liberal Associations would, in one form or another, provide the basis of any scheme for a national demonstration, whether 'parliamentary' or more modestly based on the example of the earlier classic agitations. The obvious danger of Stead's scheme would be that its pretensions would make it ridiculous.

As hopes of forcing the government to call an early session dwindled, the Sheffield project became increasingly accepted as the shape of the future agitation. It was natural for the parliamentarian to hold out hopes for an autumn session longest: Auberon Herbert and Chesson, as secretaries of the parliamentary committee formed at the end of the previous session, were still sounding Gladstone on ways and means on 12 October[4]; but nothing seems to have come of their efforts. The changing outlook is reflected in Mun

---

[1] *Ibid.*, 7 October 1876, p. 3.
[2] Stead to Gladstone, 7 October 1876, Gladstone Papers, Add. MSS 44303, f. 243.
[3] *Northern Echo*, 7 October 1876, p. 3.
[4] Gladstone Papers, Add. MSS 44452, ff. 47–8.

della, who had emerged as the leading spirit of the parliamentary committee. As early as 4 October he wrote to Leader that 'further efforts ought to take the form you have wisely indicated'.[1] On 7 October he wrote on the theme that Derby's 'tardy' dispatch of 21 September constituted a 'triumphant answer to all who have carped at our meetings and agitation'. 'Your idea of a National Conference', he added, 'seems to me to have taken hold of the public mind, and, if we have no Autumn Session, it will be the best means of bringing the Government up to the mark.' Mundella, a good parliamentarian, would still have preferred a session; but his acceptance of the conference idea as the only practicable prospect is indicated by his careful insistence that while 'localities' might elect representatives, they should '*request their Members* to attend the Conference'.[2]

★

The new rescuing and sustaining impulse provided by the idea of a national 'conference' thus coincided with the new phase into which Gladstone's relationship to the party leaders on the issue of atrocities had entered. These two new factors in the agitation were as yet distinct and unrelated; and they were only to come together in joint effort shortly before the National Conference on the Eastern Question on 8 December. It was essentially this disconnection which vitiated the process of agitation in the months of October and November. Gladstone had waited too long for either Granville or the government to come round. The natural energy of the agitation had expired beyond all possibility of resuscitation. It could no longer, as Wilson and Leader recognised, sustain its spontaneous' character.

In the sense that the atrocities agitation began in late August, it ended early in October. Thereafter it is 'got up', the work purely of organisers, committees. Yet Gladstone, the 'follower and not leader' of the party, the 'follower in the footsteps' of the *Daily News*, had, even after his declaration of independence of action on 7 October, meagre capacity for, and scant sense of the necessity of, a vigorous initiative on his part. The further 'utterance' of which Gladstone had warned Granville on 7 October turned out to be a letter to a demonstration of working men at St James's Hall.

[1] Mundella Papers.   [2] *Ibid.*

Like the Blackheath speech, Gladstone's letter seemed full of
fight; but, as Stead came to realise with dismay, its true significance lay in the fact that it exposed a complete absence on Gladstone's part of any positive ideas for the future development of the
agitation.[1] The career of that 'national movement' got, indeed
the benefit of but little of Gladstone's advice until almost its end
and such as he did proffer was by no means always encouraging
Eventually Gladstone was taken up by the Conference committee
in much the same way as he had been taken up by the agitation of
August and pushed into writing the *Horrors*.

[1] See below, pp. 234, 247.

5

The Structure of the Agitation, I:
The Parties of Religion

AT THIS point, the end of the classic phase of the agitation, a structural as opposed to a narrative analysis is called for. While September was, on the whole, a negative and unrewarding period so far as Gladstone's personal relationship to events is concerned, it was also the period in which, in terms of the incidence of protest demonstrations, the agitation attained its fullest dimensions. The structural analysis offered here is by no means confined to the month of September; indeed, the *Report* of the Eastern Question Conference of 8 December is the most valuable single documentary source for such analysis. But it takes September as the critical and central point of reference for the whole agitation period, as defined for the present study, of July–December.

The elements of this structural method include, first, a preliminary survey of the distribution and general composition of protest; then, beyond this, a series of studies of the 'fault lines' disclosed by the shock of the atrocities in the fabric of national life —denominational, intellectual, political. In this way, the agitation becomes more than merely a phenomenon of interest as a popular incursion into foreign affairs, reflecting certain qualities or expressing certain characteristics of mid-nineteenth-century England; it is a power and an event in its own right, a concussion which disturbs, shifts, accelerates, intensifies, the tendency and disposition of these qualities and characteristics.

1 Introductory: the General Distribution of Protest

Among the Foreign Office papers in the Public Records are six volumes of memorials and petitions addressed to Lord Derby and received between 1 September and 27 December 1876.[1] These volumes contain 455 memorials and petitions from identifiable sources[2] expressing indignation at the atrocities committed by the Turks and protesting against the pro-Turkish Eastern policy of the government. Of these protests 407 (90 per cent) fall between 1 September and 9 October.

Three memorials were presented in the name of national bodies: the British and Foreign Unitarian Association, the Baptist Union of Britain and Ireland, and the National Agricultural Labourers' Union. Nonconformity contributed 75 (17 per cent) of the 455 protests. Various workmen's organisations (trade unions, collieries, artisans' institutes, workmen's Liberal Associations[3]) contributed 21 protests (5 per cent). Almost all the rest came from city, town, or village meetings. There were no county meetings, a fact which Gladstone, with characteristic anxiety about the decline of the tradition of enlightened leadership by the landed classes, deplored strongly to Stead.[4] It was not a lack which worried Stead much. He admitted it to be an 'unfilled gap' but pronounced it, in the circumstances, inevitable. Where there was no organisation and no funds, he pointed out, there could be no county meetings.[5]

The figure of 455 expressions of protest can be taken as sufficiently representative of the total quantity of agitation for purposes of useful general analysis. It is reasonable to assume that a majority of meetings, having gone to the trouble of formulating and voting resolutions, would forward them to the Foreign Office, and not rely merely on the effect of an ephemeral newspaper paragraph. In a great many cases, indeed, a concluding resolution would direct the officers of the meeting to make sure that Lords Beaconsfield and Derby were made aware of its feelings. Never-

---

[1] P.R.O., F.O. 78, 2551-6: *Turkey, General Correspondence Respecting Atrocities in Bulgaria.*

[2] Not including private letters, mostly from religious cranks.

[3] These, with one from the Hackney Liberal Club, were the only overt Liberal protests. There was one Conservative memorial, from Maidstone. There were, however, some cases of ostensible protest meetings being managed deftly by Conservatives to prevent them from adopting resolutions hostile to the government. See e.g. the letter to the *South Wales Daily News* (9 September 1876, p. 6) of 'Indignant Sympathiser', complaining that a meeting at Newport had been reduced to a 'travesty' by 'Tory parsons and the Tory editor of a local paper' who insidiously concealed their partisanship and kept close control of proceedings.

[4] Gladstone to Stead, 18 October 1876, Gladstone Papers, Add. MSS 44303, ff. 245-6.

[5] Stead to Gladstone, 18 October 1876, *ibid.*, ff. 247-8. Jephson, *The Platform, Its Rise and Progress*, vol. i, p. 497, also discusses this point.

theless, there are some notable gaps: Birmingham, which certainly held a strongly supported civic meeting, is for some reason not included in the Foreign Office files. Some very important memorials, for instance one signed by 43,845 women on behalf of the women of England, were addressed directly to the Queen.[1] There are other distorting factors which must be taken into account. Individual protests differ enormously in significance. The memorials of at least a dozen Wiltshire village meetings, for instance, are almost identical and are written in the same easily recognised hand. This is not to say that they were not genuine expressions of opinion; but it is evident that, owing presumably to the zeal and energy of an individual, Wiltshire is thus grossly over-represented compared to the general level of protest throughout the country. A single petition of the women of Coventry, on the other hand, includes well over a hundred pages of signatures, and indicates clearly a most elaborately organised street-by-street operation.[2] Another large and elaborately planned petition came from Frome, in Somerset.[3]

On the whole, however, the protests registered in these files are sufficient in number and varied enough in origin and character to offset largely such distorting factors; and although the data provided is crude in quality, precluding any analysis more sophisticated than the broadest kind of regional survey, they form undoubtedly the best and most complete source of information about the general distributional composition of the agitation.

Distribution of Protests against the Turkish Atrocities in Bulgaria
Addressed to the Foreign Office, 1 September–27 December 1876, on a Regional Basis [4]

	SE.	SW.	Mid.	N.	Wales	Scot.	Ir.	National	Total	Average per day
–13 Sept.	31	26	15	59	8	6	2	2	149	11
4–18 Sept.	22	16	7	25	2	4	—	1	77	16
9–25 Sept.	21	20	22	20	8	2	1	—	94	13
6–28 Sept.	12	8	6	12	2	1	—	—	41	14
9 Sept.–9 Oct.	11	3	9	12	7	5	—	—	47	4
0 Oct.–27 Dec.	6	6	5	23	4	2	1	—	47	– 1
	103	79	64	151	31	20	4	3	455	

[1] D. Zancov and M. D. Balabanov, *Bulgaria* (pamphlet, 1876), pp. 71–2.
[2] P.R.O., F.O. 78, *Turkey*, 2554.   [3] *Ibid.*, 2555.
[4] The regional divisions are defined as follows:
    Southeast   the 15 counties bounded by Norfolk, Cambs., Hunts., Beds., Bucks., Oxford, Berks., and Hants. (pop. 8·4 million).
    Southwest   the 6 counties west of, and including, Gloucester, Wilts., and Dorset (pop. 2·3 million).

This regional analysis confirms the prominence of the north of England. This was in fact even more clearly marked in the earliest days: of the first 50 protests, 25 came from lands north of the Humber. The north contributed 40% of the 149 protests in the first two weeks of September as against 38% from the more heavily populated southern regions, and a mere 10% from the midlands. And the north finished more strongly than the south, contributing half the protests delivered between 10 October and 27 December. Yorkshire alone accounted for 64 of the protests sent to the Foreign Office, and Lancashire for 40.

When relative weight of population is taken into account, however, it is the southwest of England which emerges with by far the most frequent proportional incidence of agitation,[1] even when allowance is made for possible distortion from the 33 Wiltshire protests. Wales follows in second place, with the north of England close behind. In these three regions, frequency of protests exceeded the median average in terms of over-all population. Conversely, both the southeast and the midlands of England drop below the median level. Scotland lags hopelessly; and for Ireland, of course, the agitation can scarcely be said to have existed.

An analysis of the denominational composition of the protests confirms the prominence of Nonconformity. That 17% of the total number of protests were specifically Nonconformist in origin has already been noted; but this figure is significant not so much in itself as in relation to the fact that the number of protests interpretable as coming from Anglican sources is minute.[2] There is nothing at all from Roman Catholic or Jewish bodies. Noncon-

North	the 7 counties north of Dee-Humber (pop. 8·1 million).
Midlands	the 11 remaining English counties (pop. 4·2 million).
Wales	including Monmouthshire (pop. 1·5 million).
Scotland	(pop. 3·5 million).
Ireland	(pop. 5·2 million).

[1] Comparison of proportions of population with incidence of protest in regions of Great Britain:

	% Population	% Protests	Ratio of protests to population (000s)
Southeast	30	23	1 : 80
Southwest	8	18	1 : 29
Midlands	15	14	1 : 69
North	29	34	1 : 54
Wales	5	7	1 : 48
Scotland	13	4	1 :175

[2] There were 9 protests under the names of clergymen or parishioners which could be regarded in some degree as representative of distinctively Anglican feeling.

formist consciousness of a special mission is by far the most conspicuous feature of the agitation as revealed in the Foreign Office files. So far as the regional analysis is concerned, the most interesting fact which emerges is the tendency for a positive correlation between regions of Nonconformist strength and relatively more frequent incidence of protest. The north and west were traditionally the regions in which Nonconformity had most of its English strongholds; and Wales was overwhelmingly Nonconformist. To some extent this correlation is reflected in the provenance of the Nonconformist memorials: they accounted for a third of the Welsh protest and a fifth of the north's. But they were a strangely exiguous proportion of the west-country total.[1]

The general and tentative conclusion to which these particular findings point is thus a reasonably distinct disparity in intensity of agitation, so far as England and Wales are concerned, between the less intense inner or 'metropolitan' regions and the more intense outer or fringe regions of the west and north. Calculations and conclusions based on the limited quantity of evidence available can be used only with the greatest caution. Still, there is no lack of impressionistic confirmation, for what it is worth. It was after having attended 'many great meetings in the North & West' that Ellis Ashmead Bartlett wrote to Gladstone of the unparalleled popular enthusiasm at the beginning of September.[2] Gladstone himself found on a progress through what he rather tendentiously described to Bryce as the 'rural & Tory' counties of Wiltshire and Somerset, to his equal surprise and satisfaction, that the people there were 'as sound and as warm in the Eastern question as the men of the North & North East'.[3] And Ambrose Phillipps de Lisle of Loughborough lamented to Gladstone how sad it was 'to see how Turkish Leicestershire People are, especially among Farmers and labouring People!'.[4]

Certainly it is beyond dispute that the north, like Nonconformity, was peculiarly conscious of a special rôle in the agitation, whatever the figures may show. Stead was the loudest exponent of this northern self-consciousness. If the north owed its initial promin-

---

[1] The regional distribution of Nonconformist protests is as follows: north, 29; southeast, 17; Wales, 11; midlands, 8; southwest, 5; Scotland, 2; Ireland, 1; national, 2.
[2] See above, p. 104.
[3] Gladstone to Bryce, 29 January 1877, Bryce Papers, E 6.
[4] Purcell, *Ambrose Phillipps de Lisle*, vol. ii, pp. 195–6.

ence largely to the activity of Stead, he in turn owed the striking success of his campaign to the ready response of the north to an appeal which stressed its alleged prerogative of giving a lead to the country. Stead exemplified the north-country mystique as much as he exploited it. It was in equally proud consciousness of the distinctive reputation of the north that George Otto Trevelyan, M.P. for the Border Burghs, wrote assuring Gladstone at the height of the jingo hysteria in 1878 that the people of the north 'neither share, nor understand the folly of the South'.[1] Nor even did Liverpool, headquarters of the robust Toryism of Lancashire, stand out conspicuously against the atrocities agitation as it had against anti-slavery and anti-corn laws.[2]

Yet there remains only dubious validity in the traditional interpretation of the conflict over foreign policy touched off by the atrocities in 1876 as being in terms of a struggle between the metropolis and the provinces. The indications of a distinct pattern of regional disparity, interesting and perhaps significant as they are, must be set against the obvious fact of an equally impressive general incidence of agitation throughout England and Wales as a whole. The principal determinants in the vast majority of specific instances of agitation—the effect of habitual political reflexes, the extent of chapel influence, the particular colour (usually Anglo-Catholic) of the clergy, occasionally the lead of a local worthy or magnate—have but tenuous relevance to any regional pattern. Chapel influence cannot in itself be adduced conclusively as the general dynamic of anti-metropolitan feeling when it would appear to be far from the forefront in the case of the south-west of England. The violently eccentric anti-government opinions of the Marquess of Bath on the Eastern question undoubtedly contributed much to that popular enthusiasm for the Bulgarians in Wiltshire and Somerset which surprised Gladstone so pleasantly, and, in particular, to the efficient machinery of agitation in Bath's political bailiwick, Frome.[3] And London itself was the scene of a very

---

[1] Trevelyan to Gladstone, 18 April [1878], Gladstone Papers, Add. MSS 44335, f. 29.

[2] See the comments of George Melly, *Recollections of Sixty Years (1833–1893)* (Coventry 1893), pp. 62–3. Liverpool was the scene of the famous incident when, during a performance of *Othello*, the line, 'The Turk is drowned', was greeted with enthusiastic cheering. 'These things', as Gladstone remarked rather sententiously to Granville, 'are not without meaning' (Gladstone to Granville, 26 November 1876, Granville Papers, 30, 29/29).

[3] See above, p. 149, and below, pp. 186, 256.

respectable amount of agitation: thirty-three protests were·delivered from the metropolitan area, a third of them Nonconformist.

Such validity as there is in the thesis of the metropolis versus the provinces lies rather in the circumstance that London was the one place in which opinion critical of the agitation could develop a prominent degree of articulateness and activity. The despondent secretaries of the 'Westminster and Turkish Atrocities' movement lamented to Liddon the barren prospects of agitation in the West End; their efforts to get the High Steward of Westminster to convene a meeting were foundering on the hostility of most of the aristocracy and gentry, and the timidity of the dependent 'trading class'.[1] The metropolitan tone was set by three great agencies: the court and attendant society,[2] the press, and the 'Cockney mob', a phenomenon which included genteel elements as well as working men.[3]

Of these the press was the most important. The *Daily News*, controlled by a group headed by the Nonconformist philanthropist Samuel Morley, alone of the greater metropolitan papers remained consistently behind the agitation which it had done so much to bring into being, though Hill eventually found Freeman's violence and extravagance insupportable, and dropped him.[4] *The Times* did great service for a while, but Delane, ill and tired, was prone to shuffle. The Conservative *Standard* and *Morning Post* were furiously hostile. But thus far the balance is not overwhelmingly unfavourable; and of the political reviews, the inimical *Saturday*, *Quarterly*, *Blackwood's*, and *Pall Mall* under Greenwood, and the cold *Economist* under Bagehot, were answered with reasonable adequacy by the *Spectator*, the *Contemporary*, *British Quarterly*, *Westminster*, *Fraser's*, and the *Fortnightly*.

The pivotal position was held by the *Daily Telegraph*, the greatest of the new dailies. The choice of allegiance of the Levy-Lawsons and their editor Edwin Arnold was decisive in giving a particular colour to the metropolitan press. The *Telegraph's* pro-Turkish influence was enormous, partly because of its great circulation,[5]

---

[1] Atherley-Jones and Griffiths to Liddon, 28 October 1876. Liddon Papers.
[2] George Lansbury remarked that it was quite generally appreciated at the time of the Eastern question crisis that the Queen strongly supported Disraeli and his policy. *My Life*, p. 43.
[3] *Ibid.*, pp. 41–2.   [4] See below, p. 244.
[5] See H. J. Hanham, *Elections and Party Management, Politics in the Time of Disraeli and Gladstone* (1959), p. 110.

even more because it abandoned its traditional Liberal connection. This defection introduced a peculiar bitterness into the controversy.[1] Henry Labouchere, in particular, stung the *Telegraph* mercilessly in his newly-founded gadfly, *Truth*.[2] But the *Telegraph* was little hurt by the bitterness against it. Goldwin Smith wrote anxiously to Gladstone about a reported 'vast increase' in the *Telegraph*'s circulation since it 'turned Turk' and a corresponding decline in that of the *Daily News*, as attested by W. H. Smith's.[3] Gladstone summed up his impression: 'London is the great focus of mischief: through money, rowdyism, & the Daily Telegraph.'[4]

Turcophile politics achieved its highest refinement, however, in the committee at Stafford House, the London home of the Duke of Sutherland, and in *Vanity Fair*, the organ of fashionable society and the clubs. It was as natural for these elements to associate themselves, more or less, with a pro-Turkish point of view as it was for Nonconformity, with its 'long and bitter history as a second-class citizenry, to sympathise with the cause of what Palmerston once referred to as the 'Nonconformists of Turkey'.[5] The Turcophiles of the clubs did not object to the Russians as tyrants: their evocation of Poland in 1876-8 rang, to say the least, rather hollow; they objected to them as competitors in imperialism. The security of India was always the keynote of this attitude.[6] The other side of the Turcophile coin was practical sympathy with an imperial nation in its problems with refractory subject peoples. In this case Ireland naturally came to mind. Thus one pamphleteer, attacking Gladstone, pointed out that the Irish might well demand what the Bulgarians were demanding. It did not follow, however,

[1] E.g. Thompson, *Public Opinion and Lord Beaconsfield*, vol. i, pp. 435-40.
[2] H. Pearson, *Labby (The Life and Character of Henry Labouchere)* (1936), pp. 133ff. It did not go unnoticed that in the libel suit which resulted Labouchere's statement that the proprietors of the *Telegraph* had large interests in Turkish bonds was not denied. See also G. C. Thompson, op. cit., p. 437.
[3] Smith to Gladstone, [4 July 1877], Gladstone Papers, Add. MSS 44303, ff. 206-7. Gladstone told Stead in the autumn of 1877 that of some 3,000 letters which he had received from 'abusive correspondents', nine-tenths, or even more, came from the metropolitan area; and an immense proportion of these letters quoted the *Daily Telegraph*. At that time Gladstone was getting 40 or 50 of these 'horrible letters' every day (Estelle Stead, *My Father*, pp. 79-80).
[4] Gladstone to Bryce, 6 October 1877, Bryce Papers, E 6.
[5] E. Ashley, *Life of Henry John Temple, Viscount Palmerston, 1846-1865* (1876), vol. ii, p. 89.
[6] Sir Ronald Storrs remarks that 'As a factor in British policy, the doctrine of the Caliphate—of pan-Islamic Theocracy—was mainly the creation of the India Office' (*Orientations* (1937), pp. 96-7). But for evidence that 'Moslem susceptibilities' was not entirely a bogey, see below, p. 190.

ıe asserted, 'that because a vassal state becomes discontented, that
every absurd demand it makes on the parent country is to be
granted'.[1]

Metropolitan Turcophilism was self-contained, self-confident,
ittle affected by the feeling of the provinces. Exponents of a
national' policy assume without question that they represent the
nation. Derby, thanking Disraeli for a welcome word of encouragement, noted wishfully that they were 'fairly well supported in the
press', which he suspected was 'a better test than provincial
meetings'.[2] The 'large-print-and-lumbering-sentence foolish'
Saturday Review observed with pain and surprise at the beginning
of 1877, reported Freeman to Bryce, that a careful survey of the
constituencies' revealed that Gladstone was far more popular
here than the criticism 'justly and freely bestowed on him in
London' would lead the intelligent public to believe possible.
Always prone to be infuriated by the insularity of the metropolis
and the two universities, Freeman commented: 'The noodle has
just awakened to the fact that his own silly club is not all England,
and that there are wiser men out of it than in it. I could have told
him that many months back. Cardiff, Frome, Glastonbury,
Manchester, Exeter, London itself outside of clubs—all the same;
Gladstone *the* name.'[3] Certainly not the least important consequence of the furious hostility to Gladstone engendered by the
Eastern question in the clubs and in the 'plutocratic' social order
and outlook represented by them was that it quickened the impulse
o Gladstone's rediscovery of the moral and political virtue of the
masses as represented by the 'constituencies'.

*

Three circumstances are of particular importance in making the
Welsh participation in the agitation disproportionately large. The
irst is undoubtedly the vitality of Welsh Nonconformity. This was
he dynamic force behind the politically emergent Welsh national-
sm. Both Nonconformity and nationalism found logical political
expression in Liberalism. Everything in Wales favoured the agi-
ation, as everything conspired against it in Ireland. The most

[1] A. A. Daly, *Greater Lessons in Massacre* (pamphlet, 1877), pp. 18–19.
[2] Derby to Disraeli, 1 October 1876, Disraeli Papers.
[3] Freeman to Bryce, 15 January 1877, Bryce Papers, E6.

notable of the eleven Nonconformist protests were those of the
Baptist Union of Wales, the South Wales Wesleyan Methodists
and the Calvinistic Methodist bodies of both South and North
Wales. Four of the staff of the Calvinistic Methodist College at
Bala later became conveners of the National Conference on the
Eastern Question.[1]

The second important factor in Wales was the personal leader
ship and inspiration of Henry Richard. A prominent Congregation
alist, Richard was a leader both of Nonconformity and Welsh
nationalism. Though secretary of the Peace Society, he found it
impossible to restrict himself to the orthodox non-interventionism
of John Bright. He later became a convener of the National Con
ference on the Eastern Question, at which he spoke, and a member
of the Eastern Question Association, for which he wrote a pro
paganda pamphlet.[2] He took a leading part in at least two big
atrocity meetings in Wales, at Aberdare[3] and Merthyr.[4]

Finally, there was the strong and consistent patronage of the
agitation by the *South Wales Daily News* of Cardiff, which played
an important part in getting up the Cardiff meeting of 7 September
that set the ball rolling in Wales. This paper was a very self
conscious exponent of Welsh nationalism. A typical article, in the
course of denouncing the 'Mohammedan' press of London, de
clared the satisfaction of the *South Wales Daily News* that through
out the length and breadth of Wales there was but one paper
which identified itself with the pro-Turkish viewpoint. This was
an oblique reference to the Conservative *Western Mail* of Cardiff.
Apart from this blot, Welsh journalism, Conservative as well as
Liberal, was, as the *South Wales Daily News* proudly affirmed
'thoroughly sound on questions of humanity and morals'. It was
creditable, also, that the *Western Mail*, though published in Wales
was not Welsh 'in taste, sympathy, or faith', but was established
to ridicule Welsh habits and customs and to write down Welsh
Nonconformity. Its proprietors were aliens, with an alien cause
to serve.[5] More completely and effectively than Stead in the north

[1] The list of conveners is given in the E.Q.A. *Report*, pp. vii-xxv.
[2] *Evidences of Turkish Misrule* (Eastern Question Association Papers, No. 1, 1877
partly reprinted from 1855).
[3] *South Wales Daily News*, 13 September 1876, p. 5.
[4] *Ibid.*, 14 September 1876, p. 5.
[5] *Ibid.*, 9 September 1876, pp. 4–5.

of England, pro-agitation opinion in Wales could identify regional sentiment with a moral cause in politics.

★

The apparent quietness of Scotland compared with England and Wales as a whole is one of the impressions most decisively confirmed by an analysis of the Foreign Office files. The Baptist *Freeman*[1] and the *Spectator*[2] both noted this backwardness and commented severely upon it. Scotland, the *Spectator* concluded rather sadly, was no doubt 'sound' in its Liberalism; but it lacked the necessary element of 'comprehensive generosity'. Apart from a meeting at Glasgow led by Argyll and Shaftesbury, there was little warmth of feeling in evidence; and the main Liberal papers in both Edinburgh and Glasgow supported the government. Even Bryce, who took some pains to impress upon Gladstone the essential if undemonstrative soundness of Scottish public feeling—'at least among the middle classes'—could not deny that the 'so-called gentry and the military and a certain proportion of the new rich men in places like Glasgow' were 'no better than West End Society in London'.[3]

The obvious problem is to reconcile this apathetic state of 1876 with the fervour displayed during Gladstone's Midlothian campaigns in 1879–80. The solution lies in the simple process of jettisoning the widespread myth that the general election of 1880 was dominated by issues of foreign policy.[4] The Scots were fervent in 1879–80 whereas they had been apathetic in 1876 because behind Gladstone's platform rhetoric the issues of 1879–80 had to do with much more immediate, pressing, and practical considerations than the moral issue raised by the atrocities question.

Partly, no doubt, this marked obtuseness of moral reaction is to be explained in the very dominance of Liberalism in Scotland. Its position had not been seriously shaken, as in England, by the Conservative resurgence of 1874. It lacked the stimuli which religious and nationalist grievances gave to Welsh Liberalism: It had about

---

[1] 22 September 1876, p. 462.
[2] 7 October 1876, p. 1240; and 14 October, p. 1281, for the defence of Scotland's good name by 'Scotus'.
[3] Bryce to Gladstone, 22 September 1877, Bryce Papers E6.
[4] For examples of this myth, see Fitzmaurice, *Granville*, vol. ii, p. 198; Seton-Watson, *Britain in Europe*, p. 544; Taylor, *The Trouble Makers*, p. 86. See Hanham, *Elections and Party Management*, pp. 228–9, for a discussion of this point.

it a somewhat dry, orthodox air,[1] very like the *Edinburgh Review*
itself, or the established Church of Scotland. There was, moreover,
no comparable political equivalent of the Free Church. It is not
without significance that the only two protests to the Foreign
Office from religious sources in Scotland were from Free Church
presbyteries, at Paisley and Lockerbie.

*

The contrast between England and Scotland was as nothing to
that between Britain and Ireland. Four Irish protests only were
addressed to the Foreign Office. Three came from Ulster, where
Liberalism maintained a last foothold after its electoral collapse in
1874. One was Nonconformist, from the Congregational Union of
County Down. Two others, from Belfast and Ballymoney in
County Antrim, indicate almost certainly a Protestant-Liberal
initiative. The fourth protest, from remote Bandon in County
Cork, is more instructive. Bandon was founded in the early seven-
teenth century as an Anglo-Scottish Protestant plantation, and it
remained thereafter an exclusive and hostile enclave amidst the
Roman Catholic Irish. Given the declared policy of the Roman
Catholic Church in the Eastern question, a place as famed for its
resistance to Catholic encroachment as Bandon would feel almost
obliged to assert itself in the opposite direction. There seems little
likelihood that there was anything more behind the Bandon protest
than that. Outspokenly Protestant opinion in Ireland on the Eastern
question usually took the form of resolutions from Orange Lodges
denouncing Gladstone's 'unpatriotic' behaviour.[2]

The Dublin press, led by the Protestant, anti-nationalist *Irish
Times*, was generally very hostile to the agitation.[3] The Roman
Catholic, pro-Home Rule *Freeman's Journal* took a rather more
friendly line, though it defended the Pope's attitude.[4] One of the
most revealing manifestations of Irish feeling arose out of a debate

---

[1] Hanham, op. cit., pp. 162–3.
[2] Resolutions to this effect were sent by the Orange Lodges of Armagh, Wicklow
and Wexford, Londonderry, Antrim, Ballymena, Lisburn, and O'Neiland East, and
from several Lancashire Lodges.
[3] E.g. 2 September 1876, p. 4.
[4] 20 September 1876, p. 5. The Conservative *Daily Express* was incautiously
friendly to the agitation at first (25 August 1876, pp. 2–3; 28 August, p. 2), but
Gladstone's pamphlet caused it to swerve suddenly into violent hostility (8 September
1876, p. 2).

in the Dublin City Corporation. Alderman McSwiney refused to support a proposal to present an address to the government on the atrocities because it would have a 'prejudicial effect on the Christians of the East, especially on the Roman Catholics of the East'. References in quick succession to the English 'Bashi-bazouks' of 1798, the Indian Mutiny, Jamaica, China, and the 'bottomless pit of Russian rule' concluded with a bitter attack on Gladstone, who would not, McSwiney asserted, he supported by the Catholics of Ireland 'although the question had been before them for months'.[1] That McSwiney did speak for the greater part of Irish Catholic opinion is indicated by the fact that none of the Nationalist members of parliament became conveners of the Eastern Question Conference; and very few supported Gladstone's resolutions of May 1877 denouncing the Turkish government.[2]

Nevertheless, the situation was not quite as simple as it appeared on the surface. The atrocities question became almost invariably entangled with Home Rule: but there were wide differences of approach. Thus, in contrast to McSwiney, there was a meeting in Dublin to denounce the 'brutal conduct of England's ally, Turkey'. It became in fact a Home Rule demonstration with speeches denouncing the English and the Turks, 'blackguards, ruffians both', but with most attention devoted to the record of English atrocities in Ireland.[3] Richard Pigott,[4] in the nationalist *Irishman*, took the line that Ireland ought to sympathise with the Bulgarians as a fellow struggling nationality: the Irish knew what oppression meant.[5] The nationalist *Nation* added a further twist: in an article on 'Irish Opinion and the Turkish Atrocities' it excused the apparent apathy of the Irish by arguing that, as an oppressed country itself, Ireland could not be expected to take a share in the direction of policy. The 'provincialism' which had been forced upon Ireland, the *Nation* asserted, deprived its counsels of 'their legitimate and independent weight'.[6]

Whatever the approach, the moral drawn was always the same: the English were in no position to criticise the Turks.[7] The clearest

[1] *Times*, 26 September 1876, p. 8.
[2] The *Nonconformist* reckoned 11 (16 May 1877, p. 505).
[3] *Times*, 11 September 1876, p. 11.
[4] Later the forger of the 'Parnell letters'.
[5] 7 October 1876, p. 232.
[6] 30 September 1876, p. 9.
[7] E.g. *Times*, 28 September 1876, p. 9.

illustration of this facility for exploiting all aspects of the Bulgarian issue is afforded by Parnell himself. Speaking at a United States Independence Day rally in Dublin on 4 July, he attacked English oppression and declared that the Irish would never support Muslims against Christians in the East, to an accompanying chorus of hisses at the mention of Muslims and cheers for Russia.[1] Later, however, it would appear that Parnell's view had developed in line with that of the parliamentary Irish party, whose leadership he was about to assume: he was one of the crowd who looked on approvingly while Gladstone's windows were being smashed during the jingo phase in 1878.[2]

2 Nonconformity

The figure of 17 per cent of the total number of protests received by the Foreign Office gives no really adequate idea of the weight contributed by Nonconformity to the agitation. Far more revealing is the fact that of the 75 Nonconformist protests, 54 were official, representative of national or regional Nonconformist bodies.[3] It is hardly possible that there was a Nonconformist in England and Wales not directly and officially represented in formal protest.

To Liddon this Nonconformist zeal and solidarity seemed all the more impressive in that it had to surmount a far more formidable

---

[1] *Freeman's Journal*, 5 July 1876, p. 7.

[2] T. P. O'Connor, *Memoirs of an Old Parliamentarian* (1929), vol. i, p. 8.

[3] The memorials of the Baptist Union and the Unitarian Association have already been mentioned, as have also those of the major Welsh bodies. To these may be added the following selection of the more notable memorials in the Foreign Office files: the General Body of Protestant Dissenting Ministers of the Three Denominations in and about London and Westminster, the Wesleyan Methodist Connection in the Liverpool district (comprising 300 congregations), the Chester Ministerial Association (comprising Wesleyans, Primitive Methodists, United Free Church, Baptists, and Congregationalists), the Board of Congregational Ministers of London, the United Methodist Free Churches of the Leeds and Bradford districts (representing 150 congregations), the London Presbytery of the Presbyterian Church of England, the North Midlands Presbyterian and Unitarian Association, the Second London District Committee of the Wesleyan Conference (representing 100 ministers and as many laymen), the Executive Committee of the Congregational Union of Gloucestershire and Herefordshire, the Wesleyan Methodist ministers resident in London (165), the Northern Association of Baptist Churches, Wesleyans and Methodists of the Notts. and Derby district, and the North Staffs. Congregational Union.

Other Nonconformist protests not apparently forwarded to the Foreign Office might also be mentioned, particularly the resolutions of the Congregational Union of England and Wales (*Nonconformist*, 6 September 1876, p. 894), and later the resolution by acclamation of the Congregational Union at its autumn session (*Congregational Year Book*, 1877, pp. 122, 130), and the Connexial Committee of the Union of Independent Methodist and Free Gospel Churches in England and Scotland (*Times*, 12 September 1876, p. 10).

barrier of theological and ecclesiastical prejudice than that which faced Anglicanism as a whole.[1] There is, however, little evidence that Nonconformists had difficulty in overcoming any such prejudices. One explanation of this is undoubtedly the fact that Nonconformists could more easily (even eagerly) identify themselves with a form of religion legally discriminated against by the state. Accounts of the humiliating procedures through which Christians under Turkish rule had to go in order to secure burial of their dead[2] chimed in appositely with the contemporary struggle in England over the Burials Bill. Nonconformist self-consciousness always had about it a certain element of what might be called the martyrdom complex. This had its captious side, made especially prominent in the controversies of the time over education; but it had also a side which, on extraordinary occasions, could evoke something approaching greatness of spirit.

A second reason was, paradoxically, the very vastness of the theological and ecclesiastical gulf between English Nonconformity and Greek Orthodoxy. There were no crotchets, no reunion negotiations, no jealousies, no rivalries. Nonconformists were, in effect, placed in a position of having to accept the Eastern Christians totally, without reserve, as Christians pure and simple, or rejecting them, in the manner of their fellow evangelicals, the Low Churchmen, as 'so-called Christians', worshippers of the 'wafer-God'. The peculiar and complex arrangement of circumstances, political and ecclesiastical, which led the Low Church to reject the Eastern Christians led Nonconformity to accept them. The further, double paradox thus arose that Nonconformity and Anglo-Catholicism were allied in opposition to the equally incongruous coalition of the Low Church and Roman Catholicism.

Another, comparatively minor, factor helping to overcome any possible Nonconformist prejudice against the Eastern Christians was the influence in studies of Biblical prophecy. Nonconformists were especially prone to this eminently evangelical discipline, all the more so with the East in turmoil, and with the additional incentive of being able to link the Pope with the Successor of the Prophet. St Paul's Man of Sin, the False Prophet of Revelation, the Babylon of the Apocalypse, St John's Antichrist, and the Big

---

[1] Liddon to Guinness Rogers, 28 January 1878, Liddon Papers.
[2] See e.g. MacColl, *The Eastern Question*, p. 113.

and Little Horns of the Prophet Daniel, all seemed to fit the case satisfactorily—Russia in particular emerged with credit from the prophecies of Daniel.[1] This kind of approach was not confined to Nonconformists: Newman himself had predicted the doom of Turkey on the same grounds in 1854, in a deliberate effort to prove to Protestants that Catholics could handle and interpret Apocalyptic matters as well as they[2]; and he was followed by his disciple, Ambrose Phillipps de Lisle, who pressed these prophetical considerations strongly upon Gladstone in 1876.[3] The High Churchman Christopher Wordsworth, Bishop of Lincoln, delivered a sermon in September 1876 pointing out that Russia had these prophecies 'in her hands', and that they seemed clearly to prefigure her occupation of Constantinople.[4]

Far outweighing all these considerations, however, was the fulfilment by Nonconformity of its function as the greatest institutional exemplar of the temper of moral seriousness in the public life of nineteenth-century England. In his tribute to the incomparable contribution of Nonconformity to the agitation, Liddon lamented all the more bitterly the failure of the Established Church to do itself justice in what seemed 'so plainly the cause of righteousness'.[5] Certainly, the capacity for cutting the Gordian knot of human affairs with a simple stroke of moral decision has never been more strikingly displayed on so large a scale as by Nonconformity in 1876.

No one was more deeply impressed by the 'exertions made by the Nonconformists in the cause of humanity and justice'[6] than Gladstone. He never forgot their 'noble support' for his Bulgarian

[1] E.g. *The Eastern Question. Turkey, its Mission and Doom: A Prophetical Instruction* (pamphlet, 1876).

[2] Purcell, *Ambrose Phillipps de Lisle*, vol. ii, p. 192; and below, p. 195.

[3] Purcell, op. cit., p. 99.

[4] C. Wordsworth, *The Mohammedan Woe and its Passing Away* (pamphlet, 1876). For the Low Church aspect of these exercises, see *Rock*, 22 September 1876, p. 717; 13 October, p. 766.

[5] Liddon to Guinness Rogers, 28 January 1878, Liddon Papers.

[6] Gladstone to Newman Hall, 12 October 1876, in Newman Hall, *Autobiography* (1898), pp. 292–3. See Guinness Rogers, *Autobiography*, pp. 210–11: 'Shortly after my return to London [? from Whitby, September 1876] a friend came to me and said that Mr. Gladstone, with whom I was then but slightly acquainted, had said that the Nonconformists might, if so disposed, help very materially in awakening the opinion of the country upon the question, and my friend had therefore come to me in order to consider what was possible to be done. I immediately, in co-operation with two or three others, convened a meeting of well-known Nonconformists, and to them I submitted a series of resolutions on the subject.' A 'vigilance committee' was consequently formed, which 'acted quietly and vigorously throughout the whole of the agitation'

campaign.[1] His social contacts with Nonconformist ministers became more frequent, cordial, and close.[2] In 1881 he actually proposed some kind of formal commemoration of the great part taken by Nonconformity in the Eastern question.[3]

1876 was the decisive moment in the relations between Gladstone and Nonconformity. For the past few years especially, Nonconformity had figured in Gladstone's mind largely as the mortal enemy of the religious Establishment of England, which above all other things he held dear. Nonconformists crossed him rudely on the education question and had abetted most cruelly his electoral discomfiture in 1874. There was no very long or well-established tradition of co-operation between Gladstone and the Nonconformists. On some of the greatest questions which had exercised the moral energies of Nonconformity Gladstone had been hostile or indifferent, or at best a tardy convert: anti-slavery, the first reform movement, the corn laws, the American Civil War, education. On certain other questions they had moved along parallel lines: Italy, the second reform movement, disestablishment of the Irish Church. Relations were friendly, but did not converge into deep mutual appreciation.

This mutual appreciation came as a fruit of the Bulgarian atrocities. Thus the two greatest forces in English public life asserting the moral obligations inherent in political action at last came together in full sympathy. Nonconformists hailed Gladstone with fervour as the spokesman of their highest public ideals. One wrote to Newman Hall in February 1877: 'How grandly Gladstone carried himself last night. He becomes more & more a prophet of the most high God. We ought to be devoutly thankful to God for having called to the side of truth, righteousness & humanity, the most splendidly gifted man in Europe. . . .'[4] This, Newman Hall assured Gladstone, was 'only a specimen of the way in which all Non-Cons. think & feel'.[5]

---

[1] See W. T. Stead, *Gladstone, 1809–1898, A Character Sketch* [1898], p. 47.

[2] *Ibid.*; and Newman Hall, op. cit., pp. 273–4.

[3] See Allon to Gladstone, 30 March 1881, Gladstone Papers, Add. MSS 44095, ff. 379–80. Allon rather gingerly steered clear of anything dramatic and suggested a portrait of Gladstone in the library of the new Congregational Memorial Hall, Farringdon Street. Mr Bernard Honess, Manager of the Memorial Hall Trust, kindly informs me that no such portrait seems in fact to have been presented.

[4] R. Wilson to Newman Hall, n.d. [1877], enclosure in Gladstone Papers, Add. MSS 44188, f. 163.

[5] Newman Hall to Gladstone, 20 February [1877], *ibid.*, ff. 161–2.

The new and enhanced status which Nonconformity acquired in Gladstone's eyes was the greatest single stimulus, it is safe to say, in his resumed and developing mystique of the moral superiority of the masses as against the classes. Nonconformity was foremost and decisive in accelerating this tendency because it was, on the one hand, the most massive, organised body of articulate 'popular' opinion that existed before the era of the great trade unions; and on the other it represented a moral and religious before a democratic ethos. Gladstone gave indications of a growing preoccupation in the following years with this line of thought by such things as his patronage of Chamberlain's National Liberal Federation (which tended to be markedly Nonconformist in tone)[1] and in a controversy with Lowe on the question of extending the county franchise.[2] This controversy stimulated a series of symposia in the newly-founded *Nineteenth Century* on the subject, 'Is the Popular Judgment in Politics More Just than That of the Higher Orders?'[3] In these discussions Gladstone's view of the essential justness of the popular judgment was most explicitly asserted. His final word ran thus: 'The superiority of the popular judgment in politics, so far as it is superior, is, according to my view, due mainly to moral causes, to a greater mental integrity, which, again, is greatly owing to the comparative absence of the more subtle agencies of temptation.'[4] To a long list of examples of the superiority of the popular judgment—all the great reforming and philanthropic movements of the nineteenth century, excepting possibly Catholic Emancipation—Gladstone could now add the Eastern question.[5]

This conviction at no time implied on Gladstone's part a recognition of the moral virtue of democracy in itself. The Labour movement did not interest Gladstone except as evidence of the growing collectivism and 'Constructionism' which he deplored; but Labour acting in politics and speaking with the voice of, say, Primitive Methodism, appealed immediately to his imagination. It was thus that he spoke at Blackheath of the lead given to the country by the

[1] See *Nonconformist*, 6 June 1877, p. 581.
[2] It was in this controversy that Gladstone first described Nonconformity as the 'backbone of British Liberalism'; see his article on 'The County Franchise and Mr Lowe Thereon', *Nineteenth Century*, November 1877, p. 552. See also J. F. Glaser 'English Nonconformity and the Decline of Liberalism', *American Historical Review* **63** (1958), p. 352.
[3] *Nineteenth Century*, May 1878, pp. 797ff.; July 1878, pp. 174 ff.
[4] *Ibid.*, July 1878, pp. 185–6.
[5] 'Last Words on the County Franchise', *ibid.*, January 1878, pp. 200–1.

working men. Gladstone attributed, on the basis of this moral and emotional attitude, a quite exaggerated importance to the rôle of working men in the agitation. In the same way, though with a far more accurate appreciation of its true weight in the agitation, Nonconformity assumed in Gladstone's eyes a new dimension of moral and political significance.

Gladstone's religious Catholicism went far beyond the range of the ordinary High Churchman. In temperament he shared more with Nonconformity than perhaps even he realised. He formed a real link between Anglo-Catholicism and Nonconformity, quite apart from the issues of the agitation which had brought the two religious groups into association. It was in this sense, more than any other, that Gladstone was the supreme individual representative of the spirit of the Bulgarian atrocities agitation.

*

Nonconformist participation in the agitation reflected accurately the outstanding characteristics of its denominational composition: the numerical preponderance of the Wesleyan Methodists,[1] the political vitality and sophistication of the Congregationalists, the influence of the strategically-placed Unitarian élite.

All the connections were affected profoundly by the shock of the atrocities; but for the Wesleyans especially it was of consequence as a powerful accelerating impulse to their tendency away from the traditional insistence on historical distinctiveness from the older connections and the traditional link with Conservatism. It was important and significant that Hugh Price Hughes, the most prominent of the younger school of leaders representing the new orientation in connectional and political attitudes, should have followed Gladstone enthusiastically throughout the Eastern crisis, but even more important and significant that P. W. Bunting, grandson of Jabez and heir of his tradition, should have rallied the Methodist district meetings and the Wesleyan Conference itself

---

[1] The denominational composition of the Nonconformist protest is as follows:

Wesleyan Methodist	22	Primitive or Independent	
Congregationalist	11	Methodist	3
Baptist	11	English Presbyterian	2
Calvinistic Methodist	5	Free Church of Scotland	2
Quaker	4	Groups representing two	
Unitarian	3	or more denominations	8
		Unidentified chapels	4

in support of the agitation.[1] No less than nineteen district meetings responded to Bunting's call, as endorsed by McCaulay, the president of the Conference.[2] The more strictly working-class Wesleyan connection, the Primitive Methodists, made a comparatively small contribution, considering their numbers. The General Committee and the *Primitive Methodist* were unexceptionably staunch,[3] but the greatest service rendered to the agitation by Primitive Methodism lay in the activity and example of such influential working-class leaders as Joseph Arch and Thomas Burt, both later conveners of the Eastern Question Conference.

For all Bunting's activity, and for all that the Baptist protest was in form no less than that of Congregationalism, no Nonconformist denomination could match the sheer weight and quality of the leadership provided for the agitation by the Congregationalists. Stead himself was the son of a Congregational minister. Edward Miall, though retired from active affairs, still edited the weekly *Nonconformist* and made it one of the most potent of the organs behind the agitation. Samuel Morley was as munificent in this cause as he had been in so many others.[4] Henry Wilson was the original begetter of the idea of a National Conference. Henry Richard, the leader of Welsh political life, became president of the Congregational Union in 1877. Of the 57 Nonconformist ministerial conveners, 25 were Congregationalists,[5] including such prominent figures as Henry Allon, Aveling (president of the Union in 1876), Morton Brown, R. W. Dale, Baldwin Brown, Joseph Parker, Guinness Rogers, and Newman Hall. Notable lay Congregationalists among the conveners were the Jeremiah Colmans, uncle and nephew, of Norwich, Samuel Plimsoll, and F. Schnadhorst, Chamberlain's Birmingham lieutenant. Newman Hall

---

[1] *Methodist Recorder*, 15 September 1876, pp. 554–5; *Methodist*, 6 October 1876, p. 3. Bunting later became a convener of the Eastern Question Conference. Of particular interest is the appeal of a Wesleyan lay reader for advice as to the proper procedure for denouncing the atrocities: *Methodist Recorder*, 15 September 1876, p. 555.

[2] *Ibid.*, p. 553.

[3] *Primitive Methodist*, 14 September 1876, p. 615.

[4] See e.g. *Times*, 15 September 1876, p. 7.

[5] Based on the list in the *Congregational Year Book* (1877). The other large connections, the Wesleyans and Baptists, provided, so far as can be determined from their respective year books, only four each. See also *Congregational Year Book* (1877), pp. 122, 130; Memorial of Board of Congregational Ministers of London to Gladstone (Gladstone Papers, Add. MSS 44451, ff. 194–5); and *Nonconformist*, 6 September 1876, p. 894.

provides an excellent example of the zealous Congregational agitator. He wrote to Gladstone on 7 September:

> Availing myself of your valuable counsel, I secured a Memorial to the Queen last night, which was carried by acclamation.
>
> Extracts from your pamphlet were listened to with eager attention & received with enthusiasm.
>
> The Clergy were all well represented. The working men were there in crowds. I could not prevent the resolution for the recall of the Ambassador—the feeling was too strong.
>
> I have written both to Methodist & Congregational friends in Bucks. The Non-Cons. are active everywhere. At Weigh House Chapel last Sunday, Mr. Braden, instead of a sermon, read Mr. Schuyler's report!
>
> The enclosed notice is only a specimen of a movement which I doubt not will be universal. Next Sunday I shall refer to it at 'Christchurch' & we shall hold the first public meeting in our new Hall, on this subject.[1]

The Unitarians alone could begin to vie with the quality of this contribution: P. W. Clayden, founder of the Free Church Union, formerly preacher at the Free Christian Church, Kentish Town, above all assistant editor of the *Daily News*; P. A. Taylor of Leicester and T. B. Potter of Manchester; Joseph Chamberlain in Birmingham, with the power and organisation of the Education League behind him. The much less sophisticated political (and social) stature of the Baptists as compared with the Congregationalists is indicated by the fact that only a light sprinkling of notables of the connection became conveners of the Eastern Question Conference: Landels (president of the Union), Maclaren (past president), and J. S. Wright (president of the Birmingham Liberal Association). Conspicuously absent from the list of conveners, moreover, was the greatest ornament of the 'strict and particular' side of the connection, Charles Haddon Spurgeon. Spurgeon declined to co-operate with Stead and Dale in the movement for a 'Bulgarian Sunday'.[2] Mundella later mentioned Spurgeon as a very desirable representative figure to grace the list of conveners of the Conference[3]; and Spurgeon's absence from the list indicates fairly clearly that he declined to co-operate in that project also. Spurgeon indeed did pray for the annihilation of Muslim power and for relief from the 'extraordinary folly of our rulers'— 'change our rulers, oh God, as soon as possible'[4]; but there is little

---

[1] Gladstone Papers, Add. MSS 44188, ff. 148–9.   [2] See above, p. 138.
[3] Mundella to J. D. Leader, 11 October 1876, Mundella Papers.
[4] *Bedfordshire Times and Independent*, 2 December 1876, p. 3.

evidence of deep moral involvement in the question. It was, no doubt, characteristic of the spirit of Nonconformity at large that the anonymous author of *The Great State Trial of Great Britain versus Benjamin Beaconsfield and Others* should have sentenced Disraeli to be deprived of office and committed for two years to 'Mr. Spurgeon's excellent Reformatory, the Tabernacle, at Newington'; but it was not an accurate reflection of Spurgeon's status in the agitation.[1] The principal Baptist contribution to the agitation lay rather in the practical zeal of the *Freeman*.[2]

Even the minor connections made a not negligible showing. John Bright's ambivalent attitude to the agitation—he did not become a convener of the Conference—illustrates a difficulty in which many Quakers must have found themselves. Nevertheless, the list of conveners does not lack notable Quaker names: Henry Pease, prominent in the Peace Society; the banker Edmund Backhouse, M.P. for Darlington and a steady supporter of Stead's atrocity campaigns. The Tukes were represented by Daniel Hack, the Gurneys by Samuel, the Sturges by Edmund, secretary of the Anti-Slavery Society. Again, despite the editorial coolness of the Presbyterian *Weekly Review*,[3] which seems to have taken its cue from the Scottish Establishment, evidences are not rare of English Presbyterian solidarity with the crusade of the greater Nonconformist connections in 1876. The weighty protest of the London Presbytery was echoed by persistent and subversive opinions in the non-editorial columns of the *Weekly Review* itself.[4] And certainly the Calvinistic Methodists in no degree lagged behind their Nonconformist brethren in Wales.

*

How does that Nonconformist crusade of 1876 figure in the perspective of Nonconformity in the nineteenth century? Nonconformists universally regarded it at the time as a sign of increased vigour, the herald of greater triumphs to come. The *Methodist Recorder* saw in its 'profound moral significance' the 'happiest augury and promise' for the future.[5] Miall in the *Nonconformist*

[1] See also the comment of the *World*, 11 October 1876, p. 3.
[2] E.g. 8 September 1876, pp. 432–3, demanding that all Baptist congregations be 'duly instructed' to denounce the government's Eastern policy, and urging the Union Committee to lose no time in giving a lead.
[3] E.g. 5 August 1876, p. 765; 16 September 1876, p. 909.
[4] E.g. 9 December 1876, pp. 1198–9.
[5] 22 September 1876, p. 566. Nor, in such a mood, were Anglo-Catholic suscepti-

thought it 'by no means improbable' that, in some such manner as this agitation, disestablishment and disendowment would be achieved.[1] The mood of Nonconformity was distinctly one of pride and confidence—even elation. In the near future seemed to lie not only disestablishment, but also an educational settlement conformable to Nonconformist consciences, and, associated intimately once more with the Liberal party, a heightened influence in politics and English life generally. This optimism seemed fully justified by the Liberal electoral triumph of 1880.

The Bulgarian atrocities agitation was certainly one of the finest hours of Nonconformity—in some ways perhaps its finest. Yet the perspective view puts the atrocities agitation at the end of the high period of Nonconformist effort and vigour, rather than at a beginning. It was by no means a happy 'augury and promise'. The crusade of 1876 and the election of 1880 were in fact respectively the climax and the finale of the era, extending back to the reform agitation of the eighteen-twenties and thirties, in which politically-mature Nonconformity derived positive strength from a dynamic of genuine and genuinely-felt grievance. The Bulgarian affair evoked a profound and instinctive response from Nonconformists as a matter related integrally to their moral system and their political traditions. Liddon's pathetic analogies between the Bulgarians and the Ritualists, the *bashi-bazouks* and Lord Penzance, have about them an element of querulous pettiness and absurdity which never tainted the Nonconformist crusade, even at its most hysterical under Stead.

But 1876 was for Nonconformity a false dawn. It encouraged overconfidence and raised extravagant hopes. Fully emancipated yet still aggressive, Nonconformity after 1880 failed to remain true to itself. Its obsession with disestablishment contradicted the fundamental principle of Dissent—that a religious settlement ought not to be imposed by state compulsion. Its social and intellectual élite increasingly eroded away by the 'subtle agencies of temptation', its spiritual narrowness exposed with rare literary sensitivity by William Hale White ('Mark Rutherford'), its

bilities always treated with scrupulous tenderness, even for the sake of the Bulgarians. One 'County Rector' felt obliged to protest to the *Daily News* about certain uncalled-for remarks by Samuel Morley on the subject of Ritualism. Internal dissension in the anti-Turk party at such a juncture, especially with the National Conference coming up, would be, he pointed out, 'eminently impolitic' (*Daily News*, 4 December 1876, p. 3).

[1] 13 September 1876, p. 905.

middle-class Radicalism less and less relevant in an era of emerging democracy, Nonconformity became essentially a sterile and debilitated force, and in turn infected Liberalism with its sterility and debility. The cashiering of Parnell and the successful sniping at Rosebery were but poor compensation for the failure to get disestablishment and the failure to secure an acceptable solution to the education question.

Ironically, it was Gladstone, hailed by Nonconformity in 1876 as the incarnation of the virtuous passion of the English people, who proved the greatest single stumbling block to Nonconformist aspirations. Guinness Rogers comments in tones of resigned but regretful bewilderment:

Unquestionably there were two separate occasions when Mr. Gladstone's policy did seem to check the Nonconformists' hopes. The first was that passionate movement on the Eastern Question which began in 1876, and which, for the time, occupied the public mind almost to the exclusion of every other question. At that time, Dr. Dale and myself had just completed our Disestablishment campaign, and it is not too much to say that there was an amount of interest and excitement on the subject which led us to hope, not certainly for immediate action, but for greater prominence being given to it both inside the circle of Dissent and in the Liberal Party itself. But, as has been seen, the Nonconformists, so far from regarding Mr. Gladstone as responsible for this unhappy *contretemps*, were among his most loyal and vigorous supporters.[1]

The second occasion which Rogers had in mind was of course Gladstone's final adoption of the policy of Home Rule for Ireland. Rogers concluded, a little wistfully: 'Let me add that those who, like myself, steadily adhered to him, never for a moment suspected that the Irish question was introduced to evade the demands of the Nonconformists. Circumstances were unfortunate, that was all.'[2]

Circumstances were indeed unfortunate, but in a deeper sense also than Guinness Rogers would have been willing to admit. The Nonconformist drive for disestablishment no doubt found in Gladstone a very awkward obstacle. Yet Gladstone, as long as he remained in active politics, remained the essential and inevitable spokesman of the political morality of Nonconformity. Nonconformists could neither do with Gladstone nor do without him. But Gladstone in himself is by no means adequate as an explanation of

---

[1] Guinness Rogers, *Autobiography*, p. 214.
[2] *Ibid.*, p. 215.

the Nonconformist failure. Even had he not helped to stem the drive for disestablishment, there is every likelihood that it would have petered out in much the same way and in much the same atmosphere as the Armenian atrocities agitation, which he did his best to promote.

3 Anglicanism

The Anglican presence among the protests addressed to the government was confined to memorials sent under the names of the Dean of Winchester, the Archdeacon of Canterbury, and a few rectors and vicars, all acting as chairmen of public protest meetings. The Church of England, as a Church, had nothing to say. The effect of the Archbishop of Canterbury's commendation of the 'strictly neutral' Eastern War Sufferers Relief Fund[1] was to dampen the agitation with faint aid. There did, of course, come from within the Church an immensely important fund of support and guidance for the agitation. Of the 137 ministers of religion among the conveners of the Eastern Question Conference, no less than 80 were clergy of the Church of England.[2] But the unsympathetic attitude of the great majority of the bishops and lesser clergy gave to the Church as a body a tone more or less hostile to the agitation.

Three primary elements combined to form this tone. The first was the Church's status as an establishment, together with Archbishop Tait's perhaps inordinately Erastian stress on its responsibilities to the state. The second was the traditionally Conservative sympathies of the clergy as a class. The third lay in the peculiar position of Anglo-Catholicism in relation to the Church as a whole on the one hand and the atrocities agitation on the other.

These factors interacted upon each other in a way which tended to intensify the Church's estrangement from the agitation. The circumstance that the government assailed by the agitation was a Conservative one gave an additional incentive to Tory parsons to rally all the more solidly behind Tait's doctrine of the duty of the 'national' Church to endorse the 'national' policy. It was the working of this 'state connection' as displayed in the atrocities

[1] *Times*, 15 September 1876, p. 10.
[2] Based on the *Clergy List* for 1877. There is at least one case (W. R. W. Stephens, later Freeman's biographer) of a clergyman not listed as such among the conveners.

agitation and in the Eastern question crisis generally which drove Freeman, the mildest of High Churchmen and no Ritualist, 'utterly' against all his predilections, towards accepting dis-establishment.[1] Freeman expressed a mood of dissatisfaction shared by many. And the further complicating and intensifying fact was that the one substantial party among the clergy which had an ecclesiastical as well as a moral motive for special sympathy with the agitation was also the party which had, 'under existing cir-cumstances', as Liddon delicately put it to Guinness Rogers,[2] the least motive for gratitude and loyalty to the government and to Archbishop Tait.

The shock of the atrocities agitation, like that of an earthquake, acted naturally along existing fault lines in religion as well as politics. With Nonconformity the effect of this had been to close the rift between it and Liberalism; with the Church of England the fault line of Ritualism became an even wider rift between the ecclesiastical parties. The line of conflict was not exposed quite where it lay in 1874, but there tended to be an ominous similarity. As the High Church *Church Review* pointed out, it would not be true to say that any party, religious or political, could be defined simply as pro-Turkish; yet one had only to look at the two most conspicuous instances where 'philo-Turkism and pure Protestant-ism' were 'ostentatiously displayed in conjunction': Disraeli and the *Standard* newspaper, those two pillars of the Public Worship Regulation policy.[3]

The inescapable outcome was that, in the Church, dissent from the government-Establishment nexus on the Eastern question had about it a predominantly Anglo-Catholic tone. Most of the eighty Anglican clerical conveners were of the Catholic party, some of them the most famous. Pusey himself was one; Denison also. R. W. Church, Dean of St Paul's and mentor of the party, applauded Liddon's activities warmly.[4] Liddon of course took a most prominent part in the Conference as one of the principal speakers. Also well to the front were Malcolm MacColl, Knox-Little, Lowder, Mackonochie, Portal (domestic chaplain to the Earl of Carnarvon), Talbot (Warden of Keble College)—all of

[1] Freeman to Liddon, 7 April 1878, Liddon Papers.
[2] Liddon to Guinness Rogers, 28 January 1878, *ibid.*
[3] *Church Review*, 30 September 1876, pp. 491–2.
[4] See e.g. Church to Liddon, 16 February 1877, Liddon Papers.

the Catholic wing. Members of the Eastern Church Association would feel a special interest: committee members of the Association among the conveners were Denton, Littledale, George Williams, and, of the laity, the Hon. C. L. Wood, heir of Lord Halifax and president of the Anglo-Catholic Church Union.

The organ of extreme Evangelicalism, the *Rock*, far surpassed the *Church Times* or the *Guardian* in the simplicity of its interpretation of events. The Eastern question had converted the Anglo-Roman conspiracy into an Anglo-Greek conspiracy. 'Everywhere', announced the *Rock*, 'we encounter traces of the deep-laid plot.'[1] Foremost were the utterances of Liddon, and the 'breathless haste' with which he and his henchman MacColl rushed to the scene. Liddon's views were echoed from across the Indian seas by the 'treasonable invectives' of the Anglo-Catholic Bishop of Bombay. The plot could be detected in the *Church Quarterly Review* no less than in the accredited organs of the 'priest-party'. It had its adherents at court—'(we need not particularize)'—and in the government, especially in the persons of Carnarvon and Salisbury. And of course there was Gladstone. The *Rock* had not forgotten the disgusting veneration with which he had treated the Greek clergy when High Commissioner in the Ionian Islands.[2]

It is certainly true that among the extreme Ritualist party there was a tendency towards a fairly complete and naive identification of the merits of the Eastern question and Anglo-Catholicism. Wood illustrates this tendency well. Thus he wrote to Liddon in January 1877:

> Mr. J. Baring said to me the other day, he is nothing of a churchman but one of the shrewdest people I know & a partner in that house:
> 'The real reason why so many people side with the Turks is because they cannot bear the idea that Christianity should have anything to do towards shaping men's sympathies.'
> It is precisely the same feeling that causes Lyulph Stanley Edmond Fitzmaurice etc. to oppose Keble Coll.[3]

Again, in January 1878, after referring to a 'splendid' speech on the Eastern question by the Duke of Argyll: 'The working men's meeting was also splendid—& I was not insensible, over & above the real and overpowering interests at stake, to the pleasure of

[1] 10 November 1876, p. 861.   [2] *Ibid*.
[3] Wood to Liddon, 21 January 1877, Liddon Papers.

feeling that *we* were helping to turn the tables on the author of [the] P.W.R.A.'[1] And it was characteristic of Wood to remark, shortly after the Russian capture of Kars from the Turks, concerning a technical legal success in the case of a prominent victim of the Public Worship Regulation Act, the Rev. Mr Tooth: 'I feel as if we had taken our Kars.'[2]

Another minor but illuminating instance of Anglo-Catholic axe-grinding is disclosed by F. A. G. Eichbaum, of the Clergy House of Rest, Malvern Link. He was discussing with Liddon in October 1876 a scheme of his to take orphaned Bulgarian children to England to educate them as clerks and school-masters, or perhaps 'put them out to service'. He elaborated:

My idea with the children was to train them up to believe that the religion of their forefathers & our own were essentially the same, & that if they did eventually return to their country it would be to return to their own communion, at the same time with a thorough belief that the Church of England was Catholic as well as their own.[3]

It became a matter of surprise, worthy of note, that a High Church vicar could yet be a jingo[4]; and one correspondent of Liddon's recommended his brother, who, despite being an army officer, was quite sound on the Eastern question, 'though a *decided* Evangelical'.[5] Their predominance among Churchmen supporting the agitation became to the High Church agitators a distinct embarrassment. Canon Bright of Oxford wrote to Liddon urging the desirability of getting up a memorial of 'some "representative" clergymen, not exclusively of the High Church side', in favour of neutrality in the Russo-Turkish war.[6] Liddon was prominent also in getting up a committee to organise a Russian Sick and Wounded Fund; and in a letter to *The Times* protested that the names comprising the committee could be 'referred to no one of our political or religious parties'.[7]

---

[1] Wood to Liddon, 18 January 1878, *ibid*. See also MacColl to Gladstone, 21 August [1876], Gladstone Papers, Add. MSS 44243, ff. 173–6: 'I believe that the workingmen's association against the Publication [sic] Worship Regulation Act will play a part in the next Election wh. Dizzy little anticipated.'

[2] Wood to Liddon, 22 November 1877, Liddon Papers.

[3] Eichbaum to Liddon, 21 October [1876], *ibid*.

[4] MacColl to Liddon, 23 January [1877], *ibid*.

[5] Plummer to Liddon, 28 December [1877], *ibid*.

[6] Bright to Liddon, [6 January] 1878, *ibid*.

[7] *Times*, 31 August 1877, p. 7. The most notable members of the committee were the Duke of Westminster (president), the Marquess of Bath (vice-president), the

Despite the rather excessive Churchmanship of Wood and Eichbaum and the embarrassment of Bright and Liddon, Anglo-Catholicism did not, in itself, determine the nature of the conflict in the Church over the Eastern question. Wood did appreciate that there were 'real and overpowering' interests at stake, however much these tended to get obscured in the immediate struggle against Archbishop Tait and Lord Penzance. Liddon himself was categorical in his denial that the theological and ecclesiastical aspect of the question had any bearing on the central issue.[1] Liddon and his school ascribed the failure of the Church to protest against the atrocities to a simple failure of moral nerve. 'We of the Church of England', he protested, 'are too frightened about Education, the Burials Bill, or Disestablishment, to do justice, *as a body*, to the plain moral aspects of the Eastern Question.'[2] Tait defended his position in terms of the duties of a national Church to uphold its secular partner. When asked in 1878 to address the Queen against war with Russia on behalf of Turkey, he refused on the grounds that the Church was 'bound to strengthen the hands of the authorities'.[3]

The fundamental division in the Church arose substantially from these opposing theses, rather than the issues of 1874. Many of the strongest anti-Turks among Churchmen were also enthusiastic supporters of the Public Worship Act. Many others, if not enthusiastic for Tait's policy, were distinctly unsympathetic to the ideals of Anglo-Catholicism. The relation of Anglo-Catholicism to the Public Worship Regulation policy and the Eastern Churches, though it bulked large in the public eye and tended to give a particular colour to clerical participation in the agitation, was, if far from being as inconsiderable an aspect as Liddon implied, still essentially a contributing influence, quite distinct from the feeling which animated Shaftesbury and Henry Montagu Butler and Stop-

---

Duke of Rutland, the Marquess of Bute, the Earls of Strathmore, Shaftesbury, and Glasgow, the Bishop of Ely, Lord Richard Grosvenor, Sir R. Phillimore, R. W. Church, Professor Stubbs, Thomas Carlyle, Ambrose de Lisle, E. A. Freeman, Liddon, Allon, Professor Bright, R. H. Hutton, Auberon Herbert, J. A. Froude, Bryce, Samuel Morley, Newman Hall, Baldwin Brown, Humphry Sandwith, Herbert Spencer, MacColl and Stopford Brooke (hon. secretaries). See Liddon Papers. Russian Sick and Wounded Fund.

[1] See Liddon to Guiness Rogers, 28 January 1878, Liddon Papers.
[2] Liddon to Freeman, 26 February 1878, *ibid*.
[3] R. Davidson and W. Benham, *Life of Archibald Campbell Tait* (1891), vol. ii, p. 326.

ford Brooke and Frederick Temple just as much as Pusey, Liddon, or Charles Wood.

★

The rather awkward posture of the Anglican Church with regard to the atrocities agitation fascinated Stead. It would perhaps be too much to say that, though a zealous and pugnacious Nonconformist, he derived malicious pleasure from the divisions and embarrassments of the Establishment. Nevertheless, he displayed an almost morbid interest in its difficulties, pressing Liddon and other Churchmen at various times for their explanations of its moral shortcomings. Eventually he denounced the 'lamentable apostasy' of the Establishment in an outspoken article in the *Northern Echo*, contrasting its delinquency with the righteous solidarity of Dissent.[1]

Stead's interest in this matter is no doubt partly explained by the fact that he contemplated writing a study of the agitation. Liddon replied to one of his queries in November 1876: 'As to the feelings of the clergy, I am not a vy. good judge. Politically speaking, most clergymen are Conservatives. They are hard at work in their parishes, and do not know enough about European politics to entertain strong opinions: they put themselves into the hand of the Government.' This was regrettable; but Liddon obviously felt a duty to defend the Church of which he himself was an unsparing critic from the disparagement of outsiders. It would be a mistake, he told Stead, to assume that all the clergymen who took in the *Standard*, and accepted its opinions without having any means of ascertaining their value, would agree with it if they 'knew more'. The line taken by the *Guardian* was a fair index to the opinion obtaining 'among the more thoughtful section of the clergy'. These were not keener politicians than the others, Liddon emphasised; it required only, for a matter of this kind, 'sufficient knowledge of the facts and a fair exercise of the moral sense'.[2]

When Stead suggested in 1878 that he might discuss with Liddon the 'clerical aspects of the "atrocity agitation" of 1876', Liddon was careful, in spite of his often expressed disappointment with the mass of the clergy,[3] not to minimise unduly the contri-

---

[1] 14 November 1877, pp. 2–3: 'Church and Dissent on the Eastern Question.'
[2] Liddon to Stead, 15 November 1876, Stead Papers.
[3] E.g. Stead, *The M.P. for Russia*, vol. i, pp. 393–4.

bution of the Church. Rather he emphasised the sacrifices which participation involved.

It was, I think—so far as the clergy took part in it—a spontaneous act of homage to what was believed to be the cause of righteousness; and it had the effect of sharply separating many clergymen from their old political associates, and of producing a great deal of discomfort or worse. Those who joined the agitation—not because it was for the moment popular, but because they believed it to be right—have not, so far as I know, regretted the course they took, or swerved from it subsequently.[1]

The reference to the 'popularity' of the agitation was to some extent evasive; Liddon knew as well as Canon Bright that with the coming of the Russo-Turkish war and the crises which this produced many clergymen had 'relapsed since the autumn of 1876 into indifference as to the interests of Christianity and humanity in the East'.[2] It was this consideration, together with a letter from R. W. Dale suggesting that Churchmen might well emulate the activity of his Birmingham committee of Nonconformist ministers,[3] which prompted Canon Bright to suggest to Liddon the idea of a declaration by the clergy against Britain's going to war on behalf of Turkey.

On 2 February 1878 Liddon reported to Freeman that this 'Clerical Declaration' had just received its thousandth signature. 'But the abstentions, many of them, are very sad. Either men do not see the moral and religious interests at stake: or they sacrifice their Christianity to politics.'[4] Among the saddest of the abstentions were the bishops. Three only signed the Declaration. Even

---

[1] Liddon to Stead, 19 July 1878, Stead Papers.

[2] Canon Bright to Liddon, [6 January] 1878, Liddon Papers.

[3] R. W. Dale to Canon Bright, 4 January 1878, in A. W. W. Dale, *Life of R. W. Dale of Birmingham* (1898), pp. 423-4.

[4] Liddon to Freeman, 2 February 1878, Liddon Papers. The number of clergy of the Church of England at that time was in the region of 22,000 (with another 1,900 in Ireland). This is an estimate based on the *Clergy List* of 1877. The Declaration was as follows:

'We the undersigned Clergymen of the Church of England desire to express an earnest hope that the policy of neutrality hitherto observed by England towards the Powers now engaged in war may not be departed from.

To identify English interests with the maintenance of a cruel and oppressive government like that of Turkey is in our judgment dishonourable to the English name; and we trust that the blood of our countrymen will not be shed in an endeavour to uphold an empire, which is the traditional enemy of Christian civilisation and progress.

        H. P. Liddon, D.D., Canon of St. Paul's.
        Wm. Bright, D.D., Canon of Christ Church.
        Wm. Denton, M.A., Vicar of St. Bartholomew, Cripplegate.'

Liddon Papers.

then Mackarness gave his name with the greatest reluctance, worried about the political implications of the Declaration, even more worried that it might do harm to the cause by revealing nakedly what little support the agitation had among the clergy.[1]

*

The bench of bishops, as the special guardians of the Church Establishment, represented with fidelity the cold or hostile spirit of that Establishment towards the atrocities agitation. Freeman, as ever, was ready to over-dramatise his disillusionment. He wrote to Bryce on 5 June 1878:

> I quoted the first lesson of to-day. Does not the whole story in Chroni-cles read as if the history of the two or three last years should be recast by an ultra-clerical pen which should put all Gladstone's & Goldwin's preaching of righteousness into the mouths of Tait and Thomson? 'Tis the lay prophets that speak, both in Israel & Britain.[2]

For Tait and Thomson to have crossed the government would not have been an unprecedented act. In this matter, putting aside the merits of the Eastern question, Liddon and Freeman had a genuine grievance against Tait's doctrine of the Church being 'bound to uphold the authorities'. This was no mere prejudice on Tait's part. There was no question of his being influenced by parsonical Toryism, for both in theology and politics his tendencies were Liberal. The circumstances of his promotion to Lambeth in 1868 and the late and rather cynically opportunist support accorded to his Public Worship Bill in 1874 put him under very little personal obligation to Disraeli.[3]

Tait's Erastianism had a Presbyterian flavour about it which intensified to excess the already narrow attitude to the Church-state relationship imposed upon him by political constraint. In his attempt to cope with the crisis in the Church compounded of the legacy of the Oxford Movement and the new militancy of Non-conformity, Tait's necessary ally was a government combining

---

[1] Liddon to Freeman, 26 February 1878, *ibid.*; Mackarness to Liddon, 27 January 1878, *ibid.* The other two bishops would very probably have been Temple and Woodford. Fraser tended to be less to the front after 1876.

[2] Bryce Papers, E4.

[3] Even Freeman went some way towards recognising Tait's good faith. To Liddon, 24 August 1877, Liddon Papers: 'The Abp. is like his brother of New Rome, set up by the circumcised, though he cannot be so easily set down again. Therefore he is not so bound to say what the circumcised tell him. Let us hope that it is through a rude sense of honour that he does what the other does through constraint.'

the two qualities of not having at its head a High Churchman who would block action to discipline Ritualism by legislation, and of not being embarrassed by the presence of a truculent and unruly corps of Nonconformists in the mass of its adherents. Disraeli and the Conservatives, however distasteful to Tait on many grounds, were indispensable for his Church policy. This circumstance did not determine Tait's attitude to the Eastern question. As far as he was concerned, the 'National Established Church for the great English people', to quote a characteristic phrase from one of his charges of 1876,[1] was committed, by the very principle and nature of its existence, to the 'national' line. But Tait's attitude was, in a very real sense, justified by the spectacle of the unholy alliance of the leaders of disruption from without and within, R. W. Dale and Guinness Rogers, Liddon and MacColl, in the vanguard of the atrocities agitation.

Undoubtedly Tait took the prudent, proper course in the interest of the greatest possible unity of the Church. Magee, Bishop of Peterborough, expressed the orthodox episcopal attitude of the hard core of Low Church or 'Derby-Dizzy' bishops. 'I doubt', he wrote on 18 September 1876, 'if the whole history of democracy, rife as it is with instances of passionate injustice, supplies a grosser one than the cry against the Ministry of the last three weeks.'[2] Lightfoot, the great Cambridge theologian, recently elevated to the see of Durham, represented a less hostile but equally firm attitude. He agreed with Liddon that it would be a 'grievous crime' for England to go to war merely to uphold Turkey, but refused to sign the Declaration of the Clergy because it implied a confidence in Russia which Lightfoot could not share. Also—and here something of the Establishment mentality is exposed—Lightfoot felt that the Declaration cast doubt on the good faith of almost every influential member of the ministry who had 'declared against war in the most explicit terms, & I am bound to believe that they mean what they say'. Disraeli's bellicose flourishes were regrettable; but not enough to justify giving the lie to the government.[3]

[1] A. C. Tait, *Some Thoughts on the Duties of the Established Church of England as a National Church* (1876), pp. 104–5.
[2] J. C. Macdonell, *The Life and Correspondence of William Connor Magee* (1896), vol. ii, p. 49.
[3] Lightfoot to Liddon, 16 January [1878], Liddon Papers. See also, in the same vein, Capetown to Liddon, 18 November 1876, *ibid.*
In a sermon before the University of Cambridge Lightfoot's comment was that the

One party among the bishops could be defined as the reluctant non-participators in the agitation. Chief among these was Christopher Wordsworth, Bishop of Lincoln. As the one fully-accredited Anglo-Catholic on the bench, as an enthusiastic patron of the Eastern Church Association, as a strong opponent of the Public Worship Regulation Act, Wordsworth might have been expected to emulate or surpass Woodford or Mackarness.

Wordsworth was not, however, for all his radiant visions of St Sophia restored to Christianity,[1] prepared to go beyond the expression of these ideals to an active pursuit of them. When Wood wrote asking him to become a convener of the Eastern Question Conference, Wordsworth would not take the plunge. 'He sympathises with its objects', his son wrote to Liddon, 'but feels some hesitation in entering into an association which has rather a political aspect.'[2] Episcopal traditions still counted for something; and, after all, Wordsworth had been promoted to the bench—even if only for tactical reasons—by Disraeli.

By the same token, the four openly 'atrocitarian' bishops, the moderate High Churchmen Fraser and Mackarness, the more pronounced High Churchman Woodford, and the Liberal Temple, were all thoroughgoing Gladstonians, both in that they had been appointed by Gladstone as part of his policy of redressing the episcopal balance against the preponderance of Low 'Derby-Dizzy' bishops, and in their admiration of Gladstone's personality and the moral emphasis of his politics. Woodford wrote to Liddon in November 1876: 'I cannot help adding one line more to say how heartily I have gone with you upon this Eastern Question. How nobly and chivalrously has Gladstone shone through the whole controversy!'[3]

★

atrocities agitation might encourage too much self-righteousness and complacency; humility rather than self-righteous wrath was the attitude more suitable for Christians. See T. L. Henly, *Christianity, as Set Forth by His Grace the Archbishop of Canterbury, together with a Few Remarks on the Turkish Atrocities* (pamphlet, 1877), p. 18.

[1] *The Mohammedan Woe and Its Passing Away*, pp. 25–8.
[2] John Wordsworth to Liddon, 1 December 1876, Liddon Papers.
[3] Woodford to Liddon, 2 November [1876], *ibid.* Woodford 'gladly' gave his name for the committee of Liddon's Russian Sick and Wounded Fund in 1877 (to Liddon, 21 August 1877, *ibid.*) when Fraser and Mackarness both held back (Fraser to Liddon, 22 August [1877], *ibid.*).

The Evangelical party in the Church matched in hostility to the agitation the solidarity of Nonconformity on its behalf. A Nonconformist, let alone a prominent Nonconformist, is hardly to be found opposing the movement; apart from Shaftesbury, there is hardly a Low Churchman to be seen among the agitators. The Low Church was not as solidly Tory (or Whig) as Nonconformity was Liberal; but on the other hand the Evangelicals were bitterly suspicious of Anglo-Catholic axe-grinding in the agitation—with good cause. And naturally the party most deeply committed to the *status quo* in religious affairs as by law established—and that in a very real and immediate sense—would have least incentive to challenge the attitude of the government, the court, and the episcopate, all of which in great degree shared its religious viewpoint and patronised it as the inner Establishment.

The *Rock* took great pride in the 'almost total absence' of Low Churchmen from the Eastern Question Conference.[1] Evangelical clergy, indeed, as the *Rock* observed with swelling pride, were 'conspicuous' by their total absence,[2] especially by contrast to that 'treacherous clerical ingredient',[3] the phalanx of Anglo-Catholics. The *Rock* much regretted that Shaftesbury should have marred the patriotic completeness of the Low Church's repudiation of the agitation: 'though a good philanthropist, he was always a bad politician'.[4]

Shaftesbury indeed was made to suffer most keenly for his bad politics. The conflict between his own conscience on the Bulgarian question and the Evangelical repudiation of the cause to which his conscience was committed more than any other single event exposed his isolation in the new dispensation of things. Shaftesbury represented the heroic era in which Evangelicalism had struggled against odds; he had survived into the era in which the Low Church, too successful for the health of its spirit, was on the defensive. He

---

[1] 15 December 1876, p. 957. Sir Thomas Chambers, M.P., and Mr Whalley, M.P. (the great champion of the Tichborne Claimant and violent anti-Roman Catholic) were the only two detected by the *Rock* (8 December 1876, p. 949).

[2] 8 December 1876, p. 949. The *Church Times*, however, detected the Rev. Francis Morse of Nottingham at the Conference, and expressed thanks that at least one Evangelical clergyman had risen 'superior to his school' (15 December 1876, p. 641). The *Church Times* commented generally on this point: 'We suppose that just as the Evangelicals backed Lord Palmerston in the last Chinese War in payment for his episcopal appointments, so now Lord Beaconsfield is reaping the profits of his investment in the Public Worship Regulation Act, in the support of the faction in whose interest it was passed.'

[3] 15 December 1876, p. 957.   [4] 8 December 1876, p. 945.

O

wrote in October 1876, after sending off the miserable sum of
£128 3s 2d (including £10 of his own) to the Consuls' Fund for
Bulgarian Relief, the fruit of his personal appeal for subscriptions:
'This, and other things of late, are "notice to quit". The public
have had enough, and indeed, too much of a good thing in me.'[1]
And though Shaftesbury was later one of the chairmen of the
Eastern Question Conference and a zealous supporter of Liddon's
Russian Sick and Wounded Fund,[2] the disillusionment of 1876
and his greatly increased awareness that he had outlived his time
and generation made a decisive break in the continuity of his public
career.

★

The Liberal Churchmen were too few in number and too diverse
in theological tendency to make a 'party' on the Bulgarian question in the same way as the Catholics and the Evangelicals. Yet
in so far as the doctrines of Thomas Arnold constituted the central,
guiding tradition for the Broad Church, the weight of Broad influence, heavy with intellectual distinction, was thrown against
the atrocities agitation. Tait, in repudiating the agitation, was as
true to his intellectual heritage as to his sense of the necessities of
the Church; and Temple was almost as much a renegade as
Shaftesbury.[3]

The Arnoldian ideal of a comprehensive, liberal Establishment,
in its negative aspect, had two sides to it: one, a black and total
distrust of Anglo-Catholicism; the other, a regret, tinged with
contempt, for the persistence of Nonconformity. These were the
two groups standing stubbornly apart from what the school of
Arnold conceived to be the mainstream of the national life and
culture of England. Their exclusive pretensions and jealous obstinacy were the greatest barriers to the realisation of the truly
'National Established Church for the great English people'. The
alliance of Anglo-Catholicism and Nonconformity in the Bulgarian
atrocities agitation could thus most naturally be represented as an

[1] Hodder, *Shaftesbury*, vol. iii, p. 376.
[2] Shaftesbury to Liddon, 4 September 1877, Liddon Papers.
[3] Very few prominent Liberal Churchmen followed the atrocities agitation. Henry
Montagu Butler, Headmaster of Harrow, became a convener of the Eastern Question
Conference, as did also Mark Pattison (see below, p. 220). Stopford Brooke was a
convener and later one of the secretaries of the Russian Sick and Wounded Fund; and
perhaps it is significant that in 1880 he lapsed into neo-Unitarianism.

aggressive combination of quasi-Romanism and provincialism
against the national interest. This is how Tait viewed it, and
Lightfoot, and Westcott,[1] and Jowett,[2] and above all Stanley,
brightest ornament of the Broad Church and in this, as in so many
other matters, its spokesman.

Stanley had many of the qualifications of a Bulgarian atrocities
agitator. A sympathetic historian of the Eastern Churches, he
knew and admired the Russians. In politics he had Liberal leanings.
And indeed his first reaction to the agitation appears not to have
been hostile. He later admitted that it originated in a burst of
righteous indignation, which was, however, soon 'coloured and
perverted as it rolled on, partly by personal and political animosity
. . . partly by various small ecclesiastical influences'.[3] As 'A
Liberal English Churchman', he wrote to the *Northern Echo* in 1877
sharply attacking Stead's strictures on the clerical 'apostasy' over
the Eastern question. He dwelt suggestively on the 'mingled and
complex flow of human motives', and the 'secondary influences'
inevitably 'intertwined with the primary causes of political action':
all a scarcely-veiled attack on the good faith of Anglo-Catholicism.
Gladstone he denounced flatly as a bad Churchman.[4]

Stanley's very tolerance set him against the agitation. He could
not abide any of the 'aroma of the fourth century' relished by
Liddon, nor the element of patristic fanaticism which Liddon cultivated to match his fond attachment to the damnatory clauses of
the Athanasian Creed. To Stanley, the High Church's zeal for the
agitation bore much of the character and spirit of its zeal for the
bullying of Jowett and the hounding of Colenso. And there were
other features of his outlook apart from what Liddon liked to think
of as his deficiency in the 'logical faculty'[5]: he had intimate relations with the court; he respected Disraeli.[6] He had, moreover, a
very prescient sense of foreboding about Gladstone. He wrote
early in 1877:

Gladstone is filled with a genuine enthusiasm for the Eastern Chris-

[1] See A. Westcott, *Life and Letters of Brooke Foss Westcott* (1903), vol. i, p. 338.
Westcott's associate, Hort, was rather more sympathetic to the agitation: A. F. Hort,
Life and Letters of Fenton John Anthony Hort (1896), vol. ii, pp. 215–16.
[2] See below, pp. 213–15.
[3] R. E. Prothero, *The Life and Correspondence of Arthur Penrhyn Stanley*, D.D.
(1893), vol, ii, p. 502.
[4] *Northern Echo*, 17 November 1877, p. 3. See also Estelle Stead, *My Father*, p. 79.
[5] Johnston, *Liddon*, p. 274.
[6] Prothero, *Stanley*, pp. 397–8, 447–9.

tians; but, combined with this, he has a hold on the masses, and the masses have a hold on him, that makes his future career, now that he is disengaged from the control of his party, a phenomenon at once most interesting and most portentous.[1]

★

The incisive 'logical faculty' of the High Churchmen often proved strong enough to override traditional political attachments; and there seems little doubt that such support from Conservative quarters as the agitation did enjoy derived from Churchmanship more than anything else. MacColl had told Gladstone, attempting to entice him into the agitation, that a 'very large portion of the clergy & of lay churchmen (till now Conservatives)' had 'vowed vengeance' on Disraeli.[2] This is undoubtedly an exaggeration; but Conservative High Churchmen were apt to bolt the party on this question.[3] As early as July 1876 the Rev. P. G. Medd anxiously wrote to his fellow High Churchman, Lord Carnarvon: 'I cannot forbear expressing to you ... the profound anxiety which many (I am persuaded) who, like myself, are Conservatives by birth and education, and by every conviction, regard the risk of England's having again been committed to the policy of upholding ... the Turkish Empire....'[4]

Several notable Tory names adorned the list of conveners of the Eastern Question Conference or the committee of the Russian Sick and Wounded Fund. The Earl of Glasgow, a former Conservative M.P. for Bute, seems a clear case of Anglo-Catholic motivation. He was in 1873 chairman of the committee of the Eastern Church Association. He worked closely in the Eastern question with the great Roman Catholic magnate (newly converted), the Marquess of Bute, also a Conservative.[5] The case of the Duke of Rutland is rather less clear. Formerly a Conservative and Protectionist M.P., he was the elder brother of Lord John Manners, one

---

[1] *Ibid.*, p. 503.

[2] MacColl to Gladstone, 21 August [1876], Gladstone Papers, Add. MSS 44243, ff. 173–6. See also MacColl, *The Sultan and the Powers*, pp. 1–2.

[3] Thus 'A Tory No Longer' wrote to the *Church Times*, 1 September 1876, p. 435, pointing out indignantly that England was on the eve of committing a great crime, and that something would have to be done to convince Disraeli that the English people would not tolerate the betrayal of the Eastern Christians. This meant that Bucks. must be wrested from the Conservatives.

[4] Medd to Carnarvon, 13 July 1876, Carnarvon Papers, P.R.O., 30, 6/22; Carnarvon to Medd, 17 July 1876, *ibid.*   [5] See below, pp. 193, 195.

of the more violent Turcophiles in Disraeli's cabinet. Rutland's views, as Ambrose de Lisle reported to Gladstone, exactly squared with de Lisle's own.[1] De Lisle, whose own view on the Eastern question derived so intimately from his Catholicism, is a good indication that the same was true of Rutland. The case of the Earl of Strathmore is more obscure. A Conservative representative peer of Scotland, the only suggestive feature in his background seems to be that he was an 'ardent supporter of the Scottish Episcopal Church',[2] a body whose High leanings matched the Lowness of the Church in Ireland.

The most important of the Conservatives compelled by Anglo-Catholic religious feelings to diverge from the party on the issue of the Eastern question was Thynne, fourth Marquess of Bath. A great magnate in Wiltshire and Somerset, a former Conservative Whip in the Lords, he was an extreme High Churchman,[3] distinguished especially as a violent enemy of the Public Worship Regulation policy.[4] Bath's home at Longleat became a centre of 'plotting' for agitation. Gladstone, Liddon, and Freeman spent three days there in January 1877 talking 'incessantly' about the Eastern question.[5] Bath exemplified well the High Church tendency to complement dislike of the Turks with an uncritical Russophilism,[6] though his Toryism made him a somewhat reluctant convener of the Eastern Question Conference.[7] Some work had to be put in to keep him straight. MacColl, invaluable in these matters, reported to Gladstone in October 1878 that Bath, whom MacColl had recently met, was in 'some perplexity' as to his present relations with the Conservative party and his future political prospects. The organisation which he had built up in Wiltshire and Somerset was going to pieces, and unless he bestirred himself would inevitably be lost to the party. It would be a terrible wrench for Bath to break with his old political associates for good; yet he 'utterly loathed' their tactics and policy on the Eastern question. MacColl suggested to Gladstone that it might

[1] Purcell, *Ambrose Phillipps de Lisle*, vol. ii, p. 168.
[2] J. B. Paul (ed.), *The Scots Peerage* (Edinburgh 1911), vol. viii, p. 314.
[3] He was especially interested in the peculiar semi-theocratic situation in Montenegro. He sent large sums of money there on two occasions. See W. J. Stillman, *The Autobiography of a Journalist* (1901), vol. ii, p. 164.
[4] Buckle, *Disraeli*, vol. ii, p. 662.
[5] Johnston, *Liddon*, pp. 214–15; Freeman to Bryce, 15 January 1877, Bryce Papers, E 4.   [6] E.g. Bath to Liddon, 15 December 1878, Liddon Papers.
[7] Bath to Probyn, 3 December 1876, E.Q.A., *Report*, p. 1.

help to overcome Bath's perplexities if he were invited to Hawarden, at the same time, say, as the Duke of Argyll.[1]

Bath himself wrote to Carnarvon in November 1876, 'in great trouble', for the Conservative M.P. for Frome, Lopes, had been made a judge, thus leaving an embarrassing vacancy.

I have with those who work with me [Bath told Carnarvon] the power of preventing a Conservative being returned (it will require all we can do to return one). I am most anxious for general reasons of home policy to keep our majority, on the other hand I cannot but be true to my own long held and now avowed opinions on the Eastern question. I hope whoever stands as a Conservative will declare himself against going to war under any pretext for the maintenance of the Turkish Empire—and in favour of securing the local freedom & protection of life person & property to the Christians . . . on a better security than good will & fidelity of the Turks in which case we may avoid a split fatal to Government interests down here.

This Carnarvon passed on to Disraeli, who was probably little impressed by the threat and less by Bath's added proviso that if he supported the government candidate at Frome, his opposing the government in public and in the Lords next session was not to debar him from asserting claims which he 'might otherwise be supposed to have on them'.[2] Disraeli well knew that he took no risks by treating Bath's feeble effort at blackmail with contempt. Bath's influence and standing among Conservatives at large was negligible; and he gathered behind him no following whatsoever in the party. He 'believed', as Granville rather sardonically reported to Gladstone after a call at Longleat in December, that 'some' Tory M.P.s 'agreed' with him, though he had not taken the trouble to get in touch with them; and in any case he found such peers as he had sounded 'very strong the other way'.[3]

★

[1] MacColl to Gladstone, ?12 October [1878], Gladstone Papers, Add. MSS 44243, ff. 250–3.

[2] Bath to Carnarvon, 3 November 1876; Carnarvon to Disraeli, 4 November 1876, Disraeli Papers.

[3] Granville to Gladstone, 3 December 1876, Gladstone Papers, Add. MSS 44171, ff. 25–7.

The total number of Conservative peers who became conveners of the Eastern Question Conference or members of the Russian Sick and Wounded committee was seven: the Duke of Rutland, and Lords Bath, Bute, Glasgow, Seaton, Shaftesbury, and Strathmore. Conservative M.P.s were an even rarer breed: Lord Robert Montagu, definitely of an eccentric cast of mind, appears to have been the only one. See his *Foreign Policy: England and the Eastern Question* (1877), very anti-Russian, but

Another, very different, facet of Anglo-Catholicism in relation
to the atrocities agitation is revealed in the case of Oscar Wilde.
At this time an undergraduate of Magdalen College, Oxford,
Wilde was deep in the contemporary fashion in the university for
Catholicism—Anglo merging into Roman. His letters of this
period are full of references to religious points, to Liddon and
MacColl, Newman and Manning.[1] Wilde appears to have had but
faint moral indignation against the Turks, and his poems on the
atrocities are hardly more than literary exercises in the manner of
Milton.[2] It would not be fair, however, to dismiss Wilde as a mere
poseur, attempting to exploit the atrocities agitation to secure a
'literary interest' in London. The agitation, and particularly
Gladstone's part in it, attracted powerfully a particular kind of
youthful idealism. Ellis Ashmead Bartlett is one example which
has already been cited; another was the London clerk at Black-

strong on the point that states are 'moral persons', which perhaps gives the clue to
his critical attitude to Disraeli's handling of the atrocities issue. Montagu was a Roman
Catholic convert, who later seceded and became a bitter anti-Catholic propagandist.
In the parliament of 1874–80 he was the only Conservative supporting Irish Home
Rule.

[1] See V. Holland, *Son of Oscar Wilde* (1954), Appendix A.

[2] Wilde to Gladstone [14 May 1877], Gladstone Papers, Add. MSS 44454,
ff. 124–5:

'Your noble and impassioned protests, both written and spoken, against the
massacres of the Christians in Bulgaria have so roused my heart that I venture to send
you a sonnet which I have written on the subject.

I am little more than a boy, and have no literary interest in London, but perhaps
if *you* saw any good stuff in the lines I send you, some Editor (of the Nineteenth Century perhaps or the Spectator) might publish them: and I feel sure that you can
appreciate the very great longing that one has when young to have words of one's own
published for men to read.'

He subscribed himself with 'deepest admiration'. This sonnet, 'On the recent
Massacres of the Christians in Bulgaria', does not appear to have been published in
either the *Nineteenth Century* or the *Spectator*, or any other literary journal of the time.
It came out, in an altered form, in Wilde's first published collection of poems in 1881.
The sonnet in Wilde's holograph (Gladstone Papers, *ibid.*, f. 126) is as follows.

> Christ dost thou live indeed? or are thy bones
>   Still straightened in their rock-hewn sepulchre?
>   And do we owe thy rising but to Her
> Whose love of thee for all her sin atones?
> For here the air is heavy with men's groans,
>   The priests that call upon thy name are slain;
>   Dost thou not hear the bitter wail of pain
> From those whose children lie upon the stones?
>
> Our prayers are nought: impenetrable gloom
>   Covers God's face: and in the star-less night
>   Over thy Cross the Crescent moon I see.
> If thou in very truth didst burst the tomb,
>   Come down O Son of Man, and show thy might,
>   Lest Mahomet be crowned instead of thee.

heath. George Russell, Lord Russell's nephew, young, Anglo-Catholic, remarked on the feelings of himself and many of his generation: 'If ever Mr. Gladstone had the passionate devotion of young men and young Churchmen, it was during the years of his great crusade—1876–1880.'[1]

★

It was in the combination of High Churchmanship with political Liberalism that Catholic appreciation of the atrocities agitation attained its ripest form of expression. Felicitously representative of this ripeness is Frederic Rogers, Lord Blachford, former great civil servant, an old friend of Gladstone, and one of those who founded the Anglo-Catholic *Guardian* as a counterblast to Newman's secession. A convener of the Eastern Question Conference, Blachford wrote in February 1877: 'This Turkish question is the first in which I have felt a real interest for years.' Here at last was a matter free from the distractions of administrative detail, where large principles were at variance and the course of righteousness could hardly be in doubt, one in which Blachford could 'feel a clear faith and strong interests on the merits'.[2] To him the issue was one of fundamental morality to the point almost of abstraction. Liddon had prescribed a 'sufficient knowledge of the facts' as the complement to 'a fair exercise of the moral sense'; Blachford's moral sense was fully exercised and committed before he appreciated the strength of the 'case' for the agitation. 'Till lately', he wrote in December 1876 to Dean Church, one of his co-founders of the *Guardian*, 'it has been mainly instinct.'[3]

Freeman is better considered as a historian rather than as a Churchman[4]; yet the two sides of his personality and activity were intimately linked. No one had a vision of a restored St Sophia more bright and clear than he. 'Russia must move now', he wrote to Liddon in November 1876, in a mood of joyful anticipation. 'When St. Sophia is cleared out, make a pactia with the Orthodox that

[1] G. W. E. Russell, *Sketches and Snapshots* (1910), p. 44.
[2] G. E. Marindin (ed.), *Letters of Frederic Lord Blachford* (1896), p. 377.
[3] *Ibid.*, p. 374. Blachford's enthusiasm for the agitation was followed, if not matched, by two other notable Anglo-Catholic laymen, the judges Sir John Coleridge and Sir Robert Phillimore. See E. H. Coleridge, *Life & Correspondence of John Duke Lord Coleridge, Lord Chief Justice of England* (1904), vol. ii, p. 261. Phillimore, a friend of Liddon, was a member of the committee of the Russian Sick and Wounded Fund.
[4] So also is the case with Stubbs. See below, pp. 223–5.

their εἰκονόστασις shall not be so high as to hide the apse. Fancy
St. Mark or Torcello with such a εἰκονόστασις as I saw at Cattaro
& Cettinje.'[1] He was bitterly disappointed at the failure of the
Russians to push right through to Constantinople in 1878. 'But
how', he inquired plaintively, 'can men turn round in the sight of
St. Sophia?'[2]

Towering above all High Churchmen, lay or clerical, was, of
course, Gladstone. It is enough to add this further comment by
George Russell:

I have often been driven to ask myself what accounted for the undeserved and exceptional kindness with which Mr. Gladstone always
treated me, even when he thought me in error. Something, no doubt, was
due to hereditary association and Auld Lang Syne, to which he was always
passionately loyal; but I think the main cause must have been that he
knew that I shared, from the depths of my heart, his convictions about
the Christian religion, and the Church of England in particular, and that
my views on the Eastern question were dominated by my religious
beliefs.[3]

*

Liddon occupied among the High Church clergy in the agitation
a place of inspiration and influence comparable to that occupied by
Gladstone among High Churchmen as a whole. It is quite clear
that, without Liddon, the contribution of Anglo-Catholicism to
the agitation would have been very considerably less, both in
weight and quality. Freeman told Liddon in October 1876 that
Liddon's name had helped him 'mightily' in his gathering of
money for the Eastern Christians: 'I am much amused with a large
class who clearly imply that they would not have looked on me as a
trustworthy person but for your recommendation.' Again, in
November, not without a suggestion of pique: 'Mark also how
utterly I am but a thing—a medium—recommended by you.'[4]
Numerous illustrations of Liddon's influence could be cited from
the Liddon Papers. A typical case was that of the Rev. E. Wellsford
who sent a subscription for the Russian Sick and Wounded Fund
to Liddon, 'as I see your name in the paper as one of the committee'.[5]

[1] Freeman to Liddon, 1 November 1876, Liddon Papers.
[2] Freeman to Liddon, 29 March 1878, *ibid*.
[3] Russell, *Sketches and Snapshots*, p. 48.
[4] Freeman to Liddon, 15 October and 24 November 1876, Liddon Papers.
[5] Wellsford to Liddon, 13 September 1877, *ibid*.

An old pupil at Cuddesdon commended Liddon's 'noble stand' on the Eastern question as well as his noble support for the unfortunate Rev. Mr Tooth, victim of Lord Penzance, whom Liddon had recently visited in gaol.[1] Liddon's great sermon of 13 August provided a model for many zealous Anglo-Catholics. One of the most zealous was Mylne, Bishop of Bombay. 'Our chivalrous Bishop', Liddon was informed by one of Mylne's clergy in October 1876, 'is just now (literally) leading a crusade against Turks & the Mussulman population are indignant.' Dr Mylne was obviously set fair to get embroiled with the government of India, relations with which, Liddon was also informed, 'in *this* land are peculiar, & to an ardent "Crusader" embarrassing'.[2]

It was natural for Liddon, who had first tasted the full 'aroma of the fourth century' in St Isaac's Cathedral, St Petersburg,[3] and who had assured the Metropolitan of All the Russias that many English Churchmen longed for the day when 'Sancta Sophia' would be 'again in the hands of the Œcumenical Patriarch',[4] to take the lead in organising support for an Address to the Czar.[5] Others—even Auberon Herbert—tended to find the pace of Liddon's zeal a little too fast.[6] Another instance of this can be seen in Liddon's passionate campaign to celebrate Carnarvon's resignation from the cabinet in 1878 by having his portrait put in the Bodleian.[7] Only the strongest disapprobation of his Oxford friends and supporters could deter him.[8] Perhaps, however, the most telling tribute to Liddon's status in the agitation came from the *Methodist*, which thus joined the *Freeman* in unwonted praise of their Anglo-Catholic mentor, the 'preacher of the Gospel, the subtle theologian, who is now our political oracle'.[9]

---

[1] Poole to Liddon, 4 February 1877, *ibid.*

[2] Walford to Liddon [8 October 1876], *ibid.* See also *Guardian*, 8 November 1876, p. 3, and Buckle, *Disraeli*, vol. ii, p. 916. For other examples see Liddon Papers: C. Wray to Liddon, 18 April 1877; R. G. Penney (Anglican Chaplain in Moscow) to Liddon, 27 August 1877; A. J. Butler to Liddon, 23 November 1876; D. Grieg to MacColl, 30 November 1876; R. H. Cave to Liddon, 12 October [1876]; G. Lidgett to Liddon, 27 October 1876; Bishop of Gibraltar to Liddon, 20 May 1877.

[3] Johnston, *Liddon*, p. 102.   [4] *Ibid.*, pp. 104–5.

[5] Liddon to Freeman, 7 July 1877, Liddon Papers.

[6] Herbert to Liddon, 29 July 1877, *ibid.*

[7] See Lyulph Stanley to Liddon, 26 January 1878; Liddon to Lyulph Stanley, 27 January 1878; R. W. Church to Liddon, 30 January 1878, *ibid.*

[8] President of Magdalen to Liddon, 30 January 1878; Warden of Keble to Liddon, 30 January 1878; W. B[right] to Liddon, 30 January 1878; Lyulph Stanley to Liddon, 31 January 1878, *ibid.*

[9] *Methodist*, 8 September 1876, p. 3.

4 Roman Catholicism

On the surface, Roman Catholicism presented to the world an aspect as uniform in opposition to the atrocities agitation as Nonconformity was favourable to it. The stillness of Ireland seemed almost a dramatic affirmation of this. But the outward appearance of firm and unruffled discipline belied the reality. It was not merely that Roman Catholics were to be found among the supporters of the agitation—Lord Acton, Lord Bute, Ambrose de Lisle, even Bishop Clifford. The fault lines of Roman Catholicism were more submerged than those of Anglicanism, and fissures never quite broke the surface; but the tremors were palpable and the subterranean rifts widened dangerously.

The main Roman Catholic fault line ran along the endemic dispute between the 'English' and 'Roman' schools of thought about the nature of the Church in England. The victory won by the Romans Wiseman and Manning had reduced Newman, the symbol of the English spirit, to silence and insignificance; but resentment still smouldered among English 'Old Catholics'.

When both the Vatican and the government of Disraeli spoke with one voice on the Eastern question, Manning would be the last person to raise objections. He owed his position directly and personally to Pius IX, who had appointed him to succeed Wiseman at Westminster in the teeth of the massed opposition of English Catholicism. He concerted his policy intimately with that of the Roman Curia. Politically, he had transferred his allegiance from Gladstone to Disraeli, using as an excuse Gladstone's attacks on the Vatican.[1] His speech at Leeds in September 1876 laid it down unequivocally that it was the duty of every wise and patriotic subject to support the government.[2] For this aid and comfort he received due thanks from ministers. His 'lot', as Derby remarked to Carnarvon, had 'behaved very well in the Turkish row; I suppose because they love a Mahometan better than a heretic'.[3] Derby was less flippant but no less appreciative in his thanks to Manning himself.[4]

Manning welcomed unreservedly Disraeli's Aylesbury on-

---

[1] E. S. Purcell, *Life of Cardinal Manning* (1895-6), vol. ii, p. 521.
[2] *Times*, 27 September 1876, p. 6.
[3] Hardinge, *Carnarvon*, vol. ii, p. 340.
[4] Purcell, op. cit., pp. 525-6.

slaught. To the Catholic Lord Ripon he waxed sarcastic at the expense of the argument that the sinister power of the Slavonic Secret Societies was a mere 'hobgoblin'.[1] Vaughan, Bishop of Salford and eventually Manning's successor at Westminster, developed with vigour the line laid down by Manning in favour of Disraeli.[2] *The Crisis in the East and the Attitude of Catholics*, a pamphlet published in 1876 by one J. G. Kenyon, represents the extreme Roman Catholic viewpoint. Kenyon pointed out with pride that Catholics had shunned the insurrectionary movements in Bosnia and elsewhere in the Balkans.[3] Bitterly attacking the 'Greek Schismatic Churches', Kenyon alleged that the atrocities were much exaggerated; and in any case the Bulgarians had brought retribution on their own heads.

All this certainly gave an impression of solidarity. Gladstone, who never ceased to lament the cruel fate of Döllinger, and who knew, from Liddon's tour in the East, of the pressures being put both from Rome and Budapest on Strossmayer,[4] was indignant. He wrote to Döllinger in August 1876 denouncing the Vatican attitude: 'Surely Bp. Strossmayer will not lend himself to it.'[5] He wrote also to Acton: 'It was an act of some self-denial on my part, when writing on the Eastern question, to abstain from all notice of the conduct of the Court of Rome respecting it.'[6] Yet exceptions to the rule kept obtruding themselves: 'Most Papists are bad,' Freeman wrote to Liddon, 'but not all, as our Bishop Clifford [of Clifton], also Lord Bute, which is more wonderful in a pervert.'[7]

Clifford is interesting as the one Roman Catholic prelate who showed sufficient public sympathy for the agitation to be rebuked soundly by the *Rock*.[8] A member of one of the greatest of the Old Catholic families of England, ever a staunch friend of Newman and

[1] Manning to Ripon, 27 September 1876, Ripon Papers, Add. MSS 43545, ff.20–1.
[2] *Bedfordshire Times and Independent*, 14 October 1876, p. 3.
[3] Elliot remarked to Derby on the 'very striking' feature of the situation in the East 'which is the very strong feeling against Servia that is shown by the Catholics' (Elliot to Derby, 20 July 1876, Disraeli Papers). Salisbury wrote to Gathorne Hardy (14 September 1876) about a project for an international supervisor of reform in Turkey to be escorted by Belgian troops: 'As strong Catholics the Belgians will be rather grateful to the Turks than otherwise: and certainly rather partial to them' (Salisbury Papers).
[4] See Strossmayer to Gladstone, 1 October 1876, Gladstone Papers, Add. MSS 44452, ff. 21–4 (in Acton's hand).
[5] Gladstone to Döllinger, 11 August 1876, *ibid.*, 44140, ff. 421–3.
[6] Gladstone to Acton, 16 October 1876, *ibid.*, 44093, ff. 192–3.
[7] Freeman to Liddon, 15 July 1877, Liddon Papers.
[8] 15 September 1876, p. 708.

one of Manning's most prominent opponents in the struggle for power as Wiseman's life slipped away, he was eminently representative of the 'English' spirit.[1] He would have liked to join the committee of the Russian Sick and Wounded Fund, but, as he explained regretfully to Liddon, in the circumstances it would not be in his power 'to take an active part in promoting it'.[2] More than a hint of his feelings can be gathered, however, from a letter by the Marquess of Bute to Liddon of a few days earlier in which he enclosed a hundred guineas for the Russian Sick and Wounded Fund. Bute advised Liddon to approach both Bishop Clifford and his brother, Lord Clifford, who Bute thought would probably be sympathetic also. He added by way of illustration: 'All I know is that he [Bishop Clifford] wrote to me once asking for money for widows &c. in Bulgaria, in wh. matter he was co-operating with Mr. Freeman, & in his letter I remember he used language ab^t ^e_y Turks worthy of the Roman Breviary on Jan. 30 or ^e_y 1st Sunday of October.'[3] Bute, an immensely wealthy magnate and model of Disraeli's *Lothair*, had, for a recent convert, an independence and self-confidence which put him quite out of the reach of the normal clerical influences or sanctions.

Of the same order of independence, though for rather different reasons, was Acton. As befitted the earlier disciple of the excommunicated Döllinger and the present admirer of the Gladstone of *Vaticanism*, he became a convener of the Eastern Question Conference. Though his Catholicism was of a cosmopolitan kind, with a bias leaning to Munich rather than Shropshire, it was thoroughly 'English', for practical purposes, in its rejection of the spirit represented by Wiseman and Manning.[4]

In Ireland there were far fewer evidences of this kind of independence. It availed little that all the priests, as far as MacColl could determine, took in the *Freeman's Journal*, 'sound' on the Eastern question,[5] when the bishops so clearly discountenanced support for the agitation. Yet the ranks of Irish Catholic nation-

[1] See A. W. Hutton, *Cardinal Manning* (1892), p. 99, and G. A. Beck (ed.), *The English Catholics, 1850–1950* (1950) p. 201.
[2] Clifford to Liddon, 31 August 1877, Liddon Papers.
[3] Bute to Liddon, 23 August 1877, *ibid.*
[4] Baron Friedrich von Hügel, like Acton a Liberal Catholic and linked with the great Whig world, seems also to have shared Acton's attitude on the Bulgarian question. See Mirehouse to Liddon, 20 July [1876], Liddon Papers.
[5] G. W. E. Russell (ed.), *Malcolm MacColl, Memoirs and Correspondence* (1914), p. 56.

alism were not closed completely against it: Justin McCarthy became a convener of the Eastern Question Conference; and T. P.
O'Connor, 'filled with a passionate desire to rescue the Christians
of the East from the yoke of Turkey',[1] found in the crisis of the
Eastern question the inspiration for the biographical indictment of
Disraeli which first made his name.[2] A third, John Pope-Hennessy,
is all the more significant in that he was, at this time, a devoted
supporter of the Conservative party.[3] As Governor of the Wind-
ward Islands he took it upon himself to have copies of the *Horrors*
and the Blackheath speech broadcast, to the scandal of his bitter
enemies, the planters.[4]

There were indeed many Roman Catholics, as one of them
assured Shaftesbury in offering to speak at the Eastern Question
Conference, who did 'not approve of the alliance between Rome
and Constantinople'.[5] Lord Camoys, a convener of the Conference,
became a vice-president of the Eastern Question Association,
where he made a representative third with Bath and Shaftesbury.
Lord Ripon, one of Gladstone's former colleagues and a recent
convert, stood firm against the attempts of Lord Denbigh, put up
to it by Manning at a meeting at Stafford House, to entice him
into a committee in aid of the Turks 'on Catholic grounds'.[6] In
the columns of the *Catholic Times* itself there was a persistent
clash between the opposing viewpoints.[7]

*

The most active leading spokesman of self-consciously 'English'
Roman Catholic feeling against the policy imposed upon the Church

[1] *Memoirs of an Old Parliamentarian*, vol. i, p. 8.
[2] *Ibid.,* p. 11: *Lord Beaconsfield. A Biography* (1879).
[3] See McCarthy, *Reminiscences* (1899), vol. ii, pp. 148–61. Pope-Hennessy later
became a Nationalist.
[4] Pope-Hennessy to Gladstone, 30 September 1876, Gladstone Papers, Add. MSS
44451, ff. 259–60. This indiscretion was indeed the undoing of Pope-Hennessy's
Caribbean career: complaints against him reached such a pitch that he was in November transferred to Hong Kong.
[5] W. Nevins to Shaftesbury, n.d., Mundella Papers. See also *Westminster Gazette*,
26 May 1877, pp. 380–1. *Voce della Verita* published in September 1876 a long letter
from an English Catholic protesting against Vatican policy, together with a rebuttal
of it. *Times*, 35 September 1876, p. 5.
[6] Denbigh to Ripon, 29 December [1876], Ripon Papers, Add. MSS 43626,
ff. 3–4; Ripon to Denbigh, 1 January 1877, *ibid.*, ff. 5–6, and 2 January 1877, *ibid.*,
ff. 7–8. Denbigh was a strong Turcophile, used by Disraeli in 1878 as an unofficial agent
to Andrassy to concert a war policy against Russia.
[7] E.g. 29 September 1876, pp. 4–5.

in England by Manning was Ambrose Phillipps de Lisle.[1] A wealthy convert of long standing (married to a Clifford) and an enthusiastic worker in all Catholic activities, de Lisle, though Conservative in politics, was Liberal on such ecclesiastical issues as the temporal power, and a good friend of Gladstone. He became a convener of the Eastern Question Conference and a zealous worker for the Russian Sick and Wounded Fund.[2]

De Lisle took the leading place really by default. The natural leader of the 'English' party was Newman. The Eastern question was, moreover, one in which Newman had an old and deep and anti-Turkish interest. Nothing could have been more attuned to the spirit of the agitation of 1876 than Newman's Dublin lectures of 1854, on the *History of the Turks in Its Relation to Christianity*. Christopher Wordsworth had quoted Newman with reverence in his sermon on the *Mohammedan Woe*.

Pledged by the very principles of their existence to barbarism, the Turks have to cope with civilized governments all round them, ever advancing in the material and moral strength which civilization gives, and ever feeling more and more vividly that the Turks are simply in the way. They are in the way of the civilization of the nineteenth century.[3]

When Newman wrote that in 1854, of course, he did not reckon with the possibility of anything like the *Syllabus Errorum*.

He had learned much since 1854: disillusionment in Ireland, in Oxford; the termination of his connection with the *Rambler*; the fading of his plans for a new version of the Bible; coldness at Rome. He was in no mood for new ventures. The Anglo-Catholic Lord Glasgow, closely associated with his fellow Scottish peer, Bute,[4] wrote to Liddon much in the hope that Newman might be persuaded to give his name to the Russian Sick and Wounded Fund. It is desirable that there should be a few noble exceptions to the bad philo-Turkism of the general tone of Roman C.s at home & abroad.'[5] But Newman had been burned once too often. He replied to a letter from Gladstone asking him to join in the movement for the Eastern Question Conference:

[1] For de Lisle's 'English' Catholicism see Purcell, *Ambrose Phillipps de Lisle*, vol. , p. 161.
[2] *Ibid.*, p. 178.
[3] The Author of 'Loss and Gain' [J. H. Newman], *Lectures on the History of the Turks in Its Relation to Christianity* (Dublin 1854), p. 272.
[4] See Bute to Liddon, 22 August 1877, Liddon Papers.
[5] Glasgow to Liddon, 30 August 1877, *ibid.*

I thank you for the kind thought which has led to your sending me a list of the names of the 'Conveners of a National Conference on the Eastern Question'. I have rejoiced to see so powerful a demonstration in behalf of so great a cause, and have felt a strong temptation to offer my own name, as you wish me, but on consideration I do not see my way to do so.

Considering some of the names which appear on the list, such as Mr. Holyoake's and specially Mr. Suffield's,[1] I could only add mine as viewing the movement as of a purely *political* character, and I do not think Catholic priests have much to do with politics, certainly not when, as in this case, their Bishops discountenance such a step.

And I reconcile myself to my silence now by reflecting that I have on religious grounds been preaching in print against the enormity of the presence of the Turks in Europe for the last 23 years.[2]

Newman's refusal to associate himself with the agitation, despite his obvious inclinations, rather shocked Gladstone. It continued to prey on his mind to the end of his life. He referred to it in 1895 in a conversation with his friend Stuart Rendel as an outstanding example of what he called the 'deadening and perverting influence of Rome upon the individual mind and conscience'.[3]

*

The emphasis placed by Gladstone on the religious aspect of the Eastern question was very characteristic of him; and nothing in the religious development of his time worried and pained him so much as the tendencies in the Roman Catholic Church as expressed most prominently in the Syllabus and the dogma of Papal Infallibility. Gladstone was full of reverence for the Roman Church; to him no disaster would seem so great as the abdication of the Roman Church from its place at the head and centre of a dynamic European civilisation. His expostulations against the policy of the Vatican were always composed in an effort to save the Church from making a false step, away from the path of true Catholicism and the true 'European sense'. The Vatican's policy in the Eastern question seemed to Gladstone yet a further false step. In his perturbation he turned to his friend Ambrose de Lisle. 'I have a request to

---

[1] The Rev. R. R. Suffield, a former Roman Catholic priest.
[2] Newman to Gladstone, 3 December 1876, Gladstone Papers, Add. MSS 44452 ff. 210–11.
[3] Hamer, *Personal Papers of Lord Rendel*, p. 113.

make', he wrote on Sunday, 3 September 1876, when in the throes of composing the *Horrors*, 'and to urge upon you strongly.' De Lisle was to write to Manning and beg him to induce the Vatican authorities to bring the Pope 'back from the wretchedly false position into which they have betrayed him, and with him the Roman Church, and with the Roman Church a large part of (what I will think) our common faith, in regard to the Eastern question'. There was still time, Gladstone insisted, for the Pope to recede with credit and dignity. He concluded: 'Do not, at the most solemn moment of religious offices, forget the Bulgarians.'[1]

De Lisle responded enthusiastically. He wrote to Manning on 4 September endorsing Gladstone's views, and enclosing—perhaps a little tactlessly—Gladstone's letter. Manning reacted most unpropitiously. He thought Gladstone's coming pamphlet (which Gladstone had mentioned to de Lisle) 'at this crisis a simple disaster'. It would 'heat men's passions' and blind their understandings 'as he did about the Neapolitan Prisons and Garibaldi'. In a further letter, suitable for publication and answering Gladstone directly, Manning denied any awareness of a position 'wretched' or otherwise taken up by the Pope. He had therefore no grounds on which to rest a communication to Rome; and the present 'clamorous and vituperative agitation' seemed to him 'blind', without any 'intelligible policy'.[2]

De Lisle retorted boldly with expressions of disappointment as well as regret. This provoked from Manning a most snappish denunciation of Gladstone's original letter as an 'insolent and slanderous accusation of the Holy Father', and a final refusal to have anything to do either with Gladstone's or with Garibaldi's 'injurious conduct'. De Lisle remained unshaken, concluding a spirited defence of Gladstone on a note of clear defiance which implied much more than a mere difference of opinion on the Eastern question. 'I have never shrunk from expressing my convictions, and if I continue to serve the Church as I have served her for 50 years, I must do so as a free and outspoken Englishman.'[3]

Gladstone was 'more concerned than surprised' at the failure of his and de Lisle's efforts to sway Manning. But, with very characteristic persistence, he tried another tack. De Lisle brought

---

[1] Purcell, *Ambrose Phillipps de Lisle*, vol. ii, pp. 155–6.
[2] *Ibid.*, pp. 157–8.   [3] *Ibid.*, pp. 159–60.

to his attention a Roman Catholic periodical, the *Westminster Gazette*, subsidised by de Lisle[1] and reasonably 'sound' on the Eastern question.[2] Its editor was one Edmund Sheridan Purcell. After much discussion, Gladstone interviewed Purcell, at de Lisle's instigation, and went into the problem of what could be done to help Roman Catholicism into a more worthy appreciation of the moral issues at stake in the question. He spoke of consulting Acton before committing himself to any action.[3]

Whatever action Gladstone may have taken, if any, the *Gazette* certainly displayed a much more prominently pro-agitation attitude throughout 1877–8.[4] But Gladstone did not, in any case, achieve his object. And Manning had Purcell's paper suppressed in 1879 'by means of his influence privately exercised'.[5] Edwin de Lisle, one of Ambrose's sons and editor of Purcell's unfinished biography of his father, commented on this transaction: 'It is said that to make amends for this wrong, the chivalrous Cardinal afterwards gave Mr. Purcell the materials for his famous biography [of Manning].'[6] That biography, which pilloried the Cardinal in a way which made the hierarchy almost welcome the diverting efforts of Lytton Strachey, is in one sense a revenge of the 'English' spirit of Catholicism for, among many other things, Manning's 'Roman' policy in the Eastern question.

5 English Jewry

The Jewish community in England was, almost of necessity, traditionally Liberal in politics. Even more as a matter of necessity, it was pro-Turkish in the Eastern question. In the days of Palmerston this had been a convenient arrangement of sympathies.

[1] *Ibid.*, p. 162. The *Newspaper Press Directory* of 1876 lists the *Westminster Gazette* as representing the 'Old Catholic traditions and principles' (p. 34).
[2] E.g. the letter of 'Catholicus', *Westminster Gazette*, 2 December 1876, p. 338.
[3] *Ibid.*, p. 176.
[4] A striking evidence of a change of outlook is notable in the issue of 19 May 1877, p. 369, on the undesirability of Catholics being associated with the Turkish cause. Also 26 May 1877, pp. 385–6, 'Catholics and Turkey'; 7 July 1877, pp. 4–5, 'Observer'.
[5] Purcell, *Ambrose Phillipps de Lisle*, vol. ii, p. 169. S. Leslie, *Henry Edward Manning* (1921), pp. ix–x, has it that Manning permitted Purcell to write a contemporary biography, under supervision, 'to recoup him for his losses'. It was intended that J. E. C. Bodley should write the authorised Life. But on Manning's death Purcell made off with the materials. Purcell is very difficult to trace. Leslie remarks on the 'curtain of mystery' around his memory (*ibid.*, p. ix). There is, however, a useful entry on Purcell in J. Gillow's *Literary and Biographical History, or Biographical Dictionary of the English Catholics* (n.d.), vol. v, pp. 381–2.
[6] Purcell, op. cit., p. 169.

In the days of Disraeli there was some embarrassment; but there could be no real doubt that the Jewish community would uphold the Eastern policy of the Conservative government. The revolt of the Rothschilds in the Bucks. by-election was symbolic of this. So also was the apostasy of the *Daily Telegraph*. With very few exceptions, such as two prominent members of the bar, Serjeant Simon[1] and Arthur Cohen,[2] both conveners of the Conference, Jews remained aloof from the atrocities agitation. More often, as in the case of the leading member of the community, Sir Moses Montefiore, they gave active assistance to the Turkish cause.[3]

Jewry had a great practical stake in Turkey. Turkish rule allowed them a degree of tolerance far beyond anything conceded by Orthodox Christianity. The oppressive legislation against Jews in Romania particularly served as a stern warning in this respect.[4] Less important, but still important, was the large financial investment which the Jewish community had in Turkey.[5]

Jewish criticism of the agitation was always discreet, never approaching the violence of the 'Protestant' *Standard* or *Rock* or the Roman Catholic organs. The fundamental Jewish objection was that, too often, the Bulgarians were sympathised with because they were Christians, rather than on grounds of simple unalloyed humanity.[6] Though Jews, naturally, could share nothing of the fervent Byzantinism of the High Churchmen, they were far from unconscious of the failings of the Turkish régime. It was characteristic of the general attitude of the Jewish community that it should have reserved its energies in protesting against Turkish misrule for an international Jewish conference. Over forty Jewish organisations in Europe and America were invited to send representatives to Paris late in 1876 to discuss ways and means of improving the condition of the Eastern Jews by taking advantage of the reopening of the Eastern question.[7]

---

[1] He represented Jewry at the National Conference on the Eastern Question.
[2] See Cohen to Dicey [1877], enclosure in A. V. Dicey to Bryce [1877], Bryce Papers, E 2.
[3] L. Wolf, *Sir Moses Montefiore* (1884), pp. 271–3, and L. Loewe (ed.), *Diaries of Sir Moses and Lady Montefiore* (1890), vol. ii, p. 288.
[4] *Jewish Chronicle*, 20 October 1876, pp. 457–8: 'Roumanian Persecution'.
[5] See *ibid.*, 8 September 1876, p. 355. Mundella, for instance, took it for granted that the 'Jews and Turkish Bond-holders' were intimately associated groups. Mundella to R. Leader, 4 May 1877, Mundella Papers.
[6] *Jewish Chronicle*, 4 August 1876, p. 281; E.Q.A., *Report*, p. 49.
[7] *Jewish Chronicle*, 1 December 1876, p. 553; 8 December 1876, p. 570.

Some Jewish consciences were a little troubled at the Jewish attitude to the Bulgarian atrocities. A letter from a Jew in the *Jewish Chronicle* of 20 October raised the question as to whether, by adopting this attitude, Jews were doing themselves full justice. Though they had a right to complain against persecution by Orthodox Christianity in Russia, Romania, and to a lesser extent Serbia, they had no right to hold this against the Bulgarians. Perhaps, it was suggested, Jewish names ought to be more weightily represented than they were on subscription lists for Bulgarian relief funds.[1] This letter prompted a large discussion on the fundamental morality of the Jewish attitude to the agitation, with Gladstone taking a prominent part.[2] As with the Roman Catholics, Gladstone was anxious to guide Jews as far as possible to a position of moral irreproachability on the Eastern question.

The situation was of course complicated by the fact that Disraeli was, in the proud words of the *Jewish Chronicle*, a 'Jew of Jews' despite his baptismal certificate.[3] T. P. O'Connor certainly read rather too much into this when he attempted to prove that Disraeli treated the whole Eastern question 'from the standpoint of the Jew'.[4] Yet though it is not necessary to derive Disraeli's Eastern policy from his Judaism, this undoubtedly added a special depth and flavour to his contempt for Balkan nationalism, and, in conjunction with the very 'Protestant' character of his Christianity (such as it was), did much to blind him to all appreciation of the appeal which the traditions of Orthodoxy and the Eastern Roman Empire made to Gladstone, Liddon, Freeman, and Carnarvon. Gladstone shared in part O'Connor's attitude. One of the few things for which he admired Disraeli was the courage and honesty of his Judaism.[5] Carnarvon also was convinced that Disraeli's proud sensitiveness to his racial heritage was very important in forming his peculiar emotional attitude to the Eastern question.[6]

The anti-Semitic aspect of the atrocities agitation was prominent but superficial. Freeman was its loudest and most constant exponent. William Morris inherited it as a time-honoured feature

[1] *Ibid.*, 20 October 1876, p. 453.
[2] See *Times*, 13 October 1876, p. 7; 14 October 1876, p. 11.
[3] 18 August 1876, p. 312.
[4] *Lord Beaconsfield*, p. 609.
[5] E.g. Gladstone to Granville, 26 November 1876, Granville Papers, 30, 29/29.
[6] Hardinge, *Carnarvon*, vol. ii, p. 343.

of the Radical tradition. Froude, who of course echoed Carlyle in this as in all else, wrote sneeringly of 'd'Israeli'.[1] Goldwin Smith questioned the patriotism of Jews in relation to the demands of an essentially tribal religion.[2] The *Church Times* did not scruple to attack Disraeli as the 'Jew Premier'.[3] But there was beneath this nothing of the substantial bulk of prejudice which in France produced the Dreyfus Affair.

[1] Russell, *Malcolm MacColl*, p. 321.
[2] See *Nineteenth Century*, **3** (1878), for a series of articles on this topic.
[3] 25 August 1876, p. 426.

6

The Structure of the Agitation, II:
The High Victorian Intelligentsia

1 Problems of Interpretation

PERHAPS only the Dreyfus Affair among political *causes célèbres* can compare with the Bulgarian atrocities agitation for the brilliance of the patronage and the opposition which it evoked publicly among the greatest contemporary names in literature, art, science, and philosophy.[1] Indeed, the intervention of the 'intellectuals' in the agitation may be said to have marked the beginning on a considerable scale in Britain of the phenomenon described by Julien Benda in his *La Trahison des clercs*: the new and historically unprecedented prestige of the 'clercs' in politics in the later nineteenth century. Benda's indictment against the fashionable and influencial 'clercs' of Europe during the fifty years before 1927 was that they called upon mankind—he uses the phraseology of Tolstoy—to 'sneer at the Gospel and to read Army Orders'.[2] The relevance of this kind of postulate to the intellectual conflict generated by the atrocities agitation is immediately apparent. The agitators of 1876, political evangelists, represented traditional, and in this context 'conservative', currents of thought: humane, liberal, bourgeois, morally punctilious, optimistic, even utopian. Their critics were the men of the emerging era of idealism, imperialism, power, of challenge to the assumptions of mid-century Liberalism, question of its values

[1] Also as with the Dreyfus Affair, dispute entered into private as well as public life. One supporter of the agitation wrote in April 1877: 'I never remember anything equal to the bitterness already dividing *friends & families* on this question' (enclosure in Liddon to Freeman, 18 April 1877, Liddon Papers). There was tension also in clubs. J. R. Green, the historian and great friend of Freeman, pluckily stood up to being questioned 'a little roughly' about his Eastern politics: 'At present, mainly Russian' (L. Stephen (ed.), *Letters of John Richard Green* (1901), p. 452). See also M.C. Church, *Life and Letters of Dean Church* (1895), p. 252.
[2] J. Benda, *The Betrayal of the Intellectuals* [1927], trans. R. Aldington (Boston 1959), p. xi.

and achievements. It was the more faithful disciple of John Stuart Mill, Henry Sidgwick, who wrote in October 1876, just after settling at Chesterton Road to resume his Cambridge career: 'Altogether I have to fight against optimism rather vigorously: or should have to, except for Bulgarian atrocities and the like.'[1] And it was Leslie Stephen, the less faithful disciple, who complained in December 1876: 'Why the devil we should trouble our heads about these (unspeakable) Turks is a question to which I see no reasonable answer.'[2]

An analysis of the structure of the 'secular' aspect of the response to the atrocities agitation is not assisted and guided by such relatively clear demarcations as define the religious denominations. The fault lines along which the shock of the agitation ran in the non-religious areas are correspondingly less easy to interpret. There is no simple, coherent pattern in terms of schools of thought, very little preservation of group identity amid the fragmentation of the intellectual reaction. As with the religious denominations, though on an individual level and with much less discipline and order, there was seemingly as much a tendency for a coalescence of disparate elements as for a predictable association of 'like minds'. Thus Freeman and Froude actually appear on the same platform; Henry Fawcett and Henry Sidgwick are at one with T. H. Green; Carlyle unites with the hated Charles Darwin and the despised Herbert Spencer.

Nevertheless, the broad interpretive theme suggested in terms of Benda's thesis remains fundamentally intact. As a phenomenon exercising the thoughts and in many cases the activities of the High Victorian intelligentsia, the Bulgarian atrocities agitation performed the function, untidily perhaps, but effectively enough, of dividing the followers of the older tradition from those of its critics and repudiators. It was no mere fortuitous concatenation of random chances which united against the agitation such an otherwise oddly-assorted collection as Fitzjames Stephen and Swinburne, Hyndman and Jowett, Matthew Arnold and Marx.

[1] A. and E. M. Sidgwick, *Henry Sidgwick* (1906), p. 325. See also *Guardian*, 8 November 1876, p. 1474, for Sidgwick's defence of Gladstone.
[2] F. W. Maitland, *Life and Letters of Leslie Stephen* (1906), p. 294. Leslie Stephen did however become a convener of the Eastern Question Conference, probably at the instance of his former mentor, Henry Fawcett, whose zeal for the agitation Stephen himself describes as 'characteristic' (L. Stephen, *Henry Fawcett* (1885), p. 406).

Freeman defined the sources of support for the agitation in these terms:

> My allies are, I think, chiefly 1. High Churchmen 2. Dissenters 3. Thoughtful and consistent Liberals, irrespective of theology or lack of theology. The common bond of these three classes is that they all believe in right and wrong, which your ranting and roaring Tory and your cut and dried Whig do not.[1]

'Thoughtful and consistent Liberals' is not very useful as a working definition; and Freeman's use of 'right and wrong' again rather begs the question. Still, there is in Freeman's formula at least a basis of an approximation to the truth of the matter. At its innermost core, the mass of intellectual support for the agitation derived from very simple motives: Liberal humanitarianism with a moral revulsion against cruelty, a 'progressive' outlook in politics combined usually with personal admiration for Gladstone. Certainly no more elaborate explanation than this is needed to account for the presence among the conveners of the Eastern Question Conference of Browning, Trollope, Darwin, and Spencer.

It was not, of course, always so simple as this. Freeman's obsessional reiteration of the 'right and wrong' theme—we find him in November 1876 once more dilating to Bryce of his 'delight' in a cause in which he and Bryce and Liddon '(whose creed is of the longest)' and Cox and Sandwith '(whose creed is of the shortest)', could 'all pull together, simply because we all believe in something greater than creeds, namely right and wrong'[2]— becomes so insistent a motif of his correspondence only because he could not persuade many worthy men that there was so clear a choice between good and evil as he assumed. Freeman revealed obliquely, in characteristic terms, a puzzlement which other agitation-mongers expressed more directly. 'It is truly marvellous', wrote the Rev. C. Wray to Liddon, 'how many otherwise fair & intelligent men believe only, in this matter, the gospel of the Standard Newspaper and the traditions of our present Government.'[3] It was in the same puzzled spirit that Auberon Herbert

---

[1] Freeman to Liddon, 1 November 1876, Liddon Papers.
[2] Freeman to Bryce, 13 November 1876, Bryce Papers, E4. Sir G. W. Cox was the historian and biographer of Colenso.
[3] Wray to Liddon, 16 October 1876, Liddon Papers.

called for Liddon's assistance in an attempt to define convincingly
'the reasonableness of our way of looking at things'.[1]

Henry Nettleship, soon to become Corpus Professor of Latin at
Oxford, exemplifies well the kind of cautious arrival at a conclusion
on the 'great question' which suggests that many others, not very
different in outlook and approach, could easily have ended on the
opposite side of the issue. Instinctively unsympathetic to what he
described to Bryce, a trifle apologetically, as 'superficial Liberalism', and by no means uncritical of the 'somewhat blind but perfectly earnest & sincere' agitation of the autumn of 1876, Nettleship was brought over to Bryce's side ultimately by the consideration that war with Russia on Turkey's behalf 'must lower us
morally, for what should we be fighting for but the most obvious
material advantage?' Emancipation of the serfs had made Russia
clearly more 'progressive' than Turkey, 'in spite of Poland'; and
as a choice had to be made, Nettleship, however reluctantly, would
be on the side of morality and the Russians.[2]

Still, for all Nettleship's judicious weighing of juxtaposed moral
and material considerations, his decision emerged with sufficient
clarity. In the case of a much greater critic of 'superficial Liberalism', Fitzjames Stephen, the clarity of decision against the agitation has an almost blinding quality.

I never have believed, since I knew anything about it, that the Turks
were capable of governing otherwise than as barbarians—but to say the
truth, I never could bring myself to care two straws whether the Bulgarians, Servians, Montenegrins & others were barbarously treated or
not. . . . As to the 'unspeakable atrocities' one does not expect a savage
not to use his scalping knife, & the ill treatment of people a long way off
of whom one knows little, does not naturally move one. I rather despise
an animal facility of being so moved.[3]

These ingredients—rejection of the allegedly inapplicable moral
pretensions of the agitation, contempt for humanitarian emotionalism in public affairs, insistence that the world is divided strictly
between the minority worthy to rule and the rest, fit only to be
ruled, if they are lucky—form the most common single complex of
attitudes repudiating the agitation. In Acton's later words, in

---

[1] Herbert to Liddon, 29 July [1877], *ibid.*
[2] Nettleship to Bryce, 10 May 1877, Bryce Papers, E2.
[3] Fitzjames Stephen to Lytton, 13 August 1876, Fitzjames Stephen Papers, Cambridge Add. MSS 7349.

another context: 'Thus Maine, Stephen, Dilke, all men who live
in diplomacy, all men concerned with India, all men belonging to
the Services.'[1]

*

Some valuable insights into the nature of the intellectual involvement in the Bulgarian atrocities agitation are provided by the comparatively minor agitation which stirred intellectual circles in
1865–6 over the affair of Governor Eyre in Jamaica. The Jamaican
and Bulgarian cases are broadly analogous: attempted (or allegedly
attempted) insurrections were put down with great ruthlessness
and carelessness for forms of law by an alien ruling authority.
Broadly analagous also are the agitations which developed among
English intellectuals in consequence of the incidents. To establish
this point it is necessary only to mention the names of some of the
leading personalities who sympathised actively with the movement
to prosecute Eyre and who ten years later were equally active in
their sympathy with the Bulgarian atrocities agitation: Edward
Miall, Goldwin Smith, Herbert Spencer, Thomas Hughes, Henry
Fawcett, T. H. Green, Charles Darwin, P. A. Taylor, T. B. Potter,
F. W. Newman, Thorold Rogers, Justin McCarthy, F. W. Chesson.[2]
Gladstone, though not publicly prominent, left no doubt as to his
sympathy.[3] Bright might be added as at least a partial supporter
of the Bulgarian agitation. Stead wrote bitterly in the *Northern
Echo* in 1876 against those who attempted to defend the Turks by
reference to Eyre in Jamaica.[4] Clearly he regarded himself as an
heir of the Jamaica Committee tradition.

[1] L. Kochan, *Acton on History* (1954), p. 85.

[2] On the Eyre case generally see Lord Olivier, *The Myth of Governor Eyre* (1933);
J. S. Mill, *Autobiography* (1873), pp. 296–9; Justin McCarthy, *Reminiscences*, vol. ii,
p. 318; Harrison, *Autobiographic Memoirs*, vol. i, p. 313.

[3] There is an interesting account of Gladstone's attitude to the Eyre case by John
Addington Symonds, the writer and art historian. He described an occasion on 8
December 1865, in the house of the sculptor Woolner, when Gladstone and Tennyson
argued the matter. Gladstone attacked Eyre for needless brutality to the Negroes,
Tennyson defended him on the grounds that he had to deal with a savage mob.
Gladstone had been reading the official papers on the question that morning and said
'with an expression of intense gravity', 'and that evidence wrung from a poor black
boy with a revolver at his head'. 'He said this', Symonds commented, 'in an orator's
tone, pity mingled with indignation, the pressure of the lips, the inclination of the
head, the lifting of the eyes to heaven, all marking the man's moral earnestness.'
Throughout this Tennyson muttered, *obbligato, sotto voce*, 'niggers are tigers, niggers
are tigers'. See H. F. Brown (ed.), *Letters and Papers of John Addington Symonds*
(1923), pp. 1–2. Symonds became a convener of the Eastern Question Conference in
1876.   [4] 13 July 1876, pp. 2–3.

The relationship between the two agitations is not, however, simple. Two of the most distinguished intellectual defenders of Eyre, Carlyle and Ruskin, were enthusiastic against the Turks in 1876. Several of Eyre's prosecutors (Bagehot, Joseph Cowen, Frederic Harrison and the other Positivists, perhaps Huxley) were cold or hostile to the movement of 1876. This has been called an 'odd contrast',[1] though it hardly deserves the name.

Much of the hostility to the Bulgarian agitation of a few of the prosecutors of Eyre can be explained in terms of special circumstances. To Frederic Harrison and his fellow disciples of Comte, the Bulgarian agitation caused pain by touching on two spots especially tender to Positivists: it offended their prejudices against religious motivation in politics, and it contradicted their dogma that Russia was inherently barbaric and Oriental. Extreme sensitivity about Russia accounted for Cowen's inability to follow his fellow Radicals Potter and Taylor in the Bulgarian case.

A more important circumstance, however, was that initially much of the campaign to prosecute Eyre was based on legal rather than moral or humanitarian grounds. This legalism comes out particularly in the cases of Bagehot, Huxley, and Frederic Harrison.[2] It is illuminating to note in this connection that one as remote from humanitarian emotionalism as Fitzjames Stephen was an early supporter of J. S. Mill's committee to prosecute Eyre—on strictly legal grounds. Stephen withdrew his support when he became aware that the movement was being influenced by emotional attitudes.[3] Bagehot, as editor of the *Economist*, and Frederic Harrison both joined Stephen in 1876 in denouncing the emotionalism of the atrocities agitation.[4] Freeman remarked that he had known Bagehot for many years: 'a clear-headed fellow, but I could not get him to give me a penny for the Refugees'.[5] The case of Huxley is rather more obscure. He was away in America during the height of the atrocities agitation. But it is almost certain that he would have been invited to become a convener of the Eastern Question Conference; and the fact that he was not a convener,

[1] Taylor, *The Trouble Makers*, p. 75.
[2] W. Bagehot, *Works* (ed. Mrs R. Barrington), vol. ix, p. 44; L. Huxley, *Life and Letters of Thomas Henry Huxley* (1903), vol. i, pp. 404–5; and Harrison, *Autobiographic Memoirs*, vol. i, p. 313.
[3] L. Stephen, *The Life of Sir James Fitzjames Stephen* (1895), pp. 228–30.
[4] See Harrison, loc. cit.; and *Economist*, 12 August 1876, p. 943; 9 September, p. 1054.
[5] Freeman to Bryce, 8 April 1877, Bryce Papers, E4.

combined with his quite definitely anti-Gladstone attitude in 1878–80,[1] indicates that in the decade between the agitations he had tended to swing away from the Liberalism of Darwin towards the Conservatism of Tyndall.[2]

The seeming paradox of the attitudes of Carlyle and Ruskin does equally little damage to the logical connection between the two agitations. Instead of equating Eyre with Achmet Aga, and the oppressed Negroes with the oppressed Bulgarians, as Gladstone and the great majority of the others did, Carlyle and Ruskin equated the Negroes with the *bashi-bazouks* as ravaging barbarians. Their overriding concern was to support the cause of a stern and just authority against the powers of evil and degenerate indiscipline, cruelty, and animalism. For Carlyle especially, Russia in 1876 occupied the equivalent position of Eyre: the embodiment of the sacred principle of obedience, the bringer of righteous retribution on the transgressor.

Allowing for the difference of circumstances in the cases of people like Bagehot, Huxley, and the Positivists, and the rather special position of Carlyle and Ruskin, the Eyre episode stands clearly in a natural relationship to the atrocities agitation. To a limited extent it performs in the intellectual sphere a function somewhat similar to the conflict over the Public Worship Regulation policy in the ecclesiastical sphere: it indicates the general direction in which the fault line lies; it provides a certain basis, though hedged with every variety of cautious reservation, for prediction. It enables one to make, for instance, the definite assertion that had John Stuart Mill been alive in 1876, he would have been prominent in support of the Bulgarian atrocities agitation. The historian Goldwin Smith, a representative of the most characteristic spirit of both movements, made a special point in 1876 of looking back to the Eyre case as comparable with the atrocities agitation as an expression of those 'two great Liberal sentiments—the love of justice and the love of humanity'. The Bulgarian agitation Smith interpreted as a despairing rally of the declining forces of true Liberalism against insurgent doctrines of national idealism and imperial aggrandisement.[3] It is above all this sense of an em-

---

[1] Huxley, *Huxley*, vol, ii, pp. 241–3.
[2] See J. Morley to Gladstone, 7 April 1880, Gladstone Papers, Add. MSS 44255, ff. 13–14.
[3] 'The Defeat of the Liberal Party', *Fortnightly Review*, 1 July 1877, p. 15.

battled intellectual conservatism resisting the currents of the future that both the Jamaican and, even more, the Bulgarian agitations most convincingly convey.

★

There are few more illuminating specific illustrations of this general thesis than the contrasting attitudes to the Bulgarian agitation of Carlyle and Matthew Arnold, the two greatest social critics of their era. The grounds whereon the agitation opened a fissure between them are not the issues of 'Liberalism' as Goldwin Smith would have defined them, but rather the wider issues of acceptance or rejection of the essential qualities and *mores* of Victorian society. For all his denunciation of parliaments and advocacy of the heroic will in politics, Carlyle was a conforming Victorian in a sense that Arnold, in many ways the more profound social critic, was not.

The widespread surprise at Carlyle's attitude in 1876[1] arose largely from misapprehension. Carlyle, no doubt, was at one with Fitzjames Stephen in his contempt for the sentimentality that so often accompanied the humanitarianism of the agitation—the touching picture drawn, for instance, by Florence Nightingale, with her visions of the innocent Bulgarian women and children 'in the midst of their rose-garden industry' being 'all at once' attacked and butchered with 'never-to-be-forgotten horrors or worse'.[2] But there was, even on the surface, little enough reason for astonishment at Carlyle's enthusiasm for the movement of 1876. He had been strongly anti-Turk at the time of the Crimean War,[3] than which there was no more respectable credential for an atrocities agitator. For all the 'force-worship' of his writings, Carlyle in practice recoiled from violence and war. Fundamentally

---

[1] E.g. Gladstone (Hamer, *Personal Papers of Lord Rendel*, p. 70). Fitzjames Stephen commented disgustedly to Lytton on 30 November 1876 on 'our old prophet' Carlyle's regrettable attitude to the Bulgarian affair. Carlyle had been requested by George Howard, one of the secretaries of the Conference, for an 'utterance' on the question. Carlyle asked Stephen, the latter reported, 'about what he should say, & I said "Silence is golden", but he has a sort of craze about the Russians representing the principle of obedience etc. etc. and this seems to me to lead him quite wrong' (Fitzjames Stephen Papers, Cambridge Add. MSS 7349). It was in this 'utterance' that Carlyle coined the famous phrase, the 'unspeakable Turk' (E.Q.A., *Report*, p. 123).   [2] *Times*, 18 September 1876, p. 6.

[3] D. A. Wilson, *Carlyle to Threescore-and-ten* (1929), pp. 93–4. See also E. Bentley, *A Century of Hero Worship* (2nd ed. 1957), p. 51, and E. Lyttelton, *Alfred Lyttelton* (1923), p. 63.

he was an isolationist; this is consistently true of his attitudes to the Crimean, Italian, American, Franco-German, and Russo-Turkish wars.[1] And the agitation could hardly have failed to be congenial to one who was both an editor of Cromwell and a professed admirer of Russian autocracy. But, more profoundly, Carlyle found the agitation congenial because it fulfilled an essential demand of his criticism; it worked, like a leaven, to release the enormous moral potential of Victorian society, to disclose its inner, latent virtue. The agitation, sin-obsessed and guilt-ridden, appealed to the 'old prophet' because it exaggerated, even caricatured, this moral element in nineteenth-century English life, just as Carlyle himself was caricatured by Arnold as a 'moral desperado'.[2]

The agitation repelled Arnold, it is perfectly safe to assume, for precisely this reason. Even the element of caricature made his picture of the rampant Philistinism of the Nonconformist middle class a frighteningly faithful mirror reflection, no longer a literary and sociological concept conceived in hyperbole and executed in irony. From Arnold's viewpoint the agitation would be functionally vicious in exactly the way that Carlyle was: because, to quote Arnold on Carlyle in another context, he preached 'earnestness to a nation which had plenty of it by nature but was less abundantly supplied with several other useful things'[3]; because, to quote Arnold again, the agitation expressed 'that regular Carlylean strain' of hysteria which 'the clear-headed among us have so utter a contempt for'.[4] It was this insistence on 'clear-headedness' that led Arnold to dislike the 'passion' of Gladstone.[5]

To Arnold, who had never ceased to fight his father's good fight against the divisive 'outsiders', the Tractarians and the Dissenters, the agitation was of course unlikely, *prima facie*, to be attractive. But clearly, beyond this, the agitation was an unmistakable manifestation, in Arnoldian terminology, of the already too dominant 'Hebraic' forces of rigid moral conscientiousness, of 'fire and strength', so much preferred by Henry Sidgwick, for instance,[6] as against Arnold's own prescription of 'Hellenic' 'sweetness and

---

[1] Bentley, op. cit.
[2] H. F. Lowry (ed.), *The Letters of Matthew Arnold to Arthur Hugh Clough* (1932), p. 111.
[3] *Ibid.*, p. 47.   [4] *Ibid.*, p. 151.
[5] E. K. Chambers, *Matthew Arnold* (Oxford 1947), pp. 130–1.
[6] Matthew Arnold, *Culture and Anarchy*, ed. J. Dover Wilson (Cambridge 1961), p. 148.

light'. Arnold had just (in 1875) brought out a second edition of his *Culture and Anarchy*, that shrewdest blow ever struck against middle-class Nonconformity in England. Nonconformity was the head and front, to Arnold, of the Philistinism and provincialism which he diagnosed as the most dangerous elements in the anarchical tendency of English life—every man for himself in economics, politics, and religion, with no thought of a higher, national good. The atrocities agitation could not be other, to Arnold, than a manifestation of this anarchy; it was 'anti-national' in the same sense as it was to Stanley and the Broad Churchmen, to whom indeed Arnold, though lost to the faith, remained intellectually and emotionally attached with almost desperate affection. If the Church —'a great national society', in Arnold's phrase, 'for the promotion of goodness'[1]—were attacked, as on the Bulgarian issue, by the combined 'Hebraic' forces of the 'priest party' and the Puritans, Arnold would be the first to pledge his allegiance in its defence.

2 The Agitation and the 'National Idea'

It is clear enough that the atrocities agitation in all its aspects— ecclesiastical, political, intellectual—conflicted frontally with the concept of the nation or the state as an 'ideal'. Essentially this is the reason why the agitation made but little impact on the Conservative party. On its crudest level, Goldwin Smith echoed a characteristic attitude of the agitation when he remarked to Freeman that 'the "National" clergy generally will of course go with Islam, as at the last general election they went with Intemperance'.[2] The Conservative Alfred Austin was as flatulently 'national' on the agitation issue as might be expected[3]; but his case makes no great matter. A study of intellectual responses to the atrocities is necessarily concerned almost exclusively with varieties of 'Liberals'.

The new 'national' idealism being developed from Hegel or neo-Hegelianism by people like F. H. Bradley chimed in with the

---

[1] Quoted by B. Willey, *Nineteenth Century Studies* (1949), p. 280.
[2] Goldwin Smith to Freeman, 28 September 1876, Bryce Papers (detached).
[3] *Tory Horrors, or the Question of the Hour. A Letter to the Right Hon. W. E. Gladstone, M.P.* (12 September 1876), and *Russia Before Europe* (1876). See Gladstone to Austin, 15 September 1876, Gladstone Papers, Add. MSS 44451, ff. 196–7; and to Granville, 16 September 1876, Granville Papers, 30, 29/29.

current of idealism represented by Arnold and the Broad Church school generally, with Jowett in the centre linking the two. On the other side, no purer examples of the anti-idealist, individualist, anti-'imperialist' enemies of the state and enthusiasts for the atrocities agitation could be cited than those conveners of the Eastern Question Conference, Herbert Spencer, Henry Fawcett, and Goldwin Smith.[1] When the *Saturday Review* expressed surprise that Fawcett should have betrayed his intellectual heritage of high and dry utilitarianism by joining in the agitation,[2] it omitted to take this kind of consideration into account. Similarly, the ruthlessness of the evolution theories of Spencer and Darwin is equally irrelevant to their attitude to the atrocities issue. But the case of T. H. Green, also a convener, because it raises something of a problem, serves perhaps as a more useful illustration of this point.

One of the earliest of the neo-Hegelians, Green was far from being intellectually conservative in the manner of Spencer, Fawcett, or Smith; but the particular form of political Radicalism at which he arrived through his philosophical idealism was yet perfectly attuned to the spirit of the agitation. At the centre of Green's political philosophy was a theory of obligation. Green demanded that the Turk be put down and the Bulgarians liberated on much the same grounds as he demanded that the liquor trade and related social evils be put down in England, and the working class rescued from their clutches. Green repudiated emphatically, however, the side of the new idealism which exalted the state; instead he developed a social ideal emphasising the supreme importance of national life while repudiating with contempt all doctrines of national 'interest' or 'honour'. Moreover, a moderate, rather unorthodox Churchman, Green admired Nonconformity for exactly those qualities of deep moral conscientiousness which it displayed so strikingly in 1876. His remark on the Eyre affair might have been applied to the Bulgarian agitation with equal appositeness:

---

[1] Spencer, a member of the committee of the Russian Sick and Wounded Fund, wrote to Gladstone on 17 June 1877 thanking him for having saved England from a war on behalf of Turkey which would have been alike 'disastrous and disgraceful' by his efforts in arousing public opinion (Gladstone Papers, Add. MSS 44454, ff. 203-4). Less pure, perhaps, as an example in this category, but hardly less notable as an enemy of the 'imperial idea', is Trollope. See A. P. Thornton, *The Imperial Idea and its Enemies* (1959), p. 35.

[2] 23 September 1876, p. 372.

'It's a great thing when the religious public, as seldom happens, really gets stirred up in the right direction.'[1]

It was Jowett who introduced Hegel to Oxford and England, who taught Green; and it is Jowett, of all the enemies of the Bulgarian atrocities agitation, who best represents the kind of hostility to the agitation and all it implied deriving from an intellectual conviction of its dangerously inadequate conception of the national idea.

When, in 1878, Gladstone took the opportunity to present his case on the Eastern question at the inauguration of the Palmerston Club in Oxford, young Alfred Milner of Balliol, who presided, in moving a vote of thanks retorted 'with cool emphasis' that Gladstone had neglected a very important aspect of the question—'the interests of the British Empire'.[2] Milner's retort well expressed the Balliol outlook, already a clearly-shaped phenomenon under Jowett. 'The intelligent part of the nation', wrote Jowett of the agitation on 22 October 1876, 'is beginning to feel itself humiliated.'[3] It was natural for Jowett to be irritated by the prominence of his old enemies the Anglo-Catholic clergy, 'who, having a good deal of sham Medievalism, would like to have a sham crusade'. But a more important revelation of his underlying stock of assumptions was his conviction that the 'semi-barbaric' Eastern Christians would be quite incapable of governing themselves. And he was indignant at what he considered the hypocrisy of the agitation in view of the British record in India, Jamaica, and elsewhere.[4] Russia he regarded as bolder and more openly treacherous than ever.[5] But he reserved his sharpest criticism for Gladstone: 'Never was there such a power of self-delusion.' Where was Gladstone, demanded Jowett, a little unreasonably, in the Eyre case? 'Gladstone', he wrote in 1877, 'does not appear to me to have gained so much with the mob as he has lost with the upper and educated classes, who after all are still the greater part of politics.'[6]

It is hardly enough to say that Jowett disliked enthusiasm, moral or otherwise, and that for this reason, as well as his distrust of

---

[1] R. L. Nettleship, *Memoir of Thomas Hill Green* (1906), pp. 18, 55.
[2] J. E. Wrench, *Alfred Lord Milner* (1958), p. 46.
[3] E. Abbott and L. Campbell, *Letters of Benjamin Jowett, M.A.* (1899), p. 80.
[4] Abbott and Campbell, *The Life and Letters of Benjamin Jowett, M.A.* (1897), vol. ii, p. 117.
[5] Abbott and Campbell, *Letters of Benjamin Jowett*, p. 79.
[6] Abbott and Campbell, *Life and Letters of Benjamin Jowett*, vol. ii, p. 119.

'system-building', he regretted the outlook, method, and influence of T. H. Green,[1] and that for this reason also the narrow limitations of his range of sympathies should have led men of explosive moral energy like Freeman to despise him as a crabbed cribmonger.[2] The significance of Jowett's attitude is clearly much wider and deeper. Together with people like Fitzjames Stephen, Matthew Arnold, Bagehot, and Maine, Jowett stood at the head of a considerable section of the higher Liberal intelligentsia becoming increasingly uncomfortable in the company of Gladstone and developments associated with Gladstone—'vulgar, impulsive, unreflecting' democracy,[3] threats to property, irresponsible emotionalism in politics, far too much concern for popular liberty and the rights of subjects, far too little appreciation of the nature of political power and the rights of authority as wielded by the natural conservators of society and civilisation, the 'intelligent part of the nation', the 'upper and educated classes'. Like Fitzjames Stephen, Jowett undoubtedly regarded the existence of a Conservative government in 'these days' of 1876 as a 'fortunate anomaly'.[4]

More specifically, this section of opinion condemned the agitation because it ran contrary to the imperial factor. Here again Jowett is linked particularly with the 'men of India', Fitzjames Stephen and Maine, as well as the classic Balliol products of the younger generation personally associated with him, led by Lansdowne, Milner, Asquith, Grey, and Conservatives like Curzon. Jowett's contemptuous dismissal of the Eastern Christians as unworthy of the privilege of self-government is eloquent, in its way, of the exponent of the Platonic doctrine of guardianship, the member of the committee which reported in 1855 on the Indian Civil Service, a prime instigator of the Indian Institute at Oxford. For Fitzjames Stephen, Gladstone's 'cursed rubbish' on the 'Horrors' and the spectacle of Disraeli 'degrading' himself with 'blarney about Secret Societies' evoked indeed a painful nostalgia for the austere pleasures of empire. India, after all, had been the inspira-

---

[1] G. C. Faber, *Jowett* (1957), p. 356.
[2] *Ibid.*, p. 388.
[3] Fitzjames Stephen to Lytton, 28 September 1876, Fitzjames Stephen Papers, Cambridge Add. MSS 7349.
[4] *Ibid.* Though he considered himself a Liberal and regretted that a 'charlatan' like Disraeli should be in power, Matthew Arnold remained undismayed at the prospect of the disruption of the Liberal party over the Eastern question. G. W. E. Russell (ed.), *Letters of Matthew Arnold, 1848–1888* (1895), vol. ii, p. 137.

tion of his great critical assault on Mill, *Liberty, Equality, Fraternity* (1872–4). 'India', he wrote to Lytton amid the din of agitation, 'has an unspeakable charm & attraction for me.'[1]

The Bulgarian atrocities agitation was the baptism of fire of Liberal imperialism. By minimising the problem of the relations between the powers and insisting on a utopian international morality, by harking back to simple libertarian patronage of movements of national freedom—by everything, in short, summed up by Gladstone when he resigned finally in 1894 on the issue of preserving the principles of his 'European sense' against the demands for increased armaments in a Europe which he refused to recognise was in the grip of a struggle for mastery—the agitation declared, to the satisfaction of the school of Jowett and Stephen, traditional Liberalism's inadequacy to cope with the tasks imposed on Britain as a power in the later nineteenth century. The most interesting illustration of this fault line opened by the agitation is the controversy that developed in 1877 between Gladstone and Edward Dicey in the *Nineteenth Century*. Dicey, in advocating British occupation of Egypt to secure the possession of India, anticipated Seeley in formulating a doctrine that the power and greatness of Britain depended on its imperial position. In mystic strain Dicey interpreted empire as a necessary fulfilment of national destiny. He rejected entirely the theory that the privilege of empire could be justified only by the benefits which it conferred, directly or indirectly, on subject peoples. This attitude was the one which Gladstone—in Dicey's phrase the leader of the 'anti-imperialist theory of English statecraft'—opposed to Dicey. To Gladstone empire was a trust, a burden of honour, a source of national weakness, and in the case of the Eastern question, a cause of positive evil when misinterpreted by people like Dicey to necessitate a policy of expansion and assertiveness which involved, in spirit and practice, the sacrifice of the freedom of the Bulgarians.[2]

---

[1] Fitzjames Stephen to Lytton, 6 September 1876, Fitzjames Stephen Papers, Cambridge Add. MSS 7349.

[2] See E. Dicey, 'Our Route to India', *Nineteenth Century*, June 1877, pp. 665–85; 'The Future of Egypt', *ibid.*, August 1877, pp. 3–14; and 'Mr. Gladstone and Our Empire', *ibid.*, September 1877, pp. 292–308. W. E. Gladstone, 'Aggression on Egypt and Freedom in the East', *ibid.*, August 1877, pp. 149–66.

3 Intellectual Rifts

John Morley was as reverently sceptical of the atrocities agitation
as he was of most other things. Though sympathising 'wholly'
with the objects of the Eastern Question Conference, he declined
to become a convener because he felt uncertain as to Russian aims
and he doubted that a 'convention of doctrinaires' could achieve
anything practical.[1] Yet he could not but be sensible of the weight
and brilliance of the intellectual support for the movement. It
would be an interesting sight, as he remarked to his old friend
Frederic Harrison, the Positivist, 'to see *Mind* in such force'.[2]

Morley's long-standing links with the Positivists were indeed
responsible for the anxious equipoise of his attitude, for on the
other side, pulling strongly for the agitation, was Chamberlain.
The Positivists, as has been indicated, were the one important
group of the intelligentsia who did not respond either way to the
shock along the 'national' fault line. Both the Christian religiosity
and the open or implied Russophilism of the agitation affronted
them too directly to permit the co-operation for which in almost
every other respect they would have been supremely well qualified.
Apart from everything else, they were emphatically anti-imperialist in outlook, severe critics of policies of 'national interest'.
But Professor Rolleston, the Oxford physiologist and strong up-
holder of Liddon's views on the Bulgarian question, was almost,
if not quite, justified when he remarked to Liddon à propos of the
Liberal members of parliament, Sir John Lubbock and M. E.
Grant Duff, that 'like the Positivists they feel that opposition to
Christianity is the first thing to be sure of'.[3]

Though a small group, the Positivists were formidable in their
coherence—they were indeed the one section of the intelligentsia to
unite in a concerted attitude to the agitation—and in their influence.
George Potter, the editor of the *Bee-Hive*, the most important
working-class Radical paper, was a Comtist; and Morley's *Fortnightly*, the spearhead of 'secularism', was often available to them

---

[1] Hirst, *Early Life and Letters of John Morley*, vol. i, p. 35; and E. V. Lucas, *The
Colvins and their Friends* (1928), p. 99.

[2] Hirst, op. cit.

[3] Rolleston to Liddon, 29 August 1877, Liddon Papers.

The Positivist mystique about the spiritual primacy of Western Europe gave them
curious links with the surviving Russophobe 'Foreign Affairs Committees' established by David Urquhart. See M. Quin, *Memoirs of a Positivist* (1924), p. 63.

as a platform. Frederic Harrison wrote to Morley in September 1876: 'I should be sorry if you fall into the mere *Spectator* vain— or encourage the silly, Christian cry of "down with the beastly Turk".'[1] Though he remained essentially Gladstonian in outlook, Morley was quite receptive to Harrison's advice that the crusading spirit of the agitation needed dampening, and that Russian pretensions must be given no countenance. It took Mark Pattison's prompting to get Morley to send for a copy of Schuyler's report; and Morley was careful to see that an article in the *Fortnightly* by Freeman should be balanced by one by the senior apostle of Comte in England, Richard Congreve.[2]

But even among the Positivists the atrocities were too big a shock to leave relationships quite undisturbed. However contemptuous of Freeman's 'crusading bluster', Frederic Harrison could not bring himself to swallow entire the official Comtist Turcophile line. He was 'rather distressed', as he told Morley after reading Congreve's article, 'to find Positivism (for Laffitte is worse than Congreve) officially crying out for "more Pashas" in the midst of the welter'. Positivism, he insisted, did 'not need the Ottoman Empire for its future'.[3] In this respect he remained a rather lonely dissenter.

★

It was as a Positivist that George Eliot judged the Bulgarian agitation. She thought the Liberals cut a 'bad figure' in their 'readiness to impeach' and their 'barrenness of any definite recommendations as to a policy to be pursued'.[4] And the authentic note of the Positivist scale of values is unashamedly evident in her further comment that the 'prospects of our Western civilization' seemed 'more critically involved' in the maintenance of the French Republic against the clericals and Marshal MacMahon than in the 'result of the Bulgarian struggle—momentous as that too is felt to be by prophetic souls'.[5]

[1] Hirst, *Early Life and Letters of John Morley*, vol. i, p. 29.
[2] Morley to Pattison, 26 September 1876, Bodleian MSS, Pattison, 35660 (57), 311–12. Congreve's article, 'England and Turkey' in the *Fortnightly Review*, 1 October 1876, pp. 517–36, was in effect the official Positivist statement of the reasons for their hostility to the agitation. The *Spectator*, 7 October 1876, pp. 1238–9, 'The Positivists and the Turks', attacked it.
[3] Harrison to Morley, 6 October 1876. Frederic Harrison Papers, L.S.E., A, 2, xiii. See also his article in the *Fortnightly Review*, 1 December 1876, pp. 709–30.
[4] G. S. Haight (ed.), *The George Eliot Letters* (1956), vol. vi, p. 343.
[5] *Ibid.*, p. 409.

George Eliot's rather barbed reference to the 'prophetic souls' doubtless found many echoes—for instance, in the aloof contempt for the 'accursed Eastern question' of Edward Fitzgerald, who resolved to treat it as Boccaccio's tellers of tales did the plague.[1] And Fitzgerald's friend Tennyson was obviously unenthusiastic, to say the least, for the agitation. It can be assumed confidently that he declined to become a convener of the Eastern Question Conference. The Crimean Russophobia of Tennyson, an old defender of Eyre, his fear of the 'mob' in politics, put him essentially on the 'national' side of the issue. The most that Gladstone could do was persuade him to write the sonnet *Montenegro*.[2] Here the contrast with Browning is complete. Browning was at once a Gladstonian whose Liberalism was still wholly intact, who shared little of the distaste of Arnold, Stephen, Jowett, and Tennyson for 'the Democracy', and who at the same time contrived to remain a firm admirer of Carlyle. There is little evidence of Browning's precise opinion on the Bulgarian affair; but probably it is clearly enough reflected in that of his disciple Alfred Domett (Browning's 'Waring'). Domett was moved to compose a sonnet against the 'miserable taunt of the Philo-Turkish press that the agitation and excitement about the "Bulgarian atrocities" was mere "sentiment" '.[3]

The fissure dividing Tennyson's ground from Browning's ground was an extension of the same fault line, though here rather wider and deeper, that divided Jowett's protégé Swinburne from Browning's hero Carlyle. Like Arnold, Swinburne objected to the 'Hebraic' tone of the agitation. He objected, more idiosyncratically, as a Radical and a republican, to its pro-Russian tendencies. Above all, like Jowett, Swinburne detested Carlyle, at whose hands he had suffered much. It was Carlyle's public blessing on the agitation which moved Swinburne to speak out against it.[4] Typically enough, Swinburne lunged at the wrong target. Chary of attacking Carlyle directly—a restraint rather regretted by

---

[1] Wright, *Letters of Edward Fitzgerald to Fanny Kemble*, p. 118, and *Letters of Edward Fitzgerald* (1894), vol. ii, p. 203.

[2] Stillman, *Autobiography of a Journalist*, vol. ii, p. 162, and J. M. Moore, *Three Aspects of the Late Alfred, Lord Tennyson* (Manchester 1901), p. 61.

[3] E. A. Horsman, *The Diary of Alfred Domett, 1872–1885* (1953), p. 175. It was published as 'On a Recent Cry About "Sentiment"' in Domett's *Flotsam and Jetsam* (1877), p. 101.

[4] C. Y. Lang (ed.), *The Swinburne Letters* (New Haven 1960), vol. iii, p. 221.

Jowett—Swinburne selected Bright as his chief victim, under the false impression that Bright represented the spirit of the 'Muscovite Crusade'. The eighteen stanzas of the *Quest of Sir Bright de Bromwicham, Knight Templar, A Ballad of Bulgaria, Sung at the Feast of Notre Dame de Bon Marché by a Perishing Savoyard,* include attacks on Carlyle and Gladstone.[1] Failing to get it published in London,[2] Swinburne had to content himself with Jowett's and Dilke's praise. Eventually he published a pamphlet, *Note of an English Republican on the Muscovite Crusade* (1876), in which he made a special point of ridiculing Carlyle's 'inconsistency' as between Eyre and Achmet Aga.[3]

Ruskin's enthusiasm against the Turks derived less from the lead of his 'father' Carlyle, as Gladstone supposed,[4] than from the zealousness of William Morris, who shepherded into the agitation practically the entire pre-Raphaelite movement and its associated Chelsea and Hampstead coteries: Burne-Jones, Ford Madox Brown, G. F. Watts, William De Morgan, William Allingham, W. B. Scott, Henry Wallis, Philip Webb, George du Maurier.[5] Morris was motivated by much the same anti-'national' social

[1] Dilke Papers, Add. MSS. 43949 (a copy in Dilke's hand).

[2] Gosse printed the 'Ballad of Bulgarie' in a private edition of 25 copies in 1893 as 'The Quest of Sir Bright de Brummagem'.

[3] This pleased Herbert Spencer, who, though a supporter of the agitation, had also suffered much at the hands of Carlyle. See D. Duncan, *Life and Letters of Herbert Spencer* (1908), p. 220.

Swinburne's sado-masochistic excitement about the atrocities has already been alluded to (above, p. 34). See Lang, *The Swinburne Letters*, vol. iii, p. 225, and also Swinburne's comments to his friend Monckton-Milnes, Lord Houghton, proud owner of the finest private collection of erotica in England: J. Pope-Hennessy, *Monckton-Milnes, The Flight of Youth, 1851–1885* (1951), pp. 244–5. As it happened, Houghton endorsed Swinburne's opposition to the agitation; but the solidarity of what might be called the eroticist school of thought on the atrocities was gravely impaired by the pro-agitation attitude of their friend and fellow sexologist, Richard Burton. Undoubtedly he most bizarre of the literary patrons of the agitation, Burton, orientalist and explorer, was at this time British consul in Trieste—'that amazing creature Burton at Trieste', as Freeman described him to Bryce, 'who surely once was a Mussulman and till calls himself a Conservative' (Freeman to Bryce, 23 November 1876, Bryce Papers, E 4). Freeman ranked Burton on a level with Lord Bath for zeal in the service of the agitation. This zeal was probably a consequence of Burton's Arabic, as opposed o Turkish, sympathies, and the fruit of his experience of Turkish misrule when consul at Damascus.

[4] Hamer, *Personal Papers of Lord Rendel*, p. 70. Ruskin very curtly refused, for instance, to join the committee of the Russian Sick and Wounded Fund (to Liddon, 10 September 1877, Liddon Papers), though Carlyle did so with great enthusiasm to Liddon, 1 September 1877, *ibid.*).

[5] Others in the same group were F. S. Ellis, Morris's publisher, and C. J. Faulkner, a friend and Fellow of University College, Oxford. Perhaps Alfred Waterhouse's name among the list of conveners is due to the influence of his fellow architect, Webb; though certainly Morris was not among the admirers of his work.

ideal as T. H. Green. For Morris, the criticism of Victorian society implicit in the pre-Raphaelite revolt against Victorian taste was transmuted into Socialism by the pressure of the Eastern crisis. This was a romantic misconception, shared by Gladstone in a rather different way, that the working classes provided the dynamic of the virtuous protest against the Eastern policy of the Jew and the Empress Brown.

★

Though the prevailing tone of the universities, especially Oxford, was, not surprisingly, antagonistic to the agitation,[1] the more strictly academic section of the intelligentsia did itself fair justice in the list of conveners of the Eastern Question Conference. Among the 22 fellows of Cambridge colleges were Bateson (Master of St John's), Peile (a future Master of Christ's), Oscar Browning of King's, Fawcett of Trinity Hall, and no less than 18 Fellows of Trinity, including J. Willis Clark, Sidney Colvin, Walter Leaf, and Michael Foster. The more notable of the 20 Oxford Fellows, apart from Liddon and Bryce, were Mark Pattison (Rector of Lincoln), Talbot (Warden of Keble), Monro (Vice-Provost of Oriel), Rolleston of Merton, T. H. Green of Balliol, Thomas Fowler of Lincoln, Pusey of Christ Church, and Humphry Ward of Brasenose. Among the 19 professors outside Oxford and Cambridge were F. W. Newman, Croom Robertson, Ray Lankester, Thorold Rogers, and Henry Morley.[2]

In many ways the historians provide the most rewarding field for investigation in the academic sphere. They form a relatively

---

[1] Professor Bright 'presumed' that the majority of Oxford M.A.s would be 'reckoned as supporters of the Prime Minister' (to Liddon, 30 January 1878, Liddon Papers). Among the undergraduates, as Liddon noted, it was considered 'good form' to be Turk (Liddon to Freeman, 2 February 1878, *ibid.*). Oscar Wilde was not a typical undergraduate in any respect. Stanley Lane Poole must have been the only undergraduate among the conveners of the Eastern Question Conference. His uncle Reginald Stuart Poole, lectured against the Turks as early as 8 July 1876 (Thompson *Public Opinion and Lord Beaconsfield*, vol. i, p. 346).

There is evidence of considerable support for Gladstone among undergraduates in Scotland and Cambridge. See Macphail to Gladstone, 27 March 1877, Gladstone Papers, Add. MSS 44453, ff. 257–8; P. M. Laurence to Gladstone, 2 March 1877 *ibid.*, ff. 161–3. There was a quite well supported 'Turkish Atrocities Relief Fund' in Cambridge, patronised by the Masters of Downing and Christ's as well as Bateson of St John's. See *Oxford and Cambridge Undergraduate's Journal*, 19 October 1876 p. 17, and 30 October, p. 30.

[2] There were in addition 37 masters of public schools, with a particularly strong contingent from Harrow including the headmaster, Montagu Butler. Arthur Sidgwick was one of the Rugby names.

closely-knit group with a professional identity and, most important, a reputation for having taken part in the Bulgarian agitation as 'secular missionaries' of the Victorian cult of progress.[1] Certainly there is much, on the surface at least, to encourage such a view. It was altogether fitting that John Webb Probyn, historian of Italian unification and author of *National Self-Government in Europe and America* (1870), should have been one of the secretaries of the National Conference. The shock of the atrocities agitation produced, however, the same kinds of torsions and tensions among the better-known historians as in any other professionally identifiable section of the intelligentsia.

Gladstone, like Morley, was very conscious of the force of 'Mind' operating in the Bulgarian question. He liked drawing up lists, and he asked Freeman about historians. Freeman responded:

> In this controversy, as in some others, I have all along had the pleasure of finding that nearly everybody whose opinion I had learned to value about other matters is with me about this. I find it true, not only of historical students, but of all who think of every kind.
>
> I could make such a list as you ask for a very long one; but it is hardly worth mentioning any but those who are pretty well known to the world.

Freeman offered the names of Stubbs, Bryce, Goldwin Smith, J. R. Green, G. W. Cox, W. Bright, as having all 'distinctly spoken or acted'. He was not sure about Guest[2] or Merivale[3]; but 'the world might be more moved by Carlyle and Froude, though what right Froude has among us I don't see. The panegyrist of Flogging Fitzgerald has no right to blame any Turk.'[4] Freeman might also have added the names of Acton and Lecky, both conveners of the Conference. Gladstone had in fact already made a notable reference to the 'gentlemen who represent the historical school of England' in his speech at Birmingham in May 1877. He cited their authority in refuting the charge that the atrocities agitation and the policy it advocated were 'sentimental'.[5]

J. R. Green indeed commented that it was 'certainly well worth remarking that every conspicuous historian in England goes with

---

[1] Taylor, *The Trouble Makers*, pp. 76–7.
[2] Edwin Guest, Master of Gonville and Caius.
[3] Dean of Ely. In fact hostile to the agitation; see below, p. 278.
[4] Freeman to Gladstone, 21 September 1877, Gladstone Papers, Add. MSS 44455, ff. 86–7. Freeman added a postcript by postcard: 'I forgot R. W. Church: but of course you have got him down already' (*ibid.*). I have not been able to find any list or lists in this connection among the Gladstone Papers.   [5] *Times*, 1 June 1877, p. 10.

Gladstone in this matter'.[1] But the solidarity of the historians as imagined by Freeman and Green was deceptive; much more so if the historians are conceived of as spokesmen of a nineteenth-century Liberal *Zeitgeist*. Freeman's instinct in fact was sound; he was quite justified in his resentment at Froude's being on the same side. There is no doubt that, left by Carlyle to his own devices, Froude would not have supported the agitation, probably, indeed, would have attacked it. On 19 September he applauded Derby's policy privately, making slighting references to the 'intoxication' of the public without real reason, and to the 'thorough unscrupulousness' with which Gladstone and his 'satellites' were taking their 'opportunities'. Froude approved Disraeli's Aylesbury speech, though his historical conscience was rather shocked by Disraeli's belief in the guilt of secret societies.[2] All Froude's tendencies of thought and outlook ran contrary to the agitation. Emphatically a 'national' historian, he had no cosmopolitan sympathies in the sense either of Acton's Whiggish Catholicism or Goldwin Smith's Cobdenite Radicalism. Froude added moreover the bitterness of a renegade to his dislike of Anglo-Catholicism. Even when fixed there by Carlyle, Froude's mask would occasionally slip, as in the case of the scandal of his preface to Madame Novikov's book, *Is Russia Wrong?* (1878),[3] which he had consented to write under protest only at Carlyle's direct command.[4]

Froude consoled himself for having to make a pretence of joining in the agitation by asserting later that Carlyle's motive in attacking Disraeli's policy in 1876 was simply that it would, by being absurd, lead to Gladstone's return to power and more mischief in Ireland.[5] This was certainly Froude's own view, at least as far as Gladstone and Ireland were concerned. He wrote to Carnarvon, whom he knew well in connection with South African policy, sketching the great rôle which he could play in a policy of working with Russia, thereby averting war and earning the gratitude of Europe. Otherwise, Froude warned him, 'you will have Gladstone back at the head of the Democracy'.[6]

[1] Stephen, *Letters of John Richard Green*, p. 466.
[2] H. Paul, *The Life of Froude* (1905), pp. 279–80.
[3] W. Tuckwell, *A. W. Kinglake* (1902), pp. 94–5. Froude attempted to make amends in the preface of her next book, *Russia and England* (1880).
[4] D. A. Wilson and D. W. MacArthur, *Carlyle in Old Age* (1934), p. 394.
[5] J. A. Froude, *Thomas Carlyle. A History of His Life in London* (1884), vol. ii, p. 440.   [6] Froude to Carnarvon, 19 December [? 1876], Carnarvon Papers, 30, 6/22.

Here Froude is, of course, at one with Jowett and his school; and it is not surprisingly the other eminent historian of the 'national' or 'imperial' idea, Seeley, who exhibits a marked coolness, at best, to the atrocities agitation. Regius Professor at Cambridge since 1869, Seeley was conspicuously absent both from Freeman's list and Gladstone's list in the Birmingham speech. Seeley's precise opinion of the agitation is difficult to ascertain. Carslake Thompson, an active agitator in 1876, dedicated to Seeley, as a 'grateful pupil', his *Public Opinion and Lord Beaconsfield, 1875–1880*. This work, an essay in using historical writing as a direct aid to political understanding, attempts to practise a doctrine much preached by Seeley. But the dedication concludes with the caveat: 'For the particular opinions arrived at [Seeley] is in no way responsible.' Certainly, nothing we know of Seeley would suggest that he agreed with his pupil that in the events of 1876–8, 'Public Opinion' was deprived, by unconstitutional behaviour on the part of Disraeli, of its 'due influence on the foreign policy of England'. On the contrary, Seeley's main concern with the atrocities agitation was to observe the phenomenon of 'popular' political opinion; and he drew from his observations a conclusion precisely the opposite of Gladstone's. The masses, it was clear to Seeley, were incapable of judging on great national questions. They had no more competence to make a reasoned, informed decision on a matter of foreign policy than on a matter of technical law. Seeley wrote contemptuously of the 'animal instinctiveness' lying at the bottom of such agitations.[1] The 'public' simply did not understand foreign affairs; and everything pointed to the need for a more systematic and scientific study of politics.[2]

★

As Carlyle dragged the unwilling Froude into the agitation, so Freeman dragged the reluctant Stubbs. Stubbs' lack of enthusiasm, however, derived not so much from the 'national' dissent of Froude and Seeley as from simple Tory clerical prejudice. He was not a convener of the Eastern Question Conference; but under Freeman's relentless pressure he joined the committee of the

[1] Thompson, *Public Opinion and Lord Beaconsfield*, vol. ii, p. 109.
[2] J. R. Seeley, 'Political Education of the Working Class', *Macmillan's Magazine*, May-Oct. 1877, p. 144.

Russian Sick and Wounded Fund, 'although I see many names upon it', as he wrote plaintively to Liddon, 'with which I have no sympathy in anything else'.[1] There is more than a hint of self-conscious evasiveness in his excuse to Freeman in January 1877 that he had nothing in particular to say about the Eastern question, as he was 'quite smothered by the Wars of the Roses at present'.[2]

Freeman was the natural leader of the Gladstonian historians. Proud and more than a little vain of the stir he had made in giving a lead to the agitation, eager to build a public and political reputation,[3] even sensitive at being overshadowed by Gladstone, he lamented bitterly the lack of recognition given him by the *Daily News* because, as he supposed, he did not belong to any London club or clique.[4] Freeman's 'antiquarian crotchets', his wild temper, his carrying the 'piques and prejudices of the British archaeological factions into the councils of Europe', often cancelled out the unquestionably valuable contributions which he could make to the agitation by virtue of his expert historical knowledge of the Near East. Still, on balance, his 'learned rage' did not override the ultimate conclusion of so hostile a witness as Frederic Harrison that, at bottom, Freeman was right as to what he said about Turks, Slavs, and Greeks.[5] No one could have been more Gladstonian in his concern for struggling nationalities, particularly 'dear Montenegro'.[6] Freeman took up the cause of the Armenians, of whose national potentiality he had been unaware, immediately on Bryce's assurance of its feasibility.[7]

Freeman's Russophilism had in it nothing of Carlyle's admiration for autocracy. Nor did Russia represent for Freeman primarily the cause of Orthodox Christianity. Rather he looked upon Russia as the emancipator of the Southern Slavs as the Czar Alexander had been emancipator of the Russian serfs. 'Here is a nation', Freeman wrote to Bryce after seeing a letter to Bath from Prince

---

[1] Stubbs to Liddon, 28 August [1877], Liddon Papers. Liddon was convinced that Stubbs' failure to get the Regius Chair of Divinity in Oxford in 1878 was due to his joining this committee. See Liddon to Freeman, 26 February 1878, *ibid*. Disraeli did, however, give Stubbs a canonry in 1879.

[2] W. H. Hutton, *William Stubbs* (1906), p. 106.

[3] See Bryce to Freeman, 28 February [1877], Bryce Papers, E4. Bryce deprecated —rightly—Freeman's parliamentary ambitions.

[4] Freeman to Stead, 25 December 1879, Stead Papers.

[5] Harrison to Morley, 6 October 1876, Harrison Papers, A, 2, xiii.

[6] Freeman to Liddon, 9 November 1876, 21 August 1877, Liddon Papers.

[7] Freeman to Bryce, 25 March 1878, Bryce Papers, E4.

Voronzov, 'in the freshness of a new life, burning to go on the noblest of crusades and our loathsome jew wants us to stop them.'[1] Freeman eagerly anticipated the approaching abolition of Turkish power in Europe: 'I have a heap of difficulties ahead which I fancy that the diplomatists have not yet thought of. New Rome must be European, Christian, Orthodox—but Greek or Bulgarian? There is one puzzle.'[2] Montenegro must be enlarged; but not so as to rob it of its tribal character. 'A tribe and its prince civilizing themselves with next to no bother from outsiders is one of the greatest things in the world. . . .' Then there was the problem of reconciling Slav and Greek claims in Macedonia.[3] Freeman was almost boyishly eager to hear all about 'New Rome' from Bryce as the latter passed through on his way back from the Caucasus.[4] It is in this capacity as prophet of 'New Rome' that Freeman is of the first importance as an intellectual figure in the agitation.

J. R. Green and Bryce were the historians most closely associated with Freeman's activities in the Eastern question. Both were members of the sub-committee, with William Morris, Stopford Brooke, and Sir George Young, appointed to draw up the manifesto convoking the Eastern Question Conference.[5] Green had none of the expert knowledge of Bryce; nor did he share Freeman's hobby-horse enthusiasms or political ambitions. His zeal was the pure, uncomplicated zeal of an amateur.[6] But Bryce was a natural man of affairs, not quite ardent enough for Freeman's taste— 'Scot & lawyer & therefore cautious', as Freeman put it when resolving to 'stir Bryce up' at the beginning of November.[7] But even Bryce, who would, as he told Freeman, as soon worship Zeus or Apollo as be an Eastern Christian, was deeply moved at the sight of St Sophia, and 'longed even for Russia to drive out these

---

[1] Freeman to Bryce, 23 November 1876, *ibid.*
[2] Freeman to Liddon, 9 November 1876, Liddon Papers.
[3] *Ibid.*
[4] Freeman to Bryce, 22 October 1876, Bryce Papers, E4.
[5] J. Bryce, *Studies in Contemporary Biography* (1903), pp. 140–1. This committee met at Bryce's house, and H. A. L. Fisher is probably correct in suggesting that as Bryce was the most 'politically-minded' of its members, he would have taken the largest part in drafting the manifesto (*James Bryce* (1927), vol. i, p. 167). A further special contribution by Bryce was his bringing of the Armenian question to the front. He caused a petition of the Armenians in London to be circulated at the Eastern Question Conference (E.Q.A., *Report*, pp. 133–6), and was founder and first president of the Anglo-Armenian Society.
[6] Stephen, *Letters of John Richard Green*, pp. 446–7; and Bryce to Freeman, 10 and 22 September 1876, Bryce Papers, E5.
[7] Freeman to Liddon, 1 November 1876, Liddon Papers.

misbelievers': 'It stirred one's spirit to see the false prophet in Justinian's Church.'[1]

If Freeman stood out as the natural leader of the historians in the agitation, Goldwin Smith remained their oracle and mentor. Freeman ranked him with Gladstone as a 'lay prophet', a 'preacher of righteousness'. There was certainly something prophetically portentous about his presence in England in 1876. Returning from Canada for a visit (he had settled eventually at Toronto after resigning the Regius chair at Oxford in 1866), Smith reappeared rather as a ghost at a banquet. No one embodied more completely than he the ideals of the Manchester Liberal heyday. The significant point is that he was fully aware of this. He returned very self-consciously a representative of the golden era of Liberalism which he could see passing away. The failure to secure the prosecution of Governor Eyre he interpreted as the critical turning-point; and Gladstone crusaded in 1876 for a cause already doomed. This heavy pessimism Smith explained to Freeman by arguing that the repeal of the corn laws had resulted in the fusion of the old landed and new commercial aristocracies. Previously, their antagonism had weakened the forces of reaction and permitted much progress; now the ranks of reaction were closed, as the election of 1874 convincingly demonstrated. 'I hope', Smith wrote to Freeman in September 1876, 'I need hardly say that I still feel with my old friends in England, though I cannot help feeling pleased that I am out of the regime under which I am afraid they are destined long to live.' He concluded gloomily on the prospects of the agitation: 'You will be beaten of course. No philanthropic or religious movement can shake a government so strong as the Tory government in the active support of the double aristocracy and the general apathy of all the wealthier classes.'[2]

4 Radicalism

Goldwin Smith's diagnosis of the agitation as an essentially Radical movement struggling against the forces of the 'double aristocracy' and all the wealthier classes found wide acceptance at the time, and has since become the more generally received interpretation. Rather as Swinburne fired wildly at the comparatively

---

[1] Bryce to Freeman, 10 and 22 September 1876, Bryce Papers, E5.
[2] Goldwin Smith to Freeman, 28 September 1876, Bryce Papers (detached).

inoffensive Bright, the Hon. Algernon Egerton M.P., at a rally of Lancashire Conservatives in October 1876, denounced the 'Radical section' of the Liberal party, together with Gladstone, for having misled the country.[1] A typical Turkish interpretation takes for granted the guilt of Radicalism.[2] Recent scholarship tends also to assume an integral relationship between Radicalism and the agitation.[3]

The Radical contribution to the agitation certainly appeared imposing enough to make this kind of assumption understandable. In his book *Eminent Radicals In and Out of Parliament*, published in 1880, J. Morrison Davidson discussed the careers and opinions of 24 'Men of the Left', salt of the political world. Of these at least 19 (including that very dubious man of the Left, Gladstone) had been supporters, more or less, of the Bulgarian atrocities agitation.[4] 12 were actually conveners of the Eastern Question Conference.[5] The outstanding exceptions were Dilke, Joseph Cowen, and the Positivist Professor E. S. Beesly. This proportion of 19 out of 24 undoubtedly exaggerates the strength of the sympathy for the agitation on the political Left. Davidson's own bias in the Eastern question is clear. He remarked that only Cowen's life-long dedication to the cause of Poland could account for the 'deplorable action' he saw fit to take in adhering to the Eastern policy of Lord Beaconsfield.[6] Davidson's inclusion of Freeman among the number of eminent Radicals is also probably indicative of this bias.

Of the 32 or so members of parliament who made a special point of listing themselves in *Dod's Parliamentary Companion* for 1876 as 'Radical' or 'Advanced Liberal', or whose profession of political principles aligned them fairly closely with the more 'Advanced' section, 19 were conveners of the Eastern Question Conference.[7]

---

[1] *Times*, 30 October 1876, p. 6.
[2] H. Halid, *A Study in English Turcophobia* (1904).
[3] E.g. S. Maccoby, *English Radicalism, 1856–1886* (1938), Chap. XIV. Robertson Scott speaks of Greenwood of the *Pall Mall Gazette* as being 'Anti-Radical' on the Eastern question (*The Story of the Pall Mall Gazette* (1950), p. 235).
[4] Gladstone, P. A. Taylor, Wilfrid Lawson, Fawcett, Chamberlain, Burt, Richard, Leonard Courtney, Mundella, Dale, Arch, Spurgeon, Moncure Conway, Bradlaugh, F. A. Maxse, Auberon Herbert, Freeman, Morley, John Bright.
[5] Gladstone, Taylor, Fawcett, Chamberlain, Burt, Richard, Mundella, Dale, Arch, Maxse, Herbert, Freeman.　　　　　　　　　　[6] Davidson, op. cit., p. 51.
[7] Burt, Cameron, Colman, Fawcett, J. F. Harrison, Hodgson, W. Holms, Hopwood, Jenkins, Mundella, C. M. Palmer, Pennington, Plimsoll, P. A. Taylor, T. B. Potter, Richard, Samuelson, T. E. Smith, Whitworth.

Dilke and Cowen were again the most conspicuous exceptions, together with Bright, though his was rather a special case. This proportion of 19 to 32 in favour of the agitation among the more advanced parliamentary Radicals is probably a closer approximation to the true balance of Radical sympathies on the Eastern question.

To the names in Davidson's list and those among the parliamentary Radicals could be added such as Holyoake, Thomas Hughes, Miall, H. J. Wilson of Sheffield, Stead, Baxter Langley, Lyulph Stanley, and prominent trade unionists like George Howell, Henry Broadhurst, F. W. Campin, and W. R. Cremer, former secretary of the First International and prominent in the Workmen's Peace Association. Other than the 19 Radicals or advanced Liberals already noted, a majority of the 69 Liberal members of parliament who accepted convenership of the Eastern Question Conference could be described as moderate men of the Left. George Lansbury recalls that the London Radical clubs, heirs mainly of the Chartist tradition and 'powerful institutions in those days', led by the Eleusis Club of Chelsea, supported Gladstone in every possible way in 1876–8.[1]

Yet Radicalism was by no means in the same integral relationship to the agitation as Nonconformity. To some extent, no doubt, in its function as an attack on a policy identified with the 'ruling class', the agitation represented, or implied, as it did to Ambrose Phillipps de Lisle, a conflict between the 'Democracy' and the 'Aristocracy'.[2] But this did not constitute a fault line of any marked clarity upon which a general interpretation of Radicalism in relation to the agitation can usefully be based. An anti-Russian policy was, traditionally, hardly less to be identified with Radicalism than with the ruling class—certainly much more than with the older Toryism or Peelite Conservatism. This tradition had begun to weaken: Dilke was scandalised at the readiness of many Radical newspapers 'which for years had been the enemies of Russian autocracy' to express 'their confidence in the disinterestedness of Russia, and their support of the speeches of Canon Liddon'.[3] But even among Radicals who supported the agitation, only an eccen-

---

[1] Lansbury, *My Life*, p. 41.
[2] Purcell, *Ambrose Phillipps de Lisle*, vol. ii, p. 354.
[3] *Times*, 10 January 1877, p. 7.

tric like Stead or an historian with neo-Byzantine enthusiasms like Freeman could be positively Russophile. Opposition to the agitation among Radicals was not, as was the case among Nonconformists, negligible or perverse. A well-known parliamentary Radical like Torrens had no hesitation in rejecting a request by his constituents to take part in the agitation.[1] The first point that struck Annie Besant about the Eastern Question Conference at St James's Hall was the 'absence of well-known Radicals'.[2] No less than the anti-slavery movement could the Bulgarian agitation avoid the taunt that its philanthropy increased as the square of the distance from social injustice at home.[3] Morley's lukewarmness to the St James's Hall movement derived much from his contempt for 'that set of men—London academic radicals', 'full of good ideas and good will', but 'impotent', all their activity ending in 'mere fuss'.[4]

Bright, isolated from anti-Russian Radicalism by his Cobdenism[5] and estranged from the agitation by his strict non-interventionism, remained awkwardly and rather painfully balanced, declining to become a convener of the Eastern Question Conference,[6] yet trusting that Gladstone would not 'fail of his part and duty' there.[7] His obsession with the Crimean parallel heightened his appreciation of Gladstone's own embarrassment of conscience. A correspondent of Bryce on vacation at Menton reported in February 1877 that Bright, also at Menton that winter, seemed 'touched at Gladstone's evident pain & perplexity & thinks he feels his responsibility (or his share of it) for the Crimean War, and the present position of the Christians in Turkey'.[8] Bright's sympathy for Gladstone's perplexity, and his dislike of the implications of the way in which Gladstone was resolving that perplexity, made his own position more difficult—though he was inclined somewhat to overdramatise his problem, much as Lansbury did in 1935. The begin-

[1] W. McCullogh Torrens, *Twenty Years in Parliament* (1893), pp. 190–2.
[2] *National Reformer*, 17 December 1876, pp. 385–6.
[3] E.g. J. Combe, *Home Horrors, inscribed to the Right Hon. W. E. Gladstone* (pamphlet, Edinburgh 1876).
[4] Morley to Chamberlain, 28 November 1876, Chamberlain Papers, Birmingham University Library, J.C. 5/5.
[5] The Cobden Club reprinted in 1876 Cobden's pamphlet *Russia, Turkey, and England* (1836). For examples of Bright's Cobdenite attitude to Russia in 1876 and after see *Times*, 5 December 1876, p. 4, H. E. Carlisle, *Correspondence of Abraham Hayward*, vol. ii, pp. 276–7, and H. J. Leech, *The Public Letters of the Right Hon. John Bright, M.P.* (1885), pp. 195–6.
[6] Carlisle, op. cit., p. 277.   [7] *Ibid.*
[8] E. Winkworth to Bryce, 9 February 1877, Bryce Papers, E25.

R

ning of a letter to Gladstone in December 1877 well illustrates the
moral and intellectual conflict within his mind: 'The day before
yesterday I wrote a long letter to you—& then burnt it. Yesterday
I began a letter to you, & did not finish it. Now I am again attempting to write to you—so you will see how undecided I am, & in
what a puzzle I find myself.'[1]

Even in the hard core of Russophobe parliamentary Radicals,
represented in the older generation by Joseph Cowen and in the
younger by Dilke, there were stresses and strains. Cowen, at first
cautious, described the agitation as 'honourable to the people'
and likened it to the enthusiasm for Poland of forty two years before.[2] But, as he remarked to Dilke, increasingly Cowen found
himself unable to ' "go in" for the Muscovites so strongly as some
of our friends'.[3] One result of Cowen's option to defy the 'threats
of furious partisans' and support 'Lord Beaconsfield's patriotic
foreign policy'[4] was the sharp conflict between himself and James
Annand, the editor of his paper, the *Newcastle Daily Chronicle*.
Annand remained pronouncedly Gladstonian, and the direct contradiction between his editorial policy and Cowen's 'London
Letter' became so acute that Cowen gave his editor an opportunity
to resign towards the end of 1877.[5]

Cowen and Dilke had often worked together in the past; but
both Cowen's emotionalism and Polonophilism betrayed the
widening gap between their generations. Dilke's approach was
much more sophisticated; he was a 'national' Radical in the latest
manner. The rift which divided him from Chamberlain on the Bulgarian issue was 'imperial' as much as anything else: Dilke had
published his *Greater Britain* as early as 1868. On Russia Dilke
was dispassionate and took pains to be well-informed.[6] While
keeping in touch with the pro-agitation group with whom he normally operated—Chamberlain, George Otto Trevelyan, Leonard
Courtney—he worked mainly with Harcourt, and through Harcourt, Granville. Following Harcourt's tactical lead, he maintained

---

[1] Bright to Gladstone, 21 December 1877, Gladstone Papers, Add. MSS 44113,
ff. 107–8.
[2] *Newcastle Daily Chronicle*, 7 October 1876, Cowen Papers, Newcastle Public
Library.
[3] Cowen to Dilke, 2 January 1877, Dilke Papers, Add. MSS 43910, f. 173.
[4] Maltman Barry, *The Catechism of the Eastern Question* (pamphlet, 1880).
[5] Watson, *A Newspaper Man's Memories*, pp. 45–7.
[6] See his letter to Harcourt, ca. September 1876, from France, Dilke Papers, Add.
MSS 43890, f. 81.

a kind of distant diplomatic relationship with the agitation. Naturally Dilke would not be a convener of the Eastern Question Conference—'I dare say', Trevelyan wrote drily on 7 December, 'you do not object to be away from the Conference tomorrow'[1]— but his pre-sessional speech at Chelsea in January 1877 displayed warmth enough in its references to the agitation to please the *Spectator* and, more to the point, 'A Radical Elector of Chelsea'.[2]

*

The working-class aspect of Radicalism in relation to the atrocities agitation, though not strictly conformable to a study of intellectual attitudes, is, however, inseparable from such a study. For it raises the parallel question of the basic social composition of the agitation. It would be impossible to arrive at a satisfyingly precise solution to this problem without a great deal more detailed investigation of local and regional activity than can be undertaken here. But even an attempt to provide an approximate answer raises many points of value for a general interpretation of the agitation.

The five per cent of the total number of protests received by the Foreign Office undoubtedly under-represents the working-class contribution. Equally, Gladstone's wishful vision at Blackheath of the working men forming the head and front of the agitation exaggerates the extent and misconceives the nature of their participation. The *Spectator* commented most appositely on this point:

It is not so easy as it might at first seem to discover what is the real feeling of the English Working-men about the Eastern Question. The agitation aroused by the atrocities has pervaded all ranks in society, and though the meetings which have been held have been fairly representative ones, yet, as usually happens in such cases, they have almost unconsciously adopted the attitudes and given expression to the sentiments of the middle-class.[3]

The characteristic local leaders of agitation were, as the *Spectator* pointed out, ministers of religion, mayors, a few magistrates and members of parliament. Similarly, when in a letter to Freeman Bryce wanted to express his sense of the 'sound' element of society with regard to the agitation, he referred instinctively to

[1] *Ibid.*, Add. MSS 43895, f. 33.
[2] *Spectator*, 13 January 1877, p. 34, and 20 January 1877, p. 82.
[3] *Ibid.*, 14 October 1876, p. 1273.

'the bulk of the nation—the Liberalism of the middle class'.[1] And a revealing symptom of a general working-class backwardness in this respect appears in the puzzled (and somewhat self-contradictory) complaint of the *Spectator* that the representatives of the greatest and best-defined Radical working-class constituencies, such as Jacob Bright of Manchester (no longer the ally of Mundella) and Cowen of Newcastle, should with impunity be able to treat the agitation far less respectfully than representatives of small and 'unpopular' constituencies like Samuelson of Frome, Hayter of Bath, and Cohen of Lewes.[2] The top hats and cloth coats of which Lord Sydney had written to Granville after the Blackheath affair were indeed neatly symbolic of an essentially bourgeois respectability which not even Stead could compromise.

The official attitude of the trade union movement—the Trades Union Congress in Newcastle in September 1876 passed a resolution condemning the atrocities[3]—is not necessarily a reliable indication of working-class feeling, since only a small minority of workers were organised. In any case the resolution has every appearance of being perfunctory; and certainly the atrocities were not a live issue at the Congress. The trade unions, undergoing a period of sharp decline in numbers and effectiveness, had about them little of the aggressive political spirit of Nonconformity.

Indeed it is more than likely that the vital factor determining the quantity of working-class participation in the agitation was the influence of the chapels. 'The working men', as Newman Hall had written to Gladstone of one of his meetings, 'were there in crowds.' A meeting at Monmouth, as another instance, is described as being 'composed principally of the working classes'; and it is notable that whereas Anglican clergy were conspicuously absent, the Congregational and Wesleyan ministers took a leading part.[4] Possibly the comparative strength of anti-agitation feeling among the working class in London reflects a corresponding weakness of chapel influence. One of the few instances outside London of massive working-class opposition to the anti-government crusade occurred in Sheffield: a large rally early in 1878 protesting against war on behalf of the Turks was completely swamped by organised working

---

[1] Bryce to Freeman, 12 April [1877], Bryce Papers, E5.
[2] *Spectator*, 3 February 1877, p. 139. Cowen was candidate, not M.P.
[3] W. J. Davis, *The British Trades Union Congress—History and Recollections* (1910), vol. i, p. 60.   [4] *Ross Gazette*, 5 October 1876, p. 4.

men, to Mundella's great humiliation.[1] It seems that the Archbishop of York, who had considerable personal standing in Sheffield, took great credit for this setback to the anti-government cause.[2] Stead, not without justification, attributed it to the workers with a direct interest in the armaments industry.[3]

Chapel influence may well have contributed towards the peculiar prominence of the agricultural labourers in the working-class participation in the agitation. East Anglian agricultural labourers under Arch, as has been noted,[4] formed some of the very first protest meetings at the beginning of July 1876. As well as the National Union, three local unions (Ewell, Salisbury, and Alderton in Suffolk) sent protests to the Foreign Office; no other union, except the Cleveland miners, so distinguished itself. In the prosperous years before the beginning of the agricultural depression in 1873–5, chapel life had developed vitality concurrently with the development of agricultural labourers' unionism itself; now, with the coming of bad times, chapels would tend to become focal points of protest activity on an issue of moral excitement against a background of economic uncertainty and anxiety.

*

Behind the official caution of the Trades Union Congress a great deal of unofficial work on behalf of the agitation was done by some prominent members of the junta, particularly George Howell and Henry Broadhurst. With Howell, former secretary of the parliamentary committee of the Congress, support for the agitation was far from being a simple reflex of Liberalism. For his years as parliamentary lobbyist had disenchanted him with the Liberals. The Conservatives, on the other hand, as Howell impressed upon Goldwin Smith, were doing their best to conciliate the artisan class, and would be repaid with gratitude.[5]

Howell was yet one of the pillars of the agitation, from the Willis's Rooms meeting of July to the Eastern Question Confer-

[1] See Mundella to R. Leader, 29 January 1878, Mundella Papers. See also Mundella to R. Leader, 30 January 1878, *ibid.*, for H. J. Wilson's comments on the influence of drink and organisation. Mundella wrote to J. D. Leader on 3 March 1878 describing the astonishment of Henry Broadhurst on receiving a letter from Turner, secretary of the Sheffield Trades Council, advocating war with Russia. *Ibid.*

[2] Mundella to R. Leader, 3 October 1878, *ibid.*

[3] Stead, *The M.P. for Russia*, vol. i, p. 479.   [4] See above, p. 42.

[5] Howell to Goldwin Smith, 6 July [1877], Howell Papers, Bishopsgate Institute, Letter Book, 1877–8, p. 65.

ence, where he represented Labour as one of the speakers. But his
support was neither uncritical nor unqualified. It was typical of his
attitude, and that of the T.U.C. junta, that the meeting of representatives of the leading working-class organisations in London on
7 October to discuss the attitude of the two political parties on the
Eastern question, at which Howell presided, should carefully have
abstained from anything like political commitment. It set up a
committee for the purpose of helping to obtain self-government
for the oppressed provinces of Eastern Europe, and a 'vigilance'
subcommittee under Henry Broadhurst.[1] The Positivist Henry
Crompton wrote to Howell in terms which illuminate the character of this gathering very clearly: 'I think the resolutions of your
meeting on the Eastern Question wise & prudent. It would never
do to let the Gladstonians come back without a single pledge—&
with nothing more wrung out of the Conservatives.'[2]

It is instructive to compare the tone and character of this
meeting of 7 October with that of a larger but far less important
demonstration of working men a few days later, at St James's Hall,
under the direction of the London Committee on Eastern affairs
led by one of Farley's early associates, the solicitor J. J. Merriman,
and a trade unionist, Mottershead. The Nonconformist Radical
Stansfeld presided, diverted temporarily from his crusade against
the Contagious Diseases Acts. Gladstone sent an encouraging
letter. Freeman harangued the workers. Two Bulgarian delegates,
touring Europe under the discreet aegis of the Russians, were
displayed on the platform.[3] Malcolm MacColl, who was present,
reported to Gladstone that nothing could have been more enthusiastic. 'The hearts of the working men are evidently still in
the right place, as Dizzy wd. speedily find out if he were to appeal
to them.'[4]

This cannot, any more than Lord Bath's equally firm conviction
that the 'artisan class' were solidly in support of the agitation,[5]
sustain a generalisation; yet it is clear that Liberalism and 'Labour'
were beginning in these years to move towards a reconciliation.
Somewhat as for Nonconformity, though on a far less monolithic

    [1] *Daily News*, 9 October 1876, p. 6.
    [2] Crompton to Howell, 24 October 1876, Howell Papers, Letters, Folio 40 (1876).
    [3] *Daily News*, 10 October 1876, p. 3.
    [4] MacColl to Gladstone, 10 October 1876, Gladstone Papers, Add. MSS 44243,
ff. 203–4.   [5] Bath to Liddon, 1 January 1877, Liddon Papers.

scale, the Bulgarian atrocities became for Labour a political as well as a moral symbol. Undoubtedly also the tendency for *rapprochement* was hastened by the deteriorating situation in certain sectors of the economy, notably agriculture and iron. The agricultural labourers and the miners who made the Cleveland region a 'hotbed of agitation' almost certainly expressed a protest which went beyond the immediate issues of the Eastern question. Howell's attempt to preserve sufficient aloofness from the Liberals to maintain Labour's independent bargaining power—itself crumbling fast—was bound to give way to the tide of the Liberal reaction, of which the atrocities agitation in many indirect ways was a portent.

Henry Broadhurst, who had recently succeeded Howell as secretary of the parliamentary committee of the T.U.C., emerged as the foremost representative of the reviving warmth towards Liberalism among the leading elements of the trade union junta. As chairman of the vigilance committee set up by the meeting of 7 October, Broadhurst worked closely with the committee organising the Eastern Question Conference, and later with the Eastern Question Association formed at the Conference.[1] Mundella, who became executive chairman of both the Conference committee and the Eastern Question Association, was *persona grata* with the T.U.C. and had co-operated closely with Broadhurst in sessional work in 1876. Though Broadhurst developed his own machinery of agitation independent of Mundella's organisation[2] it still remained essentially auxiliary—which indeed sums up the general nature of the specifically working-class contribution to the agitation.

*

George Potter, founder and editor of the Radical *Bee-Hive*, 'The People's Paper and Organ of Industry', forms a link between trade unionism and middle-class intellectual Radicalism.[3] A trade

[1] *Henry Broadhurst M.P. . . . Told by Himself* (1901), pp. 79 ff., 188. Broadhurst became a Liberal M.P. in 1880, and received an undersecretaryship from Gladstone in 1886 in recognition of his services in the Eastern question.

[2] Mundella to J. D. Leader, 11 October 1876, Mundella Papers: 'I saw Broadhurst by appointment this morning, and found that he and his friends in London were already in communication with our indefatigable friend H. J. Wilson, and were at work on a movement of their own.'

[3] For an account of Potter and the early years of the *Bee-Hive* (which became the *Industrial Review* at the end of 1876) see S. Coltham, 'The *Bee-Hive* Newspaper: Its Origin and Early Struggles', in A. Briggs and J. Savile (eds.), *Essays in Memory of G. D. H. Cole* (1960), pp. 174ff.

unionist himself in origin, Potter made the *Bee-Hive* the organ of the parliamentary committee of the Trades Union Congress in its campaign for labour legislation in the eighteen-seventies. As a believer in the Comtist creed, Potter had many connections with fellow Positivists like Beesly, Crompton, Harrison, and Congreve. Positivist interest in the development of trade unionism made Potter's position natural and useful, though there was occasional friction between the Positivists and union leaders like Howell and Broadhurst, who deprecated middle-class interference.[1] On the Bulgarian issue Potter wavered between his Positivism and the Howell-Broadhurst line. The *Bee-Hive* maintained a more or less Gladstonian strain until the middle of September. Then, however, the first really Positivistic sour note was struck by Beesly. After characterising the agitation as an 'unprecedented outburst of pity, horror, and indignation', Beesly announced that he would take no part in it and did not mind 'confessing' his reason. He thought the government's policy had been correct throughout: it was right in rejecting the Berlin Memorandum; right in sending the fleet 'where it could prevent the Russians from swooping on Constantinople and violently ousting the jurisdiction of the united West'. Disraeli, Beesly thought, might with advantage be dropped, but Derby must stay; and on the whole he thought the Conservative government much to be preferred to the 'so-called' Liberals, who above all must not be allowed to 'trade' upon the agitation and wriggle themselves back into office.[2] By October, Potter had brought the *Bee-Hive* round to orthodox, anti-agitation Positivism; and he entered into public dispute with Howell on the subject of 'Working Men and the Eastern Question'.[3]

Disapproval of the agitation on grounds of social Radicalism became indeed almost an orthodoxy also in Socialist circles. H. M. Hyndman, later a Marxist propagandist, emerged as the loudest exponent of this line.[4] Lansbury recalled that Hyndman's name first came to his notice at an obscure meeting of working men on the Eastern question in Newman Street Hall, off Oxford Street.

---

[1] See R. Harrison, 'Professor Beesly and the Working Class Movement', *ibid.*, pp. 205ff.   [2] *Bee-Hive*, 16 September 1876, pp. 17–18.

[3] *Contemporary Review*, October 1876, pp. 851–72.

[4] Fittingly, Hyndman was first given a copy of *Capital* by Munro-Butler-Johnstone, a wealthy Turcophile M.P. and Disraeli's agent in several intrigues against Russia. See H. M. Hyndman, *The Record of an Adventurous Life* (1911), p. 209; and below, p. 259.

Gladstone, who went so far as to attend (a significant departure from his usual habits noted by Granville with surprise and misgiving[1]), read a letter from Hyndman to the meeting, attacking the agitation.[2] Hyndman himself recalled that throughout the Eastern question controversy he opposed the 'folly' of Gladstone and his followers 'on democratic grounds'.[3] Middle-class Liberalism was the most immediate danger to working-class progress; and what seemed to Hyndman the moral cant of the agitation well expressed its essentially bourgeois character and complexion. Hyndman respected Disraeli's 'realism' and looked to the Conservatives for a socially constructive policy.[4]

Marx himself was of course 'anti-Russian in the highest degree',[5] and shared fully Hyndman's detestation of Gladstone personally and politically. Marx had begun to think seriously of the prospects of a fundamental social revolution in Russia, and hoped that it would be provoked by defeat at the hands of the 'gallant Turks'.[6] For Turkey itself he cherished even more extravagant hopes. Hyndman recalled with pained regret that Marx accepted David Urquhart's fantastic theories about Turkey 'with a lack of direct investigation that surprised me in a man of so critical a mind'.[7]

★

That people such as Hyndman opposed the agitation was far less embarrassing to its proponents than the support and assistance of Charles Bradlaugh. With Annie Besant, at this time in her secularist phase, Bradlaugh, most notorious of Radical, atheistic, re-

---

[1] Fitzmaurice, *Granville*, vol. ii, pp. 175–6.
[2] Lansbury, *My Life*, p. 40.
[3] Hyndman, *The Record of an Adventurous Life*, p. 201.
[4] *Ibid.*, p. 240.   [5] *Ibid.*, p. 274.
[6] K. Marx and F. Engels, *Correspondence, 1840–1895* (1934), pp. 348, 355–6.
[7] Hyndman, op. cit. Several of Urquhart's 'Foreign Affairs Committees' were still active, especially in the north. Urquhart himself was too ill to take an active personal part in the controversy (he died in May 1877). The committee at Newcastle under David Rule, the Turkish consul, challenged an atrocities meeting at Newcastle on 7 September, but secured only 6 votes for its amendment (Thompson, *Public Opinion and Lord Beaconsfield*, vol. i, p. 391). Resolutions condemning the atrocities agitation and supporting Disraeli's Eastern policy were addressed to the Foreign Office by the Foreign Affairs Committees of Yorkshire and St Pancras, and by a conference of the committees of Keighley, Bingley, Shipford, Bradford, Cononly, Glusburn, and New Road Side, at Keighley in September 1876 (P.R.O., F.O. 78, *Turkey* 2555–6).
  The former Chartist leader, G. J. Harney (whose pamphlet *The Anti-Turkish Crusade* is cited above, p. 27), is an interesting link between Cowen, Marx, and Urquhart. See A. R. Schoyen, *The Chartist Challenge, A Portrait of George Julian Harney* (1958).

publican propagandists, had recently been prosecuted for advocating birth-control. Bradlaugh's Radicalism was in fact shallow; but he ranked as perhaps the major Victorian demon-figure.

The presence in the list of conveners of the Conference of the much milder 'Secularist', Holyoake, provided Newman with a good debating point in his rejection of Gladstone's plea that he join the agitation. It is doubtful whether either Liddon or Shaftesbury would have stomached Bradlaugh's formal enrolment in the Eastern Question Conference movement. However this may be, Bradlaugh was not invited to be a convener by the Conference organisers, who went to great lengths to assert the respectability of the movement—to the point, indeed, of misnaming it a 'conference' rather than invite associations with the Chartist Convention.[1] Bradlaugh's and Annie Besant's attempts to speak at the 'conference' were promptly suppressed by the agitation establishment.[2] The Irish Roman Catholic Nationalists felt much the same embarrassment at Bradlaugh's enthusiastic patronage of the Home Rule movement.

Bradlaugh was not completely whole-hearted in his support of the agitation.[3] Like the Positivists he found its religiosity repellent. But the scope it offered for assaults on Disraeli and the monarchy more than counterbalanced this defect. In most matters, political, economic, international, Bradlaugh shared the views of a rigid libertarian anti-imperialist Radical of the older generation like Goldwin Smith. There was always, however, a prominent element of special pleading in his articles and activities on the Eastern question.[4] He never quite rose above his level as a 'Secularist, Freethinking, Republican' agitator-journalist in his *National Reformer*.[5]

---

[1] See below, p. 252.   [2] See below, p. 260.

[3] H. B. Bonner and J. M. Robertson, *Charles Bradlaugh* (1895), vol. ii, p. 192.

[4] E.g. *National Reformer*, 3 September 1876, p. 145; 10 September 1876, p. 168.

[5] Also very characteristic of this approach was the letter of H. Crofts on the 'Bulgarian Agitation' (8 October 1876, p. 231): 'I see, from the National Reformer, this subject is attracting the attention of Secularists, and have been thinking the present excitement should not be allowed to pass without some effort to utilise it in the cause of Freethought.' Crofts quoted 31 Numbers and 20 Deuteronomy to prove that the Deity's instructions to the Israelites were exactly comparable to the instructions which (as it was alleged) the commanders of the *bashi-bazouks* had received from Constantinople at the beginning of May 1876. Moses, in fact, was a 'double Bashi-Bazouk'. It followed therefore either that the God of the Jews and Christians was neither moral nor benevolent, or that the Pentateuch was not divinely inspired.

7

Last Phase of the Agitation, October - December 1876

1 The Agitation in Difficulties

INEVITABLY the immense volume of protest which characterised the month of September began to slacken. At the same time the volume of counter-agitation in support of the government's Eastern policy became more prominent.[1] The agitation, however, did not die in October any more than it was born at Darlington on 25 August. In its widest sense it continued until the closing of the chapter of the Eastern question at Berlin in 1878; indeed its ghost was not finally laid until the dismissal of Disraeli's government in 1880. But there is a special unity of agitation between July and December 1876 which defines the bounds of the present study. Two circumstances in particular determined this unity. The first was that after the failure of the attempt by the powers to induce Turkey to accept a supervised programme of reform at the Constantinople Conference in December-January 1876-7, and the consequent Russian declaration of war against Turkey in April 1877, the centre of gravity of public interest shifted away from the direct

---

[1] This dual process can be observed clearly in the files of the memorials addressed to the Foreign Office. In the period 1–28 September only 4 memorials supported the government while 361 opposed it. In the period 29 September–9 October 7 memorials supported the government as against 47 protests. Between 10 October and 27 December 43 memorials endorsed the government's policy compared with 47 protests. In terms of daily averages, protests against the government declined from just over 13 per day in the period 1–28 September to 4 per day in 29 September-9 October, to slightly more than 1 every two days thereafter.
Of the 54 memorials supporting the government, 18 came from Conservative Associations, 10 from Orange Lodges, 3 from Foreign Affairs Committees, 6 from various working-men's Conservative or Constitutional clubs. The 17 others included such as 'The Loyal and Constitutional Tory Eldon Club of Norwich'. For an example of Conservative counter-measures against the agitation see H. Drummond Wolff, *Rambling Recollections* (1908), vol. ii, pp. 139–40.

question of Turkish misrule towards the issues and fortunes of the war.

The second circumstance was the reassembly of parliament in February 1877. The atrocities agitation was essentially a pheno-menon of the recess. At first it attempted to compensate to some extent for the absence of parliament; later it asserted itself in the form of the Eastern Question Conference as a sufficient substitute for parliament. But in any case, the beginning of a new session, combined with the failure of the Constantinople Conference and the outbreak of war, opened a new era distinct from the period dominated by the 'Bulgarian atrocities'.

There was also an internal aspect of this unity of the agitation in July–December 1876. The National Conference on the Eastern Question of 8 December was the culminating expression of the pattern of public demonstrations inaugurated in the obscure Willis's Rooms meeting on 27 July. The National Conference, as has been shown, had its roots in September, in Sheffield; more, it was a deliberate attempt to concentrate in one great demonstration the moral force and persuasiveness of the series of demonstrations of September. The slackening of the volume and pressure of agitation in October and November in no way interrupts the line of develop-ment from September to December.

October and November formed, however, a period commonly designated as one of 'reaction'. Critics and opponents of the agita-tion were proclaiming its demise and welcoming a healthy counter-agitation from the end of September. Manning noted happily on the 27th: 'I think a reaction is setting in.'[1] This claim of a repudia-tion of the agitation was only partly valid. Doubtless there was, as Liddon suggested in the case of Oxford, some backsliding: 'all sorts of people talking like Turks, who would have talked differently some weeks ago'.[2] Without further stimulus from Gladstone the agitation of September would naturally flag. As the Rev. W. G. Rushbrooke commented sadly to Liddon, it was difficult to keep 'humane persons of leisure', even with the best of good will, at a sustained pitch of activity.[3] There was certainly something of a

---

[1] Manning to Ripon, 27 September 1876, Ripon Papers, Add. MSS 43545, ff. 20–1.
[2] Liddon to Freeman, 16 October 1876, Liddon Papers.
[3] Rushbrooke to Liddon, 2 December 1876, *ibid.*

counter-agitation[1]; but there developed no 'great reaction' such as Disraeli had promised Salisbury on 26 September.

Nevertheless, the contrast between the tumult of September and the comparative stillness of October and November could not but be painful to the pro-agitation sensibility. James Macaulay, editor of the *Leisure Hour*, wrote to Liddon on 23 November: 'It is strange and humiliating to witness the present recoil from the generous and Christian view of the Eastern question.' He could account for it only by the 'interested anxiety' of the multitude whose Turkish bonds were in peril, and those whose vision was restricted to the 'nearer horizon' of worldly policy. 'We must', Macaulay concluded, 'have another agitation for the true and the right.'[2]

Several particular incidents contributed to this general sense of malaise. The Russian proposals for joint military and naval operations to coerce the Turks, published early in October, had the opposite effect to the reassurance they were intended to convey.[3] Russell immediately took fright, denouncing the Czar as an enemy of civil and religious freedom.[4] And two even more damaging occurrences were Forster's speech at Bradford on 7 October and Delane's reversal of *The Times*'s policy of supporting the agitation.

Forster returned from Constantinople (like Hartington, he had not been to Bulgaria itself[5]) convinced, as Granville reported to the Duke of Devonshire, that Gladstone's proposal for the dismantling of Turkish executive power in Bulgaria and the other European provinces would be 'impracticable'.[6] Granville regarded Forster's attitude as justifying his own persistent refusal to fall in with Gladstone. Manning took care to sound Forster immediately on his return, and was quite satisfied with his outlook and policy proposals.[7]

As Forster prepared his Bradford speech, Delane cut short his usual holiday at Dunrobin, the seat of the Turcophile Duke of

[1] Stafford Northcote wrote to Disraeli on 28 September decribing an 'Anti-Atrocitarian' rally at Nostell Priory, near Wakefield, on the 27th. There were more than 60,000 persons in the park, and from 12 to 15,000 tried to hear the speeches. They would, added Northcote, have cheered for a policy of clearing out the Eastern Christians 'bag and baggage'. Disraeli Papers.
[2] Macaulay to Liddon, 23 November 1876, Liddon Papers.
[3] Seton-Watson, *Britain in Europe*, p. 521.
[4] *Daily News*, 6 October 1876, p. 2.   [5] *Times*, 6 October 1876, p. 8.
[6] Granville to Devonshire, 5 October 1876, Devonshire Papers, 340/675.
[7] Manning to Ripon, 4 October 1876, Ripon Papers, Add. MSS 43545, ff. 22–3.

Sutherland, and hurried back to Printing House Square. According to Granville's version of the event, Delane had been thought 'rather wanting' by the pro-Turkish set about the Duke.[1] The Prince of Wales was one of this set[2]; and Acton wrote later to Gladstone of the 'pleasant story' he had heard 'of the way in which the Prince pressed Delane to go against you'.[3] Delane was especially perturbed, at a time of increasing suspicion of Russian designs, at the leaders being inserted by Macdonell, the most pro-agitation of his writers.[4]

While Delane prepared to trim the unsteady *Times*, Forster damned the agitation with faint praise at Bradford. The essence of his speech was reaffirmation of all Gladstone's strictures against the Turks, admission of the desirability of complete autonomy, together with the despairing conclusion that it was impossible. In effect he endorsed Derby's attitude as represented by the dispatch of 21 September admitting in principle the need for minor administrative reforms.[5]

Supporters of the agitation felt much about this speech as Nonconformists had felt about Forster's Education Act of 1870. It was a disappointment so disconcerting as to produce bitterness rather than regret. It had been assumed widely that Forster would supply invaluable expert confirmation of Gladstone's proposals.

Delane seized upon Forster's speech as a heaven-sent turntable upon which he could reverse the direction of *The Times*.[6] By 10 October this operation was completed: Forster and Derby were now patterns of statesmanship; Gladstone, by failing to restrain a popular excitement which had, in Delane's view, ceased to be commendable and become purely a nuisance and a danger, forfeited the respect of the 'reasonable majority of the public'.[7]

Stansfeld answered Forster immediately at the workmen's meeting in St James's Hall.[8] Gladstone was convinced that Forster had

[1] Granville to Gladstone, 20 October 1876, Gladstone Papers, Add. MSS 44170, ff. 264-6.
[2] See J. Penderel-Brodhurst, *The Life of His Most Gracious Majesty King Edward VII* (n.d.), vol. iii, p. 203.
[3] Acton to Gladstone, 21 January 1877, Gladstone Papers, Add. MSS 44093, ff. 195-6.
[4] *History of the Times*, vol. ii, *The Tradition Established, 1841–1884*, p. 507; and Joseph Cowen's comments in Watson, *A Newspaper Man's Memories*, p. 45
[5] *Times*, 9 October 1876, p. 10.
[6] See the extraordinarily enthusiastic review of the speech, *ibid.*, p. 9.
[7] *Ibid.*, 10 October 1876, p. 7, strongly attacking Gladstone's letter (on p. 9) to the workmen's meeting proclaiming that the agitation must go on.   [8] *Ibid.*, p. 9.

done damage which would be 'very difficult to repair'.[1] To Granville Gladstone complained that Forster's speech was like everything he did—well-intentioned but mischievous.[2] Forster protested
that his motive had been merely to commit the government to the
policy of 21 September.[3] The matter rankled long. Gladstone was
still harking back to it in July 1878.[4] To Chamberlain, of course,
Forster's Bradford speech was only to be expected from the renegade of 1870.[5] On the other side of the party, Harcourt, sensing
an effort by Forster to out-point Hartington, ridiculed Forster's
'absurd speech much bepraised by the Times'—naturally enough,
Harcourt thought, since 'it mirrors its own muddy vacillation'.
Forster's 'facing both ways style' merely confirmed Harcourt's
opinion that his 'sham honesty is only the cloak of a low cunning'.[6]
Forster's true motive lay no doubt somewhere between the bland
innocence of his protestations to Gladstone and Stead and the low
cunning detected by Harcourt. Probably he saw himself in the rôle
of mediator between the parties on the Eastern question, outside
and above the battle by virtue of his Eastern tour, asserting his
rightful status as the natural if not official leader of the Liberals in
the House of Commons. But he did not have the political finesse
necessary to carry it off.

In any case Gladstone's anticipations as to the mischief Forster
would cause, anticipations echoed by others like MacColl, proved
to be well founded.[7] The greater part of the harm was done in the

[1] Gladstone to F. Cavendish, 17 October 1876, Devonshire Papers, 340/680.
[2] Gladstone to Granville, 18 October 1876. Granville Papers, 30, 29/29.
[3] Forster to F. Cavendish, 15 October 1876, Devonshire Papers, 340/679. See
also Wemyss Reid, *Forster*, vol. ii, pp. 147–51.
[4] Stead to Gladstone, 5 July 1878, Gladstone Papers, Add. MSS 44303, ff. 302–3:
'With regard to the point mentioned by you as to Mr. Forster in the autumn of 1876
there is nothing that I have more frequently discussed with Mr. F. than the wisdom
of his conduct on that occasion.
  He told me, I believe in perfect sincerity, that he had not the least intention of
weakening or opposing the agitation, that he never dreamed of setting himself up
against you, that he regarded the charge as an undeserved insult, & that he spoke as
he did because he believed that by proffering a ready support to Lord Derby the
moment he had by his September despatch publicly abandoned the noninterference-
in-the-internal-affairs-of-Turkey-policy, he could best fix the Govt. to the altered
policy, & secure them agst. a relapse into their evil ways.'
  Gladstone brought the matter up again in 1888, in a review of Wemyss Reid's
Life of Forster. See 'Mr. Forster and Ireland' in *Special Aspects of the Irish Question*
(1892), p. 236. See also Malcolm MacColl, *The Sultan and the Powers*, p. 4.
[5] Chamberlain to Dilke, 10 October 1876, Dilke Papers, Add. MSS 43885, f. 49;
Times, 13 October 1876, p. 6.
[6] Harcourt to Dilke, 10 October 1876, Dilke Papers, Add. MSS 43890, f. 82.
[7] See Mundella to R. Leader, 18 October 1876, Mundella Papers.

Liberal circles only dubiously or waveringly attached to the agitation. Like Delane, they seized upon Forster as a face-saving guide,
with impeccable credentials, to safe retreat. The Liberal mayor of
Barrow cited Forster as his authority for refusing to convene a
town meeting.[1] Wemyss Reid of the *Leeds Mercury*, Forster's
future biographer, took up Forster's line with such effect that
Newman Hall was driven to appeal to Edward Baines, former
Whig M.P. for Leeds and proprietor of the *Mercury*, to curb his
editor, but without success.[2] Liddon was more perturbed about
The Times. Jupiter's 'change of front', as Liddon observed anxiously
to Freeman, was all the more serious in that it is well known that
Jupiter 'has no opinions of his own'.[3] Freeman tried to repair the
damage in a letter to the *Daily News* of 17 October, conceding the
existence of something like a 'reaction', but pointing out how unjustified it was.

Adversity, however, could not teach Freeman caution and
sensible restraint. Liddon's brother reported to Liddon that at a
social gathering Freeman had 'hit about him', making the Bulgarian
question 'appear a party one'. Freeman thereby succeeded in
stopping all conversation and in stirring up 'much active hostility
without ingratiating himself with his own political friends'.[4] One
of the political friends not ingratiated by Freeman's heavy-handed-
ness was Frank Hill of the *Daily News*, who simply stopped publishing Freeman's letters, which the splenetic historian thought a
great 'bore', beseeching Bryce as a common friend to repair
matters.[5] Freeman, indeed, had got so beside himself with self-
conscious concern for his reputation in his 'various struggles by
pen and voice against the devil and his angels, Turkish & Jewish',
that his usefulness was seriously compromised. 'I should much
like to know what you think of all that has been going on', he
wrote in a very characteristically fishing letter to Bryce on 13
November, 'and especially of my share in it.'

I am fairly used both to praise and to abuse. But I have been both
praised and abused now as I never was before. The local Tory press seems

[1] *Barrow Times*, 14 October 1876, p. 6.
[2] Newman Hall to Gladstone, 24 October 1876, Gladstone Papers, Add. MSS
44188, ff. 157–60.
[3] Liddon to Freeman, 16 October 1876, Liddon Papers.
[4] E. Liddon to H. P. Liddon, 18 November 1876, *ibid*.
[5] Freeman to Bryce, 22 October 1876, Bryce Papers, E4.

to have no thought but to revile me. This I take as the best possible sign. I must have hit them hard or they would not yell so loud. . . . I should much like to know what is thought of my share in the matter. I have so little means of knowing, save for gushing letters (both ways, sweet water and bitter) which I constantly get. . . . Tell me all about everything.[1]

Stead in Darlington, indefatigably practical, was one of the few who attempted to challenge the growing suspicion of Russia by taking up the Russian programme for joint military coercion of Turkey as the basis of a second series of protest meetings in the north, inaugurated at Darlington on 2 October. But this approach remained a Darlington eccentricity, and certainly did not provide an effective rallying cry for the new series of meetings, which faded out rather unsatisfactorily in the middle of October. Even Stead now realised that there was no point in persisting in this course of action. 'What next?' he wrote to Gladstone on 16 October.[2]

★

Even the project for a national conference which Henry Wilson and Robert Leader had proposed was encountering difficulties. Mundella's enthusiastic reception of the scheme was not affected by Forster's speech. Soundings at the Reform Club and elsewhere convinced him that there was no general Liberal stampede out of the agitation[3]; indeed, he was now assured that Forster had '*necessitated*' the conference.[4] Accordingly, liaison was established with the Birmingham Liberal Association.[5] A meeting of all interested parties was arranged in Birmingham on 12 October 'to consider the propriety of holding a national conference & if decided to make needful arrangements'. Mundella warmed to the scheme with a spate of practical suggestions. He wrote on the 11th urging that 'such men as Canon Liddon, Mr. MacColl, Spurgeon, Newman Hall' be invited as part of the object to 'secure the widest representation possible'. Every member of parliament and every leader of public opinion must be pressed to take part. If a parlia-

---

[1] Freeman to Bryce, 13 November 1876, *ibid*.
[2] Gladstone Papers, Add. MSS 44303, f. 244.
[3] Mundella to R. Leader, 11 October 1876, Mundella Papers.
[4] Mundella to R. Leader, 10 October 1876, *ibid*.
[5] See draft in the H. J. Wilson Papers, M.D. 2588/4, 10 October 1876.

mentary session could not be procured, 'this Conference should be the next best representation of the English people'. Mundella emphasised especially that the overtly political aspect of the organisation must be kept as much as possible in the background.[1]

But the Birmingham meeting dashed the rising hopes of Mundella and his Sheffield associates. As Mundella wrote rather bitterly to Robert Leader: 'Nothing seems to go down with Birmingham that is not of *home manufacture*.'[2] There seems little doubt that Chamberlain had in effect cast a veto on the Sheffield project. He wrote to Henry Wilson on the day following the discussions at Birmingham in a tone of condescension: 'I don't like the notion of letting your idea—which is at bottom a good one—fall through entirely.' Chamberlain instead proposed a complete abandonment of any idea of a conference at London, and suggested a meeting at Sheffield in its place, composed of delegates from Liberal Associations and any other Liberal organisations and all Liberal members of parliament. Gladstone should be invited personally to assume the leadership of the movement. No limit should be put, Chamberlain suggested, on the number of delegates from each locality: he himself promised a Birmingham contingent of from twenty to forty delegates.[3]

It is clear enough what Chamberlain was getting at. He wanted to transform the Sheffield project into a prototype of his planned National Liberal Federation. For the Sheffield ideal of wide representation and diversity, as outlined by Mundella, with the distinctly Liberal element kept as much as possible in the background, Chamberlain would have substituted an exclusively Liberal political gathering, dominated by a weighty Birmingham contingent. More, his eagerness to have Gladstone's presence as a seal and a symbol prefigures his triumph at Birmingham in 1877, when he succeeded in getting Gladstone to preside over the inauguration of the Liberal Federation. A sop thrown by Chamberlain that Sheffield and its Liberal Association would thereby cover themselves with glory proved no inducement; and the Sheffielders decided, rather sullenly, to put the conference idea aside for the time being.[4] 'Next time', Mundella remarked, 'I think we

---

[1] Mundella to J. D. Leader, 11 October 1876, Mundella Papers.
[2] Mundella to R. Leader, 14 October 1876, *ibid*.
[3] Chamberlain to H. J. Wilson, 13 October 1876, H. J. Wilson Papers, 2588/5.
[4] Mundella to R. Leader, 18 October 1876, Mundella Papers.

had better decide first, and consult our neighbours afterwards.'[1]

When Stead reported to Gladstone on 16 October that his second series of meetings had exhausted that vein of agitation, he reported also that the prospects of holding a 'genuinely representative National Convention' had faded under the cold water thrown by the Birmingham people. His 'What next?' thus had a double edge to it. For Gladstone was beginning, at this stage, to reveal a hitherto unsuspected passivity and want of decisiveness which caused Stead 'much perplexity'. As Stead pointed out, Gladstone had, in his letter to the recent St James's Hall demonstration, made much of the argument that if the people were determined to make their will prevail against that of the government, the 'constitution' would provide 'adequate means' of giving effect to the popular will. But what, Stead now demanded of Gladstone, were these 'adequate means'? Stead could see none.[2]

Gladstone himself could hardly have been less perplexed than Stead. The logic of the situation did not point clearly, as it had done at the time of the *Horrors* and Blackheath, to a path of action. By 7 October Gladstone had made it clear to Granville that he would no longer consider himself bound by normal constraints of ordinary party membership; yet the period following 7 October was for Gladstone one of anti-climax. At the beginning of September his hesitation had been for want of will; now it was for want of 'adequate means'. He pottered about in a rather Micawberish way—arranging discussions between Samuel Morley and Frank Hill,[3] receiving Bulgarian and Serbian delegates,[4] getting Liddon to have a treatise written on the evil influence of the Koran on the civil government of non-Muslims,[5] supplying Stead with 'clews' for editorial policy,[6] writing an article for the *Contemporary Review* defending Russian policy in Central Asia.[7] This last made a rather bad impression.[8] Then a government success in a by-election in

---

[1] Mundella to R. Leader, 14 October 1876, *ibid.*
[2] Stead to Gladstone, 16 October 1876, Gladstone Papers, Add. MSS 44303, f. 244.
[3] Gladstone to Hill, 12 October 1876, *ibid.*, Add. MSS 44452, ff. 49–50.
[4] Gladstone to Lord F. Cavendish, 17 October 1876, Devonshire Papers, 340/680.
[5] Gladstone to Liddon, 1 October 1876, Liddon Papers; and further correspondence in the Gladstone and Liddon Papers.
[6] Gladstone to Stead, 18 October 1876, Gladstone Papers, Add. MSS 44303, ff. 245–6.
[7] 'Russian Policy and Deeds in Turkestan', *Contemporary Review*, November 1876.
[8] E.g. *Methodist*, 10 November 1876, p. 9; *Times*, 1 November 1876, p. 9. Already the *Saturday Review* had invited Gladstone to contradict the 'scandalous report' that

South Shropshire came as a further discouragement[1]; and Gladstone admitted to Granville that the great political reaction towards the Liberal party which he had hoped might arise out of the Eastern question clearly was not forthcoming.[2] And little thanks Gladstone was getting from many sections of the party for his trouble. Lord Spencer, a Gladstonian Whig, complained to Hartington from Marleston, Northants, that he was 'amazed & horrified' at the tone of the Liberals thereabouts. 'They are simply mad agst. Gladstone & Russia.'[3] A good indication of the general sense of anti-climax in the situation is John Morley's wistful half-complaint in the *Fortnightly* that if only Gladstone could be induced to place himself distinctly at the head of the movement for promoting the success of the agitation, it would gather strength and 'all indistinctness of aim would disappear'.[4]

Far from placing himself at the head of the movement, Gladstone, to all appearances quite as much out of the running as he had been in mid-August, positively discouraged proposals put to him by Mundella and the Sheffield group to stage a rally of the agitation's forces.[5] He had already forbidden Adam, the Liberal Whip, to entertain the project, mooted at Edinburgh, of a banquet in his honour, where much might have been done to revive flagging spirits.[6] More clearly than ever, Gladstone depended utterly upon an agitation in being, owing nothing to his own efforts. Hartington, who arrived back in England shortly before 20 October, and who had complained to his father the Duke about Gladstone's 'exciting the agitation',[7] now had the satisfaction of hearing from Gladstone himself that though he received 'much communication from parties anxious for further action', he deprecated such ideas.[8]

Hartington returned from Constantinople in much the same

---

he had authorised a 'friend' to translate the *Horrors* into Russian (21 October 1876, p. 493). A Russian translation did in fact appear in 1876 under the auspices at the St Petersburg section of the Slavonic Committee. The translators were C. P. Pobedonostsev, a member of the Council of State and later famous as the Procurator of the Orthodox Holy Synod, and K. N. Bestuzhev-Ryumin.

[1] Gladstone to Granville, 18 October 1876, Granville Papers, 30, 29/29.
[2] Holland, *Devonshire*, vol. i, p. 176.
[3] Spencer to Hartington, 29 October 1876, Devonshire Papers, 340/682.
[4] 1 November 1876, p. 689.
[5] Gladstone to Hartington, 28 October 1876, Devonshire Papers, 340/681.
[6] Gladstone to Adam, 4 October 1876, Gladstone Papers, Add. MSS 44095, ff. 23–4; see also Adam to Granville, 29 September 1876, Granville Papers, 30, 29/26.
[7] Hartington to Duke of Devonshire, 8 October 1876, Devonshire Papers, 340/676.
[8] Gladstone to Hartington, *ibid.*

mind as Forster, with no faith in the feasibility of political autonomy for the Christians, and convinced that Derby's policy was
sound.[1] Tactfully, it was left to Hartington's brother and Gladstone's nephew-in-law and family favourite, Frederick Cavendish,
to 'break' the news to Gladstone.[2] This would hardly have come,
as in the case of Forster, as a surprise and disappointment to
Gladstone. Both he and Hartington took pains to keep some kind
of bridge over the gap between them. Gladstone rather wishfully
stressed that there was no fundamental difference in principle[3];
and Hartington trusted that such disagreement as there was would
not be made 'too evident'.[4] Hartington's position was made more
difficult by the sudden outburst of Lord Fitzwilliam, a Whig magnate, who took it upon himself to denounce Gladstone and the
agitation in the name of the Whigs and the greater part of the
leading elements of the Liberal party.[5] The fretful Mundella, convinced of a Whig conspiracy, talked wildly for a moment of retiring into independent opposition below the gangway.[6] But Hartington succeeded in smoothing over party differences in a speech
at Keighley early in November, by which he contrived to please
not only Mundella, Argyll, Ailesbury, and T. B. Potter among the
'atrocity-mongers', but also Harcourt and Lord Grey on the anti-
agitation wing.[7] Gladstone himself recognised that Hartington
had done all that was possible: 'He could not afford to march
through Coventry with me.'[8] Compared to the shock administered
by Forster, Hartington let the agitation down very lightly. But
behind the confusing smokescreen of superficial amiability, Hartington remained as uncompromisingly negative as ever. Lord
Spencer 'guessed' that Hartington was 'more anti-Russian than
appeared'[9]; and Acton later reported to Gladstone that Hartington

---

[1] Hartington to Duke of Devonshire, *ibid.* See also Devonshire to Granville, 15
October 1876, Granville Papers, 30, 29/26.
[2] F. Cavendish to Hartington, 20 October 1876, Devonshire Papers, 340/678.
[3] Gladstone to Hartington, 28 October 1876, *ibid.*, 340/681.
[4] Hartington to Gladstone, 27 October 1876, Gladstone Papers, Add. MSS 44144,
ff. 216–17. [5] *Times*, 24 October 1876, p. 9.
[6] Mundella to R. Leader, 29 October 1876, Mundella Papers.
[7] See Mundella to R. Leader, 4 November 1876, Mundella Papers; Argyll to
Granville, 7 November 1876, Granville Papers, 30, 29/29; Ailesbury to Granville,
5 November 1876, *ibid.*, 29/26; Potter to Hartington, 6 November 1876, Devonshire
Papers, 340/685; Grey to Hartington, *ibid.*, 340/689; and Harcourt to Hartington,
16 November 1876, *ibid.*, 340/648.
[8] Gladstone to Granville, 8 November 1876, Granville Papers, 30, 29/29.
[9] Spencer to Hartington, 16 November 1876, Devonshire Papers, 340/686.

was, 'in reality', less near agreeing with Gladstone than he had chosen to say.[1] Hartington had tact and finesse, which Forster had not; but the Keighley speech damaged the agitation in much the same way, if not in the same degree, as the Bradford speech.

★

From tragedy to *opéra bouffe*: the decline and fall of Lewis Farley's League in Aid of the Christians of Turkey, which had presumed to share with Freeman the honours of the initial period of the agitation. Quite eclipsed by the magnitude of events since August, the beginning of the end of Farley's League came when its founder's financial probity began to be questioned. Much money had been passed over; nothing in the way of the promised practical assistance had materialised. There was a disquieting absence of balance-sheets and audits; and it seemed that the ostensible treasurer of the League in fact had seen none of the money: it all passed through Farley's own hands. 'Ugly' rumours were to be heard. So wrote the Rev. Sabine Baring-Gould darkly to Liddon at the end of October.[2] It was about this time, also, that Russell, Farley's original patron, severed his connection with the League— a fact made public in December.[3]

Farley met Liddon's well-meaning inquiries on the matter with indignant denials, counter-assertions of intrigue and jealousy, and a somewhat unlikely account of the bitter envy and hostility of a certain person 'whose name has been much to the front during the past few months', and who was greatly displeased at Farley having taken the lead in the agitation; 'and he does not hesitate to express this opinion openly wherever he goes'.[4] There is little doubt that Farley referred to Freeman, certainly vain about his rôle in the agitation, and certainly contemptuous of Farley.[5] To sustain this scarcely-veiled charge against Freeman, Farley quoted to Liddon a letter which he had allegedly received on 25 July 1876 from a person who described himself (according to Farley)

---

[1] Acton to Gladstone, 21 January 1877, Gladstone Papers, Add. MSS 44093, ff. 195-6.
[2] Baring-Gould to Liddon, 30 October 1876, Liddon Papers. Well-known as the author of 'Onward, Christian Soldiers', Baring-Gould also composed some stanzas on the atrocities, 'The Turk and the Tory' (Gladstone Papers, Add. MSS 44451, ff. 239-40).   [3] *Times*, 20 December 1876, p. 9.
[4] Farley to Liddon, 17 November 1876, Liddon Papers.
[5] See Freeman to Liddon, 24 August 1877, *ibid*.

as the 'orator and active agitator' of the atrocities agitation, as opposed to Farley, the 'planner, strategist, and diplomatist of the movement', threatening to demolish Farley's organisation unless he received an invitation to the Willis's Rooms meeting of 27 July.[1] Freeman, as was earlier noted, was rather sensitive about his status at that meeting, and the fact that he had not been invited by Farley[2]; but Farley's allegations, possibly with a germ of fact in them, are too extravagant to carry conviction.

Farley promised Liddon a full financial account,[3] and continued to advertise in the press for contributions.[4] But a letter in the *Nonconformist* of 22 November,[5] signed 'Merchant', casting grave doubts on the integrity of the League, together with a statement by the editor (Miall) that he could no longer recommend readers to forward money through that channel, was effectively the end of Farley's activities on any appreciable scale.

2 The Agitation Restored: To the National Conference on the Eastern Question

It was clear that the agitation could expect no constructive lead from Gladstone to extricate it from the impasse in which it found itself after the end of September. This is the ultimate confirmation of the fact that at no point in the crisis could Gladstone be said to have been in advance of events. Even the pamphlet had been, in a sense, forced from him. In August, the decisive lead was given to the agitation 'proper' by Stead; in October the agitation was saved and restored by the Sheffield group. They acted under the stimulus of diplomatic events; and henceforward the restored agitation developed in step with the quickening pace of diplomatic activity.

At a cabinet on 19 October it was decided to threaten the Russians with 'serious consequences'[6] if they persisted in any project to occupy Bulgaria as a means of coercing Turkey. On the following day Carnarvon, the leader of the opposition to this policy—'getting a little insufferable', Disraeli thought[7]—rejoined a house-party at his seat, Highclere; which fact an indignant Derby re-

---

[1] Farley to Liddon, *ibid*.   [2] See above, p. 48.
[3] Farley to Liddon, 13 November 1876, Liddon Papers.
[4] E.g. *Nonconformist*, 15 November 1876, p. 1134.
[5] P. 1159.   [6] Buckle, *Disraeli*, vol. ii, p. 954.
[7] *Ibid.*, p. 967.

ported to an incensed Disraeli,[1] for Liddon and Froude were present as well as Auberon Herbert. Carnarvon had earlier welcomed Liddon 'as always', '& particularly so now when I shall be very glad to talk to you on Eastern matters'.[2] Talk undoubtedly Carnarvon did; for the upshot of the Highclere discussions was a telegram on 20 October from an excited Auberon Herbert to Mundella to the effect that affairs were 'most serious', and that 'agitation should not cease now day or night'. Herbert was to come to Sheffield immediately for consultations.[3]

He found Mundella in a highly receptive mood. Having earlier laid himself out for some 'judicious agitation',[4] only to be disappointed by Chamberlain, Mundella seized with alacrity this opportunity of reviving the idea of a national conference. Already, indeed, he was insistent on a point of nomenclature. He asked Robert Leader to call the projected demonstration a 'Conference': 'Don't call it "Convention".'[5] 'Conference' recalled pleasantly the heroic days of anti-slavery and anti-corn laws; and undoubtedly equally prominent in Mundella's mind was the consideration that 'Convention' bore inauspicious associations with Chartism.

By 23 October it was fully agreed that the movement for a conference should be pushed ahead, with or without Chamberlain.[6] Robert Leader, carefully briefed by Mundella on the need for strict secrecy, was deputed to interview and attempt to rouse the now passive and unresponsive Gladstone[7]; and the project was adhered to despite even his lack of encouragement.[8] Within a week the members of the informal committee of members of parliament formed at the end of the session to watch developments in the Eastern question had met. Mundella, soon full of complaints about the 'total lack of organization' around him,[9] was the inevitable

---

[1] Derby to Disraeli, 14 October 1876, Disraeli Papers.
[2] Carnarvon to Liddon, 5 October 1876, Liddon Papers.
[3] Mundella to R. Leader, 20 October 1876, Mundella Papers. This particular scare, as it happened, passed over quickly. See Herbert to Chesson, 22 October 1876, Anti-Slavery Papers, Rhodes House, Oxford, Chesson C 137/257.
[4] Mundella to R. Leader, 18 October 1876, ibid.
[5] Mundella to R. Leader, 20 October 1876, Mundella Papers. Both Seton-Watson (Disraeli, Gladstone and the Eastern Question, p. 110) and Taylor (The Trouble Makers, pp. 80–1) refer, with reason, but mistakenly, to the 'Convention'. It was characteristic of Stead, who took the mock 'parliamentary' pretensions of the movement more seriously than most, that he should long have persisted in calling it a 'Convention' (e.g. to Gladstone, 27 November 1876, Add. MSS 44303, f. 256).
[6] Mundella to R. Leader, 23 October 1876, Mundella Papers.
[7] Mundella to R. Leader, 20 October 1876, ibid.   [8] See above, p. 248
[9] Mundella to R. Leader, 4 November 1876, Mundella Papers.

chairman. It was decided to gather two hundred 'good and influential' names as conveners of a conference; if successful, the committee would extend its membership and carry on.[1] Mundella, for one, travelled widely in search of support: he is mentioned as being in Worcester and Leicester.[2]

First results were encouraging. Then came a further stimulus from outside even greater than that supplied by the (doubtless discreet) revelations of the Cabinet's truculent attitude to Russia of 19 October: it was announced that, on the invitation of Lord Derby, a conference of the powers would be held to discuss the question of the Porte's relations with its subject peoples. Lord Salisbury, Secretary of State for India, would be the British plenipotentiary. So apparently new a departure in British Eastern policy naturally could not fail to be interpreted by supporters of the agitation as a victory of the moderates in the Cabinet over Disraeli.[3] This may have been so. Yet Salisbury would also be the logical choice for Disraeli once a conference became, for tactical purposes, domestically and internationally, inescapable. As one who commanded general public esteem, Salisbury's appointment strengthened the government vis-à-vis the agitation. And as formal proposer of the conference, Derby could steer the choice of its venue to Constantinople, where Elliot could be relied upon, if necessary, to restrain Salisbury's anti-Turkish tendencies. Certainly neither Disraeli nor Derby displayed any enthusiasm for the policy they had ostensibly initiated. Derby wrote to Salisbury early in November: 'We are in for a Conference: that is now to all appearance inevitable.' And though Derby was well aware that Salisbury's contempt for Elliot had reached new depths,[4] he insisted that Elliot had worked efficiently, and that Salisbury would find him 'well-informed, and useful as a second'.[5]

That Disraeli and Derby calculated on Elliot's being a hobbling ball and chain on Salisbury's restless leg there is no doubt; for Salisbury had abated none of his earlier insistence that a fundamental revision of policy was imperative. On 23 October, for instance,

[1] Mundella to R. Leader, 1 November 1876, *ibid.*
[2] Sheffield *Independent*, 6 November 1876, p. 2.
[3] Liddon to Freeman, 13 November 1876, Liddon Papers. Disraeli accepted the conference only after having failed to secure an alliance with Austria-Hungary. See A. J. P. Taylor, *The Struggle for Mastery in Europe, 1848–1918* (Oxford 1954), p. 241.
[4] See Derby to Salisbury, 26 October 1876, Salisbury Papers.
[5] Derby to Salisbury, 3 November 1876, *ibid.*

he laid before Disraeli a letter from Constantinople from George Campbell—'so shrewd an observer'—which showed why British policy had failed to manage the Turks.[1] Naturally Salisbury's appointment was welcomed by agitation leaders as a 'great gain'.[2] An Anglo-Catholic, associated with Carnarvon, and like Carnarvon with a record of opposition to Disraeli, Salisbury seemed at all points suitable as the agent of a reformed and positive British policy of co-operation with the concert of Europe for which the leaders of the agitation had never ceased to call since the rejection of the Berlin Memorandum.

The project of a National Conference immediately assumed the function of an auxiliary to Salisbury's mission to Constantinople. The circular put out by Chesson on 6 November announcing a proposed National Conference on the Eastern Question 'at an early date'[3] was in effect the official response of the agitation to the news of Salisbury's appointment. Freeman wrote to Liddon on 9 November after 'talking with Bath and Dickinson[4] about our matters', especially Salisbury's mission. Bath thought it would be useless for him to approach Salisbury, but recommended a 'moral appeal' from Liddon.[5] Liddon wrote his appeal, shrewdly, to Lady Salisbury, who was to accompany her husband: 'May I beg you, if you can & when you can do so, to entreat Lord Salisbury to keep one or two (out of many) points in mind?' Liddon's points were that there could be no autonomy for Christians without the entire abolition of Koran-based Turkish law; that Bosnia and the Herzegovina must be united to Serbia; and (at Freeman's special insistence) that Montenegro must be given proper access to the sea. After some sympathetic remarks on Carnarvon's attitude to the autumn agitation, Liddon concluded his appeal:

No doubt the higher and purer enthusiasm *has* been abused in merely political interests. But it is in reality quite independent of these interests, & it is certain to reappear, in one form or another as long as English people continue to believe in our Saviour, and to hate organised immorality, such as *is* the Turkish Empire.[6]

---

[1] Salisbury to Disraeli, 26 October 1876, *ibid.*
[2] Freeman to Liddon, 9 November 1876, Liddon Papers.
[3] Chesson to Wilson, 6 November 1876, H. J. Wilson Papers, M.D., 2587/1.
[4] Probably S. S. Dickinson, a prominent Gloucestershire Liberal.
[5] Freeman to Liddon, 9 November 1876, Liddon Papers.
[6] Liddon to Lady Salisbury, 10 November 1876, Salisbury Papers.

Freeman himself wrote to Richard Burton at Trieste to catch Salisbury on his way through from Vienna to Constantinople.[1] Bath also, after all, appealed to Salisbury, who responded with friendly protestations as to the good faith of the government, and the necessity for reticence at the Foreign Office. He agreed in substance with Bath, though more reserved about methods. 'But the time for open speaking', Salisbury added, 'has not come yet.'[2] As it happened, that time never did come for Salisbury; but in any case, his opinions weighed little in the scale. Disraeli's attitude, and Derby's unwillingness to resist it, made it virtually certain that the Constantinople Conference would be abortive.

The first major public expression of this attitude came on 9 November, in Disraeli's speech at the Guildhall. Its keynote was full moral support for Turkey and an unmistakable threat to Russia.[3] The pattern of September was thus repeated: Disraeli's Guildhall speech practically nullified the effect of the proposal for a conference of the powers in exactly the manner of his Aylesbury speech cancelling out Derby's proposed administrative reforms of 21 September. By November, however, the Russians had lost patience. Almost simultaneously with Disraeli's Guildhall speech, the Czar declared, in effect, that if the Constantinople Conference failed to persuade the Turks to submit to the advice of Europe, Russia would be compelled in honour and simple self-respect to go to war to get satisfaction.[4]

Henceforth the principal object of the St James's Hall Conference was, in Gladstone's words, to cut Salisbury 'adrift from the Guildhall speech'.[5] That speech certainly had the effect of galvanising Gladstone into a much more positive outlook on affairs, indeed, of giving the agitation as a whole a much-needed fillip. Freeman set off on stump. After a 'fling at Turks & Jews' at Bristol on 13 November, he moved up to Manchester, then back again to Exeter, bearing testimony' all the way, and greatly heartened by an apparently revived public spirit. He reassured the dour Bryce that he could not really agree with him that there was 'no strong feeling about in the country at large'. Both Manchester and Exeter, 'the

---

[1] Freeman to Liddon, 24 November 1876, Liddon Papers.
[2] Salisbury to Bath, 10 November 1876, Salisbury Papers.
[3] *Times*, 10 November 1876, p. 8.
[4] See Sumner, *Russia and the Balkans, 1870–1880*, pp. 205–6.
[5] E.Q.A., *Report*, p. 107.

new city and the old', told Freeman 'quite another story', and he
found 'there and everywhere else' that the name of Gladstone had
the 'same magic effect as it had when I was on stump in 1868'.[1]
Small events also told of a revived spirit of agitation: Catherine
Phillimore cheered Liddon by describing to him the scene in the
streets of London of a 'Guy', dressed as a 'Turk' and terrorising
several small 'Bulgarians', being pursued by people shouting 'no
peace with Turkey!'[2] The agitation again began to catch hold of
Gladstone's imagination. He was much encouraged by the *Othello*
incident at Liverpool[3]; and he cited also to Granville the Liberal
success in the recent Frome by-election, where Bath exerted himself in his own electoral interest with half-hearted distaste. The
father of the successful Liberal candidate, as Mundella hastened to
inform Gladstone, attributed his son's success entirely to the
Eastern question.[4]

But the vital aspect of the agitation remained the progress of the
movement for a national conference. Chesson and Auberon Herbert
had been busy setting up a series of provincial headquarters for the
purpose of 'working' the several regions. Robert Leader was to
establish a central committee at Sheffield to supervise the gathering of names by sub-committees throughout the north of England.
Similar arrangements were made in Birmingham, Nottingham,
Exeter, and other places in the midlands and the south.[5] Reports
from all parts of the country were considered at a meeting of the
informal parliamentary committee on 17 November. It was decided
that the numerous 'adhesions of an influential and representative
character' justified a firm plan of operation and guaranteed success.
A date early in December was decided on, and the parliamentary
committee nominated a conference committee, with Mundella as
chairman. George Howard, J. W. Probyn, and Chesson were
appointed secretaries; Henry Broadhurst was called in to co-
ordinate the working-class side of the work; and William Morris
became treasurer. The committee included, as well as Freeman and

[1] Freeman to Bryce, 13 and 23 November 1876, Bryce Papers, E4.
[2] Phillimore to Liddon, 7 November 1876, Liddon Papers.
[3] See above, p. 152.
[4] Gladstone to Granville, 26 November 1876, Granville Papers, 30, 29/29;
Mundella to Gladstone, 26 November 1876, Gladstone Papers, Add. MSS 44258,
ff. 131–2. For Bath's comments on the election see Granville to Gladstone, 3 December
1876, Gladstone Papers, Add. MSS 44171, ff. 25–7.
[5] Herbert to Chesson, 6 November [1876], Anti-Slavery Papers, Chesson, C
137/256–60.

Morris, Henry Richard (who did excellent work in shepherding somewhat bewildered Peace Society people into the movement, making sure that Chesson softened harsh resolutions), Bryce, Stopford Brooke, Froude, Denton, Auberon Herbert, and Fowell Buxton.[1] In sending Gladstone on 25 November a list of names of 'excellent quality', Mundella echoed a recurrent motif on the agitation: 'I believe that we shall have such a demonstration as England has not seen since the Anti-Corn law days.'[2] He failed, however, in his attempt to entice Lord Frederick Cavendish into the movement, and so disrupt the aloof solidarity of the Granville-Hartington set.[3]

Disraeli soon got wind of this 'organised attempt to revive agitation under the title of a Conference in London on Turkish affairs', which was (as he thought) to 'sit while the real Conference is holding its Session'; and expatiated to Salisbury on the insolence of this 'intolerable assembly'. He understood that several leading members of the Liberal party had declined to take part, ' but Lord Shaftesbury, who believes he is preparing a great career for Evelyn Ashley, is of course a leading member, & the Gladstone influence has prevailed on the Duke of Westminster to be President'. Gladstone could also, as the Queen observed severely, 'command' the Duke and Duchess of Argyll.[4]

Though Gladstone had begun to show great interest in the progress of the National Conference project,[5] the most delicate part of Mundella's task was to make sure that he did not balk at the last moment from performing the function allotted to him as protagonist of the occasion. It was not until 2 December that he could write to Robert Leader that he was 'pretty confident' that Glad-

---

[1] See Chesson to Liddon, 20 November 1876, Liddon Papers; Freeman to Bryce, 13 November 1876, Bryce Papers, E4; Bryce to Mundella, 20 November 1876, Mundella Papers.

[2] Mundella to Gladstone, 25 November 1876, Gladstone Papers, Add. MSS 44258, ff. 127–8.

[3] Lord F. Cavendish to Mundella, 24 and 28 November 1876, Mundella Papers.

[4] Disraeli to Salisbury, 29 November 1876, Salisbury Papers.

[5] He apparently provided a draft for the manifesto of the Conference (see Auberon Herbert to Gladstone, 16 November 1876, Gladstone Papers, Add. MSS 44452, . 136); he drew up also a list of subjects connected with the Eastern question which became later the basis of the series of pamphlets put out by the Eastern Question Association (see Auberon Herbert to Gladstone, 23 November 1876, *ibid.*, ff. 270–3); he provided suggestions for speakers at the Conference (see Mundella to Gladstone, 26 November 1876, *ibid.* Add. MSS 44258, ff. 131–2); he was eager to learn the names of the Conference committee (see Mundella to Gladstone, 25 November 1876, *ibid.*, ff. 127–8).

stone would speak.[1] In putting pressure on Gladstone, Mundella,
with a sure instinct, stressed particularly the fact that the Liberal
Whip, Adam, 'rejoiced' in the work, and especially in the prospect
of Gladstone's joining in.[2] Acton also truly reflected the bent in
Gladstone's mind towards linking the Liberal party as advantage-
ously as possible with the issues of the Eastern question when, in
telling Gladstone that Hartington was less near agreeing with
him than he had chosen to say, he added: 'But he can hardly fail to
see the excellent position we are in, thanks to your initiative.'[3]

In fact, Gladstone deserved no credit whatever for initiative.
Nevertheless, as in the case of his pamphlet, he inevitably became,
in a sense, responsible for the situation created by the initiative of
others. As Mundella pointed out, without Gladstone the National
Conference would be *Hamlet* without the Prince of Denmark.[4]
Gladstone could no longer even pretend seriously to resist the force
of the logic of the situation. He rejected the argument of Granville
and Hartington that he would embarrass Salisbury at Constantinople
by participating in the demonstration.[5] He asserted that, on the
contrary, his main purpose would be to buttress Salisbury's
position.[6] In this he represented with fidelity the central and
supreme function of the National Conference.

3 The Conferences at St James's Hall and Constantinople

The fortune of the National Conference on the Eastern Question
held in St James's Hall, Piccadilly, on Friday, 8 December 1876,
was thus linked intimately and inseparably to that of the Conference
of the powers which commenced its preliminary sessions in Constantinople on 14 December.[7] The conveners at St James's Hall,
called by Bryce and his committee to the 'high and glorious
mission' of vindicating the 'principles of humanity' and blotting
out the legacy of the 'fatal Crimean war', were invited to concern

[1] Mundella Papers.
[2] Mundella to Gladstone, 2 December 1876, Gladstone Papers, Add. MSS 44258,
ff. 138–9.
[3] Acton to Gladstone, 21 January 1877, *ibid.*, Add. MSS 44093, ff. 195–6.
[4] Mundella to Gladstone, *ibid.*
[5] Granville to Gladstone, 27 November 1876, *ibid.*, Add. MSS 44171, ff. 21–4.
[6] Gladstone to Granville, 6 December 1876, Granville Papers, 30, 29/29.
[7] The formal sessions, including the Turks, began on 23 December.

themselves with four general points: instant reparation must be made by the Turks to the injured and despoiled Bulgarians; the Muslim population must be disarmed; the Christians must be accorded autonomous government; and British policy should aim at fruitful co-operation with Russia.[1]

The instructions issued by Derby to Salisbury avowing the desirability of securing a minimum programme of concessions from the Turks[2] constituted, as Gladstone later described it, 'a kind of point of junction', a 'sort of union' between the agitation and the policy of the government.[3] With the Salisbury mission, Gladstone wrote to Granville, '& mainly by it, the agitation was effectually suspended. In the St James's Hall meeting, we frankly accepted it as a new point of departure'.[4] The key to the situation lay in the capacity of the moderate section of the Cabinet to maintain the new departure intact from the incessant criticism and intrigue of Disraeli.[5]

The two weighty sessions at St James's Hall set the seal of a deep sense of responsibility on the passionate movement of late August and September; the National Conference reaffirmed solemnly and deliberately, after the heat of the initial reaction to the atrocities, the principles and purposes of the autumn agitation. As a demonstration of 'Mind' applied to politics it was of incomparable brilliance; so imposing, indeed, as almost to conceal its shortcomings. The list of speakers included Trollope,[6] the Bishop of Oxford, Henry Richard, Bryce, Shaftesbury, Liddon, George Otto Trevelyan, Freeman, Fawcett, and Gladstone. But the Conference never quite succeeded in establishing its claim to a character

---

[1] Circular *To the Conveners of the Conference on Eastern Affairs*, Liddon Papers. The circular mentions also that £20,000 had been subscribed for the work of the Conference.

[2] See *Accounts and Papers, State Papers, Turkey*, XCI (1877): *Correspondence Respecting the Conference at Constantinople and the Affairs of Turkey, 1876–77*, no. 1, Derby to Salisbury, 20 November 1876.

[3] 3 *Hansard*, CCXXXIV, c. 408.

[4] Gladstone to Granville, 17 May 1877, Granville Papers, 30, 29/29.

[5] The violently Turcophile member of parliament H. A. Munro-Butler-Johnstone 'posed' as a secret emissary of Disraeli at Constantinople (see Sumner, *Russia and the Balkans, 1870–1880*, pp. 236–7); Disraeli certainly used him as an emissary, with Lord Denbigh, to Andrassy in 1877 (*ibid.*, p. 320). See also Seton-Watson, 'Russo-British Relations During the Eastern Crisis', *Slavonic Review*, 4, p. 454.

[6] Thomas Hardy attended the session of the Conference at which Trollope spoke, and noted with amusement the vain efforts of the presiding Duke of Westminster to stem the flow of Trollope's oratory. F. E. Hardy, *The Early Life of Thomas Hardy, 1840–1891* (1928), p. 148.

radically distinct from a Liberal demonstration. Of 89 members of
parliament among the 710 conveners, 88 were Liberals and only
one (Lord Robert Montagu) a Conservative. Of the 23 peers only
3 (Shaftesbury, Bath, Seaton) were Conservatives. Disraeli could
dwell with gratification on the 'very favourable' parliamentary
position of the government in spite of all that the agitation could
do. 'It is not merely, that our own men are unanimously staunch,
but the whole of the Irish party has been instructed to support the
Government.'[1] Derby remarked also on the gratifying absence of
'deserters from our side . . .' which he had feared, 'a foolish letter
from the foolish Bath being the only approach to an exception'.[2]
Nor did the Conference have the benefit of united Liberal patronage.
Disraeli cheerfully calculated the 'decided anti-Russian section' of
the Liberals as 'not less than sixty'; and Derby took comfort in
the quite 'remarkable' 'absence & silence of the Whig chiefs'.
'I hear in all quarters', he reported to Salisbury, 'that Hartington
is determined not to be factious, & does not conceal his dislike of
Gladstone's line.'[3] The only publishable indication of support
which the Conference movement could extract from the Granville-
Hartington side was a letter from the trimming Harcourt. And
many otherwise quite sympathetic Liberals must have agreed with
Morley that, while meetings throughout the country were a good
thing, a conference to 'settle details of a government for Herzegovina' was an 'absurdity'.[4]

Nor was it in any practical sense a conference, much less a convention. The very title of the occasion was a considerable embarrassment. As Gladstone later allowed, 'conference' was rather
illogical and misleading; but it had been preferred because of its
associations with anti-slavery and anti-corn laws.[5] Even so, contributions from the 'delegates' were not encouraged, as Charles
Bradlaugh and Annie Besant found to their infinite disgust.[6] Although 117 cities and towns were listed as 'represented', the St
James's Hall Conference was certainly not an anti-parliament in the
sense Stead would have wished. Nothing like a popular referendum

[1] Disraeli to Salisbury, 29 November 1876, Salisbury Papers.
[2] Derby to Salisbury, 14 December 1876, ibid.
[3] Disraeli to Salisbury, ibid; Derby to Salisbury, ibid.
[4] Morley to Chamberlain, 28 November 1876, Chamberlain Papers, J.C., 5/5.
[5] F. Cavendish to Hartington, 22 December 1876, Devonshire Papers, 340/691.
[6] National Reformer, 17 December 1876, pp. 385–6, 394.

took place in the first week of December. There were a number of town's meetings called: Birmingham, Sheffield, Manchester, and other places convened them on the 4th; Darlington and Oldham had done so earlier. Stead's meeting at Darlington to elect 'delegates' to the 'St. James's Hall Convention' was, with his more solemn view of the parliamentary pretensions of the Conference, a more elaborate affair than most.[1] Later, Stead was rather dashed by Carlyle's contemptuous deprecation of the 'elective representative element' in the movement.[2] In the vast majority of cases it was affectively the local Liberal Association, under whatever guise, which nominated representatives. J. D. Bell, proprietor of the *Northern Echo*, in forwarding to Chesson a choice selection of Durham and York North Riding names, emphasised that their desirability as convenors lay in the fact that they represented, as presidents, 'strong North Country Liberal Associations'.[3] The chief delegates from Manchester (R. Leake) and Birmingham (J. S. Wright) were respectively presidents of the Manchester and Birmingham Liberal Associations. Some meetings were of a more *ad hoc* and less professionally political character: a gathering in Exeter College, Oxford, of 'persons sympathising with the objects of the National Conference' elected Liddon as their chief representative, to be supported by a delegation consisting of Bryce, Rolleston, Thorold Rogers, and Tozer.[4]

Much was hoped for from the St James's Hall affair. In the end, all that came of it was the Eastern Question Association, another name for the Conference committee, pledged to continue the work of keeping the public informed of the true state of the Eastern question. But it promised a great deal more than this. Chamberlain, to whose help it owed all too little, was jubilant at the prospect it seemed to open up for the humiliation and discrediting of Disraeli's government.[5] Possibly even the Russians were impressed.[6] But above all it embodied the hope of peace: the feature of the

---

[1] *Northern Echo*, 1 December 1876, pp. 2–3; 2 December, p. 3.
[2] 'More About Turks and Russians' (1877), p. 8, Stead Papers.
[3] Bell to Chesson, 7 November 1876, Anti-Slavery Papers, Chesson, C 125/161.
[4] Rolleston to Liddon, 5 December 1876, Liddon Papers.
[5] Chamberlain to Dilke, 7 December 1876, Dilke Papers, Add. MSS 43885, f. 51.
[6] Milyutin, the Minister of War, in answering on behalf of the Czar a letter sent in Gladstone's name but which Gladstone did not write (and which was no doubt suitably compromising), thanked Gladstone for his expressions of sympathy, 'tant de Votre part que de celles de Vos amis de St. James's Hall'. The Emperor, Milyutin assured Gladstone, was highly gratified at 'les voeux que Vous formez en notre faveur. Mon

T

Conference that pleased Annie Besant—not easily pleased, for she was furious at the interception by Mundella, the 'chief usher', of her note to Shaftesbury requesting leave to speak—was that every mention of 'peace' evoked loud applause.[1] The fundamental condition of peace was acceptance by the Turks of the fact that they would have to come to terms with Europe. This, together with ostentatious expressions of confidence in Salisbury, support for Salisbury,[2] was the theme most insistently stressed at St James's Hall.

This also is what Salisbury, fully appreciative of the good will of the National Conference[3] and contemptuous of the Turcophile English colony at Constantinople led by Elliot—'half fanatics, half rogues'[4]—attempted to impress upon the Turks. The Turks, however, preferred to take Disraeli's Guildhall speech as the true index of British policy. They were encouraged so to think by Elliot's counterworking of Salisbury and by the immensely significant fact that Disraeli said nothing to make them doubt for a moment the certainty of his full, constant, and in the last resort belligerent, support. The Porte defied Europe. The formal opening session of the Constantinople Conference was interrupted by booming guns and the solemn proclamation of a constitution which would answer all complaints and thus render further discussion superfluous. From this initial level of farce the Conference of Constantinople never rose.

Disraeli complained bitterly at Salisbury's 'bullying' of the Turks[5] and refused his request that Elliot be removed and the

Auguste Maître est persuadé qu'ils ne peuvent rester stériles et qu'ils exerceront une influence salutaire sur l'opinion publique en Angleterre' (Milyutin to Gladstone, 25 July/6 August 1877, Gladstone Papers, Add. MSS 44455, ff. 3–4. See also on this matter of forgeries Gladstone to Shuvalov, 2 September 1877, ibid., ff. 15–16). The letter replied to by Milyutin was the second forged in Gladstone's name. It was about this time that Gladstone decided not to join the committee of the Russian Sick and Wounded Fund, because of the 'furious' state of public feeling about his relations with Russia (Gladstone to Liddon, 22 August 1877, Liddon Papers). For one wild moment there was the possibility that Tchernaiev, the pan-Slav Russian general who had commanded the defeated Serbian army in 1876, would attend the National Conference. He inquired, through Madame Novikov, about the chances of getting tickets for himself and his staff, and the likelihood of a 'fair reception'. Freeman was complacently ready to abet such foolishness (Freeman to Buxton, 5 December 1876, Anti-Slavery Papers, Buxton, C 109/141); sense, however, prevailed.

[1] *National Reformer*, 17 December 1876, p. 385.
[2] For examples of this see E.Q.A., *Report*, pp. 4, 36–7, 91, 93, 95–6, 106–7, 118.
[3] See Granville to Gladstone, 11 December 1876, Gladstone Papers, Add. MSS 44171, ff. 32–3.
[4] Salisbury to Gathorne Hardy, 5 January 1877, Salisbury Papers.
[5] Buckle, *Disraeli*, vol. ii, p. 983.

fleet sent to the Bosphorous to intimidate Abdul Hamid.[1] Derby, buffeted by the winds of Hughenden and much too irresolute to preserve intact the spirit of his own instructions to Salisbury, insisted that 'reports indicate from all quarters that Russia is ill prepared for war and ready to make considerable concessions'; and backed Elliot once more against Salisbury's demands to be rid of him.[2] Disraeli and Derby based British policy squarely and deliberately on the proposition that the Russians could be bluffed and forced to climb down. On 14 December, as the preliminary Conference got under way, Salisbury took the counter-precaution of arranging with Carnarvon to correspond by private cipher code: Salisbury would reveal the precarious state of the negotiations, and Carnarvon would redouble his pressure on behalf of Salisbury in cabinet[3] for 'powers to squeeze the Turk'.[4] 'Otherwise', as Salisbury wrote, 'we may both be involved in decisions upon a momentous policy, which neither of us in the least approves'; Russia and the Czar '*cannot*' concede more to the 'idiotic Turks'.[5] Then Salisbury had to fight against deliberate 'leaks' of his confidential telegrams: 'Somebody is playing foul. I fear the result will be to make the Turks refuse to concede anything.'[6] This indeed was the outcome. Despite Carnarvon's efforts, backed by Northcote,[7] Disraeli and Derby declined to give Salisbury powers to coerce the Porte if it refused to accept the plan proposed by the preliminary Conference: local reforms with a Commissioner of Supervision and neutral escort.[8]

The Porte duly refused; and the Conference of Constantinople broke up in hopeless failure on 22 January 1877. Disraeli, Derby, and the Turks were confident that they had called the Russian bluff. But the Russian declaration of war—after an interval of confusion which put both Lord Bath and William Morris in despair lest the Czar climb down after all, and the Turks escape retri-

[1] Mundella to R. Leader, 11 May 1877, reported Lady Salisbury 'abusing Dizzy' for checkmating Salisbury. Salisbury himself said after his return to England: 'Had I been allowed to call the Fleet to Constantinople everything would have been settled.' Mundella Papers.
[2] Derby to Salisbury, 30/31 December 1876, Salisbury Papers.
[3] Salisbury to Carnarvon, 14 December 1876, *ibid*.
[4] Salisbury to Carnarvon, 22 December 1876, *ibid*.
[5] *Ibid.*
[6] Salisbury to Derby (draft), 5 January 1877, *ibid*.
[7] Northcote to Disraeli, 15 December 1876, Disraeli Papers.
[8] Derby to Salisbury, 18/19 December 1876, Salisbury Papers.

bution[1]—came on 24 April. Musurus Pasha later complained to Bradlaugh: 'Your country led us into war by deluding us with the hope of material support.'[2]

The collapse of the Conference at Constantinople and the outbreak of war—for all that it was hailed by Bath and Morris as the coming vengeance of the righteous—registered decisively the ultimate failure of the St James's Hall Conference, and hence of the atrocities agitation as a whole, to achieve positive results. Gladstone was wrong, or at least over-sanguine, when he predicted to Elliot, in the flush of his own enlightenment at the beginning of September, that it was 'far from unlikely' that the people of England would 'have ability to obtain their demands'.[3] When Freeman wrote anxiously and sombrely to Liddon in March 1877, convinced that 'something must be done' to 'kick up another row' and so prevent the 'jew' and Derby from 'working as hard to do nothing as Canning could have worked to deliver a nation or Wilberforce to put down slavery', he reflected a growing sense of unease and an emerging suspicion that perhaps the people had indeed failed to obtain their demands. 'But I hope', he added, 'it is not

> "labor omnia vicit
> Improbus".'[4]

But so it was to prove. Goldwin Smith was right. No 'philanthropic or religious' movement could have shaken seriously a government so strong as the Conservative government of 1876 in the active support of the 'double aristocracy' and the 'national idea'. And it was the unwavering staunchness of his party that enabled Disraeli to defy the agitation, a powerful section of his own Cabinet, and the Russians at Constantinople. Disraeli in the end proved too resilient, too difficult to impress, too hard to frighten.

*

Stead addressed the Czar Alexander III in an audience on 24 May 1888 in terms which might well serve as an epitaph for the great, in some ways noble, unfortunate movement of 1876:

---

[1] Bath to Liddon, 8 January 1877, Liddon Papers; Morris to Bryce, 20 March 1877, Bryce Papers, E19.
[2] Bradlaugh to Gladstone, 7 August 1877, Gladstone Papers, Add. MSS 44111, f. 77.   [3] See above, p. 108.
[4] Freeman to Liddon, 12 March, 1877, Liddon Papers.

I remember how England has injured Russia. I feel as if my proper place was not sitting on this chair talking to your Majesty, but kneeling humbly at your feet begging your forgiveness for all the injuries which we have inflicted on your country. . . . When I think of 1876, I am full of remorse. We did our best. . . . But we were not strong enough and you had to go through it [the war with Turkey], and all for our fault.[1]

[1] Stead Papers.

8

Epilogue: Aftermath of the Agitation

THOUGH the Bulgarian atrocities agitation achieved nothing more than a temporary and superficial diversion of British Eastern policy, its consequences were profoundly significant. Critics of the agitation indeed accused it of causing the Russo-Turkish war by encouraging the Russians to advance under the impression that English public opinion would never permit Disraeli to intervene. But this, like the sinister reputation of Madame Novikov, is unduly flattering. The Czar and Gorchakov no doubt appreciated the sympathy of Gladstone and his 'friends of St. James's Hall'; but there is nothing to suggest that English domestic affairs weighed to any notable degree in their calculations, or indeed that they appreciated to any real extent the true nature of what was going on in England during the autumn and later. As Derby remarked to Salisbury on the 'unpleasantly weakened' position of Britain vis-à-vis Russia caused by the agitation: 'Luckily foreigners do not understand us . . . and they are simply puzzled by what is passing, not ready to avail themselves of the chance.'[1] The true significance of the agitation lay rather in its political consequences in England. These consequences centre about Gladstone.

Politics in England in the twenty years from 1876 turned on two fundamental facts: first, that Gladstone returned to full political life, and eventually to power; second, that Home Rule for Ireland became a moral cause for him in the same way as the Eastern question had done. It is proposed here briefly to relate these two fundamental facts to the atrocities agitation.

1 Gladstone, the Liberal Party, and 1880

The progress made by Gladstone from the *Bulgarian Horrors* to Midlothian and thence to office once more in 1880 has an appear-

[1] Derby to Salisbury, 24 September 1876, Salisbury Papers.

ance of inevitability about it which can be misleading if treated too baldly. The fact easiest to overlook is that the very failure of the agitation to sway the government was precisely the basic condition of Gladstone's continued commitment to full political life. There is no reason to doubt the complete integrity of his wish that the government would bow to the national will as expressed, in his view, by the agitation, and thus relieve him of further responsibility in the matter. He wrote to Granville in June 1877: 'My earnest hope is that this Eastern Question is to reach a close or a resting place during the summer & that then I shall be a free man again.'[1] Any attempt to understand Gladstone will be abortive which does not accept the validity of the Gladstonian scale of values as a means of judging his motives. Gladstone's complaints to Bryce that his Homeric studies were being 'hamstrung' by the Eastern question, and that he looked with 'longing' for the 'day of resumption',[2] must be accorded solemn weight in an assessment of his intentions at the beginning of 1877.

Gladstone's desire to be free was as great as his determination to see the Eastern question to a proper end. Beneath this conflict in his mind there was a further dichotomy: embarrassed by his relation to Granville and Hartington, he was yet possessed at the same time by an almost compulsive need to concern himself with the encouragement of developments 'very beneficial to the party as such'. In the course of his progress through the west country in January 1877 to confer with Bath, Liddon, and Freeman at Longleat, he stressed to a Liberal demonstration at Frome his hope that the party would continue powerful in its sentiments and principles, and become better in its organisation, 'more practical and astute' in the 'great question of shaping means with a view to ends than, perhaps, it has been of late years'.[3] Signs were not lacking of Liberal re-organisation. In December 1876 the newly-founded Young Men's Liberal Association of Liverpool forwarded a resolution signed by eight hundred members urging Gladstone to preside at its inaugural meeting[4]; in towns like Barrow, Liberal associations were founded or re-founded as a prelude to more active political life.[5]

[1] Gladstone to Granville, 1 June 1877, Granville Papers, 30, 29/29.
[2] Gladstone to Bryce, 29 January 1877, Bryce Papers, E6.
[3] *Times*, 23 January 1877, p. 6.   [4] *Ibid.*, 29 December 1876, p. 7.
[5] *Barrow Times*, 16 December 1876, p.5.

The greatest portent of this new trend was Chamberlain's project for a National Liberal Federation modelled on the Birmingham system. Gladstone's relationship to this development is of central importance in revealing the connection of the various threads of his attitude to the Eastern question, the party leaders, and the party 'as such'.

His decision to associate himself with the inauguration of Chamberlain's Federation was related intimately to his failure to carry the Liberal leaders and the parliamentary party as a whole with him, when, on the re-assembly of parliament early in 1877, he advocated a series of resolutions indicting the Turks. He made the first overture to this end in February.[1] Granville and Hartington demurred.[2] Gladstone then declared his intention to persist by publishing a second pamphlet attacking the Turks, *Lessons in Massacre*. Then, under the stimulus of reports that Salisbury and Carnarvon were losing ground to the war party in Cabinet, he decided to press again for forthright parliamentary action.[3] He proposed five resolutions, which would in effect have committed the government to impose upon Turkey the recommendations of the Conference at Constantinople. The effect of this was to transfer the crisis from the Cabinet to the Liberal party. Both the front bench and the bulk of the Whigs on one side and the peace party led by Bright on the other refused to follow Gladstone. After much backing and filling, Gladstone was induced to preserve party unity by putting forward only the first of his resolutions, which was general and innocuous. This fiasco brought home to him the hollowness of his assumptions throughout the autumn agitation that the Liberal party as a whole was far in advance of the attitude of Hartington and Forster. At the same time a strong agitation in the country on behalf of the resolutions, got up by the Eastern Question Association, Stead, William Morris, Broadhurst, and Chamberlain, reinforced his views on the moral soundness of the 'true nation'. These views now constituted a fully-fledged mystique. In a memorandum 'written in anticipation of General Ignatieff' (when the latter visited England in 1877) but 'not read to him', Gladstone averred: 'Quant au peuple Anglais—je ne parle pas du

---

[1] Gladstone to Granville, 24 February 1877, Granville Papers, 30, 29/29.
[2] Gladstone to Granville, 2 March 1877, Devonshire Papers, 340/700.
[3] See Mundella to R. Leader, 11 May 1877, Mundella Papers; Gladstone to Granville, 23 April 1877, Granville Papers, 30, 29/29.

Gouvernement, ni du Parlement, ni des riches, ni de l'armée, ni de la plupart de la presse métropolitaine—mais quant au peuple, je suis fermement d'avis qu'il s'est décidé, sur la question Orientale, dans le sens Chrétien.'[1] 'I shall ever recall', he wrote to Broadhurst, who was organising the Labour Representation League's side of the activity, 'with lively pleasure how vivid and general an energy the people of the country have exhibited' in bearing witness to the 'reality of the autumnal and recent movements.'[2] Gladstone now became more concerned than ever with the need to 'educate' the party.

Chamberlain invited Gladstone on 16 April to attend the inauguration of the National Liberal Federation at Birmingham. His letter was, as Granville remarked wryly, 'very well-written',[3] and it dwelt on the claims which Birmingham had on Gladstone for its consistent Liberalism, and, above all, its leading rôle from the beginning in support of Gladstone's 'crusade' on the Eastern question.[4] The dates are revealing: the debate on Gladstone's resolutions closed on 14 May; on 16 May Chamberlain thanked Gladstone for accepting the invitation of 16 April. Gladstone asked for, and got, assurances that he would have full scope and full support on the Eastern question.[5]

Granville had written to Gladstone: 'I presume you will not attend Chamberlain's meeting.'[6] It was axiomatic in the upper and respectable levels of the party that the enthusiasm of Chamberlain and the other 'malcontents' for Gladstone's resolutions had behind it a desire for a final rupture in the party and riddance of the Whigs once and for all.[7] Gladstone, who was certainly not under any illusion as to Chamberlain's far from disinterested part in the Eastern question, or any misconception as to his aim to promote the Radical cause at the expense of the Whigs, nevertheless thought a bargain with Chamberlain necessary. To Granville

[1] Gladstone Papers, Add. MSS 44763, ff. 85–6 (21 March 1877).
[2] Gladstone to Broadhurst, 17 May 1877, Broadhurst Papers, vol. i, no. 26.
[3] Granville to Gladstone, 21 May 1877, Gladstone Papers, Add. MSS 44171, ff. 74–7.
[4] Chamberlain to Gladstone, 16 April 1877, *ibid.*, Add. MSS 44125, ff. 3–6.
[5] Chamberlain to Gladstone, 16 May 1877, *ibid.*, f. 9; J. L. Garvin, *The Life of Joseph Chamberlain* (1932), vol. i, p. 259.
[6] Granville to Gladstone, 16 May 1877, Gladstone Papers, Add. MSS 44171, ff. 67–70.
[7] E.g. Frederick Cavendish to Gladstone, 19 May 1877, *ibid.*, Add. MSS 44124, ff. 71–2. See also, for Lord Edmond Fitzmaurice's view, Mundella to R. Leader, 1 September 1877, Mundella Papers.

he defended his decision on the grounds that he could do good by 'minimising the difference which preceded the late debate', and also that it was essential to maintain continuous pressure on the government. 'From the Birmingham meeting there will be a ramification, through the Liberal Delegates assembled there, stretching all over the country, and I wish to warn them against giving ground for a renewal of the statement which obtained so much vogue before the late Debate that "the country" had repented.'[1] Moreover, Gladstone's revived appreciation of the political virtues of the masses made him quite ready to accept a project for improved electoral organisation 'from below'. He assured Granville that he would be careful to keep aloof from any suggestion that policy should be recast, but insisted that improved electoral organisation would tend powerfully to promote unity of action, in which the party was still 'deficient'—a deficiency, Gladstone added delicately, 'now I think, after the party has been led with great judgment and caution for three years, to a degree even exceeding anything I can recollect since 1866'. The 'vital principle' of the Liberal party, like that of Greek art, he reminded Granville, was 'action'.[2] And he was hopeful that the spread of the Birmingham principle of local party organisation 'may prove a great stroke in the interests of the party'.[3]

The great demonstration at Bingley Hall, Birmingham, on 31 May, reflected a desire on the part of both Chamberlain and Gladstone to remake the party in their own terms. Gladstone was convinced that the Liberal party, 'as in so many other cases', was alone the 'instrument' by which a 'great work' was to be carried on.[4] If Granville and Hartington would not accept a policy of 'action' they rejected, in effect, what Gladstone conceived to be the essential function of the party over which they presided. When the question of loyalties and the 'higher duty than that of party allegiance' came up, Gladstone wrote to Granville in 1878 claiming that he could assert, on his own part, that he believed he had never made 'so great a sacrifice to party', as when in the previous year he 'gave up bringing forward the Bulgarian question', especially as he was, and remained, convinced that 'the negative

[1] Gladstone to Granville, 17 May 1877, Granville Papers, 30, 29/29.
[2] Gladstone to Granville, 19 May 1877, *ibid.*
[3] Gladstone to Granville, 1 June 1877, *ibid.*
[4] Gladstone to Granville, 23 May 1877, *ibid.*

decision of you all was a mistake in the view of party'.[1] Gladstone found himself faced squarely with a conflict of loyalty to the Liberal party as an establishment and loyalty to the Liberal party as an idea. Bingley Hall resolved this conflict: his speech there clearly looked forward to Midlothian, pre-eminently a campaign of 'ideas'.

Chamberlain wanted Gladstone to displace Hartington and Granville as leaders of the party; Gladstone himself, in effect, really wanted to do the same thing in the sense of wanting them to be converted into politicians of the Liberal 'idea'. The hope was forlorn. Inevitably Gladstone had to recognise the fact that his late colleagues were 'letting things slide with respect to Turkey'.[2] Nor could he, by the same token or touchstone of the Liberal 'idea', hand over in 1880 to Hartington, 'densely ignorant as to any history beyond his experience'.[3] Gladstone kept insisting: 'Nothing can please me so much as to walk in the rear',[4] or, 'I need hardly say nothing will please me so much as to fall into the rear'[5]; but these protestations, sincere in themselves, were always and increasingly coupled with a determination, powerfully sustained by a conviction of being a 'chosen vessel of the Almighty' in the Eastern question,[6] to get, ultimately if not immediately, his own way.

The contradictions of Gladstone's position came out very clearly after the end of the session of 1877, when Hawarden became a centre of pilgrimage for thousands of devout north-country Liberal excursionists.[7] The central issue presented in this 'new invention in the way of public agitation'[8] was always Gladstone's intentions for the future. Much as Gladstone disclaimed with vehemence any hope or desire to lead again, the uncertainty could not be exorcised. Gladstone's own vehemence, for all its sincerity, was merely a function of an unresolved contradiction in his own mind. His embarrassment and guilt come through clearly in an apology to Granville.

You must within these last 3 weeks have required a large fund of Christian charity not to give me up for a born fool.

[1] Gladstone to Granville, 12 April 1878, *ibid.*
[2] Hamer, *Personal Papers of Lord Rendel*, p. 86.
[3] *Ibid.*
[4] Gladstone to Granville, 17 March 1877, Granville Papers, 30, 29/29.
[5] Gladstone to Granville, 23 April 1877, *ibid.*
[6] Hyndman, *Record of an Adventurous Life*, p. 203.
[7] See e.g. *Times*, 6 August 1877, pp. 7, 8, 21 August 1877, p. 4; *Nonconformist*, 22 August 1877, pp. 847, 851, 5 September 1877, p. 895.
[8] *Times*, 21 August 1877, p. 7.

I will not explain any more now about the repeated excursions, but only say I could not help myself; & have been obliged to be rather violent in defensive measures against ten more towns which wanted to 'go and do likewise'.[1]

Nevertheless, as with his first pamphlet, his Blackheath speech, the Conference speech, the introduction of the resolutions, and the Bingley Hall speech, Gladstone persevered. The most significant expression of this pertinacity was his decision not to take the Berlin Congress in 1878 as a 'close' or even a 'resting place'. He wrote to Döllinger in October 1878 on the theme that the 'long and grave controversies on the Eastern Question', which had been a 'sore burden and hindrance' to him, were 'not at an end'. The power of the government was decaying; but the moral and political mischief they had done would 'take long to eradicate'.[2]

Gladstone was now engrossed with electoral calculations. In September Adam supplied him with a copy of the returns of by-elections from 1876 'when you may [say] practically the Eastern Question began to influence elections'.[3] Gladstone wrote to Granville in November: 'The pot is beginning to boil. I hope it will not boil too fast.' He was now convinced that the Tories were heading towards a 'great smash', perhaps greater even than the Liberal smash of 1874.[4] The final resolution of the contradictions in Gladstone's mind began with the decision at the beginning of 1879 to contest Midlothian. Gladstone told Granville that this 'turning point' involved a change in his position, 'and a coming forward'.[5]

*

1880 was clearly, for Gladstone, the consummation of a train of personal actions and decisions set in motion by the agitation of 1876. There were accretions on the way: financial extravagance, Afghanistan, Zululand. But the atrocities and what arose directly out of them remained the central and decisive issue in his crusade against 'Beaconsfieldism'. It cannot be at all assumed that, without the incentive of the agitation provoked by the atrocities and the

[1] Gladstone to Granville, 5 September 1877, Granville Papers, 30, 29/29.
[2] Gladstone to Döllinger, 23 October 1878, Gladstone Papers, Add. MSS 44140, ff. 424–7.
[3] Adam to Gladstone, 19 September 1878, ibid., Add. MSS 44095, f. 62.
[4] Gladstone to Granville, 2 November 1878, Granville Papers, 30, 29/29.
[5] Hamer, Personal Papers of Lord Rendel, pp. 91–2.

government's handling of the situation created by them, Gladstone would in any case have been impelled to the extreme point of superseding Hartington and Granville. The elections of 1880 were not fought on any direct issue arising out of the atrocities, or even of foreign policy generally; but the sense of a deep and urgent moral responsibility enunciated, fostered, symbolised dramatically by Gladstone in the Midlothian campaigns, was a direct legacy of the great movement of 1876. It is difficult to conceive any other contingency which would have given Gladstone the moral authority and prestige which his crusade beginning with the *Horrors* of 1876 gave. Even had he found it impossible to remain still under the sense of the financial and other lesser iniquities of Disraeli's government, nothing short of the extraordinary circumstances of 1876 would have justified in Gladstone's own conscience the reversal of his decision to step down from the party leadership.

The implications for the Liberal party of Gladstone's return to the leadership in 1880 were very far-reaching. In the last analysis they could be summed up as the ruin of Radicalism. If ever a political party could be said to have had a manifest destiny, it was the Liberal party after the defeat of 1874 and the retirement of Gladstone from the leadership. It was to have come under predominantly Radical inspiration and control, and its genius was to have been Joseph Chamberlain. Gladstone's return diverted the Liberal party from its logical path. He returned as the leader of a moral crusade unrelated to the standing 'interests' of Liberal politics. Against his own and Chamberlain's expectations Gladstone found himself unable to retire at an early date from what he insisted was merely a temporary interlude of office imposed upon him by the moral obligation to destroy 'Beaconsfieldism'. He then went on to launch the Liberal party into a moral crusade for Ireland. In the process Chamberlain left the party and Radicalism was wounded mortally. The unresolvable conflict of aim and outlook between Chamberlain and Gladstone had long been latent. It was not merely that Gladstone packed the cabinet of 1880 with Whigs (which neither Hartington nor Granville could have done with impunity) and delayed the major Whig secession until 1886. Gladstone himself attracted the loyalty of the great majority of Radicals while yet remaining fundamentally alien to their outlook. This contradiction was the factor which most debilitated Radicalism.

Gladstone shared with Radicals a demand for 'action', as he shared
with Nonconformists a conviction as to the moral ends and means
of politics; but from that initial point of communion Gladstone's
path diverged sharply from theirs. Like Nonconformity, Radicalism
could neither do with Gladstone nor do without him so long as he
remained a force in public life.

1876 rather than 1886 is thus the crucial year for the Liberal
party. Gladstone could not have carried the bulk of the Liberal
party with him on Home Rule had he not had behind him both the
moral prestige and—perhaps even more important—the opportunities for dramatic political leadership afforded by the Eastern
question. Moreover, Chamberlain would almost certainly have
entrenched a position which would have made dislodgment extremely difficult. Gladstone was well aware of Chamberlain's
powers—'a man worth watching and studying', he told Granville
after the Bingley Hall meeting; 'of strong self-consciousness
under most pleasing manners and I should think of great tenacity
of purpose: expecting to play an historical part, and probably
destined to it'.[1] For himself, Gladstone was no less conscious of the
rôle of destiny. He wrote later in an autobiographical fragment:

> There is a Providence that shapes our ends
> Rough-hew them how we may.
>
> I think that no one can be more deeply penetrated with these words,
> than I am or ought to be.
>
> The whole of my public and exoteric life has been shaped as to its ends
> for me, scarcely rough hewn by me.[2]

Gladstone's part in the Bulgarian atrocities agitation, and what
led out of it, could not be improved upon as an illustration and confirmation of this dictum.

2 Gladstone, Bulgaria, and Ireland

Gladstone's great campaigns for the emancipation of Bulgaria and
Ireland have an obvious relationship in terms of his 'European
sense'; yet it has never been suggested that this relationship was
in any way organic, that there was a direct and immediate and
logical connection between the Bulgarian and Irish questions more

---

[1] Gladstone to Granville, 1 June 1877, Granville Papers, *ibid.*
[2] Gladstone Papers, Add. MSS 44791, f. 19.

precise than that provided in common by the general context of Gladstone's moral passion in the cause of nationalities struggling against alien rule. It would, however, be pleasant to think that consideration of the Bulgarian case sharpened Gladstone's sensibility to the problem of Ireland. An examination of the question indicates that there are reasonably good grounds for believing this to be a distinct probability.

Two things were clear about the Irish reaction as a whole to the Eastern question as raised by the massacres in Bulgaria. From whatever point of view the massacres were regarded—as an example of how an ally of the English behaved in putting down a justifiable revolt, or as an occasion for a display of English pseudo-philanthropic hypocrisy, led by the traducer of the Holy See—the moral drawn was the same. To all sections and varieties of opinion in Ireland which could be regarded as more or less self-consciously 'Irish' in a nationalist sense, the Bulgarian case naturally and inevitably presented itself as a heightened analogy of the Irish case. The second point was that this attitude to the Bulgarian case was expressed in terms of the movement for Home Rule.

A constant characteristic of Gladstone throughout the agitation was his solicitude for the moral welfare of those who, for whatever reasons of misconception or deficiencies of moral understanding, opposed his view of the Eastern question. It has been seen how he attempted to persuade the Roman Catholic and Jewish leaders not to take the false path. He concerned himself in the same way with the Irish nationalists.

He was kept abreast of developments in Ireland. W. Vesey Fitzgerald, a Liberal Irish landowner and an enthusiastic member of the Eastern Church Association,[1] wrote to him in September 1876 outlining the plight of the atrocities agitation in Ireland. He suggested that an increased disposition on the part of the Liberal party to act more in conformity to nationalist aspirations—as represented, he was careful to emphasise, by *gentlemen* such as the Duke of Abercorn patronised, not Fenians—would have a distinctly remedial tendency on the existing Irish apathy towards the events in Bulgaria.[2] This is unlikely to have had much immediate

---

[1] See W. Vesey Fitzgerald to Gladstone, 5 September 1876, Gladstone Papers, Add. MSS 44451, ff. 122–5.
[2] Fitzgerald to Gladstone, 12 September 1876, *ibid.*, ff. 176–7.

influence on Gladstone. Without rejecting in principle the admissibility of Home Rule, his attitude, as expressed at the beginning of the session of 1875, was that so great a constitutional change could not be considered until the nationalists themselves had proposed remedial measures to deal with the specific evils they complained of; for which measures he promised his cordial consideration.[1] But he still believed that his own Irish legislation provided, as he later put it, the firm foundations of a 'national content'.[2]

Ambrose Phillips de Lisle also wrote to Gladstone, drawing his attention to the disturbing report in *The Times* of how the 'Repealers and Nationalists' cast the whole blame for the Turkish atrocities in Bulgaria upon 'English Support'.[3] Gladstone's rising concern[4] with Irish apathy was indicated by his urging of Granville to prod Law of Londonderry into action. And he caused the *Rock* great scandal by referring, in his speech at the National Conference, to the injustices consequent on the former Orange ascendancy in Ireland.[5]

The first major overt sign of Gladstone's anxiety about the Irish reaction to the Bulgarian question was a speech at Birmingham in June 1877, shortly after the Bingley Hall demonstration, on 'Ireland and Irish Representation'. The burden of his remarks as far as the Eastern question was concerned was that in the recent great parliamentary vote on the Eastern question he could not carry the nationalist members with him. He was forced to conclude that they opposed the cause of liberty in the East. He dwelt on the boons conferred on Ireland by Liberal legislation; and he thought the Home Rule movement was making a 'great mistake' in separating from the English Liberals.[6] This incident revealed that Gladstone did not as yet appreciate the depth of the Irish problem; secondly, that he was thinking mainly in terms of Liberal unity; lastly, that his inability to understand what the Home Rulers were getting at was increased by his resentment at their failure to support

[1] See Lord Eversley, *Gladstone and Ireland* (1912), p. 67.
[2] *Times*, 2 June 1877, p. 12.
[3] Purcell, *Ambrose Phillipps de Lisle*, vol. ii, p. 161.
[4] Thus, in writing to Madame Novikov on 6 February 1877 he remarks on the fact that in the House of Commons 'the Irish Roman Catholics . . . have thus far behaved badly, in deference to the trumpet sounded from Rome'. Gladstone Papers, Add. MSS 44268, ff. 148–9.
[5] *Rock*, 15 December 1876, p. 957. See E.Q.A., *Report*, p. 111.
[6] *Times*, 2 June 1877, p. 12.

his attitude on the Eastern question. This in turn formed a further block to his better understanding of the Irish question.

It took long for Gladstone fully to overcome that block; but his immediate decision to visit Ireland, announced to Granville a few days after his speech on Irish representation at Birmingham,[1] makes it clear that he intended to persist very seriously with the problem. To Granville he explained that he hoped to do good, in a quiet way, among the Irish members; also, characteristically, he had a secondary motive in sounding opinion in the Roman Catholic hierarchy on general theological and ecclesiastical matters.[2] But the Eastern question remained his consuming interest. Liddon and MacColl made a tour through Ireland a few weeks before Gladstone arrived. MacColl reported to Gladstone that he was convinced that the Irish people were on the whole 'all right' in their individual attitudes to the Eastern question, which he and Liddon had made a special point of inquiring about; and he assured Gladstone of an enthusiastic reception.[3]

If regarded quite outside the context of his consuming interest in the Eastern question, Gladstone's only visit to Ireland was indeed an odd event. And so it has been regarded. Morley dismisses it with an ironic paragraph as being perfectly pointless.[4] Sir Philip Magnus emphasises that Gladstone apparently learned nothing.[5] Hammond sees no particular significance in it, and ascribes this to the fact that Gladstone's mind was too full of the Eastern question.[6] Gladstone did indeed complain that he was looked upon as rather a notorious figure for the *Horrors* as well as *Vaticanism*, and that the '*only man*' to speak to him on Bulgaria and the East in all the three weeks was the Viceroy (the Duke of Marlborough).[7] He complained again: 'No one speaks *to me* on the subject.'[8]

But it is precisely the fact that Gladstone's head was so full of the Eastern question when he visited Ireland, however, which surely gives his tour its special significance. In 1877, among some

[1] Gladstone to Granville, [? 6] June 1877, Granville Papers, 30, 29/29.
[2] Purcell, *Ambrose Phillipps de Lisle*, vol. ii, pp. 179–80.
[3] Russell, *Malcolm MacColl*, pp. 56–7.
[4] Morley, *Gladstone*, vol. ii, p. 179.
[5] Magnus, *Gladstone*, p. 274.
[6] Hammond, *Gladstone and the Irish Nation*, p. 159.
[7] Gladstone to Madame Novikov [31 October 1877], Gladstone Papers, Add. MSS 44268, ff. 169–72.
[8] Stead, *The M.P. for Russia*, vol. i, p. 388.

U

notes on the Eastern question, Gladstone jotted down some thoughts on the problem of the relations between ruling and subject peoples.

That no conquest can be legitimate unless it is marked by the introduction of superior laws, institutions, or manners among the conquered.

No conquest ever has been permanent unless followed by amalgamation.

Saxons ⎫
Normans ⎬ in England

Franks   in France

Lombards   in Italy

The very least that can be expected is that the conquerors should be able to learn civilization from the conquered

as Romans from Greeks.[1]

It is reasonable to assume that Gladstone had the Turks in Bulgaria primarily in mind; but the inability to cite the case of Ireland as a 'permanent' conquest must have been painful. For Ireland tended to occur almost instinctively to the English mind whenever this broad question was raised. The outlined reforms of the Andrassy Note brought Ireland immediately to the minds of Disraeli and Derby, as Shuvalov was quick to note.[2] When Lord Houghton expatiated to Gladstone on the 'failure' of forty years of Greek independence he cited, as an argument against autonomy for Bosnia and Bulgaria, the absence of any basis for Home Rule or Tenant Right there.[3] Gladstone was stung to defend the Greek record as a 'signal success' when compared with the state of affairs under the Turks, and insisted on the need for 'decisive measures' for Bosnia and Bulgaria.[4] He could not have overlooked the logical implications for Ireland of this exchange. It has earlier been pointed out that Froude's explanation of Carlyle's opposition to Disraeli's Eastern policy was that its absurdity would lead to Gladstone's return and more mischief in Ireland.[5] Dean Merivale, the historian, is another example. He was pro-Turkish, as he told a friend, and deprecated a conference of the powers on the Bulgarian question, because all that Englishmen could say against the Turks 'the Irish have said, and still say, against us; and I don't want to set a precedent for a European Conference to extort Home Rule

---

[1] Gladstone Papers, Add. MSS 44763, f. 96.   [2] See above, p. 20.
[3] T. Wemyss Reid, *The Life, Letters, and Friendships of Richard Monckton Milnes, First Lord Houghton* (1890), vol. ii, p. 341.
[4] *Ibid.*, pp. 341–2.   [5] See above, p. 222.

for Ireland, and the occupation of Ulster by the Russians, and Dublin by the Americans'.[1]

Merivale's analogy was perfectly logical. So also, based on the same kind of analogy, was the opposition by Disraeli and Derby to the principles involved in the agrarian reforms suggested in the Andrassy Note. But a mind as imbued with a 'European sense' as Gladstone's would, if only the painful analogy were squarely faced, come inevitably to an equally logical but radically different conclusion.

Little enough of Ireland outside the English Pale as Gladstone saw in his three weeks in 1877, he was made sufficiently aware of a new phase of the Irish question to write to Granville about 'concessions' which might 'beneficially be made to the Irish in the matter of self-govt'.[2] Granville was much interested to find out in what direction and how far Gladstone thought such concessions might go.[3] Gladstone was probably more impressed with the Irish difficulty than Granville realised. Matthew Arnold and T. H. Huxley dined with him after his return to England. Arnold was very sorry to observe, after conversation among the three of them, that Gladstone 'seemed full of the opposition in Ireland to England and English policy—for the present at any rate—that to go contrary was the main impulse there'.[4]

There is no doubt, from his earlier anxious comments on the lack of Irish response to the atrocities agitation, that the aspect of Irish contrariness which especially worried Gladstone was the rejection of his Eastern policy. It seems clear also that he was by now becoming increasingly aware that his Irish legislation in the 1869–74 parliament was far from being a fundamental settlement, though there was yet no special sense of urgency in his attitude. But on the whole it could be said that his mind had begun to grapple with the Irish problem in a new phase; and the circumstances suggest that this was due primarily to the stimulus of the Bulgarian question. There is nothing like a single, continuous thread of development from 1876 to 1886; it is certain, however, that Gladstone went to

[1] J. A. Merivale (ed.), *Autobiography of Dean Merivale* (new ed. 1899), p. 314.
[2] Granville to Gladstone, 2 November 1877, Gladstone Papers, Add. MSS 44171, ff. 128–33. In any case, the fact that Gladstone saw little of Ireland outside the Pale may very well have been important in itself. Goldwin Smith, a strong Unionist in 1886, thought that had Gladstone gone outside the Pale he would have seen the dangers of Home Rule. Goldwin Smith, *My Memory of Gladstone* (1904), p. 61.
[3] *Ibid.*   [4] Russell, *Letters of Matthew Arnold, 1848–1888*, vol. ii, p. 141.

Ireland with his mind full of the Eastern question; that the Eastern question, whether in conjunction with the Irish visit or not, set him thinking on the general problem of the relations between ruling and subject peoples; that he became aware of a deeper hostility in Ireland to English rule than he had anticipated; and that he came to conclusions about the Irish situation which set him thinking along lines of increased self-government. Gladstone's Irish tour of 1877 was certainly not an isolated or meaningless incident, irrelevant to his contemporary interest in the Eastern question or unrelated to his later 'conversion' to Home Rule. On the contrary, the interaction in his mind between the Eastern and Irish questions was of immense significance.

It is true that he did not immediately follow up the Irish question. The analogy between Bulgaria and Ireland, however logical, would have been very distasteful to one who felt about Bulgaria as Gladstone did, and not as Disraeli or Houghton or Merivale did. And Gladstone had certainly done enough for Ireland to give him legitimate grounds for assuming that the problem in its new phase would be the task of the coming generation of political leaders. It was too much to expect him, in the circumstances of 1876–80, to admit a fundamental reassessment of the Irish question within the limits of the restricted political competence which he defined for his temporary and provisional return to full political life. Nevertheless, the analogy remained, and Gladstone in time came to accept it wholly. He addressed an Irish delegation at Hawarden in 1886 in these terms:

I feel that the man who has exposed the conduct of foreign Governments ought, on principles of justice, to pursue the same course with regard to his own country; and I could not consent to keep back or describe in qualified terms, misdeeds for which England is responsible. . . . Attacks upon the Turkish Government, attacks upon the Neapolitan Government, made by me, certainly received a very cordial and hearty welcome in England, because it was thought that they were justly made.[1]

Gladstone never stressed or pressed unduly the Bulgarian analogy, mainly no doubt because he did not want to injure his cause by

---

[1] *The Irish Question* (authorised cheap edition, 1886), p. 29. His 'Plain Speaking on the Irish Union' (1889) ranks with his *Letters to Lord Aberdeen* and *Bulgarian Horrors* in intensity of moral passion and indignation.

opening old political wounds.[1] But he kept the analogy quietly in view. In his 'Further Notes and Queries on the Irish Demand' he cited the analogy of Bulgaria, Serbia, and Greece in relation to Turkey, together with several other similar analogies; and though he emphasised that none of the analogies was 'formal and precise', he insisted that each of them sustained the Home Rule case.[2]

Many people who were enthusiastic for Gladstone's Bulgarian crusade refused to follow him in the cause of Ireland in 1886. They refused, in effect, to admit that there was an analogy, or that it was valid. But they could no more have fitted Ireland into Gladstone's category of conquests made legitimate or lasting by amalgamation than they could have fitted Bulgaria in 1876.

The very deliberation with which Gladstone proceeded in 1880 to evade the Irish question, charging Disraeli with a clumsy attempt to divert attention from the blunders of his government by alleging a dangerous situation in Ireland, indicated a conscious determination to exclude the Irish question as outside his competence. The Irish question forced itself upon Gladstone by the unexpected speed with which it came to a crisis under the direction of Parnell. The elements of the Home Rule policy had, however, long been latent in his mind. As with his conversation with Guizot in 1845, the implications raised for Ireland by Bulgaria remained an undercurrent of gnawing doubt. They too, it is not unreasonable to assume, 'helped him on' to what was later done.

[1] E.g. 'Home Rule for Ireland. An Appeal to the Tory Householder', in *Special Aspects of the Irish Question*.   [2] *Ibid.*, pp. 222–3.

Bibliography

This is a bibliography essentially of MSS and contemporary printed sources. Of later printed sources (with a few exceptions), only works referred to in the text are included. 'Contemporary' has been defined quite arbitrarily as published in or before 1886, the publication date of Carslake Thompson's *Public Opinion and Lord Beaconsfield*. Unless otherwise indicated, place of publication of printed sources is London. The material is arranged under the following heads.

      A Manuscript collections

      B Contemporary printed sources
          (*a*) Official papers
          (*b*) Works of reference
          (*c*) Newspapers and periodicals
          (*d*) Books
          (*e*) Pamphlets

      C Later printed sources

A MANUSCRIPT COLLECTIONS

Bright Papers in the British Museum.

British and Foreign Anti-Slavery and Aborigines Protection Society Papers in the Rhodes House Library, Oxford.

Broadhurst Papers in the British Library of Political and Economic Science, London School of Economics and Political Science.

Bryce Papers in the Bodleian Library, Oxford.

Carnarvon Papers in the Public Record Office.

Chamberlain Papers in the Birmingham University Library.

Cowen Collection in the Newcastle-upon-Tyne Central Library.

Courtney Papers in the British Library of Political and Economic Science.

Devonshire Papers (Eighth Duke) at Chatsworth. By courtesy of His Grace the Duke of Devonshire and the Trustees of the Chatsworth Settlement.

Dilke Papers in the British Museum.

Disraeli Papers at Hughenden Manor, Buckinghamshire. By courtesy of the National Trust.

Foreign Office Papers, 78, *General Correspondence Respecting Atrocities in Bulgaria* (2551–2556), in the Public Record Office.

Gladstone Papers in the British Museum.

Granville Papers in the Public Record Office.

Harrison (Frederic) Papers in the British Library of Political and Economic Science.

Howell Collection in the Bishopsgate Institute.

Iddesleigh Papers in the British Museum.

Liddon Papers in Keble College Library, Oxford.

Mundella Papers in the Sheffield University Library.

Nightingale Papers in the British Museum.

Pattison Papers in the Bodleian Library, Oxford.

Ripon Papers in the British Museum.

Salisbury Papers at Christ Church, Oxford. By courtesy of the Marquess of Salisbury.

Stead Papers at Little Beside House, St Day, Cornwall. By courtesy of Mr W. K. Stead.

Stephen (J. Fitzjames) Papers in the Cambridge University Library (copies).

Wilson (H. J.)Papers in the Sheffield Central Library.

B CONTEMPORARY PRINTED SOURCES

(a) *Official papers*

Hansard's Parliamentary Debates, Third Series.

Parliamentary Papers

Accounts and Papers, State Papers

LXVII (1861)	*Reports Received from Her Majesty's Consuls Relating to the Condition of Christians in Turkey, 1860.*
LXXXIV (1876)	*Correspondence Respecting the Affairs of Turkey, and the Insurrection in Bosnia and the Herzegovina. Further Correspondence Respecting Affairs in Turkey.*
XC (1877)	*Correspondence Respecting the Affairs of Turkey.*
XCI (1877)	*Correspondence Respecting the Conference at Constantinople and the Affairs of Turkey, 1876–77.*

(b) *Works of reference*

Annual Register.

Baptist Handbook.

Clergy List.

Congregational Year Book.

Dod's Parliamentary Companion.

Minutes of the Annual Conference of the Methodist New Connexion.

Minutes of Several Conversations Between the Methodist Ministers in the Connexion Established by the Late Rev. John Wesley, A.M.

Newspaper Press Directory.

(c) *Newspapers and periodicals*

Newspapers

Barrow Times
Bedfordshire Times and Independent
Daily Express (Dublin)
Daily News
Daily Telegraph
Freeman's Journal (Dublin)
Glasgow Herald
Irish Times (Dublin)
Manchester Guardian

Morning Post
Northern Echo (Darlington)
Pall Mall Gazette
Ross Gazette
Sheffield and Rotherham Independent
South Wales Daily News
Standard
The Times
Whitby Times

Periodicals

Bee-Hive
Blackwood's Edinburgh Magazine
British Quarterly Review
Catholic Times
Church Review
Church Times
Contemporary Review
Dublin Review
Economist
Edinburgh Review
Freeman
Fraser's Magazine
Guardian
Illustrated London News
Irishman
Jewish Chronicle
Macmillan's Magazine

Methodist
Methodist Recorder
Nation
National Reformer
Nineteenth Century
Nonconformist
Oxford and Cambridge Undergraduate's Journal
Primitive Methodist
Quarterly Review
Rock
Saturday Review
Spectator
Vanity Fair
Weekly Review
Westminster Gazette
Westminster Review
World

(d) *Books*

ARGYLL, Duke of, *The Eastern Question*. 2 vols. (1879).

ARNOLD, M., *Culture and Anarchy* (2nd ed. 1875; ed. J. Dover Wilson, Cambridge 1961).

ASHLEY, E., *Life of Henry John Temple, Viscount Palmerston, 1846–1865*. 2 vols. (1876).

BATH, Marquess of, *Observations on Bulgarian Affairs* (1880).

BARKLEY, H. C., *Between the Danube and the Black Sea, or Five Years in Bulgaria* (1876).

—— *Bulgaria Before the War During Seven Years' Experience of European Turkey and Its Inhabitants* (1877).

BRYCE, J., *Transcaucasia and Ararat: being Notes of a Vacation Tour in the Autumn of 1876* (1877).

CAMPBELL, G., *A Handy Book on the Eastern Question, being A Very Recent View of Turkey* (1876).

CARLISLE, H. E. (ed.), *A Selection from the Correspondence of Abraham Hayward, Q.C.* 2 vols. (1886).

CLAYDEN, P. W., *England Under Lord Beaconsfield* (2nd ed. 1880).

DAVIDSON, J. M., *Eminent Radicals In and Out of Parliament* (1880).

DENTON, W., *The Christians of Turkey. Their Condition under Mussulman Rule* (1876).

DISRAELI, B., *Lord George Bentinck* (1851; references are to ed. of 1905).

DWIGHT, H. O., *Turkish Life in War Time* (1881).

EVANS, A. J., *Illyrian Letters* (1878).

—— *Through Bosnia and the Herzegovina on Foot During the Insurrection, August and September 1875* (1876).

FARLEY, J. L., *Modern Turkey* (1872).

—— *Turks and Christians. A Solution of the Eastern Question* (1876).

FREEMAN, E. A., *The History and Conquests of the Saracens* (2nd ed. 1876).

—— *The Ottoman Power in Europe* (1877).

FROUDE, J. A., *Thomas Carlyle. A History of His Life in London, 1834–1881.* 2 vols. (1884).

GALLENGA, A., *Two Years of the Eastern Question.* 2 vols. (1877).

HODDER, E., *The Life and Work of the Seventh Earl of Shaftesbury, K.G.* 3 vols. (1886).

KINGLAKE, A. W., *The Invasion of the Crimea*, vols. i and ii (6th ed. 1877).

LEECH, H. J., *The Public Letters of the Right Hon. John Bright, M.P.* (1885).

LUCY, H. W., *A Diary of Two Parliaments*, vol. i, *The Disraeli Parliament 1874–1880* (1885).

MACCOLL, M., *The Eastern Question. Its Facts & Fallacies* (1877).

—— *Three Years of the Eastern Question* (1878).

MACKENZIE, G. M. and IRBY, A. P., *Travels in the Slavonic Provinces of Turkey-in-Europe*, with a preface by the Right Hon. W. E. Gladstone (2nd ed. 1877).

MACKENZIE, R., *The 19th Century. A History* (1880).

MILL, J. S., *Autobiography* (1873).

MINCHIN, J. G. C., *The Growth of Freedom in the Balkan Peninsula* (1886).

MONTAGU, Lord R., *Foreign Policy: England and the Eastern Question* (1877).

MORE, R. J., *Under the Balkans* (1877).

[NEWMAN, J. H.], the Author of 'Loss and Gain', *Lectures on the History of the Turks In Its Relation to Christianity* (Dublin 1854).

[NOVIKOV, OLGA], *Is Russia Wrong? A series of Letters by a Russian Lady*, with a preface by J. A. Froude (1878).

286   BIBLIOGRAPHY

—— (O[lga]. K[ireev].), *Russia and England from 1876 to 1880. A Protest and an Appeal*, with a preface by J. A. Froude (1880).

O'CONNOR, T. P., *Lord Beaconsfield. A Biography* (1879).

PROBYN, J. W., *National Self-Government in Europe and America* (1870).

SERGEANT, L., *England's Policy, Its Traditions and Problems* (Edinburgh 1881).

STEPHEN, L., *Life of Henry Fawcett* (1885).

TAIT, A. C., *Some Thoughts on the Duties of the Established Church of England as a National Church* (1876).

THOMPSON, G. Carslake, *Public Opinion and Lord Beaconsfield, 1875–1880.* 2 vols. (1886).

Transactions of the Aborigines Protection Society, 1874–1878 [1878].

WAUGH, B., *William T. Stead* [1885].

WOLF, L., *Sir Moses Montefiore* [1884].

(e) Pamphlets

An American View of the Eastern Question. A Remarkable Letter Written to a Friend in London, by an American Gentleman of Matured Experience (1878).

Anonymous Clergyman of the Church of England, *Laud and Tait* (1883).

ARGYLL, Duke of, *Conduct of the Foreign Office During the Insurrection in Crete in 1867* (Glasgow 1876).

—— *What the Turks Are and How We Have Been Helping Them* (Glasgow 1876).

ARNOLD, A., *The Promises of Turkey* [1877].

ASHBURY, J., *The Eastern Question* (Brighton 1878).

ASHCROFT, T., *The Turko-Servian War* [1876].

AUSTIN, A., *Russia Before Europe* (1876).

—— *Tory Horrors, or the Question of the Hour* (1876).

AYTOUN, J., *How to Settle the Eastern Question* (1876).

The Avita Fraus of Russia (1877).

B.C.S., *Holy Russia and Mr Gladstone. A Protest* (1877).

The Bankruptcy of the Brittain Brothers (Edinburgh 1877).

BARRY, M., *The Catechism of the Eastern Question* (1880).

BORTHWICK, A., *An Address on the Eastern Question* (1878).

BOYLE, A., *The Sympathy and Action of England in the Late Eastern Crisis and What Came of Them* (1878).

BRASSEY, T., *The Eastern Question and the Political Situation at Home* (1877).

BRIGHT, J., *Speech on the Eastern Question delivered in the Town Hall, Birmingham, December 4th, 1876.*

Britain at the Bar. A Scene from the Judgment of the Nations. A Dramatic Poem (1877).

Bulgarian Horrors and England's Duty. An Appeal (Manchester 1876).

CAMPBELL, G., *The Blue Books and What is to Come Next* (1877).
—— *The Races, Religions, and Institutions of Turkey and the Neighbouring Countries* [1877].
Catechism of the Eastern Question (reprinted from the *Pall Mall Gazette*) (1877).
CAZALET, E., *The Eastern Question. An Address to Working Men* (1878).
CHESSON, F. W., *Papers on How to Influence Members of the House of Commons . . . for promoting the Repeal of the Contagious Diseases Acts* (1870).
—— *Turkey and the Slave Trade* (1877).
COBDEN, R., *Russia, Turkey, and England* (1836, reprinted 1876).
COLQUHOUN, P., *Russian Despotism and Ruthlessness, as Disclosed in Authentic Documents* (1877).
COMBE, J., *Home Horrors. Inscribed to the Right Hon. W. E. Gladstone* (Edinburgh 1876).
A Common-Sense Radical, *The Lackeys of the Turk: an Indictment, a Protest, and a Warning* [1877].
COMUS, *The Devil's Visit to Bulgaria and Other Lands* (Brighton 1876).
[COWEN, J.], *Mr. Joseph Cowen, M.P., on the Eastern Question and a Spirited Foreign Policy etc. etc. A Few Words of Advice to Modern Liberals* (1880).
DALTON, G. W., *'Who Is To Have Constantinople?' A Prophetic Answer to that Political Question* (Dublin 1876).
DALY, A. A., *The Duty of Civilized Europe on the Settlement of the Eastern Question, or the Warning Cry to Russia* (1877).
—— *Greater Lessons in Massacre. A Reply to the Right Hon. W. E. Gladstone, M.P.* (1877).
Dame Europa's Remonstrance and Her Ultimatum (1877).
The Dardanelles for England. The True Solution of the Eastern Question (1876).
DAVIES, J. LLEWELYN, *Religious Aspects of the Eastern Question* [1877].
DAVIS, O., *Those Dear Turks. A Lecture . . . at the Congregational Church, Lee* (1876).
DENTON, W., *Fallacies of the Eastern Question* [1877].
DE WOLFFERS, F., *Turkey's Fall the Decline of England. A Suggestion and a Warning to Turkish Bondholders and Russian Moneylenders* (1875).
The Dog in the Manger, by the author of *John's Defence and Dame Europa's Apology* (1877).
The Eastern Ogre: or, St. George to the Rescue! (1876).
The Eastern Problem Solved! (1877).
Eastern Question Association, Leaflets in the Howell Collection, Bishopsgate Institute.
—— *Regulations of the National Conference on the Eastern Question* (1876).
—— *Report of Proceedings of the National Conference at St. James's Hall, London* (1876).

—— *The Treaty of Berlin and the Anglo-Turkish Convention* (1878).

The Eastern Question. Its Peaceable Solution [1876].

The Eastern Question. Speeches by the Earl of Beaconsfield and Lord Derby (1876).

The Eastern Question. The Three Great Perils of England (1877).

The Eastern Question. Turkey, its Mission and Doom: A Prophetical Instruction (1876).

EDWARDS, H. S., *The Slavonian Provinces of Turkey* (1876).

An English Liberal, *The Indignation Meetings of the Liberals and the Conduct of Affairs in the East* (1876).

An Englishman, *The Cabinet Council and the Impending War* (1876).

An Englishman, *The Question of the Day: Turk or Christian? An Answer to Mr. Gladstone's Pamphlet: With a True Narrative of the Bulgarian Horrors* [1876].

An Englishman, *The Russian 'Wolf' and his 'Sacred Mission'* (1877).

ELLIS, J. E., *The Sequence of Events in the Eastern Question* (1878).

ETHELBERT, *The Brothers Obadiah, or, Bulgaria Befriended* (1876).

EVANS, A. J., *The Slavs and European Civilization* (1878).

An Eye Witness, *A True Narrative of the Insurrection and Atrocities in Bulgaria* [1876].

FADEEF, R., *Opinion on the Eastern Question* (1876).

The Fall of Turkey (1875).

FARLEY, J. L., *The Decline of Turkey, Financially and Politically* (1875).

FAWCETT, M. G., *The Martyrs of Turkish Misrule* (1877).

A Fellow of the Royal Historical Society, *The Eastern Question* (1876).

'*The First Alarm' Respecting the Bulgarian Outrages.* Reprinted from the *Spectator* (1876).

FOLBIGG, H., *Millennial Glory: or the Doom of Turkey and the Battle of the Nations; the Restoration of the Jews; and the Coming King of Jerusalem and of the World . . .* (1877).

FREELAND, H. W., *General Klapka on the Eastern Question* (1877).

FREEMAN, E. A., *The Eastern Question in Its Historical Bearings* (1876, new ed. 1897).

FREEMAŃ, G., *The Correct Card on the Eastern Question* [1877].

GLADSTONE, W. E., *Bulgarian Horrors and the Question of the East* (1876).

—— *The Irish Question* (1886).

—— *Lessons in Massacre; or, the Conduct of the Turkish Government in and about Bulgaria since May 1876* (1877).

—— *The Sclavonic Provinces of the Ottoman Empire* [1877].

—— *A Speech Delivered at Blackheath. . . . together with Letters on the Question of the East* (1876).

—— *Two Letters to the Earl of Aberdeen on the State Prosecutions of the Neapolitan Government* (1851).

GRANT DUFF, M. E., *The Eastern Question* (Edinburgh 1876).

The Great State Trial of Great Britain versus Benjamin Beaconsfield and Others Before Lord Chief Justice Rhadamanthus and a National Jury in the Supreme Court of Public Opinion . . . [1877].

HARNEY, G. J., *The Anti-Turkish Crusade: A Review of a Recent Agitation, With Reflections on the Eastern Question* (Boston, Mass., 1876).

HARCOURT, W. V., *The Eastern Question* (1878).

HENLEY, T. L., *Christianity, as Set Forth by His Grace the Archbishop of Canterbury, together with a Few Remarks on the Turkish Atrocities* (1877).

HISTORICA, *The Imperial Triumvirate. A Warning and an Exposure of Ambitious and Unscrupulous Designs* (1877).

HISTORICUS, *A Century of Russia's Polity and Piety* (1877).

HOLMS, J., *Commercial and Financial Aspects of the Eastern Question* [1877].

HORNBY, E., *The Eastern Question. A Scheme for a Future Government of Bulgaria* (1878).

A Humble Outsider, *The Great Conference of the Intellects at St. James's Hall, Composed of the Most Influential and Distinguished Personages!! in the Country* (1876).

HYNES, M., *The Story of Russian Aggression and Turkish Defence* (Liverpool 1877).

KENYON, J. G., *The Crisis in the East and the Attitude of Catholics* (1876).

The Kidnapping of Bulgarians During the Russo-Turkish War. Correspondence with the Marquess of Salisbury, K.G. (1879).

KINNEAR, J. B., *The Mind of England on the Eastern Question* [1877].

LAURIE, W. F. B., *Remarks on the Bashi-Bazouks and Other Irregulars* [1877].

The Lion, the Monkey, and the Bear. An Apologue on the Eastern Question (1876).

A London Physician, *The Crimean War; or, The Turk Avenged* (1876).

LONG, J., *The Eastern Question in Its Anglo-Indian Aspect* (1877).

LORIMER, J., *The Denationalisation of Constantinople and Its Devotion to International Purposes* (Edinburgh 1876).

MACGAHAN, J. A., *The Turkish Atrocities in Bulgaria. Letters of the Special Commissioner of the 'Daily News', J. A. MacGahan, Esq., With an Introduction and Mr. Schuyler's Preliminary Report* (1876).

MORIER, D. R., *Turkey and the Christian Powers* (1876).

Mrs. Britannia's East-Wind Symptoms, Treatment, and Previous Medical History (Dublin 1876).

MUNRO-BUTLER-JOHNSTONE, H. A., *Bulgarian Horrors, and the Question of the East. A Letter Addressed to The Right Hon. W. E. Gladstone* (1876).

—— *The Eastern Question* (1875).

—— *The Turks: Their Character, Manners and Institutions, as Bearing on the Eastern Question* (1876).

New Light on the Eastern Question; or, The Future Centre of Commerce (1876).

The Northern Question, or Russia's Policy in Turkey Unmasked (1876).

An Old Diplomatist, *The Essence of the Eastern Question, with a Few Plain Words on the Case of the Turk and Tory versus the People of England* (1876).

Outrages in Bulgaria: the Latest Authentic Details (Liverpool 1876).

The Partition of Turkey; or, The Eastern Question According to Prophecy (1876).

Peter the Great's Last Will and Testament and Russian versus Bulgarian 'Atrocities' (Southsea 1876).

Pickles, A., *Turkey, Russia, England, and the Jews* (Rochdale 1878).

Pim, B., *The Eastern Question, Past, Present and Future* (1877).

Porter, J. L., *England's Duty in the Eastern Difficulty* (Glasgow 1876).

Probyn, J. W., *Armenia and the Lebanon* [1877].

R. A. L., *Old Nabob Pickles, the Naughty Turk, and his Little Slave Selina Serbia* (Canterbury 1876).

The Remarkable History of a Wicked Two-Headed Bird and His Associate, and How They Came to Grief. A Russian Story for the Times (1877).

Revelations from the Seat of War. Russians, Turks, Bulgarians, and Mr. Gladstone (1877).

Richard, H., *Evidences of Turkish Misrule* (1855; new ed. [1877]).

—— *History of the Origin of the War with Russia* (1855; new ed. [1877]).

Rose, P. and Staniforth, J., *Turkish Debt. A Report* (1876).

The Row in the Zoo or The Hole in the Eastern Wall (Edinburgh 1877).

Russia, Turkey, & England: Thoughts for the Times on the Eastern Situation (1877).

Russian Intrigues. Secret Despatches of General Ignatieff and Consular Agents of the Great Panslavic Societies (1877).

S., *Turkey and India, or, Our Indian Moslems. A Question of the Present Crisis* (1876).

The 'Sacred Mission' of the Russian Wolf among the Christian Sheep of Turkey. Ought We to Oppose or Promote It? [1877].

St Clair, S. G. B., *Bulgarian Horrors and Mr. Gladstone's Eastern Policy* (1876).

Sandwith, H., *Shall We Fight Russia? An Address to the Working Men of Great Britain* (1877).

Scotus, *Facts and Opinions Anent Mr. Gladstone's Relation to the Eastern War* (Edinburgh 1878).

Sinclair, T., *A Defence of Russia and the Christians of Turkey* [1878].

—— *The Great Battle of Katsh-Tartar Bazardjik!! . . .* (1877).

Skinner, J. H., *Turkish Rule in Crete* (1877).

Strangford, Viscountess, *Report on the Bulgarian Peasant Relief Fund* (1876).

SWINBURNE, A. C., *Note of an English Republican on the Muscovite Crusade* (1876).

A Syrian, *Personal Recollections of Turkish Misrule and Corruption in Syria* (1877).

TAYLOR, S., *The Conduct of Her Majesty's Ministers on the Eastern Question* (1877).

The True Solution of the Eastern Question (1878).

Turco's Little Difficulty and How He Neglected the Advice of His Numerous Friends (1877).

The Turk's Vision of the Fall of Constantinople (1876).

TURNERELLI, T., *What We Are Doing for Russia! A Few Words of Warning from 'One Who Knows the Russians'* [1876].

'Veritatis Vindex', *That Unconscionable Turk, and What To Do With Him* (1877).

WATERS, E. E., *Servia's History* (1876).

[W.E.A.A.], *What is the War About?* (Manchester 1877).

'Warsling', *Justice for Turkey and the Maintenance of Treaties versus Russian Intrigue* (1876).

WAVENEY, Lord, *Thorough* (1876).

What's To Be Done with the Turkey? or, John Bull's Dilemma (1877).

WILSON, J., *England's Duty in Relation to the Christians of Turkey* (1876).

A Woman to Women on the Turkish Horrors (1876).

WORDSWORTH, C., *The Mohammedan Woe and Its Passing Away* (1876).

WYATT, W. J., *The Eastern Question from an English Point of View* (1876).

ZANCOV, D., and BALABANOV, M. D., *Bulgaria* (1876).

C LATER PRINTED SOURCES

ABBOTT, E, and CAMPBELL, L., *Letters of Benjamin Jowett, M.A.* (1899).

—— *The Life and Letters of Benjamin Jowett, M.A.* 2 vols. (1897).

ACLAND, A. H. D. (ed.), *Memoir and Letters of the Right Honourable Sir Thomas Dyke Acland* (1902).

ACTON, Lord, Review of J. F. Bright, *A History of England, 1837–1880* (1888), *English Historical Review*, 3 (1888), pp. 798–809.

ARGYLL, Duke of, *Our Responsibilities for Turkey. Facts and Memories of Forty Years* (1896).

ARMYTAGE, W. H. G., *A. J. Mundella, 1825–1897* (1951).

BAILEY, J. (ed.), *The Diary of Lady Frederick Cavendish.* 2 vols. (1927).

BARRINGTON, R. (ed.), *The Works and Life of Walter Bagehot.* 9 vols. (1915).

BASSETT, A. T. (ed.), *Gladstone to His Wife* (1936).

BATTISCOMBE, G., *Mrs. Gladstone* (1956).

BECK, G. A. (ed.), *The English Catholics, 1850–1950* (1950).

BEHESNILIAN, K., *Armenian Bondage and Carnage* (1903).

BENDA, J., *The Betrayal of the Intellectuals* [1927], trans. R. Aldington (Boston 1959).

BENTLEY, E., *A Century of Hero Worship* (2nd ed. Boston 1957).

BONNER, H. B. and ROBERTSON, J. M., *Charles Bradlaugh*. 2 vols. (1895).

BRIGGS, A. and SAVILE, J. (eds.), *Essays in Labour History in Memory of G. D. H. Cole* (1960).

BRIGHT, J. F., *A History of England*, vol. iv, *Growth of Democracy, 1837–1880* (1888).

[BROADHURST, H.], *Henry Broadhurst. M.P. The Story of His Life . . . Told By Himself* (1901).

BROCK, P., 'The Fall of Circassia: a Study in Private Diplomacy', *English Historical Review*, **71** (1956), pp. 401–27.

BROWN, H. F. (ed.), *Letters and Papers of John Addington Symonds* (1923).

BRYCE, J., *Studies in Contemporary Biography* (1903).

BUCKLE, G. E. (ed.), *The Letters of Queen Victoria*. Second Series, 1862–78. 2 vols. (1926).

CHAMBERS, E. K., *Matthew Arnold* (Oxford 1947).

CHILDERS, S., *The Life and Correspondence of the Right Hon. Hugh C. E. Childers, 1827–1896*. 2 vols. (1901).

CHURCH, M. C., *Life and Letters of Dean Church* (1895).

CLAYDEN, P. W., *Armenia. The Case against Lord Salisbury* (pamphlet, 1898).

COLERIDGE, E. H., *Life and Correspondence of John Duke, Lord Coleridge, Lord Chief Justice of England*. 2 vols. (1904).

COLLINGWOOD, R. G., *The Idea of History* (Oxford 1946).

COWHERD, R. G., *The Politics of English Dissent. The Religious Aspects of Liberal and Humanitarian Reform Movements from 1815 to 1848* (1959).

CURTIS, G. W. (ed.), *The Correspondence of John Lothrop Motley*. 2 vols. (1889).

DALE, A. W. W., *The Life of R. W. Dale of Birmingham* (1898).

DAVIDSON, R. T. and BENHAM, W., *Life of Archibald Campbell Tait*. 2 vols. (1891).

DAVIS, W. J., *The British Trades Union Congress, History and Recollections*. 2 vols. (1910).

DUNCAN, D., *The Life and Letters of Herbert Spencer* (1908).

DWYER, F. J., 'R.A. Cross and the Eastern Crisis of 1875–8', *Slavonic and East European Review*, **39** (1961), pp. 440–58.

ELLIOT, A. D., *The Life of George Joachim Goschen, First Viscount Goschen*. 2 vols. (1911).

ELLIOTT-BINNS, L. E., *Religion in the Victorian Era* (1936).

EVANS, J., *Time and Chance, The Story of Arthur Evans and His Forebears* (1943).

EVERSLEY, Lord, *Gladstone and Ireland* (1912).

FABER, G. C., *Jowett* (1957).

FISHER, H. A. L., *James Bryce*. 2 vols. (1927).

FITZMAURICE, Lord E., *The Life of Lord Granville*. 2 vols. (3rd ed. 1905).

GARVIN, J. L., *The Life of Joseph Chamberlain*, vol. i (1932).

GATHORNE HARDY, E. A., *Gathorne Hardy, First Earl of Cranbrook. A Memoir*. 2 vols. (1910).

GLADSTONE, W. E., *The Eastern Crisis. A letter to The Duke of Westminster K.G.* (pamphlet, 1897).

—— *Special Aspects of the Irish Question* (1892),

GLASER, J. F., 'English Nonconformity and the Decline of Liberalism', *American Historical Review*, **63** (1958), pp. 352–63.

HAIGHT, G. S., (ed.) *The George Eliot Letters*. 7 vols. (1956).

HALID, H., *A Study of English Turcophobia* (1904).

HALL, Newman, *Autobiography* (1898).

HAMER, F. E. (ed.), *The Personal Papers of Lord Rendel* (1931).

HAMILTON, Lord G., *Parliamentary Reminiscences and Reflections, 1868 to 1885* (1917).

HAMMOND, J. L., *Gladstone and the Irish Nation* (1938).

HANHAM, H. J., *Elections and Party Management. Politics in the Time of Disraeli and Gladstone* (1959).

HARDINGE, A., *The Life of Henry Howard Molyneux Herbert, Fourth Earl of Carnarvon, 1831–1890*. 3 vols. (Oxford 1925).

HARDY, F. E., *The Early Life of Thomas Hardy, 1840–1891* (1928).

HARRIS, D., *Britain and the Bulgarian Horrors of 1876* (Chicago 1939).

—— *A Diplomatic History of the Balkan Crisis of 1875–1878. The First Year* (Stanford 1936).

HARRIS, S. H., *Auberon Herbert: Crusader for Liberty* (1943).

HARRISON, F., *Autobiographic Memoirs*. 2 vols. (1911).

HAULTAIN, A. (ed.), *A Selection from Goldwin Smith's Correspondence* [1913].

HIRST, F. W., *Early Life and Letters of John Morley*. 2 vols. (1927).

HOLLAND, B., *The Life of Spencer Compton, Eighth Duke of Devonshire*, 2 vols. (1911).

HOLLAND, V., *Son of Oscar Wilde* (1954).

HOLYOAKE, G. J., *Bygones Worth Remembering*. 2 vols. (1905).

HORSMAN, E. A. (ed.), *The Diary of Alfred Domett, 1872–1885* (1953).

HORT, A. F., *Life and Letters of Fenton John Anthony Hort*. 2 vols. (1896).

[HUGHES] *The Life of Hugh Price Hughes* by his daughter (4th ed. 1905).

HUTTON, A. W., *Cardinal Manning* (1892).

HUTTON, W. H., *William Stubbs* (1906).

HUXLEY, L., *Life and Letters of Thomas Henry Huxley*. 3 vols. (1903).

HYNDMAN, H. M., *The Record of an Adventurous Life* (1911).

JANOSI, F. E. de, 'The Correspondence Between Lord Acton and Bishop Creighton', *Cambridge Historical Journal*, **6** (1938–40), pp. 307–21.

JEPHSON, H., *The Platform, Its Rise and Progress*. 2 vols. (1892).

x

JOHNSTON, J. O., *Life and Letters of Henry Parry Liddon* (1904).

KILBRACKEN, Lord, *Reminiscences* (1931).

KOCHAN, L., *Acton on History* (1954).

LANE-POOLE, S., *The Life of the Right Honourable Stratford Canning, Viscount Stratford de Redcliffe.* 2 vols. (1888).

LANG, C .Y., *The Swinburne Letters*, vol. iii (New Haven 1960).

LANGER, W. L., *European Alliances and Alignments, 1871–1890* (New York 1931).

LANSBURY, G., *My Life* (1928).

LAUGHTON, J. K., *Memoirs of the Life and Correspondence of Henry Reeve, C.B., D.C.L.* 2 vols. (1898).

[LECKY] *A Memoir of the Right Hon. William Edward Hartpole Lecky* by his wife (1909).

LESLIE, S., *Henry Edward Manning* (1921).

LOEWE, L., *Diaries of Sir Moses and Lady Montefiore.* 2 vols. (1890).

LOWRY, H. F. (ed.), *The Letters of Matthew Arnold to Arthur Hugh Clough* (1932).

LUCAS, E. V., *The Colvins and Their Friends* (1928).

LYTTELTON, E., *Alfred Lyttelton* (1923).

McCARTHY, J., *Reminiscences.* 2 vols. (1899).

MACCOBY, S., *English Radicalism, 1853–1886* (1938).

MACCOLL, M., *England's Responsibility Towards Armenia* (pamphlet, 1895).

—— *The Sultan and the Powers* (1896).

MACDONELL, J. C., *The Life and Correspondence of William Connor Magee.* 2 vols. (1896).

MAGNUS, P., *Gladstone* (1954).

MAITLAND, F. W., *The Life and Letters of Leslie Stephen* (1906).

MARINDIN, G. E., *Letters of Frederic, Lord Blachford* (1896).

MARX, K. and ENGELS, F., *Correspondence, 1840–1895* (1934).

MEDLICOTT, W. N., 'Vice Consul Dupuis' "Missing" Dispatch of June 23, 1876', *Journal of Modern History* (Chicago), **4** (1932), pp. 38–48.

MELLY, G., *Recollections of Sixty Years (1833–1893)* (Coventry 1893).

MERIVALE, J. A. (ed.), *Autobiography of Dean Merivale* (new ed. 1899).

MONYPENNY, W. F., and BUCKLE, G. E., *The Life of Benjamin Disraeli, Earl of Beaconsfield* (new ed., 2 vols., 1929).

MOORE, J. M., *Three Aspects of the Late Alfred Lord Tennyson* (Manchester 1901).

MORLEY, J., *The Life of William Ewart Gladstone* (new ed., 2 vols., 1911).

NETTLESHIP, R. L., *Memoir of Thomas Hill Green* (1906).

Nonconformist Minister, *Nonconformity and Politics* (1909).

NOVIKOV, O., *Russian Memories* [1916].

O'CONNOR, T. P., *Memoirs of an Old Parliamentarian.* 2 vols. (1929).

OLIVIER, Lord, *The Myth of Governor Eyre* (1933).

PATTERSON, C. B., *Angela Burdett-Coutts and the Victorians* (1953).

PAUL, H. W., *The Life of Froude* (1905).

PAUL, J. B., (ed.) *The Scots Peerage*, vol. viii (Edinburgh 1911).

PEARS, E., *Forty Years in Constantinople* (1916).

PEARSON, H., *Labby (The Life and Character of Henry Labouchere)* (1936).

PEEL, A., *Letters to a Victorian Editor, Henry Allon, Editor of the British Quarterly Review* (1929).

PENDEREL-BRODHURST, J., *The Life of His Most Gracious Majesty King Edward VII*. 4 vols. (n.d.).

POPE-HENNESSY, J., *Monckton-Milnes, The Flight of Youth, 1851–1885* (1951).

PROTHERO, R. E., *The Life and Correspondence of Arthur Penrhyn Stanley, D.D.* 2 vols. (1893).

PURCELL, E. S., *Life of Cardinal Manning*. 2 vols. (1895-6).

—— (ed.), E. de Lisle, *Life and Letters of Ambrose Phillipps de Lisle*. 2 vols. (1900).

QUIN, M., *Memoirs of a Positivist* (1924).

RAMM, A. (ed.), *The Political Correspondence of Mr. Gladstone and Lord Granville, 1868–1886*. 4 vols. (1952-62).

REID, T. W., *The Life, Letters and Friendships of Richard Monckton Milnes, First Lord Houghton*. 2 vols. (1890).

—— *Life of the Right Honourable Edward Forster*. 2 vols. (1888).

—— (ed.), *The Life of William Ewart Gladstone* (1899).

ROBERTSON SCOTT, J. W., *The Life and Death of a Newspaper* (1952).

—— *The Story of the Pall Mall Gazette* (1950).

ROGERS, J. Guinness, *An Autobiography* (1903).

RUSSELL, G. W. E. (ed.), *Letters of Matthew Arnold, 1848–1888*. 2 vols. (1895).

—— (ed.), *Malcolm MacColl, Memoirs and Correspondence* (1914).

—— *Sketches and Snapshots* (1910).

RYLANDS, L. G., *Correspondence and Speeches of Mr. Peter Rylands, M.P.* 2 vols. (Manchester 1890).

SCHOYEN, A. R., *The Chartist Challenge, A Portrait of George Julian Harney* (1958).

SETON-WATSON, R. W., *Britain in Europe, 1789–1914* (Cambridge 1937).

—— *Disraeli, Gladstone and the Eastern Question* (1935).

—— 'Russo-British Relations During the Eastern Crisis' (unprinted documents), *Slavonic Review*, **4** (1924–5), pp. 657–83, **5** (1925–6), pp. 177–97, 433–62.

S[IDGWICK], A. and E. M., *Henry Sidgwick* (1906).

SIDGWICK, H., *The Elements of Politics* (2nd ed. 1897).

SMITH, Goldwin, *My Memory of Gladstone* (1904).

SMITH, S., *My Life-Work* (1902).

STEAD, E. W., *My Father* (1913).

STEAD, W. T., *Gladstone 1809–1898, A Character Sketch* [1898].

—— *The Haunting Horror in Armenia, or, Who will be Damned for This?* (pamphlet, 1896).

—— (ed.), *The M.P. for Russia, Reminiscences of Madame Olga Novikov.* 2 vols. (1909).

STEPHEN, L. (ed.), *Letters of John Richard Green* (1901).

—— *The Life of Sir James Fitzjames Stephen* (1895).

STEPHENS, W. R. W., *The Life and Letters of Edward A. Freeman, D.C.L., LL.D.* 2 vols. (1895).

STILLMAN, W. J., *The Autobiography of a Journalist.* 2 vols. (1901).

STORRS, R., *Orientations* (1937).

STORY, S. (ed.), *The Memoirs of Ismail Kemal Bey* (1920).

SUMNER, B. H., *Russia and the Balkans, 1870–1880* (Oxford 1937).

TAYLOR, A. J. P., *The Struggle for Mastery in Europe, 1848–1918* (Oxford 1954).

—— *The Trouble Makers* (1957).

TEMPERLEY, H. W. V., 'The Bulgarian and Other Atrocities, 1875–8, in the Light of Historical Criticism', *Proceedings of the British Academy,* **17** (1931), pp. 105–46.

—— and Penson, L. M., *A Century of Diplomatic Blue Books, 1814–1914* (Cambridge 1938).

THOMSON, E. H., *The Life and Letters of William Thomson, Archbishop of York* (1919).

THORNTON, A. P., *The Imperial Idea and its Enemies* (1959).

[*Times*] *The History of the Times*, vol. ii, *The Tradition Established, 1841–1884* (1939).

TORRENS, W. M., *Twenty Years in Parliament* (1893).

TUCKWELL, W., *A. W. Kinglake* (1902).

WALPOLE, S., *The History of Twenty-Five Years, 1856–1880.* 4 vols. (1904–8).

WESTCOTT, A., *Life and Letters of Brooke Foss Westcott.* 2 vols. (1903).

WHYTE, F., *The Life of W. T. Stead.* 2 vols. (1925).

WILLEY, B., *Nineteenth Century Studies* (1949).

WILSON, D. A., *Carlyle to Threescore-and-ten* (1929).

—— and MACARTHUR, D. W., *Carlyle in Old Age* (1934).

WIRTHWEIN, W. G., *Britain and the Balkan Crisis, 1875–1878* (New York 1935).

WOLFF, H. Drummond, *Rambling Recollections.* 2 vols. (1908).

WORDSWORTH, J., *The Episcopate of Charles Wordsworth* (1899).

WRENCH, J. E., *Alfred, Lord Milner* (1958).

WRIGHT, W. A. (ed.), *Letters of Edward Fitzgerald.* 2 vols. (1894).

—— *Letters of Edward Fitzgerald to Fanny Kemble, 1871–1883* (1895).

ZETLAND, Marquis of, *The Letters of Disraeli to Lady Bradford and Lady Chesterfield.* 2 vols. (1929).

Index